Studies in the History of Law and Justice

Volume 9

The purpose of this book series is to publish high quality volumes on the history of law and justice.

Legal history can be a deeply provocative and influential field, as illustrated by the growth of the European universities and the *ius commune*, the French Revolution, the American Revolution, and indeed all the great movements for national liberation through law. The study of history gives scholars and reformers the models and courage to question entrenched injustices, by demonstrating the contingency of law and other social arrangements.

Yet legal history today fi nds itself diminished in the universities and legal academy. Too often scholarship betrays no knowledge of what went before, or why legal institutions took the shape they did. This series seeks to remedy that deficiency.

Studies in the History of Law and Justice will be theoretical and reflective. Volumes will address the history of law and justice from a critical and comparative-viewpoint. The studies in this series will be strong bold narratives of the development of law and justice. Some will be suitable for a very broad readership.

Contributions to this series will come from scholars on every continent and in every legal system. Volumes will promote international comparisons and dialogue. The purpose will be to provide the next generation of lawyers with the models and narratives needed to understand and improve the law and justice of their own era.

The series includes monographs focusing on a specifi c topic, as well as collections of articles covering a theme or collections of article by one author.

More information about this series at http://www.springer.com/series/11794

Paulo Emílio Vauthier Borges de Macedo

Catholic and Reformed Traditions in International Law

A Comparison Between the Suarezian and the Grotian Concept of Ius Gentium

Springer

Paulo Emílio Vauthier Borges de Macedo
Universidade do Estado do Rio de Janeiro
Leme, Rio de Janeiro
Brazil

ISSN 2198-9842 ISSN 2198-9850 (electronic)
Studies in the History of Law and Justice
ISBN 978-3-319-59402-6 ISBN 978-3-319-59403-3 (eBook)
DOI 10.1007/978-3-319-59403-3

Library of Congress Control Number: 2017941465

Printed on acid-free paper

This Springer imprint is published by Springer Nature
The registered company is Springer International Publishing AG
The registered company address is: Gewerbestrasse 11, 6330 Cham, Switzerland

This work is dedicated to my daughter Amanda Vauthier Marcelino Borges de Macedo

Acknowledgements

First, I would like to thank the Brazilian CNPq for its support. This book could not be possible without it. I am also indebted to Carolina França Noronha and Ana Luíza Calil and all the others who helped me with the translation.

Especial mention should be made to Prof. Antônio Celso Alves Pereira for his keen interest on the topic of this book and for the numerous suggestions for improvement he provided. Notwithstanding all the assistance received, the responsibility for all the shortcomings lies exclusively with the author.

As often happens in enterprises such as this one, close family members ended up bearing a significant share of the personal costs involved in the writing process. This book owes much to Prof. Ubiratan Borges de Macedo, my father and the wisest man I have ever met. He was my greatest teacher and an involuntary supervisor to this work. His attemptive reading prevented many mistakes. And I shall always remember the intellectual discussions we had. This too was a sign of love.

Paulo Emílio Vauthier Borges de Macedo

Contents

Chapter 1
Introduction

According to Pierre Mesnard (author of an important work on the history of political philosophy), "we [political philosophers] were often unjust with Suárez."[1] The thought of Francisco Suárez had an overarching influence on Catholic and Reformed Theology, even though he was relegated by philosophers and jurists. If ever, the Grenadian Theologian comes to mind as the source of a François Glisson. His major juridical-political work, the **De Legibus**, served as a mere dust collector in libraries. His second greatest text in this area, the **Defensio Fidei**, was even prohibited in France and was burned in England for all the controversy it caused. This should be a clear indication of the weight of the ideas that the writer defended. Nonetheless, a long period of time passed before the books of Francisco Suárez were allowed access to the Academia of Law and Philosophy.

It was only in the second half of the nineteenth century, when it came to light that Hugo Grotius was not the sole father of International Law, that Suárez's legal and political texts were reborn. It then became clear that Suárez was not merely an important Theologian (one of the greatest of the so-called "Spanish Golden Age" and the most important of the Second Scholasticism), but also laid out fairly Modern legal and political theories such as the social contract, the popular origin of power, and the doctrine of tyrannicide. Furthermore, the writer presented a notion of natural rights adjusted to historic changes, which spared the Suarezian Natural Law from one of the most pointed criticisms that Positivism levied against Modern Natural Law. The author's thoughts were so original that some commentators (as explored in chapter II) consider him the source of an alternative Modernity. What is more, he developed a sophisticated and original concept of *jus gentium*.

Francisco Suárez was born in Grenade on January 5, 1548, and died in Lisbon on September 24, 1617. He came from a noble and Catholic family that had been providing services to the Crown since the times of the Reconquest. In 1561, he went to Salamanca to initiate his university studies. He studied Canon Law for two years until he applied for admission in the newly founded Society of Jesus—an intel-

[1]"*On a souvent été injuste pour Suarez.*" (Mesnard 1977, p. 40).

P.E. Vauthier Borges de Macedo, *Catholic and Reformed Traditions in International Law*, Studies in the History of Law and Justice 9,
DOI 10.1007/978-3-319-59403-3_1

lectual order since its creation—in 1564. Despite the examiners' unanimous recognition of a profound ecclesiastical calling, Suárez is not admitted to the order. The young man parts to Valladolid and asks for the mediation of Juan Suárez, the province of Castile (who was no relative of Francisco's, despite sharing his surname). All the counselors issue negative opinions, but Juan Suárez sympathizes with Francisco Suárez and writes a letter of recommendation in his behalf to the dean. The young man finally obtains his noviciate, but is admitted to the order as an "indifferent," which means that should he not show aptitude for studying, he would graduate as a mere assistant brother, a status short of his nobility and academic background.[2]

Unfortunately, Suárez does not stand out in his studies, revealing a considerable difficulty with abstract subjects. He tries to remain silent and avoids public debates on themes for which the other students aimed recognition. His muteness earns him the nickname "mute ox," in a clear and ironic reference to Thomas Aquinas, the first to gain such a title, albeit for being tacit and averse to strifes. His teachers designate colleagues to help him with the exams, much to the chagrin of the young man. Now sure of his vocation as a brother of service, Suárez dejectedly pleas with the director priest Martim Gutierrez to assign him physical labor and declares being satisfied in becoming a mere servant to the scholars.

Once more, the humbleness in Suárez awakens compassion. Gutierrez replies that the young man should persevere in his studies, that the apparent ineffectiveness of his efforts only strengthened his merit. He adds that he would pray every night and ask Our Lord Jesus Christ to grant him the gift of wisdom. His prayers were answered, for Suárez gradually became a better student. He finished the Theology courses in April 1570 with a reputation of wisdom among colleagues and teachers alike. Years later, in 1607, the Pope Paul V refers to Suárez as *Doctor Eximius et Pius*. Once more, the mute ox bellowed.[3]

In the same year of his graduation, his father passes away, and Suárez renounces his inheritance. He returns to the College of Salamanca and begins teaching Philosophy. He receives the priesthood in 1572, yet, due to health issues, abandons the pastoral activity and concentrates his energies solely on teaching. This renders him fruits: between 1580 and 1585, Suárez is invited to teach Theology in the Roman College, the most important college of the Society of Jesus. There, he studies many Thomist *quaestiones* that are relevant to the present thesis, such as the *De legibus,* the *De iustitia et de iure* and the *De bello.* He meets all the intellectuality of the order: Roberto Bellarmino was his cloister mate and Leonardo Lessius was his student.

In 1585, he leaves Rome to teach in Alcala in lieu of the Theologian Gabriel Vásquez, who moves to Rome. In 1591, Vásquez returns to Alcala, and while Suárez teaches, Vásquez writes. This position as writer, less prominent in the university, creates some resentment in Vásquez, and they face each other in an

[2]All the references regarding Suárez's biography were taken from Scorraille, (1912).

[3]The metaphor belongs to Cordeiro, (1918), p. 16.

intricate theological dispute regarding the doctrine of divine worship. The situation becomes tense, and Suárez's health deteriorates; the Society of Jesus, then, "promotes" the Grenadian to a post in the University of Salamanca in 1593.

In 1596, the Portuguese King Philip II requests that Suárez take the *cathedra of Prima* in the University of Coimbra. At first, the Theologian refuses, but the monarch insists in such an imperious way that Suárez accepts the task in 1597, without further ado. Coimbra means to Suárez the top of his scientific career: this is where he teaches and publishes his most prominent works, such as the **De Legibus ac Deo Legislatore**.

Still in life, Suárez earns the reputation of being one of the greatest Catholic Theologians of his time, if not the greatest. He was involved in many theological controversies, among others the *de auxilis* controversy, which divided Dominicans and Jesuits on matters of divine grace and human freedom. In 1613, the Catholic Church calls upon him to reply to the Anglicanism of the English King James I—as discussed later in chapter IV. Suárez was one of the greatest interpreters of Thomism and stood out among the writers of the Counter-Reformation.

In 1616, almost a septuagenarian, Suárez obtains his letters of retirement. He decides to travel to Lisbon in order to complete his Theological system. In May 1617, a grave conflict takes place between the Apostolic Collector and the Lisboner civil authorities regarding the right of appointing the treasurer of the Church of Saint Catherine of Mount Sinai. Suárez intervenes as mediator, solving the problem, at the cost of his already poor health. On September 24 of that year, with admirable peace and serenity of mind, Suárez passes away.

The Dutch Lawyer Hugo Grotius requires no introduction to his scientific credentials. He was born in Delft on April 10, 1583 and died on the dawn of August 28–29, 1645. Nature bestowed a precocious genius upon him. At eight, he composed his first verses. At eleven, he entered the University of Leyden, where he studied Mathematics, Philosophy, and Law. As a 15 year old, traveling to France in the company of the Grand Pensionary and the Netherlands' grand lawyer, Johan van Oldenbarnevelt, Grotius took advantage of the trip and obtained the title of Doctor of Law at the University of Orléans. The young man's culture impressed King Henry IV in such a way that he praised him as the "miracle of Holland."[4]

At the end of the sixteenth century and the beginning of the seventeenth century, the Netherlands was determined to justify its plea for independence before an educated European public. The person that would advocate this cause had to be convincing, understand a great deal about the local political institutions, be a respected authority in all Europe for his knowledge and above all, should be loyal to his country. Grotius fulfilled all the requirements. Therefore, in 1601, the young 18-year-old Grotius won a fierce dispute to write a history of the Netherlands in Latin. In 1610, he publishes the **De antiquitate reipublicae Batavae**.

[4]For more details on the life of Grotius, see Burigny, (1754). All the biographic information come from this ouevre and from the book Borges de Macedo (2006), pp. 1–32.

However, the opportunity that would consecrate Grotius' career would come only in 1604. On February 25 of the previous year, the marshal Jacob van Heemskerck, at the service of VOC (acronym in Dutch for *Vereenigde Oostindische Compagnie*, the Dutch East India Company, which had just been created), captures the Portuguese argosy Santa Catarina in the Strait of Mallaca—it was the period of the union between the crowns of Portugal and Spain. What the Company had done was nothing short than an act of war. This gave rise to an international controversy on whether the VOC had the right to seize the argosy. Even within the Netherlands, the episode caused discontent and discomfort. Some of the shareholders of the company were Mennonite pacifists, merciful Christians, and heirs of the Irenic tradition of Erasmus. They began selling their shares and donating money to charity with the deliberate purpose of censuring the VOC, because they believed that the company should not have seized the load and that any war would represent an evil. Grotius was then charged of justifying the loot.[5]

In 1605, Grotius composes a manuscript entitled **De Jure Praedae Commentarius**, of which the twelfth chapter is extracted and published in 1609 with minor amendments, a text known as **Mare Liberum**. The very existence of the entire work, composed of 163 pages, went unnoticed for two and a half centuries, until its accidental discovery in 1864. In the **De Jure Praedae**, the first traces of the just war doctrine—which will be analyzed in depth in the final chapter—are drawn. Grotius reasons that the VOC was entitled to seize the ship, since the Netherlands were engaged in a legitimate war against Spain, despite the company not being a public authority. The second argument appears in **Mare Liberum**: the free navigation of the seas. Here, Grotius needed to overcome a Papal Bull of Alexander VI dated May 14, 1493, the *Inter Caetera* Bull (modified by the Treaty of Tordesillas in June 7, 1494), that granted to the Portuguese people sovereignty over the navigational routes. It was not an easy task, yet Grotius was skillful enough to invoke Saint Thomas Aquinas and Francisco de Vitória, two icons of the Catholic thought, as authorities in the defense of his cause.

Grotius defended his country and the VOC in many other cases in the following years until 1613, when the Pensionary of Rotterdam, Elias Oldenbarnevelt, brother to the Grand Pensionary, passed away and Grotius was appointed to the prestigious post. He became so associated to Oldenbarnevelt that, should he fall, Grotius would follow the same destiny.

The collapse of Grotius would have a religious pretext, though. In 1608, Jacobus Arminius, an eminent professor of the University of Leyden deviates from the strict canons of Calvin and teaches openly that God sent His own Son to the world for the saving of all mankind and that Grace is, thus, offered to all men. However, men may refuse the gift. On this account, God would have chosen or condemned only those whom He, in his omniscience, foresaw would embrace or reject the Grace.

---

[5]The shareholders came as far as funding a rival company more conformed to the "spirit of the Gospels" in French territory, under the auspices of King Henry IV (see Haggenmacher 1983, p. 53).

This notion is consistent with the Catholic conception according to which men cannot earn Paradise by their own merit, but only by Grace, offered to all indistinctly. In his childhood, Grotius is sent to Hague, where he has his first contact with the Arminianism professed by the Cleric Utengobard.

Another teacher from the University of Leyden, François Gomar represented the Calvinist orthodoxy. Gomar firmly and strongly disputed this notion and defended the idea that God would have destined some men for eternal life and others for damnation by an eternal and irreversible decree. Human actions would not have any effect on men's fate, neither saving nor condemning them. By his own merit, man is incapable of saving himself, but neither can those elected by God resist the power of the Divine Grace. Therefore, Jesus Christ would have not died for the condemned, just for the *electi*.

The ideas of Arminius encountered immediate resistance in the vast majority of the clergy and were altogether unpopular among the people. The supporters of Gomar[6] deemed them heresy in the Synod of Rotterdam. However, magistrates and public men welcomed the Arminianism. Dissatisfied with the persecution launched by the supporters of Gomar, the Arminians gathered in secret on January 14, 1610 and sent to the States General of the Netherlands a *remonstrance*,[7] in which they expressly condemned Gomar's point of view. That was a true profession of the Arminian faith. Forty-six ministers signed the *remonstrance* and Utengobard wrote it with the likely help of Grotius himself. Its supporters were called *Remonstrants*. In response, the supporters of Gomar wrote a *contra-remonstrance*, by which they came to be known as *Contra-Remonstrants*.

As most minorities, the *Remonstrants* defended religious tolerance while the *Contra-Remonstrants* wanted a national synod. On this matter, Grotius wrote a treaty praising tolerance, **Meletius sive de iis quae inter Christianus conveniunt epistola**, in which he also defended Erastian positions. The book would later serve to justify a maneuver by Oldenbarnevelt: with the elections approaching and wanting to keep the majority of the *Remonstrants* ministers, the Grand Pensionary resurrects a 1591 legislation whereby the magistrates themselves would hold control over the nomination of ministers: the magistrates would appoint four people, and those four would choose the ministers. In the end, the process would still require the ratification of the board of magistrates.

Grotius soon became the most fervent controversialist of the Arminian cause. He demands a meeting with King James I, himself being a respected Theologian among the Reformers, to expose the compatibility of the Arminian doctrine with the Christian faith. Once more, Grotius' legendary intellect opens doors. The supporters

[6]Often, the supporters of Gomar accused the Arminians of Pelagianism, which is a grave offense: Pelagius held that good deeds could save one's soul. St. Augustine and all of Christendom countered this heresy. The Protestant Reformers showed an even greater orthodoxy than Catholics on this issue. Arminians were also purported as Papists and Socinians. Socinians embraced a Nontrinitarian Christology (denying the existence of the Holy Trinity), which means being outside of all Christianity, either Reformed or Catholic (see Latourette 1975, pp. 792–795).

[7]French term for a parliamentary speech addressing the sovereign in a tone of protest.

of Gomar also requested an audience with the King, but he refuses. Although he sympathized with the arguments raised by the Erastians, the King still had doubts regarding the core of the issue. Blinded by overconfidence, Grotius publishes in 1613 the **Ordinum Pietas**, a text so passionate that the author becomes the main target of Gomar's supporters.

In addition, the Prince of Orange's dissatisfaction (as well as his supporters') with Oldenbarnevelt's foreign policy only increased. He maintained more amicable relations with France than with Britain, because the opinions of this country regarding the Habsburgs were somewhat ambiguous and the Grand Pensionary needed a firm ally against Spain. Maurice of Nassau disapproved of the approximation with a Catholic country and his popularity as a "Protestant hero" grew. Apart from the divergences in relation to foreign policy, it displeased Oldenbarnevelt that Nassau overshadowed him. Since he held the loyalty of the army, the Prince used his military force in order to conquer the territories controlled by the Arminians. On August 29, 1618, Nassau arrested Oldenbarnevelt and two of his supporters, Hogerbeets—the Pensionary of Leyden—and Grotius. In 1619, Oldenbarnevelt was sentenced to death and Grotius to imprisonment for life.

With the help of his friends, who often lended him books, Grotius dedicated his time incarcerated to do what he did best: to read and to write. He engaged in the translation of a piece by Euripedes, and two of his works of maturity came to life in this period: **De Veritate Religionis Christianae** and **Introduction to the Jurisprudence of Holland**. Beyond that, he began writing his *magna opus*, the **De Jure Belli ac Pacis**.

The books were brought to Grotius inside large trunks by his wife, Maria Reigesberg. Unconsolable, she begins to plot her husband's escape. Realizing that the guards stopped examining the trunk over the years, Maria Reigesberg conceives a break out plan. She spreads a rumor about her husband being sick and that he would stay cloistered in his room with his readings, so that when the guards realized he was missing it would be too late. She makes a few air holes in the trunk and even demands two soldiers to carry it. Startled by the extra weight yet unsuspecting, one of the guards commented that an Arminian should be inside. Such irony. When the authorities discovered the scheme, Grotius was already out of reach. Vexed, they arrested Maria Reigesberg. However, the act was so heroic that Maurice of Nassau himself freed her.

Grotius and his wife were welcomed with open arms in France: the French authorities granted him a pension for his sustenance. But his mind had not left the Netherlands. By the time of the Synod of Dort, the Arminians were still being persecuted and accused. Grotius argues with many authorities and sends a letter to King James rebutting the arguments raised by the supporters of Gomar. He writes a treaty entitled **A Defense of the Catholic Faith concerning the Satisfaction of Christ against Faustus Socinus**, in which he distinguishes Arminianism from Socianism.

For over 10 years, Grotius refuses every work proposal and seeks a way to return to his country. Since the moment of his arrival into exile in 1621, he actively corresponds with his father and other authorities in his homeland to probe on the possibility of his return. In 1625, the year he publishes his most important work, his hopes intensify: the Prince of Orange dies. His brother, Frederick Henry, succeeds him and was allegedly inclined to some national reconciliation. Grotius returns to the Netherlands, but he received a very cold welcome. In 1632, the States General decided to arrest him again, in case he did not leave the Republic. In this moment, Grotius realizes he could never work in his homeland again.

In a letter to his brother in April 1640, Grotius appears aware of the rebuttals his **Mare Liberum** received in Portugal and in England from **De justo imperio Lusitanorum Asiatico** by Francisco Seraphim de Freitas and **Mare Clausum** by John Selden, respectively. Grotius refers expressly to the Portuguese author's work as worthy of an answer. Nevertheless, hurt by his fellow citizens, he felt discharged of wasting his time in the controversy.

Once more, Grotius's famous erudition comes to his aid. In 1634, he accepts the invitation from the Swedish Chancellor Axel Oxenstierna to be Sweden's Ambassador in France. His controversial personality, however, was a poor fit for diplomacy. Cardinal Richelieu loathed him. Grotius became involved in many a dispute for precedence. Still, he served during several years up to 1644, when he was called back due to Queen Christina's dissatisfaction with Oxenstierna's politics regarding France.

In 1645, after a quarrel with the Queen, Grotius decides to leave Stockholm. His ship faces a violent storm and sinks in August 17. Grotius survives, but falls sick. Taken to the city of Rostock, he did receive medical attention, but it was too late. On August 26, the jurist from the city of Delft dies.

What does two authors seemingly so different have in common? In a letter to his brother, Grotius shows knowledge of the thoughts of Francisco Suárez,[8] but he refers to the author's work in General Philosophy or in Theology, not to the legal ones. In all of **De Jure Belli ac Pacis**, there are only four references to the **De Legibus**, which, considering an author with such a baroque style as Grotius, is almost insignificant. They belonged to rather distinct and often contrasting cultural universes: one to the rich Spanish and Catholic Scholastic Theology, and the other to the Dutch Calvinist and Voluntarist Legal Humanism. Still, they both developed very similar notions of *jus gentium*. The Suarezian Law of Nations is more alike Grotius' than Francisco de Vitória's, the great *maestro* of all Spanish scholastic, and the Grotian Law of Nations is more similar to Suárez's than to the Italian jurist Alberico Gentili's, whose **De Iure Belli** was heavily used in the composition of **De Jure Belli ac Pacis**.

Suárez and Grotius were the first to build a notion of *jus gentium* disassociated from the Roman texts. As will be seen in chapter I, the Law of Nations in Rome was an internal law of the Empire, *intra gentes*, interwoven with Natural Law itself. There are no doubts that the Roman notion altered with the passage of time but during all of the Middle Ages the persistence of those characteristics is striking. But, due to Suárez and Grotius, the Law of Nations undeniably becomes a Positive

---

[8]Grotius (1687), Letter to Ioanni Cordesio, 1633, n. 329.

Law, focused on the peoples (or human beings in the plural, not on abstract collectivities such as States) and though separated from Natural Law, it conserves a Moral content. The writers previous to Suárez and Grotius had not departed from the Roman heritage and failed to develop an original concept of Law of Nations. And those who came after them exaggerated in the positive character of this law, setting aside all ethical consideration. Suárez and Grotius walked a narrow path: their Law of Nations is a human invention, yet imbued with an intrinsic morality.

In this book, I try to demonstrate that the similarity between the two authors is no mere coincidence. Hugo Grotius read Francisco Suárez and this reading influenced (and even modified) the grounds for his *jus gentium*. I do not imply that one plagiarized the other—as it has already been said—; but the ideas developed by one were used to solve a problem **also** faced by the other. Suárez and Grotius studied the same sources, and articulated what could be called the "state of the art" of the *jus gentium*: they shared the same concerns and their thoughts were analogous up to a certain point. Even so, the influence of Suárez was so important on the Grotius' Law of Nations that it led him to review prior concepts and arguments.

While Suárez has received little attention, Grotius was one of the most studied authors of all times. At least, there are three main currents of interpretation.[9] Three hundred years after he was born, Grotius was considered the first Modern Political Philosopher as well as the single father of a whole branch of Law, Public International Law—and his influence extended to other fields, such as Private International Law. His work was revolutionary and pioneer in all of the fields it came across. Roughly, in the last hundred years, since sir Thomas Erksine Holland's inaugural speech at Oxford, the "miracle of Holland" suffered many shakes in his reputation; he would have been merely the most important disciple of Alberico Gentili, or the "last representative of the Spanish School," inaugurated by Francisco de Vitóriain the sixteenth century.[10] Once a pioneer, Grotius became a simple follower. There is no language in which a work was not published presenting the faults in the Grotian system or insisting in what Grotius **should** have written to produce a more satisfactory work in International Law. There were a few essays in which Grotius was compared to his predecessors, among them Suárez himself. However, all comparisons endured grave imprecisions and to a certain point intended to demean the author.

These two interpretations part from a somewhat anachronic account of things: both try to identify in the Grotian thought elements of the contemporary International Law. Only recently, with the publishing of the doctorate thesis of Peter Haggenmacher in 1983, **Grotius et la doctrine de la guerre juste**, were the works of Grotius finally analyzed in the light of the concerns of his own time. Also departing from a contextualized reading of the two authors, I attempt to promote a rather punctual comparison (limited by the concept of *jus gentium*) of the Suarezian

[9]The interpretations are divided in accordance with their chronological order, but they juxtapose. As will be seen in chapter VI, still today some commentators insist on the first interpretation.
[10]Bull (2002), p. 65.

and Grotian systems of thought. After reading my book, those who are unaware of the different interpretative disputes regarding Grotius should be surprised with the similarities between him and Suárez. But those already familiar with those works will become puzzled by discovering how distinct they are.

Neither Suárez nor Grotius wrote books on International Law. One needs only to compare the summary of **De Legibus** or **De Jure Belli ac Pacis** with the most up-to-date textbooks to conclude this. Those works are part of other ideological traditions. The *jus gentium* in both authors is not what we today call International Law. The Spaniard and the Dutch Lawyer still ignored the notion of State; they did not conceive a properly international domain, but an "extra-national" one: the Law of Nations did not apply among sovereign States, but among peoples, human beings.

Notwithstanding, International Law and the Law of Nations are not sealed in separate realities. The concept of *jus gentium* is always evoked whenever International lawyers seek an ideal or an Ethic-oriented International Law. In 1958, the judge of the International Court of Justice, Moreno Quintana, expressly referred to Francisco de Vitória and to Francisco Suárez when conceiving an idea of a natural society of nations which presumes the existence of certain imperative principles of universal reach.[11] The former judge of the Inter-American Court of Human Rights, Antônio Augusto Cançado Trindade, in his concurring opinion to the Advisory Opinion 18 of September 17, 2003—as well as in other votes and decisions—referred to Grotius and Francisco Suárez's Law of Nations as a law common to mankind, relevant not just to the State, but also to the individuals. It is a law that honors the dignity of the human being.[12]

Scholars believe in this as well. Professor Cançado Trindade also addressed the relation between International Law and the Law of Nations in his academic works. He developed the thesis that contemporary International Law abandoned the Positivist-Voluntarist paradigm and now seems to have turned to the primordial matrix of its founders, the *jus gentium*. The individual reclaims his international legal capacity while the States give way in behalf of all mankind in what concerns the very purpose of International Law. This shift represents a true return to origin.[13]

Francesco Viola conceives a very singular relation between the Law of Nations and International Law. He affirms that the former consists of a specific form of law, based on rationality and aspiring morality. Viola considers it wrong to associate the Law of Nations with International Law. The Law of Nations has died and resurrected many times, remaining a constant in the history of Law and infusing other branches with its elements. An example of the influence of the *jus gentium* on

[11]See International Court of Justice, (1958) p. 106.

[12]See International Court of Justice, (2003) p. 3. See also the reference of the notion of *civitas maxima gentium* of this judge in International Court of Justice, (1999) , p. 12.

[13]See Cançado Trindade, (2002), p. 1086; see also the following aticles Cançado Trindade, (2006), pp. 11, 161 and 405. This is the thesis defended by the Brazilian jurist in his General Course of International Law (**International Law for Mankind**: towards a new *jus gentium*) in 2005 at the Hague Academy of International Law.

contemporary International Law can be found in the notion of *jus cogens*, set forth in Positive Law itself, in article 53 of the Vienna Convention on the Law of Treaties. Every time a norm safeguards goods and values that are essential to all mankind and falls upon the universality of men, there is a manifestation of the *jus gentium*.[14]

In both scholars, the main idea is that the *jus gentium* is a law with superior ethical content that inextricably addresses all men. However, not all of the so-called "founders of International Law" share this understanding. As will be seen in chapter I, in the Theologians prior to Suárez, such as Vitória, the moral content of the *jus gentium* arised out of an intermingling with Natural Law. In addition, in the most typical Humanist Lawyer, Alberico Gentili, moral considerations give way to relativism. But in a Modern author like Vattel, the subject of the Law of Nations is already the State. Suárez and Grotius developed, in fact, a rather elusive notion, which seems to be the only one that effectively corresponds to all evocations of an ideal Law of Nations. The singularity of this *jus gentium* is reason enough to investigate its basis.

A final remark must be made. This is a work on History of International Law, but not from a "world" or "global" perspective that have become current.[15] It appears that only recently scholars discovered that International Law is not merely European Public Law and began revising its history from a more comprehensive and intercivilizational approach. However, such a totalizing view would render the efforts of comparing Francisco Suárez and Hugo Grotius fruitless. One cannot use a world map to guide him on interstate highways. This is a history of the concept of *jus gentium* in two authors: how they developed that notion, what they read, against who they wrote and how one influenced the other (if he even did). This is a story of subtleties.

Not everything has been said about Suárez and Grotius. There are still a few discoveries ahead. They have been compared before, but in a manner so general that the conclusions were inaccurate or simply vague. I wanted to follow a tread on the history of legal concepts similar to the one developed by John Greville Agard Pocock and Quentin Skinner in the history of political ideas. Rather than supporting a timeless cause, a more fitting role to the historian of thought is that of an Archeologist, who brings back to the surface "buried intellectual treasures, cleaning the dust and enabling us to reconsider what we know about them."[16] No author writes to a universal audience; he writes to refute his intellectual foes or to push forward the answers of his school teachers. Concepts are embedded in very specific debates. In this book, I attempted to recreate a certain debate, to unveil the reading that Grotius did on the Suarezian concept of *jus gentium*.

I structured this book in an unpretentious manner. The first chapter aims to place the discussion on the origin of International Law and to describe the main concepts

---

[14]Viola (2004), p. 187.

[15]Fassbender and Peters (2012), p. 46.

[16]Skinner (1999), p. 90.

of the Law of Nations prior to Suárez and Grotius. In the second and third chapters, I examine the foundations of law in these authors and their legal philosophies. Such a study facilitates the comprehension of the basis of a specific law, the *jus gentium*, which constitutes the scope of chapters four and five.

References

Bull, Hedley. The Importance of Grotius in the Study of International Relations. In: Bull, Hedley; Kingsbury, Benedict; Roberts, Adam (ed.). **Hugo Grotius and International Relations**. Oxford, New York: Oxford University, Clarendon Press, 2002.

Burigny, Jean-Levesque de. **Vie de Grotius, avec l'histoire de ses ouvrages, et de négociations auxquelles il fut employé**. Amsterdam: M. M. Rey, 1754.

Cançado Trindade, Antônio Augusto. Os Rumos do Direito Internacional Contemporâneo: de um *jus inter gentes* a um novo *jus gentium* no século XXI. In: ______. **O Direito Internacional em um Mundo em Transformação**. Rio de Janeiro: Renovar, 2002, p. 1086.

Cançado Trindade, Antônio Augusto. A *Recta Ratio* nos Fundamentos do *Jus Gentium* como Direito Internacional da Humanidade, La Emancipación de la Persona Humana en la Reconstrucción del *Jus Gentium* e Memorial por um Novo *Jus Gentium*, o Direito Internacional da Humanidade. In: ______. **A Humanização do Direito Internacional**. Belo Horizonte: Del Rey, 2006, pp. 11, 161 and 405.

Cordeiro, Valério. **O Padre Francisco Suárez (Doutor Exímio)**. Porto: Livraria Magalhães e Moniz, 1918, p. 16.

Fassbender, Bardo; Peters, Anne (eds.). **Oxford Handbook of the History of International Law**. Oxford: Oxford University Press, 2012.

Grotius 1687, *Letter to Ioanni Cordesio*, n. 3290.

Haggenmacher, Peter. **Grotius et la doctrine de la guerre juste**. Genève, Paris: Heige, Presses Universitaires de France, 1983.

International Court of Justice. Opinion individuelle de 28/11/1958. Application de la convention de 1902 por régler la tutelle des mineurs (Pays-Bas c. Suède), p. 106.

International Court of Justice. Advisory Opinion AO-18/03 of September 17th 2003. Condición Jurídica y Derechos de los Migrantes Indocumentados. Voto Concurrente del Juez A.A. Cançado Trindade, p. 3.

International Court of Justice. Advisory Opinion AO-16/99 of October 1st 1999. El Derecho a la Información sobre la Asistencia Consular en el Marco de las Garantías del Debido Proceso Legal. Voto Concurrente del Juez A.A. Cançado Trindade, p. 12.

Latourette, Kenneth Scott. **A History of Christianity**. New York: Harper & Row, 1975, v. II.

Macedo, Paulo Emílio. **Hugo Grócio e o Direito**: o jurista da guerra e da paz. Rio de Janeiro: Lumen Juris, 2006, pp. 1–32.

Mesnard, Pierre. **L'Essor de la Philosophie Politique au XVIe Siècle**. 3. ed. Paris: J. Vrin, 1977.

Scorraille, Raoul de, S.I. **François Suárez de la Compagnie de Jésus**. D'après ses lettres, ses autres écrits inédits et un grand nombre de documents nouveaux. Paris: P. Lethielleux, 1912. 2 volumes.

Skinner, Quentin. **Liberdade antes do Liberalismo**. Trad. Raul Fiker. São Paulo: UNESP, 1999.

Viola, Francesco. Derecho de Gentes Antiguo e Contemporáneo. Trad. Isabel Trujillo. **Persona y Derecho**, n. 41, 2004.

Chapter 2
The Law of Nations: Between Natural and Positive Law

The history of International Law intertwines with its definition. On the one hand, if International Law is defined as a group of positive and interstate rules then it is a recent enterprise and does not correspond to the concept examined in this work. On the other hand, the idea that there exist legal rules applicable to all men is as old as Natural Law itself. Even so, unlike the majority of the authors of the sixteenth and seventeenth centuries, contemporary internationalists do not hesitate in keeping Natural Law far aside from their subject of study.

From what can be termed as an intercivilizational perspective, Onuma Yasuaki poses some relevant questions regarding the origin of International Law. Would the presence of sporadic treaties be enough to confirm the existence of International Law or would a true international order be necessary? Which criteria differentiate International Law from other normative systems? Did agreements between the Hittites and the Pharaoh of Egypt constitute international or religious norms, since gods acted as guarantors of the covenants between the parties? Powerful empires, such as the Chinese and the Roman, did not recognize de facto foreign nations as their equals; as a result, the legal nature of their treaties was regarded as mere concessions or orders of the emperor, in other words, they were unilateral actions with no regard for the will of the other party. Even as late as the nineteenth century, the existence of International Law was a pressing issue still. Treaties of cession of territory and treaties creating protectorates shaped the conquest of Asia and Africa by the Europeans. However, the internationalists of that time believed that International Law applied only to civilized nations, a definition that excluded Asia and Africa. What is, therefore, the validity of such treaties?[1] All these questions interfere with mapping out a starting point to the very existence of International Law.

Establishing a definition a priori and then searching for its elements among thinkers of the past centuries is as damaging as the lack of clarity on the above issues, for it produces a bended and distorted reading of these authors. The past

[1]Yasuaki (2000), pp. 2–3.

P.E. Vauthier Borges de Macedo, *Catholic and Reformed Traditions in International Law*, Studies in the History of Law and Justice 9,
DOI 10.1007/978-3-319-59403-3_2

cannot be examined *vis a vis* present inquiries; the past has to be investigated by itself. Then, a paradox emerges: the lack of precise parameters prevents an accurate research, but their presence can corrupt the subject thereof. In order to avoid this paradox, negative criteria should guide the search for the origin of this field of study: if it is not possible to determine what International Law is, then we must exclude what it is not. And we can only speak of International Law solely when it becomes independent from others branches of Law, such as Natural Law and Domestic Law.

In this chapter, I examine all the efforts made in determining the origin of the concept of International Law, along with the successes and mistakes in the course thereof. Our point of departure will be the issue of the paternity of International Law, a misplaced problem in my point of view. Subsequently, I will explore the attempts to restrict the origins of international law to the doctrine of Just War. Despite being correct, these are innocuous attempts, for they are too wide and do not solve the issue of the autonomy of International Law vis a vis other types of Law. Then, before analyzing the authors that are the scope of this work—and who merit separate chapters—I will shed some light on the evolution of the notion of *jus gentium*, from the Romans to Francisco de Vitória and Alberico Gentili. The purpose of displaying such a development is to present how the original Roman notion of *jus gentium* persevered in all these writers. The original notion bears little resemblance to the contemporary International Law, because it does not separate it from Natural Law nor from Domestic Law. This entire chapter plays a role of prolegomena to the others; so that all the contours and the originality of Francisco Suárez and Hugo Grotius'definitions of *jus gentium* may be grasped.

2.1 The Law of Nations and International Law

The Philosopher Jeremiah Bentham coined the term "International Law" in his book **An Introduction to the Principles of Moral and Legislation**. In the translation to French made by the Swiss Étienne Dumont in 1802, the expression became *droit international*, and the new title found immediate acceptance among most scholars and official academic programs. Dumont also inserted the adjective "*public*" to the end.[2]

In fact, the translation is imperfect. In French, the word *Nation* derives from *naissance*, birth; while in English it endorses the polysemy of nation, country, or State. Nonetheless, Bentham's emphasis was in the prefix "*inter*." He wished to highlight the idea that this branch of Law was applicable among the peoples. According to him, this notion remained ambiguous in the first name of the discipline "Law of Nations or Peoples."

---

[2]Truyol (1952), p. 19.

The Philosopher was right. The ambiguity permeates the entire history of the concept, since its origin as *jus gentium* with the Romans until its decline in the last quarter of the eighteenth century. From a law applicable to foreigners in Rome to interstate Positive Law, the variation of meanings is so grand—Natural Law, imperial common law, common European Law and Positive Law between the peoples—that one might question whether the terms Law of Nations and International Law indeed relate to the same reality. There are those who defend an absolute separation between them. Others suggest that the term "Law of Nations" is broader and represents the genre of which International Law constitutes a specie. And still there are others who see a return of the contemporary International Law to the idea of *jus gentium*, which implies that there is no absolute identity between the two.

It is possible to outline differences between the Law of Nations and International Law that go beyond the chronologic criterion. Still, due to the polysemy above mentioned, it becomes impossible to determine all distinctions with precision. The distinguishing element will always vary or be more or less evident in accordance with the author's inclination.

However, the first question that comes to mind is this: if there are so many differences, why do the two terms intertwine? The distinction between the two concepts is meaningless if one does not explain the confusion between them in advance. It is necessary to examine the reason why there appears to be a line of continuity between the Law of Nations and International Law. The answer to this question is apparently simple: because the terms share the same founding father.

2.1.1 The Issue of the Paternity of International Law

Few scholars have received as many praises as Hugo Grotius. In one of the most prominent translations of **De Jure Belli ac Pacis** into French, the translator Jean Barbeyrac spared no compliments when writing the preface.[3] Vico proclaimed Grotius the "jurisconsult of the human race." John Locke included him among the major writers that a civilized man should read.[4] In Brazil, Miguel Reale does not hide his admiration: "prior to him [Hugo Grotius] it was not possible to talk about Philosophy of Law in the proper sense, because his book **De Jure Belli ac Pacis** is the first treatise on Natural Law, or rather, the first autonomy treaty of Philosophy of Law."[5]

More than a man, Hugo Grotius became a myth: the incarnation of the Westphalia Treaty of 1648. He would have been the first author to escape of what Modern writers call "the darkness of the Middle Ages" and to rekindle the light of

[3]Grotius (1724), pp. I–XLIII.

[4]Tuck (1979), p. 63.

[5]Reale (2000), p. 103.

reason. As the first Modern man, Grotius embodies the very notion of an international society; the States relate among themselves no more in accordance with religion, but according to their own interests, and the rule of law limits these interests. Grotius became such a symbol also because he found an Europe receptive to his ideas regarding the interdependence of peoples, the lack of authority of the pope over shipping routes, the right of rulers to use force by through a consensuous right, the validity of treaties, even those entered into with non-Christian nations.

Grotius' myth is widely spread; it is even more prominent among scholars of International Relations than international lawyers. In the book **International Theory: the three traditions**, tired of the intellectual reductionism of the dichotomy between Realism and Idealism, Martin Wight proposes a tripartite division of the traditions of International Relations: the Realistics or Machiavellians, the Revolutionaries or Kantians and the Rationalists or Grotians. In doing so, the author seeks to solve two problems: to overcome the "strait-jacket" in which intellectual works were confined and to broaden the "tradition" of a new science by resorting to the authority and to the greatness of a character as eminent as Hugo Grotius.

Wight describes the rationalists as the ones who "concentrate on and believe in the value of, the element of international intercourse in a condition of international anarchy mainly. They believe that man, although manifestly a sinful and bloodthirsty creature is also rational."[6] This rational element sometimes would allow men to escape from the fate of living like beasts and to ascend to a less aggressive existence. The Grotian tradition would be in the middle ground between Realism and Idealism. Grotians as well as realists formulate descriptive—not prescriptive—theories of International Relations, but believe that law and diplomacy stem not only from the correlation of force between States and can also have a saying on International Politics. The *raison d'être* would remain unavoidable, but Grotians do not dismiss the idea of the rule of law.

In addition to distilling from the Grotian thought a somewhat dubious essence, Wight goes as far as portraying such a caricatural essence as follows:

> The older International Law writers were divided into Naturalists, Positivists and Grotians. Naturalists maintain that the only Law of Nations is in the Law of Nature, that is, in first principles, and that custom and treaties make no true law; Positivists maintain the reverse that the Law of Nations is only what is found in custom and treaty, and the Law of Nature is non-legal or non-existent. The Grotians combine the two, saying both are essential to the Law of Nations.[7]

In this excerpt, the author seeks to portray the "Grotians of International Law" as scholars halfway between Positivists and Naturalists. They would accept the existence of international rules of a moral nature along with other rules whose creation depends on the willingness of States. Soon after, the excesses of that interpretation led Hedley Bull, Martin Wight's disciple and an assumed Grotian, to affirm, in a text from 1966 entitled "**The Grotian Conception of International**

---

[6]Wight (1991), p. 13.

[7]Wight (1991), p. 14.

Society,"[8] that the connection between Neogrotians of International Relations and Grotius himself was very much faint.

This mystifying reading of Grotius drifts away from Grotius' original intent, since it stems from today's men in light of contemporary concerns who believe that the Dutch jurist was addressing International Law in his works. But during Grotius' time, the national State was under construction and the only consolidated States were those from the Iberian Peninsula. Therefore, it seems inappropriate to read the Grotian Law of Nations as a synonym for interstate law. Moreover, during this period, the idea of unity among nations was fading: the Great Navigations had shown Europeans a diversity of habits and customs much wider than the non-European cultures already known to them (mainly Muslim). In addition, the Reformation had shaken the Pope's power over Christian princes as the only supranational authority since the fall of the Roman Empire.

The Dutch jurist arose in a time of transition. On the one side, the forces of the new, embodied in the person of Cardinal Richelieu, already conceived Politics in terms of national units. On the other side, the forces of the old, the papal, and imperial writers who preached the restoration of the fallen central institutions of Latin Christendom still existed. In this context, Grotius' writings found immediate success. When Gustavus Adolphus rode by Germania during the Thirty Years' War, he would have carried a copy of **De Jure Belli ac Pacis**. Years later, the British used the arguments regarding the free navigation of the seas against the Dutch monopolies.

The success of the Dutch jurist was so resounding that it shaped his myth. In 1661, in the University of Heidelberg, Samuel Pufendorf created the chair "Law of Nature and of Nations" to teach modern Public Law and its institutions: the social contract, the Natural Rights inherent to man and the Law of Nations. As a textbook, he used Grotius' **Law of War and Peace**. During the following century, among the members of the School of the Law of Nature and of Nations, the legend of a single founder of the subject arose. It is curious that while Grotius received many compliments, the Scholastics were associated with "obscurantism" and the "Medieval past."[9]

In the first 300 years since his birth, Hugo Grotius was considered the single father of an entire branch of law, Public International Law, as well as the father of Modern Philosophy of Law as well as of the notion of subjective right. His influence also spread to other fields, such as Private International Law. His work was revolutionary and pioneer in all the fields it came across. In 1874, however, Sir Thomas Erksine Holland, in his famous inaugural lecture at Oxford took Grotius off the pedestal and placed Alberico Gentili in his stead as the true creator of International Law. According to Sir Thomas, the jurist from Delft was a mere disciple to Gentili, surely his most popular one.[10]

The decline of Grotius corresponded to the rise of Francisco de Vitória. In 1860, there is a rediscovery of all the Spanish Scholastics, of which the Theologian of

---

[8]Bull (1966), pp. 51–73.

[9]Haggenmacher (1988), pp. 27–28.

[10]Holland (1874), pp. 1–23.

Salamanca is deemed the pioneer. There were other authors such as Domingos de Soto and Francisco Suárez whose works on Theology and general Philosophy were better known than those of Vitória. Yet Vitória's lecture on the Indians and on the civil power had an appeal that was hard to ignore and quickly the Dominican would become the central character of the Scholastic movement. The other Spanish Scholastics assumed a secondary role as followers of the great *maestro*.

The 1860s mark the turning point for the studies of Vitória due to a very unusual fact: the discovery of **De Jure Praedae Commentarius**, a work that Hugo Grotius had never published and that had disappeared. Rather than calling attention to the Jurist from Delft, the several references to the Scholastics, especially to Vitória, served only to ignite the dispute regarding the paternity of the Law of Nations. The very preface to the edition of Gerhard Hamaker underlines the decisive influence of the Spaniards.[11] By the end of that century, the revisionist literature had multiplied inside and outside Spain. Within this country, Eduardo Hinojosa had emphasized the importance of the Spanish Theologians. Moreover, in Belgium, Ernst Nys and the Swiss Alphonse Rivier virtually erased Hugo Grotius's originality:

> [When it is said that Grotius is the father of Natural Law and the father of International Law], is it asserted that a whole new discipline came out of his head, that he invented or imagined as if by divine intuition, the previously unknown rules of war, peace and relations among states, among sovereigns, the covenants, the embassies? Nothing would be contrary both to the logic of things and to the truth. A number of canonists, jurists, publicists wrote, since the Middle Ages, on such diverse topics as well as on matters pertaining to the Natural Law.[12]

In the early twentieth century, the reputation of Francisco de Vitória was already quite established and no study on the history of International Law could neglect him. The Dominican Theologian ceases to be included among the forerunners of Grotius and becomes the central figure of entire theses, such as the one from Quilicus Albertini. Furthermore, studies like that of Alfred Vanderpol and Joseph Kohler honored the Catholic version of Natural Law and of the Law of Nations. The Protestants had lost the battle.[13]

A few years later, what were scattered voices became a resounding chorus. In 1927, at the Hague Academy of International Law, a disciple of Ernst Nys, Camilo Barcia Trelles teaches a course on Francisco de Vitória. In that same year, a Protestant and Anglo-Saxon author, James Brown Scott teaches lessons on Vitória in Spain. **The Hispanic Origin of International Law** is the first version of a work

---

[11]GROTIUS, Hugonis. **De Jure Praedae Commentarius**. La Haye: Hamaker, Nijhoff, 1868. p. XI. Henceforth, **DJPC**.

[12]"*Est-ce à dire qu'une discipline toute neuve lui ait jailli du cerveau, qu'il ait inventé ou imaginé, par une sorte d'intuition divine, les règles inconnues jusqu'à lui de la guerre, de la paix, des raports entre États, entre souverains, des alliances, des ambassades? Rien ne serait plus contraire, soit à la logique des choses, soit à la verité. Quantité des canonistes, des légistes, des publicistes ont écrit dès le moyen âge sur ces divers sujets, comme aussi sur les sujets appartenant au droit naturel.*" (Rivier, 1883). See also Hinojosa, 1890 and Nys, 1882.

[13]Haggenmacher (1988), pp. 32–33.

that was reviewed and published time after time. The name of the Salamanca Theologian spread to all locations. In France, several works on Public Law—such as those of Hubert Beuve-Mery, Jean Baumel and the classic work of Joseph Delos —distinctly refer to him. In the 1930s Germany, Friedrich Heydte, Heinz Kipp, and Alois Dempf devote much more attention to Vitória than Carl von Kaltenborn had done in 1848. In Spain, the Franciso de Vitória Association was founded in 1926 and then named Francisco de Vitória Institute of International Law in 1933. Shortly before World War II, the Hall of Councils of the *Palais des Nations*, decorated by José María Sert, is named Room Francisco-de-Vitória.[14]

The prestige of the Dominican Theologian was such that he became independent from the other members of the Spanish Scholasticism. While some authors advocate the existence of a true Hispanic school of International Law, others seek to raise and separate Vitória above all others.[15] Although most Theologians of that period attempt to formulate a notion of *jus gentium*, the Jesuit Francisco Suárez is often chosen for comparison purposes. In his book on the principles of Public Law, Delos compares the two writers, always to the detriment of Suárez, in order to prove that Vitória's notion of international society had an objective ground[16] while that of Suárez denoted a State-centered Voluntarism—in the sense that he would be a precursor of legal Positivism.

Even in authors who accept a line of continuity between the Jesuit and the Dominican, Suárez is but a follower. James Brown Scott, probably the writer who most fervently acclaims both the Theologians of Salamanca and Grenade and finds the origin of various institutes of contemporary International Law in their works, optimistically considers Francisco de Vitória the first expositor, Francisco Suárez the Philosopher and Hugo Grotius the organizer. Still, the epithet of Philosopher does not prevent Scott from taking away all the originality from Suarez: according to him, the famous Suárez's distinction of *jus intra gentes* and *jus inter gentes* is

---

[14]Haggenmacher (1988), pp. 34–35.

[15]Among those that deny the existence of a Spanish School of International Law are Camilo Barcia Trelles (1933) and Joseph Delos (1950). Among those who support this idea are Adolfo Miaja de la Muela (1932) and Luciano Pereña in his series *Corpus Hispanorum de Pace*. Although Luciano Pereña believes in a true *hispanorum corpus de pace*, he devotes much of his works to study Suárez in particular. Chapters III and V refer to the works of this author. It is worth verifying whether those who see such discrepancies between the legal works of Francisco de Vitória and those of the other Spanish scholastics, and of Francisco Suárez in particular, are not merely influenced by the theologian dissonance between the Dominicans (Bañez) and the Jesuits (Molina) on the issue of the foreknowledgment of God.

[16]*Or, à ce problème, il n'y a en définitive, que deux solutions: la force obligatoire du droit positif lui vient d'un fondament objectivf, le bien commun, dont il interprète les exigences idéales en fonction d'un donné historique, – ou de l'accord de volontés. Volontarisme ou droit à fondement objectif, telles nous semblent les seules branches de l'alternative. On pressent en quel sens se prononcera Suarez.*" Delos (1950), p. 270. I strongly disagree with this idea. For further information, see the final part of chapter V.

already found in Vitória, as well as his description of the international community, which Vitória allegedly already presented in a more appealing and complete way.[17]

As will be seen later, Francisco Suárez received an unfair treatment. It is Suárez, not Vitória, who occupies the most important place in the history of International Law. The Suarezian *jus gentium* refers to something new and different and influences the Grotian *jus gentium*.

The controversy over the paternity of International Law today remains unclear. In addition to Francisco de Vitória and Hugo Grotius, other authors dispute the title, though with less intensity, such as Francisco Suárez himself, Fernando Vasquez de Menchaca, and Alberico Gentili. The latter, ever since the inaugural speech of Sir Thomas E. Holland, occasionally arouses interest. However, contrary to a 100 years ago, Gentili no longer disputes the paternity of the Law of Nations, but that of the more original, more secular, more Modern or, at least, less Medieval doctrine[18] thereof.

The debate regarding the founder of International Law is insolvable. Any work that advocates a name over another is ideological: in possession of what they consider the "quintessence" of International Law (generally, either Positive Law or "Statism"), historians of today attempt to find traces of these elements in the doctrines of the authors of the sixteenth and seventeenth centuries.

It is necessary to remember that Vitória, Suárez, Gentili, and Grotius wrote for different audiences and in light of different concerns than those of today. It is strange that James Brown Scott discovers, in Vitória, the source of the principle of the legal equality of nations and today's notion of citizenship or is able to compare the thought of the Theologian with that of President Lincoln.[19]

---

[17]Scott (1934), pp. 183–184.

[18]Recently, historians of International Law have been studying the work of Gentili. Peter Haggenmacher proves that he is the one who influenced Grotius the most. He also weighs that Grotius and Gentili cannot be both considered father of International Law; however, the approach of the latter—topical and less systematic—seems less "older" than Grotius'. The question is if Haggenmacher only exalts Gentili or criticizes contemporary International Law altogether. (Haggenmacher 2002). Diego Panizza presents the difference between a teleological view, inherent to the Scholastics, and that of the Humanists such as Gentili. The author takes note of the influence of Macchiaveli—and the consequent resemblance of Gentili's *jurisprudentia* with Politics—and states that the Gentili, in addition to building the grounds for the Science of International Law, embodies the emergence of the modern paradigm (PANIZZA, 2005). The influence of Machiavelli undoubtedly explains why some authors can find elements of secularism in Gentili. Although secularism seems somewhat counterfactual in a writer of the early seventeenth century, his Realistic "tone" produces this belief. Yet, as it will be seen further, Gentili endorses a notion of *jus gentium* older than that of Grotius' or Suarez.

[19]Scott (2003), pp. 137, 147 and 254.

The problem with this discussion lies in the very approach of all sides to the dispute: the pursuit of a single founder of International Law. The solution does not stem from a book of single authorship. In 1904, Antoine Pillet (who had previously directed the thesis of Quilicus Albertini) publishes a collective work entitled ***Les fondateurs du droit international***,[20] composed of a series of essays, each regarding a founding father.

The title already indicates the change in perspective; instead of one, the discipline would entail several founders. The list opens with Vitória, then moves to Gentili, Suárez, Grotius and continues with Zouche, Pufendorf, Bynkershoek, Wolff, Vattel and ends with Martens, at the time of the French Revolution. The same perspective permeates the Classics of International Law collection, published in 1906 by the Carnegie Endowment for International Peace, under the initiative of James Brown Scott. The Belgian Internationalist Maurice Bourquin, in a conference in Geneva in 1946, summed up this new perspective well: "The father of the Law of Nations is a general partnership, if I may so express myself; is a series of thinkers and jurists, a few preceded Grotius and others magnified and developed his work during the seventeenth and eighteenth centuries."[21]

It is important to bear in mind that the concept of the Law of Nations does not correspond, necessarily, to that of International Law. If the latter refers to a Positive Law between sovereign States that are equal among themselves, then perhaps the first Jusinternationalist would have been Emerich de Vattel. Indeed, there is no correlation between the titles from a summary of a textbook of International Law and those of the works of Hugo Grotius, or those of the Spanish Scholastics. These authors wrote on a subject that resembles International Law, but does not coincide perfectly with it. This subject is the Law of Medieval warfare, the Just War doctrine.

2.1.2 International Law and the Just War Doctrine

The Just War doctrine represents the middle path between the total repudiation of war, often seen among Idealists, and the unconditional acceptance of violence for the glory of the State advocated by certain conceptions of political Realism, as if kings and *potestades* were not bound by morality and laws of nature. The supporters of the Just War doctrine recognize that war is an evil, but that there are worse evils, like the murder of innocents and the desecration of cemeteries and holy places at the hands of invading soldiers. This is a universal tradition, first developed by Christian Theologians and Canonists, but also by lay jurists.

---

[20]Pillet (1904).

[21]"*Le père du droit de gens, c'est une société en nom collectif, si j'ose ainsi m'exprimer; c'est une série de penseurs et de juristes, dont les uns on précédé Grotius, dont les autres on élargi et développé son oeuvre, au cours du XVIIème et du XVIIIème siècles.*" (Bourquin 1948, p. 77). The idea of this change in perspective is referenced in Haggenmacher (1988), p. 36.

Most historians credit the origins of the doctrine to the *jus fetiale* of the Romans *collegia fetiales*. This *corpus juris* existed from the days of the kings until the end of the Republican era. *Fetiales* were priests brought together in a form of corporation (*collegia*), and charged with a series of obligations, partly religious and partly legal (*jus sacrum*). Among their many duties, they were entrusted with pronouncing the beginning of a war. Two conditions of procedural nature were essential to that end: an official notice to the opponent insisting on the redress of the injury or offense directed to Rome and providing a term for the opponent to respond, followed by a formal declaration of war. The latter took place at an elaborate religious ceremony, marked by the recitation of legal formulas in an adequately grand tone of voice, ending with the throwing of a spear soaked in blood into the border of the enemy's territory. Rome could not go to war without the prior and express approval of the *fetiales*, since the gods only favored the *bellum iustum et pium*. Yet, as the *fetiales* were subject to the authority of political leaders, they always sought a justification for hostilities (e.g., violation of a treaty or immunity of ambassadors, violation of territorial rights or offenses against allied States).[22]

However, the influence of the law of the fetials in the Just War doctrine turns out to be so elusive that it becomes difficult to establish any sort of correlation. Its development during the Middle Ages bears no resemblance to its Roman origins. The Medieval Law of War had no formalities and was not even subject to political authority. From Rome, solely the idea of preaching to the justice or injustice of certain armed conflicts seems to have survived. Wars were no longer natural events or fatalities and began to enter the domain of morally relevant actions.

Some authors[23] find in the Medieval Law of War influences of the Hebrews of the Old Testament. Hellenic reminiscences are also undeniable. Nevertheless, there appears to be a consensus that the Law of War is a specifically Christian doctrine that began properly with Saint Augustine (354–430). There were earlier influences, but their influence is only marginal to the main aspect of this tradition: the justice of a war.

From a purely procedural matter in the ancient times, the idea of Just War acquired a material element throughout the Middles Ages. War and all the violence and destruction it engendered posed a serious moral problem for Christianity; apart from always engaging in strifes against non-Christians and even against Christians, the sacred texts can be misleading. On the one side, there is Christ's teachings about peace and "turn the other cheek" to the enemy, which could generate a radical pacifist interpretation in repudiation of any war, even those that are defensive in nature. On the other side, in the Old Testament, God reveals himself as the "Lord of the armies," a title that might legitimize any holy war.

---

[22]Fusinato (1885), p. 273 et seq.

[23]Vanderpol (1919), pp. 160–170.

For Christianity, war is not an evil in itself. According to the Spanish *maestros*, the evils that befall war are merely incidental and do not exceed the drawbacks that there would exist should war not be allowed.[24] Moreover, no religious council has ever permanently prohibited Christians from taking part in a war. There are undoubtedly some restrictions: the Council of Nicaea outlawed battles after baptism; in Isaiah, there can be no killing and no dying on the holy mountain—and in wider interpretations, in any sacred places. The reasoning behind this notion lies in the fact that war is not opposed to peace, but to the bad peace, one that endures to the detriment of justice and law. There is a substantial difference between the concepts of peace and tranquility. The latter means paralysis, the former means harmony. Harmony always presupposes equilibrium, a balance in the scales of justice. Therefore, *true* peace rests in law.

The Just War doctrine is eminently a Christian tradition, because it was developed and re-elaborated by authors of the European Christendom. After its origin with St. Augustine, other Church Fathers, St. Isidore of Seville and Pope Nicholas I, took up the doctrine of Just War. There was then a hiatus during the high Middle Ages, when the doctrine received little attention. Only in the twelfth century did the subject begin to interest thinkers again with the Gratian Decree. Writing about the war became very popular in the late Middle Ages. Canonists and Theologians began to scrutinize the arguments until the doctrine acquired its classic formula with Thomas Aquinas. Due to Aquinas' interest on the subject, the idea of Just War became an obligatory reference for all scholars. For this reason, Alfred Vanderpol prefers to call it the "Scholastic doctrine of the Law of War."[25]

---

[24]SUÁREZ, R. P. Francisci. **Opera Omnia**. *Editio Nova. Parisiis: Ludovicum Vivès*, 1858. *Tomus* XII. **De Fide, Spe et Charitate**. *Tratactus de Charitate. Disputatio* XIII. **De Bello**, 1, 2. Hencerforth, **DB**.

[25]Vanderpol (1919), p. 285. Besides St. Augustin, St. Isidore of Seville (560–636) and the Pope Nicholas I, with his letter to the Bulgarians, are both authors of this tradition, together with Bishop Rufin, in the treaty **De bono pacis** (1056), Yves de Chartres (1040–1116) and Abelardo (1079–1142). In the first half of the twelfth century, there is also the decree of the monk Jean de Gratian. Subsequently, there appears St. Thomas, Raimundo de Peñaforte (1180–1275), Pope Innocent IV (1243–1254), Hostiensis (Henri de Suse: beginning of the thirteenth century-1271), Alexandre de Halès (1170–1245), Henri de Gand (beginning of the thirteenth century-1293) and St. Boaventura (1221–1274). In the fourteenth and fifteenth centuries, there are other works which titles refer to war: Jean de Legnano (beginning of the twenty fourth century-1383)—**De Bello** (1360), Henri de Gorychum—**De Bello Justo** (1420), St. Anthony of Florence (1389–1459), Alphonse Tostate (1400–1455), Martin de Lodi—**De Bello** (fifteenth century), Gabriel Biel (1425–1495), Sivestre Prierias (1456–1523), Thomas de Vio (Cajetan: 1468–1534), Guilherme Mathiae—**Libellus de Bello Iustitia Iniustitiave** (1533), Josse Clichthove (1472–1543). Afterwards, with the Great Navigations, names such as Francisco de Vitória, Francisco Suárez and Balthasar de Ayala—**De Jure et Officiis Bellicis et Disciplina Militari** (1582) appeared. From this period, it is also possible to cite: A. Guerrero—**Tratactus de Bello Justo et Injusto** (1543), Diego de Covarruvias (1512–1577), Domingos de Soto (1494–1560), F. Martini—**De Bello et Duello** (1589), Gabriel Vasquez (1551–1604), Domingos Bañez (1528–1604), Roberto Berlarmino (1542–1621), Leonardo Lessius (1554–1623), Gregory of Valencia (1561–1603), Luís de Molina (1536–1600), P. Belli—**De re Militari et Bello** (1558), Alberico Gentili—**De Jure Belli** (1598) and Grotius himself—**De Jure Belli ac Pacis** (1625).

According to some textbooks,[26] in the beginning of Christianity, as the religion faced persecution and represented a minority, the Church adopted a peaceful posture and even forbade Christians to enlist as soldiers. However, after the spread of Christianity, when it became the official religion of the Empire and Christians started to shed blood not only as martyrs, the question of whether it would be lawful or not to engage in a war arose.

This view seems rather cynical. According to Haggenmacher, the early Church Fathers expressed objections to military service, but it is not possible to infer therefrom a radical pacifism. Most of their objections focused not on the violence but on the service itself; the religious aspect, the mandatory imperial cult in the army, seemed incompatible with the worship of the true God. Moreover, these objections appeared very sporadically. "Therefore, only a few martyrs proceeded to the end in their refusal; faithful soldiers sometimes chose to withdraw from military life, as allowed by the Roman system; but the great mass of Christian soldiers obeyed, without doubt, to the word of the Apostle that exhorts each to retain the position he occupies."[27]

The Church has never accepted the thesis of radical pacifism. Christians did not cease to swell the ranks of the legions long before the Edicts of Rome and Milan. Their large presence in the army was the main cause of the last persecutions carried out by the Romans. Moreover, as it would be, the movement that would culminate in the Edicts of Toleration of Constantine and of Licinius in the year of 313—which did not consider the military profession to be a sin—actually rose within the army. The compatibility of the military service with Christianity was such that one of the Fathers of the Church, St. Athanasius, came to preach that it was not only allowed but even glorious to give one's life in a Just War.[28]

Haggenmacher also criticizes the notion, made popular by Alfred Vanderpol, that all scholars and authors after Augustine of Hippo had simply systematized a doctrine which essence had already been conceived. It is not about contesting the relevance that the work of St. Augustine has had to the Medieval Law of War, but that it would form a true doctrine. For this to occur, for a doctrine regarding a particular subject to be established, it is necessary that this subject is investigated by itself; it must be the main scope of a precise and relatively autonomous set of coherent propositions.[29]

However, the first writings on the justice of war only dealt with war ancillarily. As seen, war itself was not the main issue that the Fathers were attempting to solve, but the legitimacy of a public service, the military service, in the light of Christian morality. Therefore, St. Augustine's statements are but a late manifestation of this

---

[26]Dinstein (2004), p. 89.

[27]"*Pourtant seuls quelques martyrs sont allés jusqu'au bout de leur refus, d'autres fidèles choisirent peut-être de se retirer de la vie militaire, comme le système romain le leur permettait; mais la grande masse des soldats chrétiens obéissait sans doute à la parole de l'Apôtre enjoignant à chacun de se maintenir dans la situation qu'il occupait.*" (Haggenmacher 1983, pp. 14–15).

[28]Nys (1894), p. 45.

[29]Haggenmacher (1983), p. 13.

concern. In the famous passage from ***Contra Faustum manichaeum***, in which he defends the campaign of Moses against the actions of Faustus of Milev, war is not the central issue. What was central in his campaign was the unconditional obedience to the unfathomable but also just divine commands: "the fact that Moses waged wars should not provoke strangeness or horror, because he had done it not on cruelty, but on obedience and respect to the divine commands."[30]

In **De Civitate Dei**, war became target of criticism because it represented one of the main tools of the Roman imperialism. St. Augustine uses it as a warhorse within the larger fight against the false values chanted by Virgil: the illusory grandeur of Rome is a result of *superbia*, not of *pietas*. The famous verse of this poet appears in the preface of the same book.[31] In truth, then Augustine's criticism is not directed to war itself, but to all pagan morality. It is from the *pax* and from the related notion of *ordo naturalis* that his understanding becomes complete. As in his Theodicy, in which evil is reduced to an absence of good, without having a proper consistency, war is merely a reflexive idea of the positive notions of *pax* and *ordo*. The human will is free to undergo *ordo,* by *pietas*, or to contest it by *superbia*. The *pietas* leads to the *pax ordinata* that is in harmony with the *ordo naturalis*; *superbia* leads to the *pax perversa*, the peace from the diabolic city. In order for the war to be fair, it has to abandon this kind of peace and build a better one, more appropriate to the *ordo naturalis* that corresponds to the divine will.[32]

In reaction to the feudal greed for combat, the Church positioned itself against war. Nonetheless, its hostility was limited to wars among the faithful. The aim was to reduce the violence and destruction caused by war. The clergy were then prohibited to shed blood. A council sentenced the companions of William the Conqueror to a 1-year penance for each person killed, 40 days for those they wounded and 3 days for all those who they wished to hurt. There was no question around the legitimacy of war itself; only the Unjust War was a true punishment from God.[33]

Historians usually consider the St. Isidore of Seville's eighteenth book of the **Etymologies** an obligatory reference in the High Middle Ages. The author distinguishes four kinds of war: *bellum justum, injustum bellum, bellum civile*, and *plusquam civile bellum* (the one between generals united by family). "Just is the war that is declared to recover things that have been taken or to repel the enemy." And, in its turn, "the war that comes from a furor and was not initiated by a

---

[30]"*(...) nec bella per Moysen gesta miretur aut horreat, quia et in illis divina secutus imperia non saeviens, sed oboediens fuit* (...)" (Agostinho. **Obras de San Agustin**. Trad. Pío de Luis. Edição bilíngüe. Madrid: BAC, 1993. t. XXXI. *Escritos antimaniqueos. Contra Fausto*. p. 604. XXII. 74).

[31]Agostinho. **Obras de San Agustin**. Trad. José Moran. Edição bilíngue. Madrid: BAC, 1958. t. XVI. *La Ciudad de Dios*, p. 62. I. *Praefatio*.

[32]Truyol y Serra (1944), pp. 57–70.

[33]Nys (1894), p. 46.

legitimate reason is unjust."[34] There are therefore two requirements for the justice of a war in this definition: a declaration of war and a just cause. The just cause may be that to repel an enemy, which characterizes a defensive war, or to vindicate a stolen property, a species of the genus injury.

Despite the significance that this definition would later acquire—mainly because it would be reproduced in the Gratian Decree—Haggenmacher points out that this formula is a commonplace in ancient literature and was not really central to the Just War tradition. The Swiss Internationalist demonstrates that the Bishop of Seville wanted to resume two sentences of Cicero and not carry on St. Augustine's thought on the war,[35] which would have little or no impact at all in this period. It is important to bear in mind that this does not apply to the Augustinian notions of *pax* and *iustitia*, which comprise the heart of the Political Augustinianism. The Christian notion of justice is rooted in the West since the end of the Empire, due to the privileged role that various popes would play in the political organization of the Frank and Germanic monarchies.

Only in the twelfth century did the Just War doctrine begin to take shape. In Bologna, in the year of 1140, the monk Gratian writes ***Concordia discordantium canonum*** that marks the beginning of the classical Canon Law. A substantial portion of the work, the *Causa XXIII*, focused on war and it has ever since been a mandatory subject for future generations of Theologians and Canonists. The **Gratian Decree** proves to be a work on both Law and Theology, which opens it to many interpretations. The Decree consolidates several subject matters—including war—and brings together a wide range of Patristic quotations. All the passages that are traditionally associated with the Just War doctrine are in the same place. If Haggenmacher is right—and both Augustine and Isidore had not dwelled on the idea of Just War—then it is in the **Decree** that this tradition begins. The mere encoding of all Christian thought on the subject in a single place is a clear indication of the desire to investigate the issue for itself. The quotes were taken out of their original context and began to acquire a value of their own, as a universal rule. This is a more generic approach, characteristic of the understanding of the time regarding the *auctoritates*: rules of a general character are necessarily found in the *auctoriates*, without taking notice of the framework of which they were only a part. Gratian comes as far as granting to the excerpts of the Patristic the same weight as the decisions of councils and the decretals of popes: they all amount to canons.[36]

---

[34]"*Justum bellum est quod ex praedicto geritur de rebus repetitis aut propulsandorum hostium causa.*" And "*Iniustum bellum est quod de furore, non de legitima ratione initiur.*" (ISIDORUS HISPALENSIS EPISCOPUS. **Etymologiarum sive Originum Libri XX**. ed. W.M. Lindsay. Oxford: Clarendon Press, 1911. XVIII, *De bello et ludis*, I, 2).

[35]The resemblance with Isidore's phrases is clear: "*Illa iniusta bella sunt, quae sunt sine causa suscepta. Nam extra ulciscendi aut propulsandorum hostium causa bellum geri iustum nullum potest. (...) Nullum bellum iustum habetur, nisi denuntiatum, nisi dictum, nisi de repetitis rebus.*" (Cicerón 1954, p. 164. Book III, 23).

[36]Haggenmacher (1983), pp. 24–25.

The *Causa XXIII* from the **Gratian Decree** is entitled *De re militari et bello* and is divided into eight issues. Unprecedented, the first issue expressly addresses the morality of wars: *an militare sit peccatum?* ("Is it a sin to make war?"). Despite evoking the Gospels that preach for sweetness and forbid revenge, the author admits that war may be legitimate. Some wars are necessary, and the necessity thereof would excuse a certain degree of violence.[37]

However, the necessity in itself is not enough to legitimize a war. Gratian borrows from the Treaty of St. Augustine against the Manichees a list of all the reprehensible actions in a conflict: the desire to destroy, the cruelty of vengeance, the ruthlessness and violence of the spirit, the savagery in combat, the passion to dominate and all other such excesses. The mere engagement in a war does not equate to a sin, but war should not be carried out with cruelty and greed, but only in the pursuit of peace. The Decree sets forth two definitions of Just War, that of Isidore of Seville, already quoted, and one borrowed from St. Augustine: "It has been the custom to call just wars those which purpose is to avenge the injustices, to punish a city or a country that did not punish an unlawful act committed by one of their own, or to restore what has been taken unjustly."[38] Therefore, just is the war which purpose is the pursuit of peace, to avenge an "in-jury" and to retrieve a good unjustly taken.

When Gratian uses the definition of the Bishop of Seville, he introduces a subtle modification. He replaces the expression *ex praedicto*, which implies the need of a declaration, by *ex edicto*, which implies the existence of an authority to order the wage of war.[39] Therefore, a vague notion begins to take shape—and would later be developed by Raymundo Penñaforte and Aquinas: the notion that a legitimate authority must declare the Just War.

Before the Gratian Decree, there are still some canonical collections relevant to the Just War doctrine, such as those of Burchard of Worms (1012), Anselmus of Lucca (1083) and Ivo of Chartres (1095), all of which influenced Gratian. However, Gratian's merits lies in the fact that he devised the justice in a war not strictly in theological or moral terms, but also legal, at least partially.

For instance, in the collections of Ivo of Chartres the **Decretum Ivonis** and the **Panormia Ivonis**, the canons on war do not form a body of rules separated from the rest of the work; they are inserted in the subjects of murder, massacre, and violence in general. Although the Gratian Decree assembles several texts of the works of Ivo, the context had changed. Although it is possible to identify objective criteria, on the works of Ivo the aura of voluntarism prevailed: justice depends on the straight intention of the combatants. The soldier cannot fight with *odium* or *avaritia* in his heart. Nevertheless, when quoting Ivo, Gratian rearranged the texts and wipes out

[37] GRATIANUS. **Decretorum Codex**. *Venetiis*: Nicolai Jenson Sallici, 1477. Causa XXIII, I, 1.

[38] "*Iusta enim bella definiri solent, quae ulciscuntur injurias, si gens vel civitas plectenda est quae, vel vindicare neglexerit quod a suis improbe factum est, vel reddere quod per injurias ablatum est.*" (GRATIANUS. **Decretorum Codex**. Causa XXIII, II, 1).

[39] Nys (1894), p. 100.

any shred of "intentionalism" from it. War makes for an independent subject of study, no longer attached to the study of murder. There exists a sketch of an objective and legal public order.[40]

Although the Gratrian Decree examines war in itself, Haggenmacher emphasizes that Gratian's purpose seems not to investigate the justice in a war. If one considers the *Causa XXIII* as a whole, then the key subject thereof is the legitimacy of coercive power among Christians in the domain of faith. War is but one manner of exercising such power. The first three questions that deal with war, especially the very question that characterizes what a Just War is, are the most concise questions. Given their extent, the two median questions are the center of attention, and they relate to the vindictive power and its ultimate consequence: the capital sentence imposed by a judge. Therefore, the core of the problem lies in the idea of coercive power. The first three questions are of a preliminary nature and discard a fundamental objection; the two median questions cope with the subject itself; the sixth and seventh questions deal with the immediate consequences of the power of repression and the eighth one addresses a particular issue that is the use of weapons by clerics. History also confirms this interpretation of the *Causa XXIII*, since all the leading decreetalists of the twelfth century also adopted it in their comments.[41]

Still, even if the *Causa XXIII* does not encompass a true Just War doctrine, the specificities of its contents—the fact that it addresses war in itself and assembles a large number of Patristic references on the subject—were decisive in the emergence of the Just War doctrine. From Gratian to Thomas Aquinas, the doctrine of war develops itself in an organic and continuous fashion. If the Church Fathers imprint no depth to the study of the subject, whereas in the Gratian Decree it is part of a larger issue, it succeeds anyhow in gaining autonomy among jurists, canonists, and decretalists.

The collection of decretals that one Spanish Dominican named Raymundo Peñaforte managed to assemble in the first half of the thirteenth century, under the orders of Pope Gregory IX, are worth mentioning. The author establishes five conditions for war to be just (*persona, res, cause, animus* and *auctoritas*), which would later be condensed by Aquinas in only three. Shortly after, two other authors produce their comments to the Gregorian decretals: Pope Innocent IV, one of the greatest jurists to occupy the seat of Peter, in the **Apparatus in quinque libros decretalium**, and Henri de Suse, known as *Cardinalis Hostiensis,* in **Summa Aurea**.[42]

Then, between the years of 1263 and 1269, St. Thomas Aquinas writes his **Summa Theologica** and introduces the classic formula of the Just War doctrine. His work would exert influence on Theologians, Moralists, and Canonists alike, even though Aquinas was not a lawyer. His research on war is encapsulated in question 40 of the Treaty of Charity *secunda secundae*, and summarized in four

[40] Bauer (2005), pp. 50–54.

[41] Haggenmacher (1983), pp. 26–27.

[42] Haggenmacher (1983), p. 38.

articles. The first article deals with the issue of the lawfulness of war; the second questions whether it would be lawful for clerics to go to war; the third addresses both the legitimacy of using stratagems and the legality of fighting on holy days. But the first article is indeed the core of his theory. For a war to be just, it must satisfy three conditions:

> First, the authority of the prince, by whose mandate it is allowed to make war. The private person is not competent to declare war because he can submit his claim to a higher court. (…).
>
> It is required, secondly, a just cause, namely, that those who are deemed guilty deserve for some fault such an impugnation. (…).
>
> Thirdly, it is required a straight intent on the part of the combatants: that they attempt to or promote good or avoid evil. (…)[43]

In light of the authority that the thought of Aquinas would acquire over time, these three conditions define the Scholastic Doctrine of Just War.

Lay jurists also began turning their interests to the law of war. At the end of the thirteenth century, Cino of Pistoia and many a French jurist of the School of Orléans began studying the subject. At the beginning of the following century, the great Medieval jurist Bartolus of Saxoferrato reinforces the doctrine by incorporating the theories of Innocent IV. A disciple of Bartolus, Iohannes Lignano wrote in 1360 the first book to exclusively address the law of war: **Tratactus de bello, de represaliis et de duello**. Lignano set a tradition that would culminate in Gentili and Grotius. This book would acquire a very practical connotation due to the many a dissemination such as those from Christine de Pisan, William Caxton, and the famous work of Honoré Bonnet, *L' Arbre des Batailles*, all written in vulgar language. From then until the time of Grotius, several works specifically addressing the law of war begin to emerge, such as the treaties of Martin of Lodi, Juan Lopes, Pierino Belli, Balthasar Ayala and Heinrich Bocer. Therefore, a progressive consolidation of the intellectual *corpus* of the Just War[44] doctrine emerges.

Despite the fact that it is Lignano's book that establishes the Just War doctrine, he does nothing more than compiling the findings of his predecessors. He introduces a period of stagnation in the discipline, dominated by a rather sterile casuistic approach, except for some isolated progresses such as those made by Lucas de Penna or Raphael Fulgosa. From the sixteenth century onwards, although the general interest on the subject only increased, lawyers were not the ones to develop the law of war. The Theologians did. Haggenmacher mentions the contributions of

---

[43]"*Primo quidem, auctoritas principis, cuius mandato bello est gerendum. Non enim pertinet ad personam privatam bellum movere: quia potest ius suum in iudicio superioris prosequi. (…) Secundo, requiritur causa iusta: ut scilicet illi qui impugnantur propter aliquam culpam impugnationem mereantur. (…) Tertio, requiritur ut sit intentio bellantium recta: qua scillicet intenditur vel ut bonum promoveatur, vel ut malum vitetur.* (Aquino, Santo Tomás de. **Suma Teologica**. Texto latino de la edición crítica Leonina. Trad. Francisco Barbado Viejo, O.P. 2. ed. Madrid: Biblioteca de Autores Cristianos, 1947. 2-2 q. 40 a.1. Henceforth, **ST**).

[44]Haggenmacher (1983), pp. 39–40.

Martin Luther and Erasmus,[45] but they appear to be somewhat eccentric to the Just War tradition. The main writers of this period are in fact the Italian Thomas de Vio —namely, Cajetan—and the Spanish Scholastics. Among these, there is no doubt that Francisco de Vitória and Francisco Suárez occupy a prominent position, especially because they developed the concept of *jus gentium*.

2.2 The Evolution of the Concept of Jus Gentium

Vitória's understanding of the law of war and of the *jus gentium* will be examined separately, in light of the author's relevance to both Suárez and Grotius. For now, it is worth mentioning that in the late nineteenth and early twentieth centuries, there begins to take shape a literature that considers the Jurist of Delft and his Scholastic precursors the legitimate exponents of the Just War tradition. The reason thereof is that this doctrine is henceforth associated with the origin of the International Law. "The Middle Ages saw some elements of the Law of Nations arise, but they were too feeble to be of any relevance. Only the law of war would be really developed; it forms the core of International Law."[46] Even before the appearance of autonomous works on the Law of Nations, there already existed books on some of its subjects: the law of embassies, the law of trade and slavery. Thus, the law of war would correspond to an early manner of investigating the Law of Nations.

However, the assertion that the contemporary field of International Law originated in its entirety from the Medieval doctrine of the law of war is overstated. Except for Suárez and Grotius (Vitória and possibly Vázquez de Menchaca and Gentili may be included between these two, but not without any controversy), the concept of *jus gentium* in the authors of the Just War tradition does not correspond to a law between nations, but to a common domestic law, still immersed in Ulpian's Roman orbit—as mentioned below. Much of these Christian writers did not even use the expression "*jus gentium.*" According to a very suggestive image of Haggenmacher's, it seems possible to compare the evolution of the Just War doctrine towards International Law with the growth of a plant: if the latter corresponds to a flower, the law of war is its stalk.[47]

Suárez and Grotius undeniably take part in the Just War tradition, and were inspired by it when developing their concepts of *jus gentium*, as will be seen in other chapters. However, they did not write solely about law of war. They offer a definition of *jus gentium* in their works that sets them apart from all their predecessors. In order for this innovation to be unveiled in all its contours and thus for

---

[45]Haggenmacher (1983), p. 42. See, in chapter VI, Grotius' critics to Erasmus' ireninsm.

[46]"*Le moyen âge voit se former quelques institutions du droit de gens, mais elles sont trop chétives pour qu'on puisse em tenir compte. Seul, le droit de la guerre se développe sérieusement; il forme le noyeau du droit international.*" Nys (1894), p. 7. In addition, see, for illustrative purposes, another work that establishes the origin of International Law in the law of war: Vanderpol (1919).

[47]Haggenmacher (1988), p. 77.

these thinkers to have stood out, it is essential to present how the concept of *jus gentium* modified over time.

When Aristotle introduces his famous distinction between Natural and Legal Justice[48] in Book V of the **Nicomachean Ethics**, he also bequeathed to posterity (especially to Scholasticism) the notion that Natural Law would be unchangeable and that Positive Law would vary from place to place. One has a universal character, the other a particular one. One is based in truth, in the eternal essence of things; the other in opinion, in *doxa*, as ephemeral as human circumstances are.

However, this division is shortlived. A third term would emerge: the Law of Nations. This Law would bring together elements of the other two: it would be positive, yet applicable to all men. For a contemporary Internationalist, the nature of this Law does not constitute a problem: its universality does not derive from the natural reason; it is a mere framework of spatial validity encompassing all States. However, this apparent simplicity is misleading. The truth is that the Law of Nations is a *tertius genus*, a middle ground between Natural Law and Positive Law. There is an ethical content in the core of this legal branch.v

2.2.1 The Roman Notion

Roman Law exerted a profound influence on the authors of International Law. Until the eighteenth century, in addition to the sources, Rome bequeathed to the entire Western civilization, including the United Kingdom, a common legal terminology. Whenever possible, writers would make use of the vocabulary and the Roman sources. In fact, these references said nothing about International Law but constituted a mandatory tradition—as well as a source of inspiration. For example, the rules on private property (*dominium*) applied irrespective of territorial sovereignty; international treaties were born out of the rules on general contracts; the provisions on *mandatum* extended to the functions of diplomatic agents.[49]

Likewise, the concept of the Law of Nations derives from the Romans: it is the literal translation of *jus gentium*. It appeared first in Rome, during the tribal organization, even before the monarchy—which was instituted at the same time of the City, in 754 BC.—bearing a meaning quite different from International Law. The social organization of the Italian peninsula relied on those principles, a system called "gentile" because it formed the right of the "gens," of the people who belonged to the same clan or to related clans. It was possible to distinguish among the "*jus gentilicum* that governed the relations between the upper and lower classes within the same people, the *jus gentilitatis* which comprised the laws in force in the senior class of the gentils and the *jus gentium* that governed relations between different '*gens*'."[50]

[48]Aristóteles (1973), p. 331. book V, 7.

[49]Nussbaum (1953), p. 14.

[50]"(...) *le* jus gentilicium *qui gouvernait les relations entre les classes supérieures et les classes inférieures au sein d'une même* gente, *les* jus gentilitatis *qui comprenait les lois en vigueur aun*

Afterwards, the Roman concept of *jus gentium* extended to the relations among foreigners (*peregrini*) and to the relations between them and the Romans *cives*. It was a set of rules addressing human beings, not political organizations. Moreover, the *jus gentium* consisted in an *intra gentes* law, not an *inter gentes* one. From 242 BC. onwards, it was given by a *praetor peregrinus*, an itinerant figure. This enabled the edicts to reconcile cultural proposals and distinct legal traditions. The Praetor needed to focus on actual agreements not formal ties, to favor the substance rather than the form, as the form is proper of one community and not easily universalized. Contracts should emphasize the *volutas*, the *consensus*, even if their form was poor. This feature stands out from the rest of the Roman law, which was formalistic in its essence. Even in its origin, the fundamental task of this field was already outlined: "to govern the relations between 'outsiders', between human beings who do not belong to the same tribe, to the same clan, to the same nation, to the same culture, but who share one common humanity."[51] From the onset, *jus gentium* has within it the requirements of an universal law, a law that should be in principle acceptable to all men; a nonnational branch, open to differences.

This branch belonged in fact to Positive Law, but it resembled Natural Law in many of its elements. As the Roman pride prevented the direct import of external legal rules, the *jus gentium* welcomed and re-elaborated the uses and customs of other peoples. Thus, a body of *jus aequum* was formed, which had little to do with kindness or mitigating the rigors of the law—it had little to do with equity, according to a common definition. It favored actual will instead of an instrumental formula; it was a requirement of universality to facilitate communication. Moreover, the notion of *bona fide*, of loyalty to one's word, held a key position. Good faith proves to be crucial for the stability and sustainability of commercial relations and constitutes a guarantee of personal credibility. Apart from trade, Rome established with foreigners relations of patronage, *amicitia* and *hospitium*. The *jus gentium* also cared about the preservation of *mores*. These ethical contents made the Law of Nations closest to Natural Law than to Positive Law.[52]

So, it is hardly surprising that the *jus gentium* was often confused with Natural Law itself, since, as a set of universal rules, its creation relates to that of custom, which can become lost in ancient times. Cicero himself offers no distinction between the *jus naturalis* and the *jus gentium*. In **De Officiis**, he investigates the nature of the obligations that prohibit men from harming others, "Why, of course it is not only by force of nature, that is, by the Law of Nations, but also by virtue of the laws of the different peoples, who hold public affairs in every city. They also set forth that it is not lawful to harm others for their own benefit." Furthermore, Cicero

---

(Footnote 50 continued)

sein de la classe supérieure des gentils et le jus gentium qui réglait les rapports entre les différents *gentes" (Laghmani 2003, p. 11).*

[51]"(...) *gobernar las relaciones entre 'extraños', entre seres que no pertenecen a la misma tribu, al mismu clan, a la misma nación, a la misma cultura sino que comparten sólo una común humanidad*" (Viola 2004, p. 166).

[52]Viola (2004), p. 170.

demonstrates the validity of this law in light of the wickedness of customs and the corruption of Civil Law[53]:

> Although I established that similar scam is not considered wicked by virtue of the perversion of the customs, nor is it prohibited by Law or Civil Law, I believe that the Law of Nature forbids it. Indeed, there is a wide society - it has been said many times, but it is worth repeating it many others - the company of all men and a more restricted one, that form part of the same family, and finally an even smaller one, of men that are of the same city. Our ancestors wanted the Law of Nations to exist on the one hand and Civil Law to exist on the other. Civil Law does not necessarily need to be the Law of Nations, but the latter does need to be Civil Law.[54]

It is possible to infer that Civil Law is opposed to the Law of Nations, the law derived from nature, from the wide society of men. All law stems from a society: Civil Law from a small society, which is the city itself, and the Law of Nations from a human *magna communitas*, the society of all men. Influenced by the Stoic philosophy, while confronting Civil Law with the Law of Nations, Roman authors made broad assumptions that significantly altered the essence of the term *jus gentium*. The Roman historical *jus gentium* applied the foreign experience to very particular cases; however, the philosophical *jus gentium* comprised norms and legal elements found everywhere, such as those relating to marriage, to the defense and protection of the property, to the duty to repair a damage. Since it was in fact a universal common law, the task of separating it from Natural Law was challenging.

The great Roman jurists also showed this lack of accuracy. In their compilations, they did not merely list the elements of the Law of Nations, but also sought to define it, and it was Greek Philosophy, not the current legal practice, that served as their matrix. It is worth noting that among the various issues covered by this philosophical *jus gentium*, some were international in nature, such as the law of embassies and the rules on war plunder and spoils of war. However, most subjects were of private law and to a lesser extent of domestic public law, such as the status of the deportees. Therefore, it does not seem possible to establish any correlation with International Law. The initial title of the **Digest** introduces two main definitions of *jus gentium*, one of Gaius and another of Ulpian; both rely on a natural basis. To Gaius,

---

[53]"Civil Law" is the law of the city and the citizens (the *cive*). In this book, I will not use this term in the sense of private law.

[54]"*Neque vero hoc solum natura, id est jure gentium, sed etiam legibus populorum, quibus in singulis civitatibus respublica continetur, eodem modo constitutum est, ut non liceat sui commodi causa nocere alteri.*" E, adiante: "*Hoc quanquam video propter depravationem consuetudinis neque more turpe haberi neque aut lege sanciri aut jure civilii, tamen natura elege sancitum est. Societas enim est (quod etsi saepe dictum est, dicendum tamen est saepius), latissime quidem quae pateat, hominum inter homines, interior eorum, qui ejusdem gentis sunt, propior eorum qui ejusdem civitatis. Itaque majores aliud jus gentium, aliud jus civile esse voluerunt. Quod civile, non idem continuo gentium; quod autem gentium, idem civile esse debet.*" (CICERÓN. **De Officiis**. Paris: Garnier, s/d. Liber III, V and XVII.)

In all peoples governed by the laws and customs, both their own law and the common law, applicable to all men, they use those rules them. Indeed, the right that each people have set for themselves is proper to the city itself; but the law which natural reason has established among all men is a rule which conforms to all and is called the Law of Nations, inasmuch is the law used by all peoples.[55]

There are thus two sets of rules: Civil Law and the Law of Nations. The first is proper to each State, which is also its source; the second one is common to all men and manifests itself equally among all peoples. The peoples do not create the Law of Nations, but it derives from a higher principle, the *naturalis ratio*. This is prior to Positive Law, created in a state of primitive innocence. The opposition between the law of a determined nation and the law common to all nations, between the law based on human will and that which results from the right reasoning, between a written law and an unwritten one, is evident. Thus, the expression *jus gentium* may be easily replaced by Natural Law.

In turn, Ulpian adds a third term to the division of sources: the *jus naturale*. He begins his work with this expression, which comprises the most basic and vital functions that nature reserves to all living beings, humans and animals alike: the union of the sexes, procreation and the education of the offspring. This *jus naturale* seems to refer to the Stoics' Natural Law. In contrast, the author defines the Law of Nations: "The Law of Nations is applied to human beings and can be easily deduced from nature by understanding, and, among all the animals, only men shares [this law] with one another"[56] The Law of Nations constitutes a portion of the Natural Law applicable only to human beings.

This division dates back to a Pythagorean notion that assumes the existence of an age of innocence, a golden age, opposed to an age of sin, an age of iron. In ancient times, all things would have been common; man would have been free and directly ingrained in Nature. Afterwards, man would have followed perversion and selfishness, and the private property, along with other excluding institutions, would have been established. In Ulpian, Natural Law is more related to the idyllic period, while the Law of Nations to the subsequent one.[57]

Despite having included this third term, both Ulpian and Gaius considered Civil Law as the *ius proprium*, opposed to an *ius commune*, following the teachings of Aristotle. Yet, there is a flaw in the comparison with Aristotle, because while Gaius considered the common law the equivalent of the Law of Nations, Ulpian regarded

---

[55]"*Omnes populi, qui legibus et moribus reguntur, partim suo proprio, partim communi omnium hominum iure utuntur nam quod quisque populus ipse sibi ius constituit, id ipsius proprium civitatis est vocaturque ius civile, quasi ius proprium ipsius civitatis: quod vero naturalis ratio inter omnes homines constituit, id apud omnes peraeque custoditur vocaturque ius gentium, quasi quo iure omnes gentes utuntur.*" (IUSTINIANUS IMPERATOR. **Corpus Iuris Civilis**. ed. Krueger e Mommsen. Berlim: Weidmann, 1908. **Digesto**, 1, 1, 9).

[56]"*Ius gentium est, quo gentes humanae utuntur, quod a naturali recedere facile intellegere licet, quia illud omnibus animalibus, hoc solis hominibus inter se commune sit.*" (IUSTINIANUS IMPERATUR. **Digest**, 1, 1, 1, 4).

[57]Barcia Trelles (1933), p. 424.

the *ius commune* as both Law of Nations and Natural Law. For this author, all that is not Civil Law is common law. Therefore, since Civil Law is specific and changeable, the *jus gentium* would share its immutability with the *jus naturale*. If this feature is a result of a higher principle, such as the natural reason of Gaius, then the Ulpian's Law of Nations would not belong to Positive Law and not correspond to the historical reality of the Roman *jus gentium*. It would only possess a philosophical and Hellenic nature. To avoid this conclusion, the "common" feature of Ulpian's *jus gentium* would need to derive from a coincidence of legal institutions among diverse nations, not from right reasoning. Either Ulpian is a bad jurist, as he did not properly and accurately describe the historical *jus gentium*, or he would be a bad philosopher, by ignoring the fundamentals of the Aristotelian bipartition.

However one interprets this matter, the fact remains that neither the *jus gentium* of Ulpian nor Gaius' resemble contemporary International Law. Even if both concepts may apply to different nations, their true subjects are not the peoples or the *populi* that the authors mention. As in Civil Law and Natural Law as well, the subjects of their *jus gentium* are the individuals. In Ulpian, the emphasis rests on the *humanae* adjective. Employing the noun *gentes* instead of *genus humanum* (a term that is present in the excerpt above, one must notice) is merely for wordplay purposes with the expression *jus gentium* and supposedly to uphold its proof of value. The same happens with Gaius. The *populi* are no equivalent to the subject of the *jus gentium*, either in law nor in syntax, because the *apud* inserted in the end transforms the word into a complement of place. In addition, the term *omnes* appears four times in the sentence. "Far from being *ius inter gentes* or *inter populos*, the Law of Nations of our two authors should be regarded as *inter homines*."[58] The individuals, more precisely freemen, are the subjects of the *jus gentium*; the *jus gentium* is thus opposed to Civil Law, which addresses men who have, in addition to their freedom, the *status civitatis*.

2.2.2 *The Medieval Notion*

The authors of the Middle Ages dismissed Ulpian's concept of Natural Law as applicable only to animals. The theme of the autonomy of the Law of Nations would also arise parallel to this rejection. As seen, the **Concordia** of Gratian is a turning point for the law of war. It also sets out a definition of *jus gentium* extracted of St. Isidore that would become famous. In chapter II of the **Etymologiae**, the Archbishop of Seville, St. Isidore, proposes a very interesting distinction between human and divine laws. The latter would arise from nature and the former from the uses. For this reason, human laws vary from place to place, according to the will of the nations, while divine laws are immutable. According to him, *lex* does not mean

---

[58]"*Loin d'être* ius inter gentes *ou* inter populos, *le droit des gens de nos deux auteurs doit s'entendre* inter homines." (Haggenmacher 1983, p. 318).

jus; *lex*, together with *mores,* constitute a species of the genus *jus*. The *jus* is divided into natural, civil and of nations, as a separate category. Civil law is the Positive law of the city, and Natural Law applies only to men. But the *jus gentium* remains unclear. Without offering a proper definition, the author begins by pointing out the etymological origin of the term and by recalling Gaius' concept thereof. However, he introduces a subtle difference: the Law of Nations presents itself as "almost" universal. Then, he proceeds to list the themes addressed by this branch of *jus*:

> The Law of Nations addresses the occupation, the buildings and the fortification of castles and cities, the war, the captives of war, the slavery, the restoration of rights by *postliminium,* the peace agreements, truces, the inviolability of embassies and the prohibition of marriage between people of different religions. And so is the Law of Nations, for it is the law of the uses of all nations.[59]

This definition of *jus gentium* by the enumeration of its themes marks a future trend that would culminate in the autonomy of the *jus gentium* from the *ratio naturalis*. The Medieval way of making Jurisprudence (Science of Law) called *mos italicus* due to the influence of jurists such as Baldo, Paulus Castrensis, and Bartolus of Saxoferrato, consisted of drafting long treaties about everything that there was to know from the Law of the current time. The first books only resurrected Roman law, which was considered the pinnacle of perfection in legal terms. Only later did they begin to combine the Roman legacy with Germanic institutions. Thus, there was an accentuated universalist feature (albeit limited to Europe), and slowly there began to emerge one or other work that would address the subject matters of domestic law. They were addressed by way of *topói* and from questions raised by authors who had already written thereon. Gradually, there appeared treaties covering specific legal issues, although retaining the old approach.[60] In the field that would come to be that of the Law of Nations, a considerable number of dissertations on the law of the embassies emerged, not to mention books on the Just War tradition.[61]

---

[59]"*Ius gentium est sedium occupatio, aedificatio, munitio, bella, captivitates, servitutes, postliminia, foedera, pacis, indutiae, legatorum non violandorum religio, conubia inter alienigenas prohibita. Et inde ius gentium, quia eo iure omnes fere gentes utuntur.*" (Isidorus Hispalensis Episcopus (1911), V, VI).

[60]That was Rhetoric, considered a true *vir civilis*, a civic virtue. Logic was solely for speculative Philosophy and Theology, which was the *magna* science. Aquinas, e.g., places the Rhetoric at the top of the well-known hierarchy of knowledge introduced by the Stagirite in chapter I of Book I of Metaphysics, for Rhetoric was more speculative than practical and superior to other disciplines. Aristotle himself had established the Metaphysics at the top of the hierarchy, but the term was used only when it dealt with the *ens commune*; "'*filosofia primera*', *en cuanto considera las causas primeras de las cosas;* '*teologia*', *en cuanto considera las sustancias que no tienen materia, Dios,* etc." (Sciacca 1976, p. 50). It is the triple aspect of a single discipline. However, practical sciences such as Ethics and Law, which researched on how to live good, are not expressed according to the canons of formal Logic, but according to another logic that seeks conviction and persuasion: the Rhetoric and the Topic.

[61]Wijffels, 1995–1996, p. 39.

Some authors[62] perceive similarities between Isidore's definition and the modern discipline of International Law. Far from being fortuitous, this enumeration marks three major thematic circles: one concerning the institution of political power, other the war and its consequences and the third concerning the law of treaties and embassies. In fact, some subjects already approached Isidore's Law of Nations to the contemporary International Law. However, others such as banned marriages between foreigners would bewilder an Internationalist. Indeed, banned marriages between foreigners do not fall within any of the major issues of today's International Law.

Therefore, other authors[63] do not find in Isidore's *jus gentium* any trace of International Law. Although Isidore disputes Ulpian's definition of Natural Law, his imagination does not lead him to other places when addressing the Law of Nations. The Bishop of Seville seemed to have simply "bumped into" the term *jus gentium* because of the authority that the ancient texts had acquired, and thus he would need to dwell on the subject lest he be deemed incomplete.

The vagueness of the text even leaves room for a speculation that Francisco Suárez would make years later with his known division between *jus inter gentes* and *jus intra gentes*, as will be seen in Chapter V. Isidore's Law of Nations would be equivalent to the *jus intra gentes*, as a sort of private law common to many nations. The adjective "common" would be a mere coincidence, and would not imply a provision binding on all States, which, in any event, is no different from the Roman *jus gentium*. Isidore's Law of Nations refer to rules already created by the human intellect—such as the uses, the custom: *eo iure omnes fere gentes utuntur*—much like Civil Law, and applicable to all different nations and men, like Natural Law.

Yet, it appears questionable that Isidore would have completely distanced himself from the Roman orbit, since much of his institutes coincide with those of the Hellenic *jus gentium* of the Roman jurists. Since the Law of Nations was not the author's main concern, it is possible that the term would allude to the legal-political reality of the High Middle Ages: a split European Christianity, ruled by the Pope and the Emperor—a more symbolic than effective authority—united by a vague commonality of interests and a positive common customary law, reminiscent of the Roman law. This could explain the positive character of Isidore's Law of Nations without distancing him from the ancient sources.

So, the issue of the autonomy of the Law of Nations was as follows: some of the themes of this law emerged from the human will, but it shared an (almost) universal character with Natural Law, which bring us to the problem of its philosophical basis. In Ulpian, the Law of Nations is a species of the genus Natural Law, but it encompasses rules of Positive Law.

The glossators tried to solve this issue by splitting either Natural Law or the Law of Nations into several species of law. This coincided with the idea of a progressive

[62]Rivier (1883), pp. 9–10.

[63]Walker (1899), v. I. § 85.

development of Natural toward Positive Law within a temporal and genetic framework. Therefore, one may find in the **Summa Institutionum** of Placentin a *prima iura naturalia* and a *secunda iura naturalia*, which correspond respectively to Natural Law and to the Law of Nations. Likewise, Etienne de Tournay, in the **Summa ad decretum**, refers to a *ius naturale primitivum*, prior to the institution of private property—an institute that was proper of the *jus gentium*. Many glosses associated with the Institutas distinguish a *jus gentium* created with man from other *jus gentium* created by men: the first is inspired in Gaius, and the second is equivalent to the Positive Law of Nations.[64]

Such way of reasoning would even reach Grotius. While this solution provided substance to a notion that wandered between two extremes, it hid the problem of the autonomy of the positive *jus gentium* from the *jus naturale* and the *jus civile* by creating another superfluous subdivision. This *jus gentium* clearly had nothing to do with International Law.

Contrary to jurists, legists or Medieval canonists, the Theologians ignored the Law of Nations. The Sentences of Peter Lombard, as well as the comments and sums of post-thirteenth century Theologians, are silent on the subject. If, by chance, there is any mention thereof, the *jus gentium* plays only an ornamental function.[65]

The great exception is Thomas Aquinas, who assigns to the *jus gentium* a privileged place in his thinking and brings together all the traditional interpretations in one concept. Like St. Isidore, Aquinas differentiates the Law from the laws. The Treatise on Laws must be read in conjunction with the Treaty of Grace, because both laws and grace are principles external to men, govern their behavior and move them towards righteousness. In Aquinas, the study of the Law is part of the Treaty of Justice; the object of the virtue of Justice is the Law itself, the *iustum* that corresponds to the Aristotelian *dikaión*. In the next chapter, in order to understand Suárez's concept of Law, I will investigate the Thomistic distinction between the Laws and the Law. For the time being, it is sufficient to bear in mind that studying the different kinds of law in Aquinas (Eternal, Natural, Divine and Human Law) means to investigate God's project for Creation, because "the law is a certain rule and measure for the acts whereby one is induced to act or to restrain from doing something."[66] Laws govern not only human social organization, but also the entire universe. In turn, the entire problem of the Law comes down to Justice. This is an issue that a modern Positivist such as Kelsen or Hart would leave out of the realm of the science of Law, but not a Medieval jurist and much less a Theologian.

Haggenmacher states that Aquinas introduced two different concepts of *jus gentium*: one in the Treatise on Laws and the other in the Treaty of Justice. The difference goes beyond the attention that each receives in its respective treaty. In the first treaty, the Angelic Doctor recovers St. Isidore's definition (according to which

---

[64]Haggenmacher (1983), p. 326.

[65]Haggenmacher (1983), p. 327.

[66]"(…) *lex quaedam regula est et mensura actuum, secundum quam inducitur aliquis ad agendum, vel ab agendo retrahitur* (…)" (**ST** 1-2 q. 90 a.1).

the Law of Nations belongs to Positive Law), while in the second treaty, he reconstructs the definition of the Romans (for whom it is intertwined with Natural Law). Since the two notions are incompatible, the unification proposed by Aquinas would seem ambiguous.[67] However, Haggenmacher's conclusion does not withstand closer examination. Reversing the order that these two texts are presented (first the Treaty of Justice, then the Treatise on Laws) may help clarifying the Dominican's synthetic proposal.

In Aquinas, as in Aristotle, law (*jus*) may proceed both from the nature of things (Natural Law) as from a convention (Positive Law). Thus, the author's questions set the Law of Nations apart from Natural Law. The natural just is that which is "adjusted" to another thing by its own nature. This may occur in two different ways:

> First, taking into account the thing utterly in itself; thus the male, by his nature, accommodates to the female to breed with her, and the parents to their child, to feed them. Second, considering the thing no longer in itself, in its nature, but in relation to its consequences; for example, the ownership of possessions [of land].[68]

In itself, Natural Law presides the relations of things that are already compatible one to another by their own nature: for instance, procreation is just by nature because women and men have reproductive organs that are perfectly compatible, and the care for the offspring proves to be just by nature because the mother feeds the child with her breast milk. The perfect fit is the very evidence of the existence of Natural Law: it requires no further confirmation. Aquinas calls this the Natural Law *primo modo*.

However, something by its own nature may also turn out to be just, even if it is not straight away. The example of the property is quite illustrative. In fact, the land in itself does not imply any need for it to belong to this or that person. Nevertheless, if one is to consider the consequences—the fact that the property may be cultivated —it becomes possible to draw an ownership title: this, and not that other person is gifted to be a farmer, and it is fair that he owns the land. This kind of justice does not escape the realm of the Natural Law, because there is no human convention establishing this or that behaviour. However, virtue does not arise from the thing in itself: human intervention (the cultivation of the land) was necessary for the perfection of justice. Aquinas calls this the Natural Law *secundo modo* or the Law of Nations.

Applying the expressions *primus* and *secundus modus* to Natural Law may remind the glossators' concepts thereof, but the author does not attribute to them any temporal or genetic meaning. They simply constitute forms of adapting one thing to another, according to their nature.

---

[67]Haggenmacher (1983), p. 328.

[68]"*Uno modo, secundum absolutam sui considerationem: sicut masculus ex sui ratione habet commensurationem ad feminam ut ex ea generet, et parens ad filium ut eum nutriat. Alio modo aliquid est naturaliter alteri commensuratum non secundum aliquid quod ex ipso consequitur: puta proprietas possessionum.*" (**ST**. 2-2 q.57 a.3).

Men share the Natural Law *primo modo* with other animals. However, the Natural Law *secundo modo* is exclusive to human beings. This is undoubtedly Ulpian's concept. However, Aquinas inserted the *jus gentium* in the realm of Natural Law; thus, he interpreted Ulpian's Law of Nations as belonging in the Natural Law, not as being part of the positive common law, as other interpretations thereof would have it. Either that, or Aquinas reconciled two Roman sources: he used Ulpian to define Natural Law, and Gaius to define the Law of Nations. In both situations, the *jus gentium* seems to belong to the nature of things and to emerge from human reason.

Notwithstanding, the wording of the Third Article of question 57 of the Treaty of Justice seems unclear. By employing the Scholastic method in his inquiries, Aquinas merely mentions the dichotomy Natural Law/Positive Law. Since he does not express the naturalness of the Law of Nations in his response, and given that he clearly distinguishes between two forms of "adjusting" one thing to another, the Law of Nations seems to be something quite distinct from Natural Law. Therefore, Positive Law could only occupy the other side of the equation. For this reason, the hypothesis raised by Peter Haggenmacher is apparently true. The fact that this adjustment occurs "according to nature" may be lost due to the lack of clarity in his reasoning.

However, this argument is incomplete. One must seek the definition of Law in the Treatise on Laws to elucidate the issue. In Aquinas, law is not a *sollen*, an "ought to be" judgement, but a measure, a standard of reference, a rational structuring project. Laws are measures by which the movement of the stars, the course of the rivers, the instinct of the animals and human life in society abide. This is no legal command, but a rational design that organizes the different spheres of life in the universe. Each kind of law (Eternal, Natural and Civil) rules over a proper sphere of existence, but they all consist of the same reality: the ordering of reason. For instance, Civil Law is not essentially different from Eternal Law, as both represent commands of the divine reason (although, in Civil Law, there is a co-causality of human reason). One applies to the entire cosmos and the other to human life in the city only. This divine organizational design affects the different domains of reality in a scaled way: Eternal Law is God's plan for all creation and proceeds directly from Him; Natural Law is the very participation of the Eternal Law in rational beings; Positive Law derives logically from Natural Law.

> (…) The force of law depends on the extent of its justice. And in the case of human things, their justice is in proportion to their compliance with the rules of reason. And the first rule of reason is Natural Law, as has been said. Thus, all human laws have the status of law in that it derives from the Law of Nature.[69]

[69]"*Unde inquantum habet de iustitia intantum habet de virtute legis. In rebus autem humanis dicitur esse aliquid iustum ex eo quod est rectum secundum regulam rationis. Rationis autem prima regula est lex naturae, ut ex supradictis patet. Unde omnis lex humanitus posita intantum habet de ratione legis, inquantum a lege naturae derivatur*" (**ST**. 1-2 q.95 a.2).

Not only are the different species of law related, but also human rights (*jus*) derive from Natural Law (*lex*). The *jus* is related to *lex*. The entire Positive Law (which is both Civil Law and Law of Nations) derive from Natural Law, but they do so in different ways. The first stems *per determinationem* and the second *per conclusionem* (1-2 q. 95 a. 4).

> But it should be noted that one thing may derive from Natural Law in two ways: first, as the conclusions derive from a principle; second, per determination, as the determinations of certain common notions. The first method resembles the sciences, which extracts demonstrative conclusions from the principles. The second is similar to what happens in the arts: abstract shapes materialize into something particular; the architect, for example, embodies the generic form of a house in this or that house model.[70]

Natural Law therefore determines the moral limits that Civil Law may not overstep. As an architect keeps in his mind the notion of "house" and uses it as a template to build a concrete house, so does Natural Law determine a model for the construction of Civil Law. The color and texture of the house are not in the original project, and there is hence a certain degree of discretion. But this does not apply to the Law of Nations. It derives from Natural Law as a theorem extracted from a logical axiom. Natural Law is the higher premise, and the Law of Nations the conclusion.

Here we find the element that harmonizes Aquinas' concepts of *jus gentium*. The derivation *per conclusionem* of the Treatise on Laws corresponds to the suitability *secundo modo* of the Treaty of Justice. Both deal on how Natural Law "creates" the Law of Nations and the manner by which this happens is not according to the thing itself, but to its consequences or its conclusions. The difference in approach lies in the fact that, in the Treatise on Laws, Aquinas aims to distinguish the Law of Nations from Civil Law, while in the Treaty of Justice he seeks to differentiate among the many forms that Natural Law may appear in reality. There are no two distinct concepts of *jus gentium.* There is merely a variety of purposes.

Indeed, Aquinas classifies the Law of Nations as Positive Law and this may be misleading. In a certain sense, the Law of Nations is natural. "First, the Law of Nations is natural to man, because it is something rational, since it derives from Natural Law (…). Yet, it is distinct from Natural Law in the sense that Natural Law is common to all animals."[71] But why does Aquinas use the word "positive"? Because he does not use it in its usual meaning; the term should be read as "human." The Law of Nations consists of a natural human law: its foundation is the

---

[70]"*Sed sciendum est quod a lege naturali dupliciter potest aliquid derivari: uno modo, sicut conclusiones ex principiis; alio modo, sicut determinationes quaedam aliquorum communium. Primus quidem modus est similis ei quo in scientiis ex principiis conclusiones demonstrativae producuntur. Secundo vero modo simile est quod in artibus formae communes determinantur ad aliquid speciale: sicut artifez formam communem domus necesse est quod determinet ad hanc vel illam domus figuram.*" (**ST**. 1-2 q.95 a.2).

[71]"*Ad primum ergo dicendum quod ius gentium est quidem aliquo modo naturali homini, secundum quod est rationalis, inquantum derivatur a lege naturali* (…). *Distinguitur tamen a lege naturali, maxime ab eo quod est omnibus animalibus commune.*" (**ST**. 1–2 q.95 a.4.)

natural reason, but natural reason is not always evident. It presupposes a certain human effort to derive it from other axioms that are actually evident. It does not depend on a formal process of positivation to exist, such as Civil Law.

> By assuming an intervention of the discursive reason to deduce what will not appear immediately and entirely to the intelligence, the Law of Nations has something from Positive Law, but taking the term "positive" in a very broad sense, which is not usual in the Theological terminology and current legal thought. The Law of Nations is formed out of conclusions deduced from primary principles of Natural Law, which are entirely obvious. There is hence a positive effort, although very easy, to derive and determine that these findings are very close to those principles and, therefore, are within the reach of **all nations**. However, the strength or validity of the requirement, in these conclusions, stems from the same Natural Law that they contain substantially.[72]

Take for example an indisputable theme of the Law of Nations: reducing the defeated enemy to slavery. In a sense, it is about a natural precept. Making the captive enemy a slave seems less cruel than murdering him out of combat, and it follows logically from the natural commandment "Thou shalt not kill." Moreover, as will be seen in the next chapter, until the time of Suárez, it was believed that man could dispose of his own freedom; nothing prevented him from losing it in a war or using it to pay off debts.

The Law of Nations is therefore not immediately natural but derives from natural precepts. This occurs because Natural Law produces in man three types of inclinations: one concerning everything that matters for the preservation of life; another (which he shares with other animals) concerning the union of the sexes, the rearing of children, etc. and the last one is a true rational inclination that refers to man's natural penchant of living in society and toward seeking the divine truths.[73] Natural Rights or the just in itself derive directly from the first two inclinations of the Natural Law, like the male fits the female, according to the excerpt above from the Treaty of Justice. In turn, the Law of Nations stems from the third inclination of Natural Law not directly and organically, but in a comparative and a consecutive manner. It does not spring from the essence of the thing; it requires the intervention of human reason. In this sense, the Law of Nations is human: the conclusions thereof are conditional and hypothetical, given that they depend on the will of men,

---

[72] "*Al suponer una intervención de la razón discursiva para deducir lo que no aparece inmediata y absolutamente a la inteligencia, el derecho de gentes tiene algo de positivo, pero tomando el término **positivo** en un sentido muy amplio, que no es usual en la terminología teológica y en el pensamiento jurídico atual. El derecho de gentes está constituido por las conclusiones deducidas de los primeros principios, absolutamente evidentes, de la ley natural. Hay, pues, un **positivo** esfuerzo, aunque muy fácil, para deducir y dictaminar esas conclusiones, que están muy próximas a los principios y por eso se hallan al alcance de **todas las gentes**. Pero la fuerza o vigor de obligación, en esas conclusiones, viene del mismo derecho natural, que substancialmente contienem.*" (Santiago Ramirez 1947, p. 148).

[73] **ST**. 1-2 q.94 a.2.

"even if that will is not that of a particular power or of a concrete society, but in a sense, of all humanity, of all nations."[74]

The Thomist conception may be confusing and complex, but never ambiguous. The Law of Nations is always Natural Law. It is simply a "less evident" Natural Law. In fact, it does not correspond to a portion of Natural Law, but to a variation thereof. What the term *jus gentium* gained in reasoning and unity with Aquinas, it lost in autonomy.

Aquinas' considerations regarding the Law of Nations found no echo among the Theologians of his time. It would be necessary to wait until the sixteenth century for Francisco de Vitória to arise. Nevertheless, the Medieval jurists continued to comment on the **Digest** and the **Institutas** and followed the tradition of the glossators in dividing Natural Law or the Law of Nations into *ius primaevum* and *secundum*, according to a chronological order.

Bartolus of Saxoferrato divides Natural Law in two and then splits the Law of Nations in two also. The *ius naturale secundum* coincides with the *ius gentium primaevum*, and it applies to all men following the *ratio naturalis* from Gaius. The *ius gentium secundum* corresponds to a law that is common to all nations and originates from them. This kind of progressive development also appears in the disciples and followers of Bartolus, as Ubaldo, Baldo and Paulus Castrensis. This terminology reaches the young Grotius, who will use it in **De Jure Praedae**.[75] Though yet to gain autonomy, there begins to grow the idea of a strictly Positive Law of Nations, which proceeds from the *usus* of various nations, not from natural reason.

2.2.3 The Vitorian Notion

From the late thirteenth century and early fourteenth century to the sixteenth century, the question of the autonomy of the *jus gentium* had no progress. Only when the **Summa Theologica** of Thomas Aquinas replaced the **Book of the Sentences** of Peter Lombard as a textbook of Theology, did the Theologians begin to look into the Law of Nations. In particular, in Spain appears a profound renewal of interest for the Scholastic that this period becomes known as neo-Scholastic, or Second Scholastic. This new-found interest coincided with the Great Navigations and Spain experiences its "golden age."

Europe underwent profound changes. In addition to the discovery of the New World, the invention of the gunpowder and artillery, the rediscovery of Classical Antiquity, the invention of printing (which spread the written word) and of the maritime compass, the development of the idea of sovereignty, and the emergence

[74]"(...) *aunque ese arbitrio no sea el de un poder particular o de una sociedad concreta, sino, en cierto sentido, de toda la humanidad, de todas las gentes*" (Santiago Ramirez 1947, p. 147).

[75]Haggenmacher (1983), pp. 331–333.

of the first national States, all date back to this very special time. With so many technological advances (which, in fact, changed the very notion of the world as people knew it) Theology began to deal with human issues too.

One of the greatest authors of this epoch was Francisco de Vitória. However faithful to the canons of Thomism he may have been, he lived in a world quite different from that of Aquinas and had to confront new issues, such as the capacity of the Indians and the fall of the universal Christian empire. The Great Discoveries had decreased the size of the planet and revealed a multitude of pagan peoples. For the first time, it seemed possible for a king to become the master of the whole world. In addition, Christianity did not seem as universal as it used to be. So Vitória had to update Aquinas.

The problem of the soul of the Indians brought a delicate legal consequence: the question of whether non-Christian peoples could validly exercise dominion over their territories. According to a highly spread notion extracted from the Old Testament from the idea of "promised land," many canonists concluded that, as God had given Palestine to a particular nation (the Jews), God had given the entire world for Christians upon the arrival of Christ. Thus, Christianity, the "true" belief, would consist of a requirement for the valid acquisition of a territory, and thus it would be legitimate to deprive the infidels of their lands.[76]

But not all Christians were intolerants. In the first half of the thirteenth century, Pope Innocent IV recognized that the infidels could hold dominion, ownership and jurisdiction.[77] However, Muslims were the only well-known infidels of that time and they were an even more advanced a civilization than Europe. Like Christians, Muslims worshipped one God, also professed a "religion of the book" and, together with the Jews, observed moral principles that a European would find no trouble in recognizing. The relationship between the peoples of monotheistic religion, though far from peaceful, was respectful. However, what can be said of those who worshipped many gods, including personifications of natural forces and those who practiced cannibalism and human sacrifices? The distance to the revealed religions was too great. There was no possible dialogue.

Since Pope Innocent IV's open-mindedness favored Islamism, it is not surprising that the Church would not bestow the Indians with the same tolerance. On May 14, 1493, in the famous bull **Inter coetera**, Pope Alexander VI donated to the Catholic Kings "remote islands and mainlands" already discovered by Columbus and "those to be discovered later," so that they could exercise "full authority and jurisdiction" to the west of a meridian known as "Alexandrian line," which went a hundred leagues west of the Azores islands and Cape Verde. On June 7, 1494, the Treaty of Tordesillas, imbued with the same spirit of dividing the world, altered the prescribed limits.[78]

---

[76] Stumpf (2005), pp. 71–72.

[77] Tierney (2004), p. 8.

[78] Bathélemy (1904), p. 15.

Yet, even in the sixteenth century, the idea that a papal bull would contain enough authority to transfer full control of these lands (the discovered and undiscovered) was challenged and argued *in lieu* that the papal bull had merely split between two princes the authority to preach Christianity. This would characterize what is called in modern language "spheres of influence." However, the propagation of the faith would be a prerequisite for the exercise of such power.

Francisco de Vitória would defend this latter thesis. But he would need to overcome almost insurmountable obstacles. The rival theory of donation appears in the **Request** drafted by the Junta de Burgos of 1512, work of the great jurist López Palacios Rubios. After reassembling the creation of the universe, the document states that God had entrusted to St. Peter all men, wherever they lived and under any law, sect, or belief, to serve them as their head and lord, and had given the whole world as his kingdom and jurisdiction. Then, reference is made, explicitly, to Alexander VI's act as "donation." In this sense, all major elements of a variant concept of the Medieval imperial monism come into light, establishing the Supreme Pontiff, instead of the emperor, as the lord of the world. Many canonists advocated this theory, such as Cardinal Hostiensis and Innocent III in the decretal **Novit Ille**, as well as some Theologians, especially the Spaniards Alvaro Pelayo and Rodrigo Sánchez Arévalo.[79] The defense of the opposite theory would not only contradict the official policy of Spain, but would also put its proponent on a collision path with the pope himself.

Vitória held the position of *prima* Professor of Theology in Salamanca, and his views warranted respect. To the chagrin of many, he did not endorse the papal monism or the war against the Indians. According to Vitória, God had distributed its authority to all peoples, not only to the Christians. The Indians could also own land and exercise sovereignty because they were in "peaceful domain of their public and private things. So, (unless there was an obstacle), they shall be considered true lords of their land and, in these circumstances, they cannot be deprived of their possessions."[80]

Therefore, when published, the Relecciones only escaped from the Index of prohibited works due to the unexpected death of Pope Sextus V. However, the King did not even wait for its publication. In 1539, the Prior of the Convent of St. Stephen, Domingo de Soto, *vespera* professor of Theology and a follower of Vitória, received a letter signed by Charles V himself forbidding the clergy of that monastery to express opinions that were against Castile's overseas policy. Any manifestation to the contrary would be regarded as a personal offense.[81] This was a very specific indisposition, limited to this issue only, because in many previous

---

[79]Viejo-Ximénez (2004), p. 365.

[80]"*(...) in pacifica possessione rerum et publice et privatim. Ergo omnino (nisi contrarium constet) habendi sunt pro dominis. Neque in dicta causa possessione deturbandi*" (**De Indis**, *Relectio* 1, 5. p. 651).

[81]Scott (2003), pp. 84–85. In this book, the author reproduces the letter.

episodes and even later the King expressed his appreciation and admiration for Vitória.

For this reason (Vitória's courage in defending his ideas) and because of the eagerness to find a new father to the field of International Law, the Dominican was portrayed in a pristine and somewhat caricatured fashion. Two exaggerations were made: just like his brother of order Bartholome de Las Casas, Vitória became a champion in the defense of the rights of the Indians and was deemed the first person to present a modern view of International Law. In other words, according to this kind of literature, the Theologian of Salamanca developed an unprecedented concept of *jus gentium*. His *jus gentium* regulated both periods of war and peace; its subjects were sovereign States. However, sovereignty is not absolute, for there would exist a higher constricting principle: the *totus orbis*, an international and organic community established by links of solidarity among men in view of the common good. This world body would be above the particular wills of the States, edit international rules and ensure their implementation. The States themselves, by virtue of a "functional split," would act as members of the *Orbis* and would deploy Just War to vindicate wrongs and to correct mistakes.[82]

This notion according to which Victoria had already developed a modern definition of International Law is based on the following reasoning. As Aquinas' legitimate heir, Vitória shares the idea of natural solidarity of man and the consequent spontaneity of the State. The international society would form a community akin to a State: "And the whole world, which somehow forms a republic, has the power to prescribe, to all subjects, just laws, as are the Law of Nations."[83]

Just as the republics consist of natural groupings of individuals, there is another natural community made up of republics and that exercises authority over them, in analogy with the State itself; such would be the meaning of the statement *aliquo modo est una republica*. The orb is a natural and organic *corpus*, whose members are all republics. Like any political community, it promulgates true laws: "the Law of Nations does not have power only by the pact and the covenant of men, but it has real force of law."[84] Thus, the *jus gentium* is independent from the will of the States. The *totus orbis* is a legislative instance above the mere sum of all its members.

Therefore, the sovereignty of States remained limited by a higher power: the common good, the reason by which the orb was created. The natural solidarity of individuals becomes a valid principle for international relations. A political event that interests a certain State affects them all. Thus, the justice of this event should bear a global assessment. "As each republic is a part of the whole world, and

[82]This corresponds to the institutionalism conception from Delos (1950), pp. 187–228. To the traditional thesis, more pure, see the whole book Scott (2003).

[83]"*Habet enim totus orbis, qui aliquo modo est una republica, potestatem ferendi leges aequas et convenientes omnibus, quale sunt in iure gentium.*" (**De potestate civili**, 21. p. 191).

[84]"*Quod ius gentium non solum habet vim ex pacto et condicto inter homines, sed etiam habet vim legis*" (**De potestate civili**, 21. p. 191).

especially as a Christian province is part of a republic, if war were useful to a province or republic but harmful to the world or to Christianity, I think by that fact that it would be unjust."[85]

However, the main argument was yet to come. The literature that sought to establish Francisco de Vitória as the new father of International Law found in the famous passage in which the Theologian of Salamanca quotes Gaius' definition of *jus gentium*: "But what natural reason has established among all **peoples** is called the Law of Nations."[86] It is worth recapping the above definition of the Roman jurist: "But the law which natural reason has established among all **men** is a rule that also conforms to all and is called the Law of Nations, inasmuch as it is the law that all men make use of." Vitória replaces the word *homines* in the original text by *peoples* and such a replacement was no error in quoting the **Institutas** by heart. Vitória does this on purpose: the subject of International Law would no longer be men—a view that associate *jus gentium* and *jus naturale*—but the peoples.

> This innovation has a major relevance. Because, with the replacement of *homines* with the word peoples, the old Roman law, which served to govern relations among all men of all parts of the world, is converted into a law that governs the relations of the various peoples considered as nations, or better, as States.[87]

Therefore, Vitória would have surpassed the Roman context permanently and would have been the first to present a concept of *jus gentium* akin to the contemporary International Law. Furthermore, to corroborate this interpretation, the sentence that follows such passage begins with *Apud omnes enim nationes*, which permitted to identify the peoples of Vitória with "nation," and no longer with "men," as it were in Gaius' text.

However, this literature produced a somewhat biased version of Vitória's work. Early twentieth-century Internationalists were looking for someone to replace Grotius and decided to make Vitória say more than he intended to. A reading from Vitória's own premises, rather than permeated by post dated preconceptions, reveals a thinker worried in promoting the "Christian values and in justifying the thing that Spaniards candidly call conquest."[88]

The very structure of the ***Relecciones'*** on the Indians shows Vitória's purpose. In the first *relección*, the first section seeks to demonstrate that the Indians validly possessed their land. This demonstration, irrespective of the profound legal

---

[85]"*Imo cum una respublica sit pars totius orbis et maxime christiana provincia pars totius reipublicae, si bellum utile sit uni provinciae, aut reipublicae, cum damno orbis aut christianitatis, puto eo ipso bellum esse iniustum.*" (**De potestate civili**, 13. p. 168).

[86]"*Quod naturalis ratio inter omnes gentes constituit, vocatur ius gentium*" (**De Indis**, I, III, 2, p. 706).

[87]"*Esta innovación tiene una importancia fundamental. Pues, con la substituición de* gentes *en lugar de* homines, *el antiguo derecho romano que servía para regir las relaciones entre todos los hombres por todas las partes del mundo, queda convertido en un derecho que rige las relaciones de los varios pueblos considerados como naciones, o bien, como estados.*" (Scott 1938, p. 20).

[88]"*(…) des valeurs spécifiquemement chrétinennes et à justifier ce que les Espagnols appelaient sans ambages une conquête.*" (HAGGENMACHER 1993, p.215).

consequences thereto, served a bigger purpose: to prove that the infidels could have the domain of things. To profess other religion that is not the true one gave no cause to depose the heretics of their goods. Ownership, property, domain, and sovereignty represented institutes independent of religion. With this, the author prepares to attack the idea that the pope could exercise jurisdiction over the whole world.

This lesson plays the role of introducing the second section, in which Vitória disputes the unlegitimate titles by which the Spaniards have conquered the "barbarians of the New World" (*barbari novi orbis*). Those are the titles set forth in the Burgo's Requirement. The first title affirms that the emperor is the lord of the world. Vitória could not accept this because he no longer lived in a feudal environment. The Roman-German Emperor already boasted a more symbolic than effective power. Thus, Charles V could not claim the Indian lands on his own authority. Regarding the second title, the author rejects the papal monism. The pope does not exercise temporal jurisdiction over the orb, because God had never made this donation. The third title corresponds to the discovery of the New World. However, those lands were not devoid of owners, so there was no new acquisition. The fourth title refers to the refusal of the Indians to receive the faith of Christ. Vitória does not accept this because he denies the legitimacy of forced conversions. Concerning the fifth title, the Spaniards could declare war on the Indians because of their sins; which went against not only divine Positive Law, but also Natural Law. The Indians would eat human flesh and would practice incest. This reason was quite serious, but the pope did not exercise spiritual jurisdiction over nonconverted people and hence could not delegate the authority to correct them. The sixth title is the voluntary submission of the Indians to the Spaniards. In addition to the fact that fear and ignorance corrupted this type of submission, the heretics already had a sovereign. So this title must be void. Finally, the last title would confer to the Spanish rights over all the barbarians by a special donation from God. Vitória does not dwell much on this title because this argument was not proven either in the Scriptures or by miracle.

So far, the writings seem to be in line with the image of Vitória as a humanist saint; however, the *relección* continues. In the third section, the author proceeds to analyze the legitimate titles by which the Spaniards could conquer the barbarians. The first title concerns the natural communication that exists worldwide. The Spaniards have the right to visit and to settle in the land of the Indians, without suffering any damage. Should they come to any harm, they would be entitled to start a war. From this title derives the legitimacy of the trade, the use of common things and migration. All these institutes would belong in the Law of Nations, and the noncompliance thereof was just cause for war. The second title refers to the propagation of the Christian religion. The Indians are not obliged to convert, but they must withstand evangelization. This duty does not derive from the Law of Nations, but from the true faith, and it seems unlikely that Vitória admitted reciprocity. The third and fourth titles also correspond to matters of faith. If some of the barbarians were to convert, their princes could not use force to bring them back to idolatry, under penalty of a Just War. In addition, after their conversion to Christianity, the pope could rightfully grant a Christian prince to the Indians. The fifth title derives from the tyranny of the barbarians' masters who enacted inhuman laws providing for the sacrifice of innocents. This may be described as the embryo of a humanitarian intervention. In the sixth title, Vitória resumes the idea of voluntary submission of the Indians to the King of Spain, but stressed that their consent must be valid. The seventh title refers to the alliances that some tribes could establish with the Spaniards against others. In this case, Spain would be entitled to assist its allies. Finally, should there be a community unable to rule itself; the Spaniards could (by charity) govern it. However, they should not do it for their own advantage, but for the sake of the barbarians.

The entire **Second Lesson on the Indians** provides for the Spaniards' right to go to war against the Barbarians.

Thus, Vitória offers new grounds to support all that he had previously refuted. The fact that the Indians possess domain does not exclude the possibility of interdiction. The pope cannot exercise jurisdiction over them, but he has an indirect power. The Spaniards may settle there in virtue of society's natural communication. Forced conversions are prohibited, but the Indians should endure evangelization. Barbaric practices, such as sodomy and cannibalism, do not justify intervention, but the intervention may take place in the defense of the innocents. These arguments do not bode well with the image of a defender of the rights of the Indians.

Vitória was a man of principles. He did not accept the official doctrine of the **Request** for the conquest of the Indians, nor the idea that the pope could exercise authority over the entire world, even over the non-Christian world. However, he was as much a patriot as a defender of the Christian faith, although his doctrine led him far from the ordinary arguments of his time. In the debate between Bartolomé de Las Casas and Juan Ginés de Sepúlveda on the rights of the Indians, Francisco de Vitória stood in the middle.

What to say about Vitória's statements regarding the existence of an international society limiting the sovereignty of States and governed by law? In fact, the Theologian of Salamanca frequently uses the expression *totus orbis* or even the variant *totus mundus*. There is no doubt that the expression works as a frame of reference, but it is strange that the author never defines it. Haggenmacher analyzes all the passages in which the words appear in Vitória's works. In some cases, they have a purely factual meaning and describe the "world" as a geographical reality. In other rarer passages, they denote a moral authority, invested with *auctoritas* or *potestas*. In these fewer cases, the *totus orbis* appears as the source of the Law of Nations or as the source of the law of war only, used by the sovereigns as a sanction.[89] Was Vitória introducing an original notion, akin to that of the international society?

On commenting Aquinas' Treaty of Justice, Vitória examines question 57, which, as seen, considers the *jus gentium* a Positive Law. Aquinas' ambivalence on the nature of the International Law reflects on Vitória's work: at certain times, the *jus gentium* belongs to Natural Law, at others to Positive Law. In this text, Vitória opts for the latter. However, it is a rather unique Positive Law due to the apparent

---

[89]Haggenmacher (1988), p. 39.

absence of legislative power. Positive Law manifests in two ways: by *condicta privata* (in ordinary contracts between private individuals) and by *condicta publica* (in conventions adopted by an entire community).[90] These usually appear in the form of laws, which ensures their publicity. But when referring to an agreement among all peoples and nations of the world, publicity is an implicit element. According to Haggenmacher, Vitória wanted to apply a Civil Law subtlety to the Law of Nations. The public aspect stems from the universality of the convention. Therefore, the author's language remains within the contractual sphere, and the *Orbis* does not designate an autonomous and superior entity. It is merely a convenient way of referring to the sum of States.[91] So, in this text, despite resembling a legislative source, the *totus orbis* does not represent a moral person.

But how to explain the passage in *Relectio de potestate civili*, the aforementioned *aliquo modo est una republica*, in which the *totus orbis* enacts true laws? Indeed, the passage is a corollary of the preceding statement. Vitória questions whether Civil Laws also bind legislators and kings ("*An leges civiles obligent legislatores et maxime reges*?"). Some believed those persons were above the republic and thus there would be no higher power constricting them. According to the Theologian of Salamanca, the sovereigns are also part of the republic and, such as the law is valid for the whole of the community, they too should abide by it. The same dynamics of the contracts apply to them: beforing entering into an agreement, the person is free, but once he does, he becomes bound to the terms thereof. Vitória thus infers the corollary: "the Law of Nations is enforceable not only by result of the covenant and agreement of men, but has real force of law. And the whole world, which somehow forms a republic, has the power to prescribe to all subjects just laws, such as the laws of the Law of Nations."[92]

With this statement, the author wishes to emphasize the legal character of the Law of Nations. However, this character does not conflict with the contractual nature outlined above, because the *condicta publica* enables such assimilation with law. The emphasis on the legal character derives from a previously developed logic. Vitória argues that Positive Law, unlike Natural Law, focuses on actions that were once morally neutral. However, after the enactment of Positive Law, the action prescribed therein becomes prohibited or required by Natural Law itself. "From that, it can be understood that all who violate the Law of Nations mortally sin."[93] Vitória did not seek to contradict a previous finding and to change the conventional source of the *jus gentium*, but he emphasized the notion that this law also obliges in conscience.

---

[90]Vitória (2003), **De Jure Gentium et Naturali**, p. cxii.

[91]Haggenmacher (1988), p. 41.

[92]"*Quod ius gentium non solum habet vim ex pacto et condicto inter homines, sed etiam habet vim legis. Habet enim totus orbis, qui aliquo modo est una republica, potestatem ferendi leges aequas et convenientes omnibus, quale sunt in iure gentium.*" (**De potestate civili**, 21, p. 191).

[93]"*Ex quo patet quod mortaliter peccant violantes iura gentium*" (**De potestate civili**, 21, p. 191).

In his Lecture on the Indians, Vitória offers a double ground of validity for the Law of Nations: in some cases, it is Natural Law, in others, the human consent. "But what **natural reason** has established among all nations is called the Law of Nations." Or: "And since [the Law of Nations] not always derive from Natural Law, it seems that the **consent** of the major part of the world is sufficient, especially if it is for the common good of all."[94] The fact that Vitória gave this lecture one decade after the previous one is significant. If he decided to look into the nature of the *jus gentium*, he has changed his opinion with the years; once Positive Law, the Law of Nations became part Natural, part Positive Law. There is also the possibility that Vitória was never worried about the *jus gentium*, and that the double basis thereof implies indifference. In both possibilities, Vitória distances himself from a more modern notion of International Law.

In the last excerpt above, the validity of the *jus gentium* does not derive from the *totus orbis*, but from the *majoris partis totus orbis*. Without any doubt, this change follows the larger frame of reference imposed by the discovery of the "barbarians of the New World." It produced very interesting consequences. The consent of the majority of mankind is enforceable on the entire world, even against the will of a minority (which is not elaborated).

It is on such enforcement that Vitória based the legitimacy of the war waged by the Europeans against the Indians, as addressed in his Second Lecture on the Indians. All the princes exercised authority not only over their subjects, but also over foreigners in order to prevent them from making wrongdoings. Their power emanated from the authority of the entire orb.[95] It is possible to draw another consequence in addition to Vitória's defense of the Spanish colonialism. In the two lessons on the Indians, the orb does seem to constitute a legislative source, sometimes of the all the *jus gentium*, others only of the vindictive power of the sovereigns.

However, Haggenmacher remarks that in no moment does Vitória investigate the figure of the orb itself. It appears always in relation to other issues (the Law of Nations and the vindictive power of the sovereigns), but never at the core of the discussion. For this reason, its notion remains unclear. As a result, in the rare occasions in which the *totus orbis* appears as an organic whole, superior to the sum of the States, the author could not be referring to a new reality that might call for a careful scrutiny. In fact, he was referring to something quite old that would require no introduction and was probably lost in an immemorial past: the *orbis christianus*.[96] The *Respublica Christiana* corresponded to an old framework, of which every European was fully aware. The *totus orbis* is a marginal abstraction of a notion that was no longer real. It means the update of a past reality (though not

---

[94] "*Quod naturalis ratio inter omnes gentes constituit, vocatur ius gentium*" and "*Et dato quod non semper derivetur ex iure naturali, satis videtur esse consensus maioris partis totius orbis, maxime pro bono communi omnium.*" (**De indis** I, 3, 2. p. 706 and I, III, 4. p. 710).

[95] Vitória (2003) **De Jure Belli**, p. lvi.

[96] Haggenmacher (1988), pp. 45–46.

entirely forgotten) due to the discovery of non-Christian people who somehow found themselves under the jurisdiction of the Christians.

The distinction between Christians and non-Christians is essential to the comprehension of Vitória's Law of Nations. Such as the Roman *jus gentium* ruled the relations between Romans and foreigners, so does Vitória's *jus gentium* govern the relations between Christians and non-Christians. In addition, just like the former bore no resemblance to the contemporary International Law, since it applied within the Roman Empire, the later focuses on a European empire expanded by the Great Discoveries. It is the Civil Law of a multi-religious community under Christian (Spaniard) jurisdiction.

Vitória developed this thesis of Spanish aggrandization of the *orbis christianus* and selected the examples accordingly. What he did was to derive consequences from the old European Christian *aliquot modo* Republic to all mankind. Thus, just like each Christian province integrated the European Christianity, so each republic was part of the orb. The example used by the author in the lecture on the civilian *potestade* to prove that each State has an organic connection with the entire world is quite revealing. Even if a State has a just cause to go to war, it may not do so at the expense of the *totus orbis*: "(…) if the war were between the Spanish and the French should cause greater damages and rupture to Christianity, with the risk of the Turks occupying Christian provinces, however just may be the reasons and however advantageous may be for Spain, it must give up on that war."[97] The author's illustration does not refer to the *totus orbis*, but only to the *Respublica Christiana*.

According to Haggenmacher, Vitória chose an example that would certainly convince his viewers, because it appealed to a general concern that hovered over the political reality of that time. However, such an example suited poorly the whole orb since the idea that the entire world would become Christian was still very remote. In Vitória's time, to imagine that the *totus orbis* could form a republic could only be *aliquo modo*. It was a distant and elusive notion, evoked only to serve as background explanation regarding other issues that were crucial to Vitória's reasoning. Different altogether was the situation within the center of Christianity, where Vitória could conceive universal monarchy without any difficulty.[98]

What to say regarding the alleged adaptation of Gaius' definition of the *jus gentium* (*Quod naturalis ratio inter omnes gentes constituit, vocatur ius gentium*) made by the Theologian of Salamanca? If this was intentional, Vitória wished to argue that the subject of the Law of Nations would be the State, not the individual. However, even without analyzing what Vitória's concept of State was, it is possible to demonstrate that such an issue was never on the author's mind.

---

[97]"*(…) ut si bellum hispaniarum esset adversus gallos alias ex causis iustis susceptum et alioqui regno hispaniarum utile, tamen cum maiore malo et iactura geritur christianitatis, puta qui turcae occupant interim provincias christianorum, cessandum esset a tali bello.*" (**De potestate civili**, 13, p. 168).

[98]Haggenmacher (1988), p. 46.

When Vitória questions whether the Indians had the public and private property of their lands before the arrival of the Spaniards, he does not investigate the international legal personality of the Indians, only their legal personality at all. Otherwise, those conquerors could not deprive them of their possessions, and the Laws of Burgos would not apply. Vitória's attention was not focused on an alleged difference between private and public properties, but on the legal capacity of the Indians. He does not seek to prove the State-like character of the barbarian communities of the New World, but the human nature of the individuals that compose it. Moreover, when the author examines the just titles for the Spanish intervention, the focus is always on the barbarity or on the infidelity of the individuals. Vitória looks for souls to convert and to save.[99]

The Theologian from Salamanca worries about men, not States; he even blurs the distinction between the Law of Nations and Natural Law. The reference to Gaius appears in the first of the fourteen arguments that aim to prove that the Spaniards could visit the Indians. In the very definition thereof, the *jus gentium* stems from natural reason. In addition, his reasoning begins with "it is proved, in first place, by the Law of Nations, which is Natural Law or derives from it."[100]

Contrary to his prior understanding (according to which the *jus gentium* derived from a tacit covenant), Vitória here sets forth a natural basis for the *jus gentium*. There was no other way. There was nothing in common between the Spaniards and the Indians, except for nature itself.

Therefore, by addressing the definition of Gaius, Vitória does not want to underline *the inter omnes gentes*, but the *naturalis ratio*. However, why did the author substitute *homines* for *gentes* (peoples)? Although Gaius refers to *homines* in the excerpt above, he also uses the words *populi* and *gentes*, and this explains the etymologic origin of the expression *jus gentium*. Vitória attempted to invoke Gaius' formula, which he quotes in an approximate manner. To the Dominican, *inter omnes gentes* does not differ from *inter omnes homines*. The extension of one, *apud omnes enim nationes habetur inhumanum* directly reflects on the extension of the other *apud omnes populos peraeque custoditur*. So Vitória wanted to evoke the Roman notion of *jus gentium*, an internal common law that is based on some kind of natural intrinsic necessity.

Even the choice of the term *nationes* does not seem random. It appears that Vitória channeled the definition of Natural Law from Saint Isidore de Sevilla: "Natural Law is common to all nations and comes from a natural instinct."[101] Following the inclination of his work, Isidore produces an etymological wordplay that may go unnoticed for a modern reader. Since **Natural** Law applies to all **nations** and originates from a **natural** instinct, there must be something common to

---

[99]Haggenmacher (1988), pp. 50–56.

[100]"*Probatur primo ex iure gentium, quod vel est ius naturale, vel derivatur ex iure naturale*" (**De indis** I, III, 2. p. 706).

[101]*Ius naturale commune omnium nationum, et quod ubique instinctu naturae*" (Isidorus Hispalensis Episcopus (1911), V, IV, 1).

all these words, the common root, the verb "*nasci.*" Thus, Natural Law is a law "of birth," which is "born" with man, and not by a legislative convention. Vitória (who knew very well the **Etymologies**) wanted to insinuate that meaning and inserted the word nation to match the *ius naturale* referred at the beginning of the passage as a direct or indirect source of his *ius gentium.*[102]

There is no doubt that here the author turns his efforts into setting forth a foundation to the Law of Nations. Nonetheless, such a foundation lies in nature, which separates the Law of Nations from International Law. It is curious that the first Vitória (the one who based his *jus gentium* on a convention) did not seem as concerned with finding the basis thereof: "first the dispute relates more to the name than the thing itself, because it matters little if someone affirms one thing [that the Law of Nations belongs to Positive Law] or another [that it belongs to Natural Law]."[103] When Vitória is concerned with foundations, the Law of Nations stems from nature, but when he considers it a matter of less importance, its origin lies on Positive Law.

Vitória is not able to overcome the Roman concept of *jus gentium.* The *jus gentium* remains the internal law of an empire that is common to different peoples (but not between those peoples) and sometimes merges with Natural Law. However, paradoxically, the weakness in Vitória's arguments regarding the law among political societies constitutes the strength of his legacy. Even if he had not conceived a law among political societies, Vitória actually replaced the word *homines* for the word *gentes.* Although he never offered a clear basis for the Law of Nations, at one point he considered it part of Positive Law. Albeit he defended the Spaniards' right of intervention on the Indians, he granted the "barbarians of the New World" the possibility of domain. Whatever mindless abstraction may have occurred, the term *totus orbis* was indeed often used. Vitória laid the groundwork for someone else to discuss a law between peoples, positive in nature, inserted into an international society that is above the States' sovereignty.

2.3 The Humanist Law of Nations: Alberico Gentili

The last character in this evolution of the concept of *jus gentium* is the jurist Alberico Gentili. Italian-born, he fled his hometown because his family embraced the Protestantism. Then, in 1581, he began teaching at Oxford, where he became *Regius* Professor of Civil Law. It seems likely that both Selden and Hobbes had attended his lessons, for he remained at that university until 1605.[104]

---

[102]Haggenmacher (1988), p. 61.

[103]"(...) *first of all the dispute concerns the name more than the thing, for it matters little whether one says this or that*" (Vitória 2003, **De Jure Gentium et Naturali**, p. cxi).

[104]Nézard (1904), pp. 39–43.

Even though he held the Civil Law chair, Gentili always dealt with the Law of Nations and wrote important books on the subject, such as the **De Iure Belli, De Legationibus** and **Advocatio Hispanica** (the first on the law of war, the second on diplomatic law, and the last one on the law of naval warfare).

Alberico Gentili greatly influenced Hugo Grotius. His name appears ten times in the **De Jure Praedae** and a dozen times in the **De Jure Belli ac Pacis**. Haggenmacher believes that, because of the confiscation of his library, Grotius would have made use of references from the Italian to compose his masterpiece. The Dutch Lawyer even repeated several quotation mistakes made by the Italian Jurist.[105] Undoubtedly, among his contemporaries, Gentili deserves a place of honor. When explaining the purpose of his work, Grotius ignores those who preceded him, but expressly acknowledges that he made use of Gentili.[106]

Due to his education at the University of Perugia, Gentili received a classic formation of an Italian Humanist: he was a true follower of *the mos italicus* and disciple of authors such as Bartolo and Baldo. This is what Richard Tuck called the "Oratoric tradition," opposed to the "Theological tradition" of the Spanish Scholastics. While the former is based on the literary and rhetorical writings of the ancient world (especially on Romans speakers who were clearly skeptical of much philosophy), the latter was inspired by Christian literature, in combination with Greek Philosophy and the legal systematizations of the Romans.[107]

Gentili embodied not only a distinct tradition, but also one that conflicted with Vitória's. Jurists and Theologians delved into the same subject (the law), each claiming preeminence of their own perspective. On the one hand, since Cicero (who is an obligatory reference for all Humanists) the "Jurisprudence" corresponded to the *magna* science and encompassed Legal and Political Philosophy, Ethics, Economics, and Social Sciences in general. On the other hand, the Theologians had placed their Theology at the summit of human knowledge and considered it the "queen of the sciences." The issue was no mere corporate jealousy, because the Theologians also studied Law. To Vitória, "the Theologian's craft is so vast that no argument, no dispute, no matter is outside his profession."[108] Thus, raids were inevitable, and Gentili could only answer: "On matters that are none of your concern, Theologians be silent!"[109]

As expected, even when addressing the *jus gentium* and the law of war, Gentili's conclusions differed greatly from those of the Scholastics. The difference was so

---

[105]Haggemacher (2002), pp. 146–149.

[106]GROTII, Hugonis. **De Iure Belli ac Pacis libri tres**. *In quibus ius naturae et Gentium: item iuris publici praecipua explicantur. Parisiis: Nicolaum Buon, 1625. prolegomenom* 38. Henceforth, **DJBP**.

[107]Tuck (1999), p. 16.

[108]"*Officium ac munus theologi tam late patet, ut nullum argumentum, nulla disputatio, nullus locus alienus videatur a theologica professione et instituto*." (**De potestate civili**, Prologue, p. 150).

[109]"*Silete theologi in munere alieno*!" (GENTILI, Alberico. **De Iure Belli Libri Tres**. Hannover: G. Antonius, 1612, I, 12, 4. Henceforth, **DIB**).

deep that if Alfred Vanderpol is right and indeed the Medieval Law of War consists of the **Scholastic** Doctrine of Just War, then Gentili does not belong to this tradition. His position is closer to political realism and far from a doctrine that seeks to determine the justice in war.

For instance, Gentili is concerned with the balance of power: "This is what the distinguished Lorenzo de Medici, an eminent scholar of peace and father of peace, always looked for, ensuring that the States of Italian princes always remained balanced among them." That is why it should come as no surprise that he devoted an entire chapter to defend the legality of the preventive defense: "to ensure that men do not grow in excessive power is safer than chasing the medicine [*sic*] after they become powerful."[110] Fear plays an important role and replaces injustice as the determinant reason. To all Scholastics, war is just if the enemy inflicts an actual injury; without actual aggression, the simple fear that the adversary would grow in power, could never justify the conflict.

Gentili widens the notion of legitimate defense: "The defense is also needed to protect our things and we have just cause to defend them during war, even if the war that endangers our things has been unjustly caused by us."[111] Within this author's law of war, injury becomes a secondary issue.

Another fundamental difference between Gentili's and the Scholastic's Doctrine of Just War lies in the problem of bilateral justice in a war: whether there could be a just cause legitimizing both sides in battle. Theologians dismiss this hypothesis because the will (or reason) of God is indivisible. The only concession possible is if one side incurs in an error of fact, which might become an invincible ignorance. As will be examined in Chapter IV, in this case, one party would be subjectively and objectively right, while the other would have no legitimate grounds to go to war despite believing otherwise. This issue was subject of careful examination, with many advices and urgings for the prince to act prudently and to know his case in depth, in order to reduce the likelihood of an error.

Yet, the Italian Jurist does not share these qualms. Chapter VI of **De Iure Belli** is dedicated in its entirety to prove the possibility of bilateral justice. This opinion could be the cause of much terror to all writers subsequent to Gratian, but not to the classical spirit. Many Romans expressed sympathy for the patriotic fight put up by their own enemies. Caesar recognized that the Gauls defended their country, because they "naturally" loved their freedom.[112] Gentili metaphorically describes war as a judicial procedure: just as law cannot be known before the award, so it was not possible to access justice in abstract before the battle came to end. In principle,

---

[110]"*Et id illud est, quod sapientissimus, et pacis studiosissimus, ac pacis pater, Laurenius ille edicis procuranit semper, ut res Italorum principum paribus libratae ponderib. forent.*" and "*Obsistendum igitur. Et cauere fatius est, ne homines augetur nimium potentia, quam contra potentiores postea remedium quaerere.*" (**DIB**, I, 14, 3).

[111]"*Res etiam ut nostras defendamus, necessária (quod et diximus) defensio haec est et iusta haec causa, etiam si bello petiti bellum promeriti nos essemus.*" (**DIB**, I, 13, 5).

[112]**De Bello Gallico**, III, 10, 3, p. 62.

both sides have standing to litigate, so that the *cause probabilis* should replace the requirement of "just cause."[113]

> To this we are forced, by the infirmity of human nature, by which everything appears veiled before us and we are not granted with that reliable perception of absolute justice that would not allow for two to truly contend between themselves and both be right, that the just should be offended by one or the other.[114]

The idea of absolute justice may even exist, but it can be perceived only by God (or gods). The weakness of the human condition does not allow man to argue coherently about it; therefore, men can only investigate possible causes.

Because he professed the Lutheran faith, Gentili did not harbor any illusions regarding the idea of a moral unity of Christendom. This disenchantment, added to his cultural heritage, approached the Italian from Oxford one step closer to ethical relativism. Had Machiavelli been committed to the study of the law of war, he would have been named Alberico Gentili.

This realistic tone of Gentili's arguments led many[115] into seeing a secularist essence in his admonition to the Theologians (*Silete theologi in munere alieno!*). Given that this is a typically modern notion, Gentili (and not Grotius) would be the real "father" of International Law.

However, this claim that the Oxford Professor would have laicized the *jus gentium* after centuries of Catholic obscurantism is at best controversial. Like any Reformer of his time, Gentili believes that the Law of Nations proceeds from the will of God, which makes for a feeble secularist theory: "a small part of the divine law is the Law of Nations, with which God has left us after sin."[116] To Haggenmacher, the admonition to the Theologians implied merely a separation between the jurisdiction of the *jurisconsulti* (which always appeared in Gentili's work as *nostri*) and that of the *theologi*. This jurisdictional distinction required the author sometimes to abandon an entire issue to the Theologians, especially when related to the first three commandments of the Decalogue.[117]

Therefore, Gentili is very careful in advocating the possibility of investigating alliances with peoples of different religions, since "this issue is in part Theological and examined by the Theologians, and in part civil, and examined by us." When addressing the issue of the legality of the duel between princes for the kingdom, he bumps into the problem of the origin of the sovereign domain of power and whether

---

[113]Panizza (2005), p. 18.

[114]"*Huc adigit nos humanae nostrae conditionis infirmitas: per quam sunt nobis in tenebris omnia: etpurissimum illud, arq; verissimu iustum ignoratur, quod non serret duo litigare iuste.*" (**DIB**, I, 6, 1).

[115]See the introduction from Diego Panizza (2004), p. 30 to the De Iure Belli of the Brazilian edition. This author insists on a distinction between *res religionis* and *ius humanum* in the Italian Jurist's thoughts.

[116]"*Et quamquam ius gentium particula est divini iuris, quam Deus nobis post peccatum reliquam fecit*" (**DIB**, I, 1, 4).

[117]Haggenmacher (2002), p. 171.

the prince may dispose of it. For fear of having to delve into the Theory of the Divine Right of the Kings and of the popular origin of sovereignty (which were a warhorse between Reformed and Catholic Theologians, as will be seen in chapter V) the Italian Jurist bluntly accepts his incompetence: "this issue, on the other hand, belongs to the first table [of the Ten Commandments] and transcends the office of a Legal Adviser."[118]

In addition, Gentili's concept of *jus gentium* is even less modern. In fact, it is older than Vitória's. While Vitória's Law of Nations came to be part of Positive Law, at times hastily so, in Gentili, there is no doubt that it belongs to Natural Law. He even uses the redundant expression *iure naturali gentium*. Gentili expressly incorporates the definitions of the Roman jurists when he states that "the Law of Nations is one that is in use among all peoples, that natural reason has established among all men and is observed by all. That is the Law of Nature."[119]

References to custom and consensus should not evoke Positive Law. They only mean that Gentili is an empiricist in his efforts to prove the existence of the Law of Nations.[120] Custom does not serve as a basis for the *jus gentium*, but as its phenomenological manifestation. Consensus and the uses of the various peoples prove the existence of Natural Law. As a Humanist, Gentili never intended to leave the Roman orbit.

2.4 Summary

Before the publication of the work of Antoine Pillet, **Les fondateurs du droit international**, academics urged to find a father for International Law. The legend of a single founder of the discipline coincided with the creation of a myth around Hugo Grotius by the School of Law of Nature and of Peoples. For 300 years, this author bore such title. However, when his innovativeness was questioned and the Spanish Scholastic rediscovered, it was found that Grotius himself had his sources, and thus the idea of a law between the peoples appeared older than him.

An old Christian tradition of universal value came to the rescue: the Just War doctrine. War corresponds to the most extreme form of contact between two peoples; then, rules of war would clearly mean an expression of International Law. Furthermore, all prospective fathers of the discipline, Grotius and the Spanish Scholastics, belonged to this tradition, which reinforces the notion that it represents the source of such law. So, one must look into the first author to defend this theory.

---

[118]"*Atque est quaestio partim theologalis, tractataque theologis; partim et nostris tractata civilis*" and "*Fortetamen hic quaestio est prioris tabulae: quae supra iurisconsultum est*" (**DIB**, III, 19, 1 and III, 15, 2).

[119]"(...) *ius esse gentium, quo gentes humanae utuntur: quod naturalis ratio inter homines constitui, et apud omnes peraeque custoditur. Hoc ius naturae est.*" (**DIB,** I, 1, 5).

[120]Haggenmacher (1983), p. 355.

Yet this task is not simple. The influences of the Medieval Law of War are lost in Antiquity. There are reminiscences, both Hebrew and Hellenistic, and several affinities with the Roman *jus fetiale*. But it seems to be a consensus in Historiography that the first writer of this tradition was St. Augustine. Despite this agreement, the nonsystematic references in the work of the Bishop of Hippo do not seem to imply a concern over the issue of justice in war. In fact, St. Augustine was preoccupied about the legitimacy of a public service: the military service. The other authors of the High Middle Ages also failed to consider the law of war as an autonomous issue.

Only in the twelfth century did this doctrine begin to take shape. Although it was not the main concern of the monk Gratian, the **Gratian Decree** holds a prominent position in the history of Just War. In this Decree, there is a range of references and quotations somewhat out of context from the Patristic, but organized around specific issues, among which war appears as *Causa XXIII*. Since then, the succeeding writers were able to investigate war by itself. Canonists, Theologians, and Decretists turned their attention to the subject.

In the following century, Thomas Aquinas, one of the most important thinkers of all time, turned his attention to the issue of the legitimacy of war. In order to be just, war must fulfill three conditions: competent authority, just cause and right intention. Although there is no further analysis of these requirements, Aquinas' conception became a mandatory reference for subsequent thinkers, due to the authority that his work acquired in the Middle Ages. Aquinas thus eventually provided the classic formulation of the doctrine. His followers claimed it in such a way that it became impossible to separate the doctrine from the Scholasticism, albeit lay jurists have also written about the law of war.

Nevertheless, the influences of the Scholastic Just War doctrine on International Law is much too fleeting for it to be possible that this law would have originated, in its entirety from this tradition. Most of the Just War authors do not even offer a definition of *jus gentium*. To infer that justice invariable leads to the existence of a law between the peoples is to neglect the role played by a universal, rational, and Natural Law. Since the time of the Romans, Natural Law provided the basis for the common law among peoples and individuals that did not emanate from the legislative will of a *civitas*. Only when the concept of the Law of Nations acquires autonomy from Natural Law may we infer that there is a modern notion of International Law.[121]

It turns out that the Romans were not good Philosophers and found it difficult to formulate nonnatural grounds for their *jus gentium*. In Rome, this law ruled the relations among foreigners located within the Empire. It did not correspond to a Law of Nations, but of the *gens*. It corresponded to law *intra gentes*, not *inter gentes*.

[121]Autonomy does not mean exclusion. As will be seen later, all the positive law (including the *jus gentium*) of Suárez and Grotius had to be in accordance with Natural Law.

The authors of the Middle Ages inherit the tripartite division of Natural Law, Civil Law and Law of Nations, but they too could find no distinct basis for the Law of Nations. In fact, the *jus gentium* was of no significant concern in the Middle Ages. It was more an annoying legacy, one people did not know what to do with or where to place it. Indeed, St. Isidore of Seville considered the *jus gentium* to be a Positive Law, but the absence of a clear definition undermines the originality of his intent. It seems likely that, influenced by the Christian imperial notion of the time, the author conceived this law as an almost universal common law, but one that did not govern the relations between the peoples.

Thomas Aquinas seems to infer the *jus gentium* from Natural Law, as if it corresponded to the very Natural Law applied to one of the many aspects of human society. The confusion with the existing law is a product of a deviant definition of the word "positive." For Aquinas, positive means human. Unlike Civil Law, man does not create the *jus gentium*. However, the *jus gentium* requires a "positive" effort of man's intellect to derive it from natural principles. It is an inclination that Natural Law arouses in men. It is a distinct inclination and exclusive to humans. It is a "human" law not because it is man-made, but because men do not share this (natural) impulse with other beings.

The literature that was looking for a father of International Law then turned to the Dominican Theologian Francisco de Vitória. In his lectures, the *jus gentium* seems to apply to the most distinct peoples of the world. This literature argued that Vitória limited the sovereignty of the State by the notion of an international community: an organic whole, greater than the sum of its parts, a legislative source of the Law of Nations. In addition, the literature concluded that he defended the rights of the Indians against the Spanish conquerors and proclaimed their international legal personality. Finally, it considered that the Spanish Theologian overthrew Gaius' definition of *jus gentium* to adapt it to the current notion thereof.

However, under a more detailed analysis, these conclusions are proven hasty. The very structure of Vitória's lectures on the Indians evidences a supporter of the Spanish conquest, though his reasons differed from the official rationale. In the rare occasions that the *totus orbis* designates a legislative body, the author conceives it according to the moral unity of the European Christendom. In addition, his alleged subversion of Gaius' definition of *jus gentium* is a mere quotation from memory. Vitória did not leave the Roman context.

Even if Francisco de Vitória cannot be called the "father" of International Law, his relevance is not to be underestimated, because he left elements that others were able to work from. Nevertheless, for the *jus gentium* to become International Law, the idea of imperial monism or *Orbis christianus* had to be buried. The emergence of the idea of "internationality" walks hand in hand with the decline of the Universal Empire.

Reformation destroyed the Christian unity of Europe and, with it, the notion of *Respublica Christiana*. Succeeding authors were then able to write about a *jus gentium* of positive nature and applicable between peoples. However, the destruction of the Christian unity would also erode a universal moral framework. This would deprive this new Positive Law of Nations and the basis thereof of any ethical claim other than the will of the States. Only authors who had experienced the Reformation, but foresaw and refused ethical relativism at all costs could conceive a positive nonvoluntary *jus gentium*. There were only two jurists to walk this narrow path: Francisco Suárez and Hugo Grotius.

References

Agostinho. **Obras de San Agustin**. Trad. José Moran *et alii*. Madrid: BAC, 1993. t. XVI. *La Ciudad de Dios*; t. XXXI. *Escritos antimaniqueos. Contra Fausto*.

Aquino, Santo Tomas de. **Summa Teologica**. Texto latino de la edición crítica Leonina. Trad. Francisco Barbado Viejo, O.P. 2. ed. Madrid: Biblioteca de Autores Cristianos, 1947.

Aristóteles. **Ética a Nicômaco**. Translation. Leonel Vallandro and Gerd Bornheim. São Paulo: Abril Cultural, 1973.

Barcia Trelles, Camilo. Francisco Suárez: les théologiens espagnols du XVIe siècle et l'école moderne du Droit International. **Recueil de Cours de l'Académie de Droit International de Le Hague**, n. 1, t. 43, pp. 386–503, 1933.

Barthélemy, Joseph. François de Vitoria. In: PILLET, Antoine. **Les Fondateurs du Droit International**. Paris: V. Giard & E. Brière, 1904.

Bauer, Dominique; Lesaffer, Randall. Ivo of Chartres, the Gregorian Reform and the Formation of the Just War Doctrine. **Journal of the History of International Law**, n. 7, pp. 43–54, 2005.

Bourquin, Maurice. Grotius est-il le père du droit des gens? (1583–1645). In: **Grandes figures et grandes oeuvres juridiques**. Genève: Librairie de l'Université, Georg & Cie., 1948.

Bruxelles: Académie Royale de Belgique, 1883.

Bull, Hedley. The Grotian Conception of International Society. In: Butterfield, Herbert & Wight, Martin (ed.). **Diplomatic Investigations**. London: George Allen & Unwin Ltd., 1966.

César, Júlio. Comentários sobre a Guerra Gálica (De Bello Gallico). Trad. Francisco Sotero dos Reis. Rio de Janeiro: Ediouro, s/d.

Cícero, Marco Túlio. **Dos Deveres**. Translation Angélica Chiapeta. São Paulo: Martins Fontes, 1999.

Cicerón. **De la République—Des Lois**. Trad. Charles Appuhn. Paris: Garnier Frères. 1954.

Delos, J. T. **La Société Internationale et les Principes de Droit Public**. 2. ed. Paris: Pédone, 1950.

Dinstein, Yoram. **Guerra, Agressão e Legítima Defesa**. Trad. Mauro Raposo de Mello. 3.ed. Barueri: Manole, 2004.

Fusinato, G. Le droit international de la République Romaine. **Revue de droit international et de législation comparée**, pp. 270–310, 1885.

Gentili, Alberico. **O Direito de Guerra**. Tradução de Ciro Mioranza. Ijuí: Unijuí, 2004.

Gentili, Alberico. **De Iure Belli Libri Tres**. Hannover: G. Antonius, 1612.

Grotii, Hugonis. **De Iure Belli ac Pacis libri tres**. *In quibus ius naturae et Gentium: item iuris publici praecipua explicantur*. Parisiis: Nicolaum Buon, 1625.

Grotius, Hugo. **De Iure Belli ac Pacis libri tres**. *In quibus ius naturae et Gentium: item iuris publici praecipua explicantur*. Parisiis: Nicolaum Buon, 1625.

Grotius, Hugo. **De Iure Belli ac Pacis libri tres**. *In quibus ius naturae et Gentium: item iuris publici praecipua explicantur*. Amsterdã: I. Blaeu, 1646. Edited by James Brown Scott. Oxford, London: Clarendon Press, Geoffrey Cumberlege, 1925. (The Classics of International Law).

Grotius, Hugo. **De Iure Belli ac Pacis libri tres**. *In quibus ius naturae et Gentium: item iuris publici praecipua explicantur*. Cum Annotationibus Auctoris, ejusdemque Dissertatione de *Mari Libero*; Ac Libello singulari *De Aequitate, Indulgentia et Facilitate*: Nec non Joann. Frid. Gronovii Notis in totum opus de Jure Belli ac Pacis, Ex altera recensione Joannis Barbeyracii. Amsterdã: apud Janssonio-Waesbergios, 1735.

Grotius, Hugonis. **De Jure Praedae Commentarius**. La Haye: Hamaker, Nijhoff, 1868.
Grotius, Hugues. **Le droit de la guerre et de la paix de Hugues Grotius**. Trad. J. Barbeyrac. Amsterdam: Pierre de Coup, 1724.
Haggemacher, Peter. Grotius and Gentili: a reassessment of Thomas E. Holland's inaugural lecture. In: Bull, Hedley; Kingsbury, Benedict; Roberts, Adam (ed.). Hugo Grotius and International Relations. Oxford, New York: Oxford University, Clarendon Press, 2002.
Haggenmacher, Peter. 1492 Le choc de deux mondes. **Actes du Colloque**. COMISSION NATIONALE SUISSE POR L'UNESCO. Genève: La Différence, 1993.
Haggenmacher, Peter. **Grotius et la doctrine de la guerre juste**. Genève, Paris: Heige, Presses Universitaires de France, 1983.
Haggenmacher, Peter. La place de Francisco de Vitoria parmi les fondateurs du droit international. In: Truyol y Serra, Antonio et al. **Actualité de la Pensée Juridique de Francisco de Vitoria**. Bruxelles: Bruylant, Centre Charles De Visscher pour le droit international, 1988.
Hinojosa, Eduardo. **Influencia que tuvieron en el Derecho Público de su pátria y singularmente en el Derecho penal los filósofos y teólogos españoles, anteriores a nuestro siglo**. Madrid: Reus, 1890.
Holland, Thomas E. Alberico Gentili: an inaugural lecture delivered at All Souls College, November 7, 1874. In: **Studies in International Law**. Oxford: Clarendom Press, 1898.
Iustinianus Imperator. **Corpus Iuris Civilis**. ed. Krueger and Mommsen. Berlim: Weidmann, 1908.
Isidorus Hispalensis Episcopus. **Etymologiarum sive Originum Libri XX**. ed. W. M. Lindsay. Oxford: Claredon Press, 1911.
Laghmani, Slim. **Histoire du droit des gens**: du *jus gentium* impérial au *jus publicum europaeum*. Paris: Pedone, 2003.
Nézard, Henri. Albericus Gentilis. In: Pillet, Antoine. **Les Fondateurs du Droit Intersternal**. Paris: V. Giard & E. Brière, 1904.
Nussbaum, Arthur. **Historia del Derecho Internacional**. Trad. Francisco Javier Osset. Madrid: Revista de Derecho Privado, 1953.
Nys, Ernest. **Le Droit de la Guerre et les précurseurs de Grotius**. Bruxelles et Leipzig: Murquardt, 1882.
Nys, Ernest. **Les Origines du Droit International**. Bruxelles, Paris: Alfred Castaigne, Thorin et fils, 1894.
Panizza, Diego. Introduction. In: Gentili, Alberico. **O Direito de Guerra**. Tradução de Ciro Mioranza. Ijuí: Unijuí, 2004.
Panizza, Diego. **Political Theory and Jurisprudence in Gentili's *De Iure Belli***. The great debate between "theological" and "humanist" perspectives from Vitoria to Grotius. IILJ Working Paper 2005/15 [History and Theory of International Law Series]. New York: New York University School of Law, 2005.
Pillet, Antoine. **Les Fondateurs du Droit International**. Paris: V. Giard & E. Brière, 1904.
Reale, Miguel. **Horizontes do Direito e da História**. 3. ed. São Paulo: Saraiva, 2000.
Rivier, Alphonse. **Note sur la littérature du droit de gens avant la publication du Jus Belli ac Pacis de Grotius** 1625.
Santiago Ramirez. Introducción a las cuestiones 95-97. In: Aquino, Santo Tomas de. **Suma Teologica**. Texto latino de la edición crítica Leonina. Trad. Francisco Barbado Viejo, O.P. 2. ed. Madrid: Biblioteca de Autores Cristianos, 1947, Tome VI.
Sciacca, Michele. **Perspectiva de la metafisica en Sto. Tomas**. Madrid: Speiro, 1976.
Scott, J. B. **The Catholic Conception of International Law**. Washington D.C.: Georgetown University Press, 1934.
Scott, J. B. **The Spanish Origin of International Law**. Francisco de Vitoria and his law of nations. 2. ed. New Jersey: The Law Book Exchange, 2003.
Scott, J.B. Conferencias del Presidente del Instituto Americano de Derecho Internacional preparadas en homenaje a la Universidad Mayor de San Marcos, Lima, Universidad Mayor de San Marcos, 1938.

Stumpf, Christoph A. Christian and Islamic Traditions of Public International Law. **Journal of the History of International Law**, n. 7, pp. 68–80, 2005.

Suárez, R. P. Francisci. **Opera Omnia**. *Editio Nova*. *Parisiis*: *Ludovicum Vivès*, 1858. *Tomus* XII. **De Fide, Spe et Charitate**. *Tratactus de Charitate*. *Disputatio* XIII. **De Bello**.

Suarez, R. P. Francisci. Granatensis è Societate Jesu, Doctoriis Eximi. **Tratactus de legibus, ac Deo Legislatore in decem Librus distributus.** Venetiis, apud Sebastianum Coleti, 1740.

Tierney, Brian. Vitoria and Suárez on Ius Gentium, Natural Law and Custom. In: **The Nature of Customary Law**: Philosophical, Historical and Legal Perspectives. Centre for Research in the Arts, Social Sciences and Humanities: University of Cambridge, 2004.

Truyol y serra, Antonio. **El Derecho y el Estado em San Agustin**. Madrid: Revista de Derecho Privado, 1944.

Truyol, Antonio. **Noções Fundamentais de Direito Internacional Público**. Trad. Ehrhardt Soares. Coimbra: Armênio Amado, 1952.

Tuck, Richard. **Natural Rights Theories**: their origin and development. New York: Cambridge University Press, 1979.

Tuck, Richard. The Rights of War and Peace: political thought and the international order from Grotius to Kant. New York: Oxford University Press, 1999.

Vanderpol, Alfred. **La Doctrine Scolastique du Droit de Guerre**. Paris: Pédone, 1919.

Viejo-Ximénez, José Miguel. "Totus orbis, qui aliquo modo est una republica". Francisco de Vitoria, el Derecho de Gentes y la expansión atlántica castellana. **Revista de Estudios Histórico-Jurídicos**, n. 26, Sección Historia del Pensamiento Jurídico, Valparaíso, pp. 359–391, 2004.

Viola, Francesco. Derecho de Gentes Antiguo e Contemporáneo. Trad. Isabel Trujillo. **Persona y Derecho**, n. 41, pp. 165–189, 2004.

Vitória, Francisco de. **Obras de Francisco de Vitória**. *Relecciones Teologicas*. Editadas por Teofilo Urdanoz. Madrid: Biblioteca de Autores Cristianos, 1960.

Vitória, Francisco de. **De Jure Gentium et Naturali.** In: Scott, J. B. **The Spanish Origin of International Law**. Francisco de Vitoria and his law of nations. 2. ed. New Jersey: The Law Book Exchange, 2003., Appendix E.

Vitória, Francisco de. **De Jure Gentium et Naturali.**. In: Scott, J. B. **The Spanish Origin of International Law**. Francisco de Vitoria and his law of nations. 2. ed. New Jersey: The Law Book Exchange, 2003., Appendix B.

Walker, Thomas Alfred. **A History of the Law of Nations**. Cambridge: Cambridge University Press, 1899. v. I.

Wight, Martin. **International Theory**: the three traditions. Leicester & London: Leicester University Press, 1991.

Wijffels, Alain. Early-Modern Literature on International Law and the Usus Modernus. **Grotiana**, v. 16–17, pp. 35–54, 1995–1996.

Yasuaki, Onuma. When was the Law of International Society Born?—an inquiry of the history of international law from an intercivilizational perspective. **Journal of the History of International Law**, n. 2, pp. 1–66, 2000.

Chapter 3
The Foundations of Law in Francisco Suárez

Francisco Suárez was an intellectual "giant." In his works, he managed to assemble and organize all the knowledge of the scholastics that preceded him. The Pope even entrusted him with the delicate task of "defending the Catholic faith against the errors of the Anglicanism sect,"[1] such was the confidence he placed in the Jesuit Theologian. Despite his aversion to controversy, Suárez obediently accepted the assignment and wrote the **Defensio Fidei**. In this text and in the **De Legibus**, Suárez puts forth his ideas on Law and Politics. Although his ideas have become well known and accepted in Theology, his theses on these two subjects are no less important.

As a jurist and a political scholar, Suárez professes naturalist ideas. However, one must proceed with caution when labeling Suárez a naturalist: though precise, such an association evokes notions that have little to do with the theories he defends. His theories occupy a unique position in the history of naturalism. By writing in the end of the sixteenth century and the beginning of the seventeenth century, Suárez succeeds in embracing both the Medieval tradition and the Modern revolution that was on its way. There are traces of the old and of the new in his Natural Law. Suárez lived during a period of transition, from a Medieval and God-centric world to a Modern and secular one; from the last wars of religion to an international system grounded in the *raison d'état* and in the balance of power; from the *Republica Christina*'s diffused realities of power to the consolidation of State sovereignty. He is thus a man of transition.

Yet Suárez is not just that. He possesses the originality of the Modern thinkers and the finesse of the Scholastics and this combination generates a different kind of thinking. Suárez does not simply repeat the old and delineates the new. These two elements blend in such a way as to form a coherent system of ideas in which the best of both worlds can surface.

---

[1]A reference to the complete title of the book written by Suárez, **Defensio Fidei Catholicae adversus anglicanae sectae errors**.

P.E. Vauthier Borges de Macedo, *Catholic and Reformed Traditions in International Law*, Studies in the History of Law and Justice 9,
DOI 10.1007/978-3-319-59403-3_3

On the particular subject of Natural Law, the Medieval man in Suárez enabled him to solve a problem related to the Metaphysical *status* of this system: the misconception of the term "nature." Since Aristotle, Philosophers consider natural the substances whose driving principle is independent from human action. However, this word has been used with two different meanings: sometimes as law *per se*, as a recurrence of the empirical world, a relation of cause and effect and other times as a Theological construction, in reference to an ideal rule or value, to what should be. In the first sense of the word, gravity and the other laws of Physics are Natural Laws. In the second sense, Natural Law coincides with its elements. Hence, health is as natural to the human body as virtue is to Morality. In line with the terminology employed by the neo-Kantian Philosophy, the term alludes to a distinction between the world of the facts, of what is, and the world of the values, of what should be.

According to Recásens Siches, Francisco Suárez does not confuse an empirical fact regarding human beings for the foundations of Natural Law, as Modern authors such as Grotius, Hobbes, Puffendorf, and Thomasius did. These thinkers drew rational conclusions of normative nature from feelings such as sociability, fear, or incapacity. They extracted the *sollen*, the *should-be* from the beings themselves. For the Grenadian Author, man is sociable, but law does not emanate from this sociability. Suárez's Natural Law is exempt from cause-effect relations.[2]

In turn, the Modern man in Suárez allows for a unique interaction between Natural Law and Positive Law, creating an earthly realm, largely deprived of divinity. In the Medieval context, Natural Law derives either direct or indirectly from God's omnipotence. Even in this case, it was possible to draw therefrom a Positive Law that aimed at placing men closer to God, other than trying to regulate society. In Suárez, despite emanating from Natural Law, Positive Law does not possess a transcendental scope.

Those statements will become clearer as this chapter progresses. In order to highlight Suárez's originality, the first step is to present Suárez's Theological starting point. Subsequently, I shall show how Suárez distances himself from the traditional ideas of the Thomist movement, so that it will be possible to perceive the uniqueness of his Epistemological assumptions regarding the concept of law. Next, I will analyze the immanency of his theory of law. This is the key aspect of this chapter, because from there Suárez's influence on Grotius will become clear. Lastly, I shall demonstrate that, though universal, Suárez's Natural Law is not short of historicity—this is especially important so that it is possible to understand what led Suárez to perceive the *jus gentium* as a law between nations.

[2]Recasens Siches (1947), p. 143.

3.1 A Theologian's Approach

This topic begins with the first sentence from Paulo Merêa's famous work on Suárez: "Father Francisco Suárez, *Societatis Iesu*, was not a jurist, strictly speaking."[3] As a youngster, before joining the Society of Jesus, Suárez studied Canons in Salamanca, but did not complete his course. It is unlikely that all his knowledge of Law came from such a short period. After all, he never achieved high scores in Law School, nor did he rise to teach Canons or Law. He dedicated his visionary spirit to Theology (the "queen of sciences"); on this subject, he taught and wrote.

Those assertions should not be understood to diminish the relevance of Suárez's works for the study of Law. He has been the subject of a considerable number of studies, both from International Law historians and from Philosophers of Law. He shared, with Francisco de Vitória, a title that once belonged to Hugo Grotius: that of the "father" of International Law. In addition, a host of writers, especially of Portuguese and Spanish origins, consider Suárez a herald for an alternative Modernity, in opposition to Descartes' triumphant view.[4] His thinking regarding Law is quite sophisticated and filled with nuances, making it difficult to categorize.

The issue here at stake is to show the difference between Suárez and Grotius' starting point. As will be seen later, Grotius adopts a different posture, though not necessarily a secular one. Yet Suárez stood amongst Catholic thinkers as the true interpreter of Thomism, against the official version set forth by Cardinal Cajetano between the years of 1502 and 1522 in his commentaries to Thomas Aquinas' **Summa Theologiae**. It was not by chance that Baltazar Álvares assembled Suárez's entire work in accordance with the Angelic Doctor's *opera magna*.[5] The **De Legibus**, which full title is **Tratactus de legibus, ac Deo Legislatore in decem Librus distributes**, dedicated to the Dean of Coimbra, *Reverendissimum D.D. Alphonsum Furtado de Mendonça Episcopum Egitaniensem... Conimbricae*, refers to questions 90 through 108 of the first part of the second part of the **Summa**.

Even in a work dedicated to the study of Law, Suárez still regards himself a Theologian:

> It should come as no surprise that laws appear to the man that profess Theology as something that ought to be studied. The truth is that Theology's greatness, which stems from the highest eminence of its subject matter, excludes any reason for admiration. On the

---

[3]Merêa (2004), p. 111.

[4]Larrainzar, 1977 and Alves, 1949. The latter compares the formation of the State on Suárez and Rousseau.

[5]"There have been two attempts to publish Francisco Suárez's full work. The first was **Sebastião Coleti**'s 23 volumes (Venice, 1740–1751); and the second was **Luís Vivès**'s 26 volumes (plus 1 volume of index) (Paris, 1856–1878). The latter was done based on the former, with only a few corrections and supplements, since both have the same general index and the same arrangement first established by Baltazar Álvares in Coimbra" (marked in the original). (Moita 2004, p. 81).

contrary, if one is to thoroughly examine this issue, it will be made clear that the study of Law is within the scope of Theology in such a way that a Theologian must study the laws in order to fully exhaust his subject matter.[6]

This enlarged notion of Theology, one that seems to encompass all of Law, as well as several other areas, is even more eloquently found in Francisco Vitória, for whom "the subject-matter of the Theologian is so wide that no argument, dispute or issue is indifferent to his profession."[7]

Theologians from Suárez's time routinely occupied themselves with legal matters, noticeably Natural and Public Law. They did not hesitate to discuss any questions relating to Legal Philosophy, relegating the exegesis, a less noble and distinguished task, to the jurisconsults. Soto, Bañez and Molina had even written treaties on **De Justitia et Jure**. In the **Summa**, Aquinas wrote a Treatise on Laws and another on Law and Justice. Theology was not just the science of God, but also the science of reason and human conscience. Pursuant to Cicero, the knowledge of the just and unjust shifted from Law to Theology.[8]

This invasion may seem arbitrary to a man of the twenty-first century, but was quite reasonable to Suárez. Laws were not foreign to a Theologian, inasmuch as they derived from God, the legislator. God created the entire world, but did not abandon it to chance. He remains present, governing all creatures and leading them towards the right path. He admonishes those who stray from Him and leads them back to the righteous path, "enlightening them with teachings, advising with counsels and enforcing with laws." This applied even to Human Laws because "much like paternity, all legislators come from God and the authority of all laws must be lead, ultimately, back to Him."[9]

This understanding was popular among Theologians due to St. Paul's statement in the Epistle to the Romans (XII, 1): "All souls must bow to higher authorities; because there is no authority that does not derive from God, and the ones that do exist, are commanded by Him [*Omnis anima potestatibus sublimioribus subdita sit: non est enim potestas nisi a Deo: quae autem sunt, a Deo ordinatae sunt*]."

---

[6]"*Nulli mirum videri debet, si homini theologiam profitenti leges incidant disputandae. Theologiae namque eminentia ab ejus subjecto eminentissimo derivata omnem excludit rationem admirandi. Imo si res ipsa recte dispiciatur, palam erit, ita legum tractationem theologiae ambitu concludi, ut theologus subjectum ejus exhaurire non valeat, nisi legibus considerandis immoretur.*" (R. P. Francisci Suarez. Granatensis è Societate Jesu, Doctoriis Eximi. **Tratactus de legibus, ac Deo Legislatore in decem Librus distributus**. Venetiis, apud sebastianum Coleti, 1740. book I, Proemium. Henceforth, referred as **DL**).

[7]"*Officium ac munus theologi tam late patet, ut nullum argumentum, nulla disputatio, nullus locus alienus videatur a theologica professione et instituto.*" (**De potestate civili**, *Prologue*, p. 150.).

[8]Merêa (2004), pp. 112–113.

[9]"*(...) doctrina illuminando, consiliis monendo, legibus cogendo (...)*". "*(...) sicut omnem paternitatem, ita etiam omnem legislatorem a Deo derivari, omniumque legum auctoritatem in eum esse ultimo resundendam.*" (**DL**. *Proemium*).

This sentence shows no trace of a theory on the Divine Right of the Kings, nor any principle of monarchy legitimity or even of a defense for a particular form of government. The Apostle was not concerned with issues of earthly politics; he was merely advising obedience to civil powers. This rationally conforms to Christ's famous statement "to Caesar what is for Caesar."

Given the vagueness of his advice, it seems possible to derive therefrom a wide range of theories related to political conformism, according to the changes in historical circumstances. However, "if we look at them [St. Paul's words] in their purest form, without intending to find more than there is," it is possible to infer that social authority is morally necessary and is a product of human association. Since all power finds its origin in God, the social authority is entirely justified by Natural Law itself. "The authority in itself, as a social institution, and as long as it does not stray from Natural Law, is something **just** (…). But this refers to the authority, to the power (whatever it is called) as an institution, not to a particular ruler."[10] For Suárez, even the authority that comes from men, and not directly from God, is natural—so he dedicates an important length of book III of the **De Legibus** to answer the question of the legality of the power one may have to command another, *vis a vis* the free will.

Therefore, since all power comes from God, it was only natural that a Theologian should write a treatise on laws. The content may pertain to a human fact and God may be referred to only indirectly, but faith and religion still remained as a hidden subject, serving as a source of inspiration and to correct errors that the rational investigation (or better yet, the investigation led by the imperfect human reasoning) may produce. At first glance, the chain of thought is unfazed by this matter of principle.

It does not follow from this assertion that Suárez made "mistakes" in his reasoning in the name of faith. Suárez's ideas have a unique logical consistency; they are even more coherent than Grotius'. Suárez does not choose faith over reason. Faith represents only the foundations upon which he built his work; everything else is subject to rational scrutiny. Besides, as it happens with all axioms in relation to the theorems derived therefrom, faith serves as parameter or as evidence of the validity of his arguments. Often it is possible to notice a "test of faith" regarding his conclusions on religion's truths: he confronts his conclusions with the dogmas of faith in order to assess their truthfulness.

Thus, it should come as no surprise that some general conclusions bear exceptions or that particular reasonings demand a greater level of sophistication. Such is the case of the waiver of Natural Law, which I will analyze further below; for now, it is important to take note that the waiver of Natural Law was a passionate discussion throughout the Middle Ages. The dogma that lies at the bottom of this

---

[10]"*Si nos dirijimos hacia ellas con el animo puro, sin deseo de encontrar allí más que lo hay*" and "*La autoridad en sí, como instituición social y mientras no se aparte de la ley natural, es algo justo (…). Pero se trata de la autoridad, del poder – llámesele como se quiera – en si, como institución, y no de este o de aquel gobernante.*" (Recásens Siches 1947, pp. 20–21).

discussion (which is very dear to Thomists) is that God is infinite in His wisdom and thus cannot contradict Himself. This axiom cannot change. However, when He tells Abraham to sacrify Isaac, He goes against Natural Law, seemingly enacting two contradictory decrees. This seems to threaten that first religious truth.

The answer that Suárez finds for this problem is not to invalidate the axiom, nor is it to resort to other faith-based truths. He resorts to reason, infusing more complexity to the equation. According to him, Natural Law is immutable, but it employs broad formulations. On the other hand, human matter and circumstances vary greatly. In a specific circumstance, acting with rectitude implies making a certain decision and, in another, following a different course of action. Therefore, when one prescribes, "thou shalt not kill," it does not follow that murder is illegal under all circumstances. This commandment bifurcates into many others, such as "thou shalt not kill on your own authority" and "it is legal to kill in self-defense." The fifth commandment forbids murder in itself, without any appreciation for justice or injustice.[11] When God told Abraham to kill his own son, there was no waiving of the law. The meaning of the act was quite different:

> He did that as Lord of life and death; because if the same God had wanted to kill Isaac Himself, He would not have needed to resort to anyone, for it is in His realm to do so. Much in the same way, He could have used Abraham as an instrument and the fifth commandment does not prohibit one from being an instrument of God to kill another, if He so wishes.[12]

The structure of his reasoning merits attention. God is the omnipotent and omniscient maker (faith-based truth). He prescribes the laws to ordain His creation, and these laws are good, immutable and hold coherence amongst them (rational development following the dogma). However, the Bible puts forth an example in which God establishes a decree that directly contradicts a previous decree (another faith-based truth). This contradiction is only apparent because though the law remains immutable, the human circumstances to which it is applied (another logical development that adds complexity to the issue) vary. Thanks to this reasoning, the integrity of the rational conclusions and of the truths remains intact. It is a rational solution to a problem raised by a religious dogma. In short, despite not discarding reason, Suárez does not treat the laws as a jurist, but as a Theologian.

---

[11] **DL**. II, 15, 13.

[12] "(...) *id fecit tanquam dominus vitae et motis. Si enim Deus ipse* per se *ipsum voluisset interficere Isaac, non indiguisset dispensatione, sed ex suo dominio id facere posset. Eodem ergo modo potuit uti Abrahamo ut instrumento; et quintum praeceptum non prohibet esse instrumentum Dei occisione, si ipse praeceperit*." (**DL**. II, 15, 20).

3.1.1 Consonance and Dissonance from the Scholasticism

To every Theologian in Suárez's time the task of discussing and further developing the **Summa Theologiae** was simply imperative; such was the authority of this text. However, during Aquinas' life his ideas were a constant source of controversy; only gradually did they gain acceptance and the **Summa** replaced Peter Lombardo's **Book of Sentences** in Schools. His ideas clashed with three different opponents: the secular professors, engaged in the struggle against the teaching by religious men; the Franciscans, ideologically affiliated to Plato and to St. Augustine; and the followers of the Averroism movement, led by Siger of Brabante, who repudiated Arab interpretations of Aristotle's work. On July 18, 1323, when the Pope John XXII, canonized Thomas Aquinas and affirmed that his doctrine was so inspiring that it must had been a product of God's miraculous intervention (*doctrina eius non potuit esse sine miraculo*), Aquinas' influence spread across the Catholic and Byzantine worlds. In the fourteenth century, the **Summa** found new strength in Francisco de Vitória, Melchior Cano, Martinho de Ledesma, Bartolomeu de Medina, Domingos Bañez and António de Sena. On April 11, 1567, Pope Pius V edicted the Bull **Mirabilis Deus** and declared that St. Thomas Aquinas had been a doctor of the Church, granting him the title "Angelic."[13]

For this reason alone, Suárez dedicated his whole life as a professor, when not interrupted by wars and other worldly controversies, to comment Aquinas' work. Furthermore, St. Ignatius of Loyola actually instructed all members of the Society of Jesus to study the Doctor Angelic. After teaching several classes on Aristotle's Philosophy, Suárez explained the first section of the **Summa** in Valladolid between the years of 1576 and 1560. Between 1580 and 1585, in Rome, he focused on the second section and afterwards, in Alcalá (1586–1590), on the third. After a period of disputes with Gabriel Vasquez, he went on to Coimbra to teach on the **De Poenitentia**, which is the last subject matter of the third section of the **Summa**. Between the years of 1598 and 1600, he went back to the beginning and teached **De Deo**. Though controversy followed Suárez until the end of his life, he still found strength to teach **De Lege** (1601–1603), **De Gratia** and **De Virtute Religionis** simultaneously (1606–1609), as well as **De Fide** (1613–1614) and **De Infidelitate et Heresi** (1614–1615). After receiving his letters of retirement in 1616, he attempted to finish his long commentary on Aquinas' work, but death interrupted him.[14]

Even if the orthodoxy of Suárez's thoughts vis-à-vis Thomism may be arguable, there is no doubt that this tradition represents a unique reference and starting point for Suárez, an intellectual heritage that belonged to him. Suárez synthesizes all of the Scholaticism in such an encompassing fashion that Bousset stated "*en lui on voit toute l'École*." In truth, Aquinas did not witness the events nor did he anticipate the issues that would challenge thinkers for over a century. The discovery of

[13]Moita (2004), pp. 77–81.

[14]Moita (2004), p. 82.

America, the issue of the soul of the Indians, the reach and the limits to the right of evangelization and the emergence of a controversial new right (defended by the Monarcomachs and, in Spain, by João de Mariana) to resist the unjust orders of the ruler. Regardless of the relevance of these events, they did not invalidate the essence of Thomism. Even the most impassionate Catholic would not deny it; the most devoted should only update it to the needs of a new era.

It is no surprise therefore that Suárez masterfully employed the Scholastic method. It is an instructive method of teaching that begins with the exposition of a Philosophical or Theological argument, followed by an objection or question thereon. The method ends with the presentation of a solution to the problem and a response to the objection.[15] However, compliance to this method was not mandatory. Suárez himself often did not follow it. Even the Author of the **Summa** deviated from this method in other works. The method was reserved to those works that were for students or that covered classroom discussions. The frequency with which it was applied is not relevant; the mere fact that it is employed in **De Legibus** is enough to establish a link between Suárez and Thomism.

Even more important than this instructive method of exposition, the greatest formal legacy left by Scholasticism was the incorporation of Aristotle into Christian Philosophy. That is the reason why Suárez is so fond of reason. While writing on matters of faith, the authority of the Bible does not replace the coherence and cohesion of reason. Theology is a true science. Not by chance, the second article of the first question of **Summa**'s prologue addresses this very issue: whether the holy doctrine is a science, since it "is based on articles of faith, which are not self-evident."[16] The Angelic Doctor answers this question in the affirmative because there are sciences based on principles known by the natural light of understanding, such as Arithmetic and Geometry, and others based on principles evidenced by a higher science. The holy doctrine and Music are amongst those (Music is based on Arithmetic whilst Theology is based on the sacred revelation). However, Theology is no mere science. Aquinas places it at the top of the scale of knowledge proposed by Aristotle in chapter I, book I of **Metaphysics**,[17] as it is more speculative than practical and thus superior to others.

Pursuant to the rigor of the Scholastics, there is nothing modern about Theology; it bears no resemblance to the modern sciences. The study of Theology is entirely about Aristotle that was rediscovered by the West. The higher science of principles and causes (the study of God) is so distant from the real world that it can only make sense through the use of Logic, which is the discipline that studies the formal

---

[15]Cedroni (1996), p. 39.

[16]"*Sed sacra doctrina procedit ex articulus fidei, qui non sunt* per se *noti*" (**ST**. 1 q.1 a.2).

[17]Ibidem, 1 q.1 a.4 and 1 q.1 a.5. It is worth noting that Aristotle himself placed Metaphysics at the top of the hierarchy, but it is only called Metaphysics when it refers to *ens commune*; "*'filosofia primera,' en cuanto considera las causas primeras de las cosas; 'teologia,' en cuanto considera las sustancias que no tienen materia, Dios,* etc." (Sciacca 1976, p. 50). It is the threefold aspect of a single discipline.

operations of reasoning. This is how one must understand what Suárez and the Scholastics set themselves to accomplish.

Here lies an important distinction between Suárez and Grotius. The practical sciences, such as Ethics and Law, which target the good living, did not follow the tenets of formal Logic. They operated in accordance with a logic that aimed at persuading and convincing others: the Rhetoric. That, in addition to the Topics, made up the civic artistry of Humanism, the art of the citizen that, blessed with a good oratory, could influence his city's politics. The most important Italian jurists, such as Bártolo, Baldo and Paulus Castrensis, from whom Grotius indirectly descends,[18] employed a method based on persuasion and casuistry. On the other hand, even when lecturing on laws, Suárez did not abandon formal Logic, because it was appropriate for the *magna* science and spread across other fields. Therefore, to study laws through Theology demanded more than a simple inversion of competences; it demanded adopting a perception quite different from that of the jurists of that time.

A perfect example of that is how Suárez treats his sources. The bibliographical structure of **De Legibus** is quite complex for an oeuvre on law of that time. There are four different types of sources: Biblical, Theological, Philosophical, and Legal. Among jurists, Suárez consults not only those who wrote about the religious canons, but also the traditional commentators of Roman law.[19] That in itself distinguishes Suárez's Treatise on Laws from other Medieval Theological works, which drew only from other Theologians. The use of nonreligious thinkers

---

[18]Haggenmacher (2002), p. 161.

[19]Pereña (1971), pp. xxxvii–xxxviii. He distinguishes only three types of sources, but it seems important to separate Biblical quotations from those of the Theologians. First, Suárez used Biblical texts (St. Peter, Proverbs, Psalms, Genesis, Ecclesiastes, Isaiah, Job, Jeremy, John, Matthew, Luke, and Mark). Second, there are Theological references to the Holy Fathers (St Augustine, Isidoro, João Crisóstomo, Cirilo de Alexandria, Jerônimo, Justino, Anselmo, and Boaventura); to the moralists (Silvestre Prierias, Antonio de Florença, Ângelo de Clavasio, João Dridoens, João Gerson, João de Medina, Alexandre de Hales, Vicente de Beauvois, Nicolau Biesius, Jerônimo Angest, Henrique de Gante); to comentators of Aquinas (Domigos Soto, Caetano, Bartolomeu de Medina, Luís de Molina, Gabriel Vázquez, Conrado Koellin), of Peter Lombardo (Duns Scoto, Gregório de Rimini, Guilherme de Ockan, João Mayr, Durant de Santo Porciano, Gabriel Biel, and Richard de Mediavilla) and of Alfonso de Castro. Third, Suárez, mentions Philosophers, such as Aristotle, Cícero, Platão, Plutarco, Sêneca, Quintiliano, Filão, Salustio, Plubio Terêncio, Cassiodoro, Donato Elio, Fabio Marcos Vitorino, Luís Vivès, and Marcílio Ficino. Lastly, he draws from Canon Law (The Gratian Decree and other decrees and councils), with Bernardo de Parma's magna gloss and the interpretation from a few decretists (Johannes Andrés, Felino Sandeo, Baldo de Ubaldo, Angelus de Ubaldo, Guido de Baysio, Domingo de Santo Geminiano, Nicolo Tudeschi, Juan de Torquemada, Diego de Covarrubias and Martin de Azpilcueta), while also paying reference to Roman Law (Digest, the Iustinian Codex, the Institutes and the Authentics) with the help of traditional comments from Acursio and Bártolo de Sassoferrato, Giassone de Maino, Rafael Fulgosio, Francisco Connan, Barnabé Brisson, Gregório López and Antonio Gómez. These authors are indirectly quoted, but that was standard proceeding of the time. Most likely, Suárez directly knew only Aristotle, Cícero, St. Augustine, St. Isidore de Seville, Aquinas, Domingos Soto, Bartolomeu de Medina, Alfonso de Castro, Covarrubias, Connan, Brisson, Bártolo, Nicolau Tudeschi, Marsílio Ficino, and Luís Vivès.

separates Suárez from other authors of his time. The indiscriminate use of sources as an exercise in Rhetoric and persuasion characterizes the Legal Humanism of this period. However, in Suárez, these sources had a positive value and not as a mere display of erudition, for he effectively explored them. They constituted real sources and Suárez even employs them according to a hierarchy, reserving the top for classical thinkers and using newer ones to exemplify or to clear up controversies.

But those who think that Suárez is a compliant commentator of past writers could not be more wrong. He borrows tradition in order to surpass it and even to dispute it, not only for historical reasons, but also due to Gnosiologic and Metaphysical differences. He carried out a profound reorganization of the structure of Aristotle's Metaphysics in **Disputaciones Metaphysicae**. Previous works of the Scholastics on Metaphysics never strayed from the list of topics set out by Aristotle. As Suárez stated:

> It is, for having always believed that a large portion of the task of understanding and discussing problems depends on choosing of the appropriate method of inquiry, that I find it would be difficult, if not impossible, to follow the path of other commentators: discussing issues randomly, as they appear on the work of the Philosopher. I find it more useful and efficient, following the order set out by scholars, to question and expose before the reader all the issues that can be drawn or studied from this wisdom.[20]

Suárez knew some would not approve of this. That is why he included an index of the issues discussed by Aristotle in **Metaphysics**, pointing where they appeared in **Disputaciones Metaphysicae**.

> However, as many would prefer to find this work in consonance to Aristotle's books, not only to understand which principles the Great Philosopher uses as basis thereof, but also to make it easier to read and understand Aristotle, I have also attempted to facilitate the understanding of readers, through this index (…).[21]

This index at the end of his book hints at the degree of Suárez's subversion. Typically, the index was at the beginning of the book, in order to facilitate its understanding by the students. By setting aside the didactic method, Suárez showed that his book was not intended for students and that it did not offer a mere interpretation of Aristotle's work. He wanted to do something new. After considering

---

[20]"*Et quoniam iudicavi semper magnam ad res intelligendas ac penetrandas, in eis convenienti methodo inquirendis et iudicandis, vim positam esse, quam observare vix aut ne vix quidem possem, si, expositorum more, quaestiones omnes, prout obter et veluti casu circa textum Philosophi occurrunt, pertractarem, idcirco expeditius et utilius fore censui, servato doctrinae ordine, ea omnia inquirere et ante oculus lectoris proponere, qua de toto huius sapientiae obiecto investigari et desiderari poterant.*" (*R.P. Francisco Suárez è Societate Jesu*, **Metaphysicarum Disputationum**, *in quibus et universa naturalis theologia ordinatè traditur & quaestiones omnes ad duodecim Aristotelis libros pertinentes accurate disputantur*, 1597. *Tomus Prior. Ratio et Discursus Totius Operis*).

[21]"*Quia tamen erunt permulti, qui doctrinam hanc universam Aristotelis libris applicatam habere cupient, tum ut melius percipiant quibus tanti philosophi principiis nitatur, tum ut eius usus ad ipsum Aristotelem intelligendum facilior sit at utilior, hac etiam in re lectori inservire studui, indice a nobis elaborato* (…)" (**DM**. *Tomus Prior. Ratio et Discursus Totius Operis*).

that Suárez belonged in the Middle Ages because he kept the practice of the *quaestiones disputatae*, Éthienne Gilson stated that **Disputaciones Metaphysicae** was, in fact, a Modern treatise on Philosophy, "because its author had deliberately freed himself from being completely subject to the text of Aristotle's **Metaphysics** (…). To be guided by the subject matter of Metaphysics itself and not by Aristotle's every word (…), is to write a treatise on Metaphysics and not on Aristotle."[22]

Suárez also strays from Aquinas in the study of the laws. As will be seen, both the authors have different concepts of law. Nevertheless, they also differed in their approach of the subject. The Angelic Doctor begins his analysis with the universal level, law in general, and from there he reaches the singular level: "About the law, it is necessary to first study the law in general to then study its parts."[23] Suárez initially seems to follow the same path: "Firstly, we shall discuss the law in general, to then reach its different parts (…)."[24] However, this resemblance is only fictional. There is a difference between comparing the law in general to its parts, such as Aquinas does, and comparing the law in general to particular classes. Here lies a problem of Gnosiology.

3.1.1.1 The Singular and the Universal

The traditional Thomist thesis on Gnosiology is similar to Aristotle's moderate realism. The universal is "the direct object of knowledge and, therefore, can be understood through the simple comprehension of the concept." The concept and the thing are directly linked: the universal exists de facto. Our concepts are universals, and these universals do exist. On the other hand, the "*ut singularis* thing can only be known indirectly or through contemplation, which transforms it into fantasy images, by way of the universally intelligible form of direct cognition."[25] The individual is reached through a complex mechanism called "individualization"; it is a process of assembling into one object several universals. This is how, e.g., the individual "Socrates" is defined by his attributes: Man, Mortal, Male, etc. For this reason, individuals consist of combined substances.

---

[22]"*(…) car leur auteur s'est délibérément affranchi de toute sujétion au texte de la Métaphysique d'Aristote (…). Se régler ainsi sur les objets mêmes de la métaphysique, et non plus sur la lettre d'Aristote (…) c'était s'engager à écrire sur la métaphysique au lieu d'écrire sur Aristote.*" (Gilson 1962, p. 145).

[23]"*Circa legem autem, primo oportet considerare de ipsa lege in communi; secundo de partibus eius.*" (**ST**. 1-2 q. 90 proemio).

[24]"*Dicemus enim primo de lege in communi et deinde at singulas species descendemus* (…)." (**DL**. *Proemio*).

[25]"*(…) objeto del conocimiento directo y, por tanto, se capta en la simple aprehensión que engendra el concepto* (…)". "*(…) la cosa* ut singularis *sólo es conocida indirectamente o por una reflexión que, a través de la especie inteligible universal propria de la cognición directa, convierte hacia las imágenes de la fantasía* (…)." (Larrainzar 1977, p. 124).

Yet Suárez does not reason like that. By using the term "species," he meant to designate a reality in itself. For him, contrary to the above method, "our understanding sees singular objects directly [without the ghosts made by our minds]." It is only afterwards that the "understanding knows the appropriate concept, separate and unconcerned with the singular objects."[26] The cognitive process follows a path contrary to what Aquinas teaches; first, one acknowledges the singular and then abstracts the universal from it.

> To say that God is prior to Jesus Christ or that the Father came before the Son is to say the truth, but not how it was experienced (Jesus paving the way to God). It is from what actually exists that our journey begins and it is in it that the essence can be perceived, as in the case of Jesus Christ, God made man, it is the concrete, singular and individual manifestation of the extreme possibility of a meeting between man and God, and other men.[27]

For Suárez, in his own words:

> [The] universal is reached through comparative knowledge, which enables the following understanding: nature, precisely understood in its abstract character, is compared to the things in which it exists and it is seen as something able to exist in inferior beings and to communicate with them.[28]

The first perception is of the singular object. One reaches the universal through the comparison of several entities that exist (singular ones); we understand their common features and extract them from a tangible reality. The universal has great value because once reached, it allows one to follow the reverse path: from the universal to the singular. When one extracts and contemplates the universal features of an object, he is able to understand it in its entirety and more clearly. After this process is completed, it is possible to establish comparisons and other relationships among these universal features found in singular objects.

However, if the universal is suitable for predication, the same does not apply to the individual. The individual unity cannot pass on to other entities—for it would stop being singular, unique. The individual unity is only equal to itself; it is impossible to divide and mistake it for other unities. It is not transmittable and hence unsuitable for predication.[29]

So, if the universal is transmittable and divisible and the individual is not, what truly exists is the singular, "because there is a contradiction in saying that an entity exists and [at the same time] that it is divisible into several other entities that are

---

[26]"*Intellectus noster cognoscit directe singularia materialia absque reflexione.*" "*Intellectus cognoscit proprio conceptu universalia, abstrahendo a singularibus seu non curando de illis.*" (Suárez, Francisco (S. I.). **Commentaria una cum quaestionibus in libros Aristotelis "De Anima"**. Madrid: Labor Sociedad de estudios y publicaciones, 1978, IV, 3, 7 and IV, 3, 11).

[27]Moita (2004), p. 89.

[28]"*(...) universale fieri per notitiam comparativam qua intellectus possibilis, postquam naturam praecise et abstracte aprehendit, confert illam sic conceptam cum rebus in quibus existit et intelligit illam ut unum quid aptum ut sit in multis inferioribus et de illis praedicetur.*" (**DM**. VI, 6, 5).

[29]**DM**. V, 1, 2.

equal thereto." Suárez reverses the Thomist reasoning by abandoning the ontological primacy of the universal in such a way that "all things that are actual things and that do exist, or can exist, are singular and individual."[30]

There are several opinions regarding this inversion carried out by Suárez: some say it is due to an "error" of interpretation of Aristotle's realism,[31] others say that it is an attempt to merge Thomism with Ockhamism and others even say that it is a result of the discovery of the autonomy of the subject, prior to Descartes.[32] Some authors[33] place such emphasis on this dissonance to the point of stating that Suárez would have preferred the inductive method, despite the deductive method being typical of Thomism. But this latter conclusion seems anachronic. In any case, this controversy does not directly related to my book. My purpose here is simply to present the differences between Suárez and Aquinas in their manner of perceiving reality.

3.1.1.2 Suárez's Immanence

These differences between the authors have important consequences. Aquinas takes Aristotle's main teleological principle (*omnes agens agit propter finem*) and adds a Theist corollary of his own: "all things aim at the divine resemblance."[34] Thus, all creatures lean towards God and all rational creatures, like men, relate to Him in a special way. Because of their distinct feature, the *telos* of all rational creatures is also rational: to meet and to know God.[35] However, as an imperfect creature, man is not able to reach that goal on his own; he needs divine assistance. Here lies a difference between Suárez and Aquinas. Suárez speaks of two kinds of goals for men: one, in a state of pure nature (*status purae naturae*), before Grace, and another ordained by God's saving power. In a state of Grace, the rational creature leans towards God, but without it, men's goals are but ordinary. "The goal of the men in nature, as Suárez sees it, is directly related to the means that he has at his disposal

[30]"(…) *quia implicat contradictionem esse entitatem et esse divisibilem in plures entitates, quae sint tales qualis ipsa est.*" E, ainda, "(…) *res omnes, quae sunt actualia entia, seu quae existunt, vel existere possunt immediate, esse singulares ac individuas*" (**DM**, V, 1, 5 and V, 1, 4).

[31]Larrainzar (1977), p. 98.

[32]Moita (2004), p. 75.

[33]Cedroni (1996), p. 40.

[34]"(…) *omnia appetunt divinam similitudinem quasi ultimum finem*" (Aquino, Santo Tomás. **Suma contra os Gentios**. Trad. Odilão Moura. ed. bilíngüe. Porto Alegre: PUCRS, 1996, III, 24, n. 2051. Henceforth, referred as **SG**).

[35]**SG**. III, 25, n. 2055. "(…) *finis cujuslibet substantiae intellectualis, etiam infimae est intelligere Deum*". This understanding applies even to God's point of view (*homo est capax visionis divinae essentiae*).

and to his 'abilities'."[36] It is possible to argue that man possess a Metaphysics of his own. In Suárez, there is a purely human sphere of reality.

The discovery of immanence and of its compatibility with theism is what unquestionably distinguishes Suárez's work from that of other jurists of his time. He had to stray from traditional Thomism in order to build a secular domain, always careful not to stray from Theology itself. His Treatise on Laws evidences this balancing act.

Because of all that, it is safe to remark that when Francisco Suárez and Thomas Aquinas write about law, they are actually talking about quite different things. When Aquinas speaks about law in general, he is referring to the kind of law that most closely resembles this concept: Eternal Law that is the rational order by excellence. On the other hand, Suárez refers to a much closer and palpable kind of law: the human Positive Law. When studying law in general, he attempts to extract the most essential aspects of this kind of law in order to create a concept and, then, to study all different kinds of law and conform them to his general definition. Compared to the traditional thought, this Epistemological choice leads to very different results and serves as the basis for Suárez's delicate balance.

Aquinas distinguishes the Law from the Laws. The Treatise on Laws and the Treatise on Grace should be read together, since both Laws and Grace are external principles that guide men towards rectitude. But for the Angelic Doctor, the study of the Law is part of the Treatise on Justice; justice's object is the right, the *iustum*, which relates to Aristotle's *dikaion*. The right is a private entity, while the law is a universal. The *jus* is *res*, something that exists in the real world. The *lex* is an exemplary cause, the design, something towards which all things lean to in conformity with our Maker's plans, not the thing itself.[37] The confusion between the two terms is Modern and has its roots in the Ockhamism. Yet the distinction is old. Even the Romans interpreted their law as *lex*, as a list of obligations.[38] The *jus* itself is a situation, a specific state of things that one might find just, but it is not something that belongs to an individual, a quality. The idea of *jus* as a subjective right would only emerge with Suárez and Grotius.

Hence, for Aquinas, law is one of the manners through which justice is done. However, this does not hold true for all kinds of law: only for human Positive Law. Other laws fulfill this and other purposes. For instance, Eternal law is the design through which divine wisdom orders creation: "Eternal Law is nothing if not divine wisdom directing **all** acts and movements,"[39] even those acts that are not human-made. For Aquinas, other laws are not a mere platonic participation of the idea of law in general on the individual object; Natural Laws and Human Laws do not represent an imperfect reflection of the Eternal Law—an imperfection that

[36]"*La fin de l'homme naturel – comme entend le rappeler Suárez – doit donc être rigoureusement commensurée à ses moyens ou mieux à sa 'capacité'.*" (Courtine 1999, p. 51).

[37]Bastit (1990), p. 163.

[38]Villey (1990), p. 125.

[39]"(…) *lex aeterna nihil aliud est quam ratio divinae sapientiae, secundum quod est directiva omnium actuum et motionum*" (**ST**. 1-2 q. 93 a.1).

augments as the distance widens. They represent the very divine order at each level of reality.

> One should not conceive the Laws in a descending order, starting with the Eternal Law, but in an order that is consistently in tension with the law of a truly perfect being. (…) Far from being a symbol of humanity's degradation, human order becomes a symbol of this fundamental tension towards perfection.[40]

For Aquinas, justice and the law are singular constructions that meet at the human order. That is how they relate to the laws. Since the divine design is present in all spheres of existence (and thus Eternal Law is expressed through Natural Law and this one through Human Law), the *jus*, which is part of an earthly order, eventually conforms to the *lex*. In other words, Natural and Human Laws are the Eternal Law in different spheres of reality. So, Natural Law and Human Law express the concrete ways through which God orders everything.

What is there in Eternal Law and Human Positive Law that make them both singular products of the same essence of law? There are two elements universal enough to assemble both formulations under a single concept: reason and externality. For Aquinas, the universal "law" refers both to an ordering idea of reason and to a drive that is external to the recipient of the obligation. "Law is a certain rule and measure of actions according to which someone is driven to act or not to act in a particular fashion."[41] This orientation or prohibition can only move rational beings because it is based on God Himself. This occurs ultimately because there are only two principles external to the rational creature: God (that drives humans towards good) and the devil (which drives them towards evil). The latter uses seduction and temptation, while the former guides us through Laws and Grace.[42] It is worth remembering that the human Positive Law leads to rectitude because it derives, logically, from Natural Law (which is, in turn, the Eternal Law's intervention in rational creatures).

According to Aquinas, the laws thus consist of a rational ordering principle that stems from God Himself. Given that it proceeds from God, its study within Theology is justifiable. However, this notion of laws differs greatly from that which contemporary jurists apply. Aquinas thinks of the laws as action of divine substance (all laws are consubstantials to God), not as a rule enacted by an authority upholding political power.

---

[40]"*Les lois ne sont plus alors à considérer dans l'ordre descendant à partir de la loi éternelle mais dans une ordre en tension vers la loi d'un être réellement parfait.* (…) *Loin d'apparaître comme l'indice d'une dégradation de plus en plus accentuée, il devient le signe de cette tension fondamentale vers la perfection.*" (Bastit 1990, p. 49).

[41]"(…) *lex quaedam regula est et mensura actuum, secundum quam inducitur aliquis ad agendum, vel ab agendo retrahitur* (…)"(**ST**. 1-2 q. 90 a.1).

[42]**ST**. 1-2 q. 90 *proemio*.

In turn, Suárez has in mind a much less transcendental and much more immanent object. "Catholic faith not only teaches to what point we must be subject to God, who rules over us all, (…) [but] establishes clearly how much we must subject ourselves to civil and church laws."[43] The study of the faith teaches men to respect the rules of a transcendental origin as well as those of a human origin. In Aquinas, submission to Human Law is indisputable because it is a way through which the divine order comes into being. But in Suárez, law may be both a product of the supernatural and divine order and of the human order (church laws are Human Laws). Law in general does not necessarily derive from divine substance.

A contemporary lawyer can already relate to this earthly concept of law. Suárez does not reach the universal sphere directly, such as Aquinas. In order to do so, he departs from the singular and Positive Law before him: the human Civil Law. It is interesting to note that he does not consider true law, other than metaphorically,[44] that part of Eternal Law that applies to irrational beings. Law is no longer a design to organize creation. Only the laws that apply to rational beings, who possess free will and can thus disobey, are truly law. It is anachronic to suggest that Suárez anticipated Kant's definition of Law as *sollen*, a "should-be." Nonetheless, a certain amount of freedom (and the greatest freedom is the possibility to disobey a rule) is essential to the existence of the law.

Despite the immanence of that notion, **De Legibus** is a treatise of Theology and is not limited to the analysis of the Eternal Law. It also investigates man-made laws. There is no trespassing of competence, because Suárez is very careful of the limits of his science. The solution to this dilemma again leads Suárez to stray from Aquinas: law is no longer a principle external to men. To study the laws, from a Theological standpoint, it its necessary "to interpret the normative or juridical information as a **bond of conscience**"[45] (marked in the original).

> Besides, it is part of the Theological duties to watch for the conscience of the travelers; the righteousness of consciences, in fact, is noted by the following of the laws and its impudence, by its transgression, since all laws, if obeyed as they should be, are rules intended to lead to eternal salvation, and if broken, to damnation. Thus, the study of laws, inasmuch as it is a bond of conscience, will also be a task of the Theologian.[46]

---

[43]"*Tandem catholica fides non solum docet quatenus parendum sit Deo supernaturaliter praecipienti* (…) *atque adeo quatenus parendum sit um ecclesiasticis legibus, tum laicis ante oculus nobis ponit.*" (**DL**. *Proemio*).

[44]**DL**. II, 2, 13.

[45]"(…) *interpretar el dato normativo o jurídico como* ***vínculo de consciência*** (…)" (Larrainzar 1977, p. 141).

[46]"*Deinde theologicum est negotium conscientiis prospicere viatorum; conscientiarum vero rectitudo stat lebibus servandis, sicut et pravitas violandis, cum lex quaelibet sit regula, si ut oportet servetur, aeternae salutis assequendae; si violetur, amittendae; ergo est legis inspectio, quatenus est conscientiae vinculum, ad theologum pertinebit.*" (**DL**. *Proemio*).

I shall explain ahead what exactly this bond of conscience is. For now, suffice it to say that, for Francisco Suárez, the recipient of the legal obligation (the subject) is important, as he must be convinced of the legitimacy of the law that he must obey.

If God is the end of all things, it is up to the Theologian to study the means through which one can reach Him. The law is but one of those means. So far, Suárez and Aquinas agree: laws are instruments of the divine providence over rational creatures; they are a means to reach salvation. That is why the theory of laws falls under the scope of Theology. "The Theologian studies all human actions that lead to happiness and, moreover, he studies God himself as the ultimate cause of all these actions, while He himself leads all creatures towards bliss."[47]

The accord between the two philosophers ends here. In Aquinas, the law is a principle that is external to men, as it stems from the divine substance. As seen, Suárez rejects that notion. Only Eternal Law (and Natural Law) derives from God, as Human Laws are born with men themselves. The transcendental order explains only Eternal Law (of which Suárez has reservations in considering a true law). The dissonance continues. Even when they do not stem from a human authority, the laws are no longer an external principle because they appeal to the conscience of men. All laws, including Human Laws, lead to salvation because (as understood from the previous quotation from **De Legibus**) they bind in conscience, meaning that they are "internalized" by men.

Thus, Suárez reverses Aquinas' argument: law is a principle inherent to men. Even if the authority responsible for issuing it is not the individual, he incorporates the law because it aims at his conscience. For this reason Human Laws can also "save." Kant's work distinguishes Law from Morality, in saying that the former demands an external conformity of action, while, for the latter, intent, and purpose are relevant. This is still the prevailing notion in the contemporary Theory of Law. However, in the epoch of Suárez, Morality was not dissociated from Law. Suárez even combines the investigation on justice with the study on law. Both law and justice become realities that are within the individual.

3.2 The Theory of Law

In essence, Suárez's theory of law differs from that of Aquinas. It is a new construction; Suárez uncovers the most singular and individual reality of the law: its subject. Such discovery is already unfolded in the division of his theory of laws. In analyzing each type of law, Suárez first ponders about the very existence of the law (*an sit*). In Aquinas, this issue is not distinguished from Suárez's second question (*quid sit*), which relates to the essence of the law. Lastly, Suárez examines the issue

[47]"*(...) el teólogo estudia, en este sentido, las acciones humanas conducentes a la felicidad pero, con más propriedad, al mismo Dios en cuanto causa de tales acciones, en cuanto El mismo auxilia a las criaturas y las conduce a la beatitud.*" (Larrainzar 1977, p. 141).

of how the law comes into effect (*quo motu*), which can be broken down into two categories: the effects of the essence of said law (*de effectibus legum*) and the issue of change in laws (*de mutatione legum*)—no similar effort is found in Aquinas' work. Even in the themes that both authors do discuss, there is much discrepancy. The issues relating to the existence of the law (*an sit*) and its transformation (*mutatio legum*), which are not found in the **Summa**, highlight the relevance that Suárez places on the subject. The law only exists and may only change by a subject who is endowed with reason and thus capable of legislative action. For Suárez, the subject is not a mere detail and it is not possible to dissociate him from the study of the laws.[48]

Therefore, it is not surprising that Suárez begins his study of the laws by criticizing Aquinas' definition thereof ("a law is a certain rule and measurement of actions according to which someone is led to do something or restrained from doing something"). He considers this too wide and generic a concept. Wide, because all things, even irrational things, have a measurement according to which they function. As seen, irrational things cannot obey. This concept is also generic because law would no longer be exclusive of moral objects or of good and honest actions: there is a set of rules guiding artificial objects (arts and techniques) and vile actions as well. Furthermore, that definition does not differentiate the strength of a law from that of an advice.[49] Advices differ because there is no need to obey them.

After refuting Aquinas' definition, Suárez begins to develop that of his own. However, he did not dispute every element in Aquinas' concept; rather, he used them as a basis for his own definition. Suárez accepts the fact that the law is a measurement, but only "of the moral actions, as it relates to their kindness and righteousness."[50] Hence, the element of the intellect is present in the law. All laws refer to an act of instruction, which moves rational beings towards good. Therefore, the law is an act of reason.

So far, there is no difference between Aquinas and Suárez. All things trend to their own good and perfection. What drives them that way is the law. However, reason measures and governs human acts; so, the quality of ordering an action towards an end belongs to the sphere of rationality.

It is then that Suárez strays from Aquinas. He analyses the meaning of the word "right" (*jus*) and notes that many scholars mistake this word for the law itself (*lex*). Suárez acknowledges both etymologies: one derives from the verb *iubere*, which means "to order," while the other comes from *iustitia*, the virtue of justice.[51]

---

[48]Moita (2004), p. 70.

[49]**DL**. I, 1, 1.

[50]"*(…) sed moralium, quoad bonitatem et rectitudinem eorum simpliciter*" (**DL**. I, 1, 7).

[51]**DL**. I, 2, 1-2.

3.2.1 Subjective Right

According to these two etymologies, "right" may have two main meanings. Pursuant to the last etymology, right is what is just and equitable; it is the scope of justice. In broad terms, justice may coincide with virtue in general (just like any justice relates to fairness), or with a particular virtue that grants the other with what is his. In this more specific sense, Suárez calls right "the moral faculty that anyone has either regarding its own thing or something due to him; thus the owner of a thing is said to have a right (*jus*) to the thing such as a workman is said to have a right to his wage."[52] This is a Modern notion of subjective right.

One of the main differences between the Medieval and the Modern Naturalism lies in the understanding of the subjective right, the power that each individual has to act. In the Middles Ages, Natural Law was a system, a set of duties that men had to abide by. It imposed obligatory tasks and activities. In a certain sense, it was the opposite of human liberty. At best, it drew the external boundaries of freedom and established the obligations that men had towards their communities.

Yet, Modern Natural Law confers to men a certain amount of power regarding the society as a whole. Subjective right is a synonym for power. The individual holds this power or freedom despite the fact that another legal order (such as Positive Law) may not grant him with it. The existence of this right is independent from any set of laws; the origin and basis thereof are man himself, not something that is external to him.

The subjective right is the distinctive note of Modern Naturalism. Nonetheless, Suárez was able to grasp this notion by reinterpreting very old scholars.

In that most strict sense of justice, as a specific virtue (not virtue in general), Thomism reclaimed Aristotle's division of justice into legal, commutative, and distributive justices. Legal justice deals with all the relationships among individuals that live in a town. The right (*jus*) to which this justice refers is the sum of the actions and goods of the subjects, which must conform to the laws. The State needs only to legislate towards the general welfare. Suárez does not discuss this notion of justice; but since he equates law and right (as shall be seen), it seems that he evokes the traditional classification and reinterprets it.

Distributive justice takes place among unequal people, between the superior and the inferior, the State and its subjects. The right with which this justice is concerned is the distribution of the *polis*' public assets. The thing that is owed to someone does not actually belong to him, only in a relative sense, according to his capacity or dignity. It is a right less rigorous, feebler and farther away from the notion of dominion. Suárez does not dwell this notion of law either, but he presents a looser notion of right: the *fas*, the lawful. The *fas* is suited for men's relationship with

---

[52]"(…) *facultas quaedam moralis, quam unusquisque habet vel circa rem suam vel ad rem sibi debitam; sic enim dominus rei dicitur habere ius in re et operarius dicitur habere ius ad sti pendium ratione cuius dicitur dignus mercede sua*" (**DL**. I, 2, 5).

God, because it is impossible to repay God in full.[53] Albeit indirectly, the concept of distributive justice does appear in Suárez's work.

Lastly, what we know today as subjective right refers to Suárez's reinterpretation of the commutative justice. This notion of justice operates between equals, between the citizens themselves. The focus is the equality in exchanges. It is a right by excellence, because it reflects the most current idea of justice ("to each his own"). Suárez does not employ the expression "commutative justice," but resumes the original statement and makes a subtle change: the "each" in the statement "to each his own" becomes a "moral faculty": "certain power or moral faculty each one has over what is theirs and what is owed to them."[54] And thus he changes the focus from the object to the subject. Classical scholars focused their discussion on the thing that was owed, not on the subject to whom it was owed. The thing or the situation was "just." Before, the most current definitions used to refer to something else entirely.

> The juridical science of the classical scholars, in order to determine someone's rights (*jus suum cuique*), did not begin with the individual, but objectively with the mass of social assets that had to be divided: someone's right was the result of that division. The right was not, therefore, an "attribute" of the individual, but something, an objective thing ("incorporeal thing"), a specific amount of prerogatives or obligations. It was not "power" to perform a certain task (walk around, express opinions, grow the land), but – and this is an important nuance – a **region** of power, a space for action limited by other spaces that were attributed to other associates [in a given society].[55]

Until then, someone's rights were a reflection of the set of obligations imposed on the rest of the society. The individual could not claim his right. He could claim for another person to fulfill the obligation that was owed to him. Suárez focuses the definition of the *jus* on the subject, on the holder of the right over the thing. The object of commutative justice then becomes a "just capacity." This capacity belonged to the individual, as if it came from within him, independently from the law (which was understood as a list of obligations) that established what others owed to him.

Incorporeal assets that were part of the commutative justice became part of the individual's dominion. The *lex* (the set of commands) and the *dominium* (the property of a liberty), in a sense, are antipodes. However, Modern Naturalists united both concepts under a single system and interpret the natural order as a set of

---

[53]**DL**. I, 2, 11.

[54]"(…) *ius vocari facultas quaedam moralis, quam unusquisque habet vel circa rem suam vela d rem sibi debitam*" (**DL**. I, 2, 5).

[55]"*La science juridique des classiques, pour établir le droit de chacun* (jus suum cuique), *ne part pas de l'individu, mais objectivement de la masse des biens sociaux à partager: le droit de chacun, c'est un quotient. Le droit n'est donc pas 'l'attribut' de l'individu, isolément considéré, mais une chose, une chose* ***objective*** *('chose incorporelle'), une quantité délimitée de prérogatives ou de charges. Il n'est pas 'pouvoir' d'accomplir telle activité (circuler – dire son opinion – cultiver l aterre), mais – voici la nuance essentielle –* ***zone*** *de pouvoir, secteur d'action délimité par rapport à d'autres secteurs attribués à d'autres associés.*" (Villey 1962, p. 160).

individual liberties, not as a set of obligations, like the Medieval Naturalists did. If not fully Modern, Suárez anticipates this trend.

In Suárez, the concept of subjective right may be traced to William of Ockham's Philosophy. Nominalism reduces reality to individual substances; only singular beings (Paul, Peter and John), who have first names, truly exist. Regular names (Men, Animals) and concepts (citizenship, paternity) do not refer to anything that actually exists. They represent an economy of language; they are useful instruments when referring to a plurality of individuals. The objective order called Law, which guides human relations, in truth, does not exist. Only in the conscience of men does law (lowercase) exist; the right should be construed from the individuals themselves.[56]

William of Ockham was engaged in a controversy between Pope John XII and the Franciscans over the poverty of the religious order. St. Francis bequeathed to his followers an obligation of poverty; yet the order, due to its size, had plenty of assets. The popes usually protected the order by way of a fiction, according to which all such assets were assigned to the Holy See, but the Franciscans were entitled to use them. John XXII took over the papacy and sought to prohibit that obligation to poverty by the decrees **Ad conditorem** and **Quia quorundam.**[57] Dissident Franciscan friars argued that in the *communio primaeva* of men there was use "of fact," but no private property. When God created everything, He gave men *dominium* over lesser creatures. These liberties existed for everyone and, thus, the Franciscans had a use "of fact" over other properties, allowing them to eat, drink and get dressed.

William of Ockham calls this use "of fact" a right: the *jura poli*, as they are the specific rights of the city of God. However, he did not anticipate that these rights were enforceable. He never studied Law and religiosity impregnates the use of the term *jura poli*. A contemporary jurist would accept this concept as a right only metaphorically.[58]

The Modern meaning of subjective right is attributed to Grotius. There is no reference in his works to a right existing only in the city of God; his understanding is secular and legal. But Suárez seems to have come first. There is no doubt that Grotius goes even further and extracts consequences that Suárez only mentions. Yet, a simple mention lacking any transcendental reference (such as in the Franciscan controversy), confers to Suárez precedence over Grotius on the history of the concept of subjective right.

The concept of *jus* as a capacity that stems from men corresponds to a profound dissonance between Suárez and Thomism. And this dissonance is just beginning.

---

[56]Villey (1990), pp. 119–120.

[57]Tierney (2001), p. 330.

[58]Villey (1990), p. 125.

3.2.2 Voluntarism and Intellectualism

In the previous section, I analyzed the concept of *jus* deriving from *iustitia*. The other etymology of the word *jus*, which derives from *iubere* (ordering) equates right with law itself. It is a very specific understanding of the term and Suárez does not mistake one for the other, like Grotius does. Suárez quotes St. Isidore de Seville, for whom right is a genus and law is a species alongside with customs and mores for the fulfillment of such right.[59] He appears to agree with the Archbishop of Seville because he notes, in the following item, that the concept of right also comprises the acts of a judge. In comparison with the other scholars of the Spanish Scholastic movement, Suárez seems to value more the nonlegal manifestations of Law.[60]

However, in this etymology in which *lex* is equivalent to *jus*, Suárez introduces one of his most important thesis for the theory of Law, one that will influence Grotius greatly. This equivalence is possible because both terms denote a command, an order. As understood in traditional Thomism, besides teaching and enlightening the law also commands. Here, Suárez strays from his own legacy and, without fully denying it, accepts the opposite tradition: the Nominalism. The debate between voluntarism and intellectualism corresponds to the Scholastic discussion regarding the relations between the intellect and the will in the constitution of Natural Law. Notwithstanding, this discussion is relevant to the study of law in general, because law comprises these two elements: intellect and will. The law is not only a rational precept, but also a command issued by an effective will.

Are certain actions sins and so God forbids them or because God forbids them, certain actions are sins? According to Voluntarism, when an action is a crime, it is because God willed it to be so. But according to Intellectualism, a crime is a crime, regardless of any divine prohibition. There is no doubt that everything, even Natural Law, stems from God, but He would have created the cosmos for a good and noble purpose, and there are rules which derive from the nature of things and lead them to their final purpose. God made intrinsically good things; the rules that flow from the nature of these things compel them to what is good. The same would take place with men. In spite of that, since men have free will, they could thwart those plans and, thus, perform actions that are evil in themselves: acts that go against nature. This is the Intellectualist explanation.

---

[59]**DL**. I, 2, 7.

[60]"*Como serían la costumbre y los usos vigentes (locales, regionales-nacionales, cuasiuniversales), los derechos personales (naturales o adquiridos) y las diversas modalidades de 'lo justo' o 'suyo' objetivo (correspondientes a otras tantas formas de titularidad jurídica, de justicia o de dominio y señorío).*" (Suñer 1974, p. lxi). Suárez equates a specific understanding of *jus* with *lex* (a reference that anticipates the Modern meaning) and this causes such an uprising among commentators that many forget that this is only one meaning of right, but not the only one.

The problem that voluntarists see in this understanding lies in the fact that, once the world is created, God's will and authority took on a merely supporting role. He could not change the nature of that He created. He could not make it so that two and two were five or change the essence of a good or a bad action. God would be submitted to Natural Law, which would mean a restriction on the powers of an omnipotent being.[61]

This debate originated in the following manner. In principle, Natural Law derives from the human nature, which is, at once, both rational and social. Thus, Theologians are faced with a hard question: when one follows the command of Natural Law, meaning an order of the human reason, is one also following God's law? Since the dawn of times, Christianity responded in the affirmative. St. Paul regards Natural Law as an authentic divine law. Several Medieval Theologians associated the Ten Commandments and others precepts from the Bible, in the Old and New Testaments both with Natural Law. The first Scholastic wave agreed with that logic.

Duns Scoto broke with that understanding. Above God there can be no superior law restraining Him. God is the only being whose *potentia absoluta* (the power to act with no limitations) is equal to the *potentia ordinata* (the power to act in an orderly fashion). Since there is no law over the Maker, which could serve as an ethic paradigm, all that manifests through His will is just and orderly. Regardless of His actions, justice is made: "Or, which is the same, his *potentia absoluta* will never surpass the limits of His *potentia ordinata.*"[62] Therefore, it is the divine will, not His wisdom, which dictates the rules of the cosmos.

By stating that, Scoto preserves the initial freedom of the divine will. In principle, things are like they are, but they could be different. However, once things are created, God's will faces limits. There are commands that constitute "necessary natural laws" that not even God may derogate. He loves himself because He is the ultimate good and if He creates a creature capable of loving, He must infuse in this creature the drive to love God, the ultimate good. The first law that exists for this creature is to love God. God cannot prescribe otherwise. Even God cannot edict a law that forces men to hate Him.[63]

William of Ockham would go even further. There is no law essentially good; there is only an essentially good legislator. The Nominalism weakened the concepts of nature and essence over God's omnipotent free will:

> Everything that is not contradictory in its form may choose to establish God's will. There were Nominalists who could not see the inconsistency in the fact that a man was simultaneously man and horse, since they are distinct, but not contradictory concepts. Nominalism is incapable of seeing the meaning of the essences, it refers everything to God's will. It is voluntarist.[64]

---

[61]Schneewind (2001), pp. 47–51.

[62]"*O, lo que es lo mismo, su* potentia absoluta *no traspasa nunca los límites de su* potentia ordinata." (Carrillo Prieto 1977, p. 16).

[63]See Carrillo Prieto (1977), p. 17.

[64]"*Todo lo que no es formalmente contradictorio, puede quererlo y estabelecerlo la voluntad de Dios. Hubo nominalistas que no veían contradicción en que un hombre fuera simultáneamente*

One of the Nominalists quoted by Suárez, Peter d'Ailly, accepts that God could not order men to disobey Him, because that would lead to a formal contradiction: the obedience would lead to disobedience. However, he does not see the impossibility of God ordering men to hate Him. There are no good or bad actions in themselves; what God wants is just and what he does not want is unjust.

Several Scholastics, including Gregório de Rimini, emphatically refuted Nominalism. Still, it exerted great influence over the Reformers. Pursuant to the Lutheran theory on justification, even if man is a sinner, the divine will may still save him and extrinsically impute justice upon him. "Then man will become *simul iustus ac peccator*. Just, by God's will that justifies him; sinner, because objectively and intrinsically man remains in sin."[65] Good deeds do not matter for human redemption. Only the divine will can save men. It is a notion that diminishes the power that men have over their own fate and salvation. One of Luther's book is justifiably entitled **De Servo Arbitrio**.

The Council of Trent condemned this doctrine and Suárez is a post-Trent Theologian. His first impulse was anti-Nominalist: Natural Law stemed from the essence of things. The righteousness of an action was not dependent on God. "If, by an impossible turn of events, there were no Eternal Law, nor a God, giving to another what is his would still be just."[66] This statement (which will play an important role in a controversial debate in Grotius) is a deviation of the "impious hypothesis," or *etiamsi daremus* because this is how the Grotian variation begins. Suárez did not accept this thesis. God exists, period. However, he used it *ad argumentandum*. There is no doubt that God exists, but the goodness or wickedness of actions do not depend of Him.

Suárez also responds to the voluntarists objections over the issue of the limitation of God's powers in his work from 1612: it is about self-limiting. As a perfect being, God cannot make mistakes and, thus, cannot issue contradictory decrees. In this issue, he remains faithful to Thomas Aquinas and Francisco de Vitória. When criticizing the pure Voluntarism, he refers to Gregório de Rimini who presents another deviation of the impious hypothesis:

> even if God did not exist or if He did not use reason or even if He did not judge things correctly, if the sayings of just reason lived inside men, constantly reassuring them that lying

(Footnote 64 continued)

hombre y caballo, ya que estos dos conceptos son distintos, pero no contradictorios. El nominalismo, incapaz de leer el sentido de las esencias, lo remite todo a la voluntad de Dios. Es voluntarista." (Suñer 1974, p. xxxix).

[65]"*El hombre será entonces* simul iustus ac peccator. *Justo, por la voluntad de Dios que lo justifica; pecador, porque objetiva e intrísecamente el hombre permanece en el pecado*." (Suñer 1974, p. xli).

[66]"*(…) si enim per impossibile non esset lex aeterna neque Deus, velle dare alteri quod suum est esset iustum.*" This quote came from a 1581 manuscript entitled **De actibus humanis et de via et ratione consequendi ultimum finem, iuxta ordinem doctrinae divi Thomae em Prima Secundae, quaestione sexta, ubi incipit agere de voluntario et involuntario**. That work may be found in **De Legibus** of *Corpus Hispanorum de Pace*, v. XIII, pp. 210–215.

> is bad, for example, these sayings would have the same legal nature that they do indeed possess, since they represent a law that indicates that evil exists intrinsically in the object.[67]

Since good and evil exist in themselves, regardless of the divine will, there is a morality set forth by nature. Even if God had not forbidden it by His will, it would still be sinful to corrupt the essence of things (the so-called "philosophical sin," that goes against morality, but not against God). Some of the authors quoted by Suárez, such as Bartolomé de Medina, explore this discussion in depth despite not accepting the impious hypothesis. They distinguish between the bad action (the one which turpitude flows from the nature of things) and sin (that bad action that law itself also forbids). Hence, bad actions are the genus and sins the species. Other authors (not named by Suárez) distinguish sins from actions free of guilt using this same reasoning. Suárez does not accept this position, deeming it too extreme.[68]

At the beginning of the chapter V of the book I, Suárez lists several arguments in favor of the idea that laws are an act of intellect. After the usual arguments of authority, he reasserts Aquinas' definition of law as an "ordering of reason." By "ordering" he meant organization, not an order or command. "Well, ordering does not refer to the will, but to the intellect, because it includes a certain amount of reasoning; hence, those who cannot reason, cannot order. Law is then an act of intellect."[69] Besides, guiding and instructing are qualities of the law and reason enables such guidance and instruction—thus, will alone cannot establish a rule.

Suárez eventually softens his conclusion and assumes a syncretic position, taking into account some voluntarists' arguments. The first condition found in the law and that makes it an act of will is the fact that the law drives its subjects to action or prevents them from doing something, and that which leads someone into acting is will itself. The understanding directs more than moves. The second feature of the law is that it has strength to compel, and such strength lies in the will, because the intellect evidences a need, but only will can create that need. Furthermore, the law is an exercise of power of the superior authority, which is, of course, a free activity. Lastly, Suárez notes that the law is an act of legal justice (Aristotle); even if prudence leads the legislator towards this or that law, with the intention of achieving the common good and fulfilling the distributive justice, it is will that choses one over several different options to accomplish that purpose.[70]

---

[67] "(…) *licet Deus non esset vel non uteretur ratione vel non recte de rebus iudicaret, si in homine esset idem dictamen rectae rationis dictantis v. g. malum esse mentiri, illud habiturum eandem rationem legis quam nunc habet, quia esset lex ostensiva malitiae, quae in obiecto ab intrinseco existit*" (**DL**. II, 6, 3).

[68] **DL**. II, 6, 16.

[69] "*Sed ordinare non ad voluntatem sed ad intellectum spectat, quia includit ratiocinationem quamdam; unde quae ratione carent, ordinare non possunt. Ergo lex actus intellectus est.*" (**DL**. I, 5, 3).

[70] **DL**. I, 5, 15.

In Suárez, the law unites both intellect and will. "There is no doubt that, firstly, to produce the law, intellect and will intervene."[71] The law is an intellectual craft, as far as it contains rational guidelines meant to order beings endowed with reason. Besides the intellect, inside the mind of the legislator, law presupposes an act of will to force its addressees.

> In fact, if in the law we see a power to compel, and, for that reason, we call that which exists in the ruler that drives people to move and act as law, then law is an act of will. However, if one sees in the law the strength to drive that which is good and necessary, it belongs to the intellect and seems to represent a practical judgment (…).[72]

Therefore, the law exercises two functions: a directive function and a perceptive function; in one, it guides, in the other, it enforces.

Though Aquinas adopted a more intellectualist standpoint, Suárez calls on his authority to legitimize his position.[73] Even Natural Law consisted of intellect and will. The natural *jus* (right) is a deontological order of conduct that stems from human nature, but Natural Law transforms it into a mandatory command. Good and bad are those actions that agree or disagree with nature. Yet, so far, reason has only pointed to what is good and to what is bad. Natural Law is the one that reaffirms its mandatory aspect, by forbidding the bad and demanding the good.

Hence, God forbids what is evil and prescribes what is good, but things are good and evil even without His will. This notion does not restrict the divine omnipotence. In the moment of creation, God's discretion is unlimited. He can create in this or that fashion: two and two could be four or five. However, once creation is complete, God may only order things in a manner that is in accordance with its nature, lest he prescribes conflicting decrees. For a perfect being, contradiction is a far graver heresy than limitation of His powers.

That is why Suárez does not accept the existence of the philosophical sin. That which is evil is evil in itself and such a condition predates the prohibition thereof (*mala in se*). Still, God must forbid that which is vile. This does not impair the divine free will, as God could have done differently before Creation. However, once everything is created in a particular way, not even Him can assault the nature of His doing, otherwise He would contradict Himself.

This is a very subtle distinction. To explain it, Suárez dives into the structure of the impious hypothesis—"even if God does not forbid or prescribes that which is

---

[71]"*In quo certum imprimis est adferendam legem intelectum et voluntatem intervenire.*" (**DL**. I, 4, 6).

[72]"*Nam si in lege attendatur vis movendi, et ideo lex dicatur id quod est in principe quod movet et obligat ad agendum, sic lex est actus voluntatis. Si autem spectetur ac consideretur in lege vis dirigendi ad id quod bonum et necessarium est, sic pertinet ad intellectum, et videtur consistere in iudicio practico* (…)" (**DL**, I, 5, 21).

[73]**DL**. II, 6, 5. Suárez states that his understanding is a generally accepted thesis among Theologians. It is an argument intended to reaffirm his authority (one that Aquinas did not endorse). However, it is possible to relent his affirmation, because Suárez was trying to defend a thesis that corrupted Thomism, but wanted to avoid being mistaken by a pre-Trent Ockhamist or a Reformer.

Natural Law, lying would still be bad and honoring your parents would still be good and obligatory."[74] Once more, he disagrees with Bartolomé de Medina, for whom the hypothesis led to a contradiction: lying, for example, would not cease to be sin because the law does not forbid it; it would remain a sin for going against natural reason. Suárez disagrees because he understands what it implies: that, in a conceptual level, the wickedness of an action exists before it becomes prohibit by law.

Still, Suárez does not accept this hypothesis, not because of its internal logic, but because of its consequences and external principles: "If God did not forbid an act, that would be because it does not displease Him and, thus, it would not be bad. Yet, we assume that it is bad. There lies the contradiction."[75] If God wanted the fire to be cold, it would be so, but God would never wanted that. There lies the difference between Suárez and the advocates of Intellectualism: God does not go against the nature of things because He cannot do so, but because He does not want to.

When discussing the impious hypothesis, Suárez realizes that it may be possible or impossible, true or false. The advocates of Voluntarism consider it possible, yet false: if He so wishes, God almighty may not forbid or not prescribe what is proper of Natural Law. By doing so, it follows that lying would not be bad, which leads to the falseness of the argument.[76]

Since Suárez has "co-opted" Aquinas (and other respected Theologians) to his cause, he does not need to elaborate on the perception that the most radical advocates of Intellectualism shared regarding the hypothesis. When discussing the position that was most contrary to that of the Ockhamists, he stated his own thesis. Yet, it seems possible to foresee a *contrario senso* conception of the latter. For "pure" Intellectualists, the hypothesis is impossible, but true. God would always prescribe or forbid what is proper of Natural Law. However, if (by an impossibility) that did not come to happen, good and evil would still exist.

Nonetheless, according to Suárez's intermediary proposal, the hypothesis is "absolutely impossible." Good and evil things are such because of their essences and because God cannot help but prescribe or forbid them.[77] Even though Suárez's position coincides with that of the most ardent proponents of the Intellectualism, the reasoning behind his assertions is different. God will always forbid what is evil and prescribe what is good, because He cannot be unfaithful to Himself.

Suárez thus answers affirmatively that initial question on whether by following a precept of Natural Law would one also be obeying God's law. Even if the justice of the action derives from itself, reason can only point towards that justice. But to coherence the correspondence of an action to its intrinsic justice is an ability of the will. In Natural Law, the will belongs to the Maker Himself. Goodness or

---

[74]"*Etsi Deus non prohibeat vel praecipiat ea quae sunt de lege naturae, nihilominus mentiri est malum et colere parentes bonum et debitum.*" (**DL**. II, 6, 14).

[75]"*Quia si opus non prohiberetur a Deo, non displiceret illi et consequenter non esset malum, et tamen alias supponitur esse malum, et ita sequitur contradictio.*" (**DL**. II, 6, 15).

[76]**DL**. II, 6, 20.

[77]**DL**. II, 6, 21.

wickedness derives from the essence of things, but the law stems from God. Hence, by accepting God as the author of Natural Law, the transcendental origin of morality/justice is ensured. On the other hand, in Suárez, there is still a morality inherent to the essence of things, independent from God. Men are entitled to morality, with no need to report to God. This moral entitlement only becomes legal through God's will. Despite being a Theologian, Suárez leaves room for an eminently immanent character in his theory of law.

This conclusion is even one of the reasons for the famous debate between Francisco Suárez and Gabriel Vásquez. Vásquez divides Natural Law into two categories: primary and secondary. The latter is a rational judgment on what is just and on what is unjust, while the former is the very rational nature of every rational being. This nature would be sufficient to create the natural right. He prefers the expression "natural right" over "Natural Law," because the term *jus* evokes the capacity of logically pointing out the good and the bad before the law comes into existence. It can only indicate that which is intrinsically good or bad (if the action conforms or not to human rational nature). Thus, the natural right does not need a legislator.[78]

Yet, Suárez's treatise is called **De Legibus ac Deo Legislatore**, implying that the legislator enjoys a position of prominence in his mind. Suárez disagrees with Vásquez because he can anticipate the consequences of his statement. If the rational nature existed on its own, it would disconnect from the eternal reason, which, in turn, would lead to a relativization of the morality. Should Vásquez want to prevent relativism, this rational nature should be conceived as something above the world we live in, which would lead to a "divinization" of the human nature.[79] Suárez's intermediary stance avoids both conclusions: there are absolute ethical precepts and they apply to an earthly reality. The rational nature is not Natural Law itself, but the basis and measure thereof.

Will and intellect are part of any law: Eternal, Natural, and Human Laws. In the first two, the will is divine. In the latter, the will is humane. Suárez does not give into the temptations of a Hobbesian voluntarism when he refers to the will behind Civil Laws. The enactment of a law by a competent authority is not enough; the law must also be just and fair. In Hobbes, Natural Laws are still present in civil societies, but the ruler becomes the only person allowed to interpret them. For instance, homicide and theft are still violations of Natural Law and Civil Laws should conform to such prohibitions. However, it is up to the ruler and to him alone to determine what kind of action constitutes a crime. Thus, he may consider illicit those actions that might seem otherwise, as well as consider licit those which appear not to be.

Although logically consistent with Hobbes' ideas, this statement undeniably leads to an unrestricted justification of State sovereignty. The problem is that when Natural Law ceases to be a role model for Positive Law, it loses its ability to

---

[78]Pace (2014), p. 280.

[79]Carrillo Prieto (1977), p. 20 and 27.

challenge it. Apart from the will of the ruler, there are no other criteria of justice to judge the actions of the State. If it were not for the social contract, Hobbes would be one-step closer to accepting that power alone creates Law.

In Suárez, the will of the prince cannot prescribe what is evil. Only the law "that is perfectly correct and straight and honest can actually be called law."[80] Power alone does not make a law. Obviously, he is aware that the ruler may eventually edict decrees that contradict Natural Law. However, he does not accept these decrees as true laws. This behavior of the ruler may lead to civil resistance and, eventually, to regicide. Albeit sufficient to produce Civil Law, the king's will is not unbounded. Since Natural Law informs the precepts of Civil Law, the will of the prince is limited by a superior will, that of the Maker. One will binds the other. Since all authority comes from God, an unjust law has no power to subject people.[81]

According to Suárez, due to this combination of will and reason in the making of a law the righteousness of a law depends on two requisites: one formal and the other substantial. In order to be just, the law must prescribe an ethical content, as well as come from an authority that has the power to enact laws. As such, Aristotle's ideas of justice take on a new meaning:

> It is understood that law in general must be passed with **legal** justice, so that it aims at the common good and gives a community what is rightfully theirs, with **commutative** justice, so that the legislator does not command beyond his legitimate powers, as well as with **distributive** justice, so that it equally shares the burdens.[82] (marked in the original)

The commutative justice encompasses the formal criterion, whilst the other two understandings of justice encompass the substantial requisite. Though there is a close resemblance, the ethical content of Natural Law is not quite the same as that of Civil Law. Suárez alters traditional Thomism with this notion: the concept of "common good" differs greatly from one philosopher to the other.

3.2.3 Suárez's Common Good

My investigation of the elements of the law in Suárez is close to establishing a formal concept. I have shown the ways in which he strays (and innovates) from traditional Thomism: the combination of will and intellect, the discovery of the

---

[80]"(…) *quae est mensura rectitudinis simpliciter et consequenter sola illa, quae est regula recta et honesta, potest lex apellari*" (**DL**. I, 1, 6).

[81]Bastit (1990), pp. 318–319.

[82]"*Se entiende, pues, de la ley en general, que debe ser dada con justicia* ***legal****, a saber: para procurar el bien común y conceder lo debido a la comunidad; con justicia* ***commutativa****, en cuanto que el legislador no mande sino aquello que lícitamente puede ordenar; y con justicia* ***distributiva****, repartiendo proporcionalmente las cargas.*" (Recásens Siches 1947, p. 127).

subject and the understanding of the law as an individual notion. Despite his Theological starting point, Suárez's definition of law bequeaths an ample room for immanence or, at least, seems to draw the line between transcendence and immanence. However, as long as Human Law incorporates criteria of justice that can be traced back to God, the distinction between the human and the divine will never be absolute. Only when the criteria of justice are exclusively human will there be a proper split.

This split will take place in Grotius, but Suárez sets the groundwork for him. He extended the distinction between transcendence and immanence as far as a Theologian could go. To understand this boundary, it is necessary to go back to item 3.1.1.1, in which I discuss the differences between the meanings of "general" and "common" and of "parts" and "singular" in Aquinas and Suárez. There, I remark the gnosiologic primacy of the singular over the universal in Suárez. The true meaning of the word "common" is yet to be discovered, though. Several authors besides Aquinas (e.g., St. Isidore de Seville) considered law to be a "common precept." Given that Suárez does not relate the term common to universal, he needed to reinterpret the idea. Thus "(…) for three reasons may law be considered a common precept: First, because it is established by common agreement or authority. Second, because it is common to all. Third, because it should conform to the common good."[83]

I will address the public authority in Suárez in another chapter. The second reasoning refers to the fact that laws should compel an entire community, not just one individual. Suárez insists on that point throughout chapter 6 of book I. His last statement is that the law should conform to the common good.

Common good is not a new expression. Aquinas had used it before. He does not study it specifically, but refers to that notion in many of his works (**De Regno**, **De Caritate**, **Ehticorum ad Nicomachum**, **Summa contra Gentiles**, **Summa Theologica**, **Commentarius in librum beati Dyonisii de Divinis Nominibus**, **Quaestiones quodlibetales**, **Politicorum**), so that it becomes possible to compile its common traits. In Aquinas, common good is a Metaphysical conceptual scheme that takes part in the idea of the good in general. And "good is what pleases everyone."[84] All things, rational or not, animated or not, lean towards good. Thus, the idea of good in general coincides with God, the ultimate good. This is the Theist tradition of the Aristotelian *telos*, to which I have referred previously.

However, there is a diversity of goods: moral, material, intellectual, and spiritual. Man, as a rational creature, made up of matter and spirit, body, and soul, and living in community for so long, searches for three goods: his individual good (that provides for his subsistence), the common good (which aims at the survival of his social group) and the divine good (because of reason, man wants to know God).

---

[83]"*(…) triplici ratione potest dici lex praeceptum commune: Primo, quia communi consensu seu auctoritate lata est. Secundo, quia debet esse communis omnibus. Tertio, quia pro bono communi*" (**DL**. I, 6, 5).

[84]"*Bonum est quod omnia appetunt*" (**ST**. 1-2 q. 94 a. 2).

These three types of good do not engender different inclinations. If that were the case, the quest for one would thwart the quest for the other. In fact, theses goods articulate themselves in a dialectical and hierarchical manner (the individual good is at the bottom of the pyramid and at its summit is the divine good).[85] Everything in a human being draws him to God and the individual and common goods are intermediate steps towards the ultimate good, the divine one.

Such as there are several communities, several goods overlap within the common good. There are common goods for the family, for the labor[86] (or the market) and for the political society; these three entities are hieratically arranged. Nonetheless, as men are also organized in a religious society, there is another order of division for the common good: the temporal common goods, proper of political gatherings, and the spiritual common goods (more important), which is proper of the Church.

These different types of goods are not conflicting, nor do they oppose each other. They refer to a same impulse (the drive to meet God), but from different standpoints. For instance, the individual good does not refer to the good of some, but to the search for the good pertaining to each individual, according to the means available to him.[87] The common good of the family is the same as the individual good, but marked by the affective union of people, which allows for a greater and better horizon of events. The gathering of people makes it easier to fight for survival and allows the individuals of that family to search higher aspirations, as taking care of the offspring and seeking the eternal truths. One good is the means through which the other nobler and higher good can be achieved.

What distinguishes the common good from the other goods is life in society. Not simply living, but living well. For that reason, the common good takes up two forms. On the one hand, the common good refers to the collection of specific common conditions for the organization of the society or for the conservation of individual goods. Here, the values of justice and of the internal and external peace, among others, provide a stable structure for life in groups. Such values enable the search for other goods. On the other hand, the common good refers to the combination of resources (material and spiritual, intellectual, and vital), which pursuit is the very purpose of the community. Among such resources, there are the material wealth and properties as well as the teaching and the growth of the true faith.[88]

---

[85]Michel (1932), p. 18.

[86]The expression is from Gabriel Chalmeta, who created it to designate those societies in which professional relations typical of the market are developed. It corresponds to a *vico* or village, a place of exchange of artisanal products needed by man that the first society, the family, cannot provide. Here, at this meeting of buyers and sellers, the commutative justice applies at its best. (Chalmeta 2002, p. 169).

[87]Utz (1961), p. 175.

[88]Michel (1932), p. 49.

Two comments are in order. Common good encompasses both the conditions that allow for the pursuit of goods (peace, justice, security, stable institutions) as well as the goods themselves that society cultivates. It is not enough to allow ownership; ownership must truly exist.

Society pursuits the common material goods because they allow men to be free of trivial concerns and search for the eternal truths and God. These goods stand in a clear rank, as the common good is the mean through which men reach the divine good. So, common good consists of an appetite, ultimately a Metaphysical and Theistic one. The different kinds of laws (even Human Laws) are all part of the Eternal Law; they are nothing if not the Eternal Law itself in different states of existence. Since law has a transcendental nature, it cannot command things toward a secular goal. One may find the term "common good" in Aquinas' shorter definition of law: "it is a precept of reason, aimed at the common good (…)."[89]

Therefore, the expression "common good" is part of Thomism. But in Francisco Suárez, the common good displays a very different nature: it is immanent. He evidences his heterodoxy by pondering about the necessity of Human Laws, since there already exist Natural Laws, which can regulate all aspects of life in society.

> [T]his need arises out of the fact that Natural or Divine Law [in contrast to Human Law] are general and only include moral principles, which are self-evident, comprising occasionally things that are plainly understood from those principles. However, the truth is that for the fair government and conservation of the human republic, much more is needed. That leads to the necessary establishment of other laws through human reason, to deal with things that are not settled by natural reasoning – that is why human laws are necessary.[90]

Natural Law regulates life in society, but insufficiently so. Its precepts are too few and too broad to govern all nuances of the daily life. Human Laws are important because they unfold these general precepts of Natural Law. And they also introduce principles other than those already provided for by Natural Laws.

The introduction of new principles is quite relevant. The ultimate purpose of the laws that come from God is different from that of the Human Laws. "It is certain that divine laws aim at making men good (…), since they prohibit everything that is bad and prescribe all virtues." However, Civil Law "does not have the goal of making men good, since Aristotle (III, **Politics**, chap. 3) affirms that one is the virtue of the good man and another is the virtue of the good citizen." Hence, Civil Law's goal is the making of good citizens, which is not the same as making good

[89]"*(…) rationis ordinatio ad bonum commune* (…)" (**ST**. 1-2 q. 90 a. 4).

[90]"*(…) necessitas manat ex eo quod lex naturalis vel divina generalis est et solum complectitur quaedam principia morum* per se *nota et ad summum extenditur ad ea quae necessaria et evidenti illatione ex illis principiis consequuntur. Praeter illa vero multa alia sunt necessaria in republica humana ad eius rectam gubernationem et conservationem; ideo necessarium fuit ut per humanam rationem aliqua magis in particulari determinarentur circa ea quae per solam rationem naturalem definiri non possunt, et hoc fit per legem humanam, et ideo fuit valde necessaria.*" (**DL**. I, 3, 18).

men. This happens because "the goal of the city is to preserve temporal life in external peace and justice."[91]

Common good, which, in Aquinas, influenced all laws applicable to human groups (that is, both Natural and Human Laws), in Suárez, becomes the ultimate goal of Human Laws. The ultimate goal of Natural Law is honesty. The common good is no longer a Metaphysical concept, because it is no longer the subject of God's immediate desire. Human Laws still cannot contradict natural precepts. Being a good citizen is a prerequisite to becoming a good man; similarly, the common good has strict relations with honesty. However, they refer to realities that are autonomous to some extent.

These are important considerations. One of the greatest criticisms directed at Naturalism is that it deprives Positive Laws of their own dignity. They should conform to Natural Laws under penalty of being null and they should accurately translate the precepts of Natural Law in men's daily life. In short, Positive Laws would have no existence of their own. But this criticism does not hold true for Suárez' naturalism. Even if Positive Law is not completely separate from Natural Law, the former is able to reflect only part of the latter, since their content differs. Suárez' common good does not refer to honesty of character *per se*.

Yet, it would seem possible to dispute this alleged autonomy of Human Laws, since they cannot contradict Natural Law. To contend this objection, it is necessary to take into account the relation between Human and Natural Law. The conclusion reached by the Grenadian Theologian reaffirms why he is known for his philosophical subtleties.[92] Human actions can be good, bad or indifferent. All laws, human or divine, express themselves through commandments, prohibitions or permissions, which correspond to the spheres of the commanded, forbidden and licit. A Human Law can never forbid something that Natural Law commands, nor can it command something that Natural Law forbids. Here lies a restriction thereto. There are several other relations that can be drawn from the normative propositions (commandments, prohibitions, and permissions) and from the moral quality of the actions (good, bad, or indifferent) that underline the autonomy of the Human Law *vis a vis* Natural Law.

Good or bad things are always subject to a prescription of nature: Natural Law forbids bad actions and orders good ones. However, there is a wide array of behaviors that find themselves in a zone of indifference, such as the rules concerning judicial procedure or norms of organization of the judicial system. Natural Law does not provide for these, but Human Law may. Nonetheless, there lies the *mala prohibita*: such behaviors may become bad, not because of an intrinsic quality thereto, but because Human Laws deemed it so. When man positively (in any

[91]"(...) *manifestum est divinas leges eo tendere, ut faciant homines bonos* (...) *nam prohibet quidquid est malum, praecipit autem omnem virtutem*" (**DL**. I, 13, 4). "(...) *saltem lex civilis non habet facere hominem bonum, propter quod Aristoteles (III,* **Politicorum**, *cap. 3) aliam dicit esse virtutem boni viri et aliam boni civis*" and "(...) *quia finis civitatis solum est huius vitae temporalis conservatio in exteriori pace et iustitia*" (**DL**. I, 13, 2).

[92]Grotius refers to Suárez as such in a letter. (Grotii 1687, p. 118).

sense) decides, he creates something new where there was only a licit possibility, among many others. Hence, for Human Law, actions and behaviors that lack moral content do matter. Ultimately, this is a human legislative domain. It is worth pointing out that while these actions are the exclusive product of Human Laws, they begin to matter also to Natural Law. They were indifferent, but after Human Laws ordered or forbade them (and because all authority comes from God), they also became ordered or forbidden by Natural Law itself.[93]

In morally relevant issues, Natural Law may command or merely allow good actions. In the first case, such a command should become paralleled by another Human Law. But the good action should never be prohibited by the Human Law, since it would be a direct contradiction. However, when Natural Law merely allows a certain good action, this permission does not necessarily entail another permission by the Human Law: it may be either licit, commanded or forbidden. The reason for that is that bad things are always malicious, but the absence or presence of a particular circumstance in good things can annul their goodness. Thus, the act of eating is good in itself, because it is healthy for the body and ensures the person's survival. However, eating meat in a day of fasting is a sin. Similarly, a donation evidences a degree of generosity, but a specific community may find it harmful to the common good. Here, the element that taints the action is the prohibition set forth by Human Law.[94]

Concerning bad behaviors, there is always a prohibition imposed by Natural Law and thus Human Laws may never turn them mandatory, yet they may allow them. "One thing is to command evil; another is to simply allow it or not to punish it."[95] Human Laws can allow or not punish them without incurring in nullity, because their content would be the permission of an evil, not evil itself. There must be a room for free will. Moral condemnation can only happen where there is freedom; if the laws oblige all goodness and prohibit all wickedness in a given society, its members would not become more virtuous. A man who obeys all the laws in this fictitious community would be a good citizen, not a good man. Virtue only arises when evil is possible.

At this point, it is possible to perceive how Natural Laws' and Human Laws' subject matters vary widely in Suárez. To seek the common good is not the same as to seek sanctity. Yet, there is one last untouched dominion that brings out the immanence of Suárez's concept of common good: the intent.

Just like man is made of body and soul, actions can be both internal and external. Internal actions are those that take place with a simple thought. Natural Law aims at goodness and moral perfecting and thus demand conformity between internal and external behaviors. However, "Civil Law is not about internal actions."[96] One cannot punish a thought; that is why it is useless to command or to forbid an

---

[93]**DL**. III, 12, 17.

[94]**DL**. III, 12, 18.

[95]"(…) *aliud esse praecipere iniquum: aliud promittere, aut non punire*" (**DL**. III, 12, 6).

[96]"(…) *jus civile* per se *non versatur circa internus actus*" (**DL**. III, 13, 2).

intention. When a law qualifies a crime based on the intention of its perpetrator, it does so because some external actions may evidence the intention. A crime does not always consist of a single action and the behavior that precedes the commitment of a crime may be punishable as well. Still, in Human Laws, purely complying with the wording thereof suffices. For that reason, Suárez states that "good actions are not needed for law enforcement; often, on the contrary, it is through sinful practices that Canon Law [which is a Human Law] is enforced; however, man can only become good through good actions; hence, abiding by the law does not make him any good."[97]

Suárez seems to contradict himself when he acknowledges that Civil Law may oblige on one's conscience. However, to oblige on one's conscience is not the same as to command or to forbid an internal action. First, he refers to the intention of the action and then to a belief in the mandatory nature of the law. Civil Laws oblige in conscience because the legislator received his authority from God. This is consistent with the idea of the legitimacy of the ruler's legislative powers. The power of the prince to pass laws comes from Natural Law. To oblige on one's conscience means to accept, in principle, the fairness of Civil Law. A "government with no coercive powers is ineffective and will easily tumble, but coercion with the power to oblige on one's conscience is either morally impossible, as just coercion implies a feeling of guilt, or it is very ineffective."[98] The power of the State lies both in its force and in the consensus. This consensus, the acceptance of Human Law, is how Human Laws oblige on one's conscience.

Thus, in Suárez, the common good refers only to external actions. Even when Human Law coincides with Natural Law and forbids an unjust behavior, one attains the common good by the mere external compliance to the law. Intention does not matter because the content on the two commands are not identical. "Positive Law cannot and should not regulate those actions that refer to the spiritual perfection of an individual, nor can it forbid certain vices that, despite their heinous nature, do not affect social life."[99] Natural Law forbids a bad action because the behavior in itself is bad; Civil Law forbids it because it affects the social life and jeopardizes the common good. For this reason, Recásens Siches notes that there exists a difference between Moral and Law in Suárez unlike the long-lived contrast between Natural and Positive Law.

[97]"*(...) ad legem implendam non est necessarius actus bonus; immo saepe per peccatum impletur etiam canonica lex; sed homo non fit bonus nisi actibus; ergo observantia legis non facit bonum*" (**DL**. I, 13, 2).

[98]"*(...) gubernatio sine potestate cogendi inefficax est, et facile corruo: coactio autem sine potestate obligandi in conscientia, vel est moralis impossibilis, quia coactio justa supponit culpam (...), vel certe est valde insufficiens*" (**DL**. III, 21, 8).

[99]"*El Derecho positivo no puede ni debe regular aquellos actos que se refieren especialmente a la perfección espiritual del individuo, ni siquiera prohibir ciertos vicios, que, por muy horrendos y detestables que sean, no tienen especial resonancia en la vida social.*" (Recásens Siches 1947, p.193).

In Suárez, the common good is autonomous from the honesty of the soul. Even a sinful action may lead to the common good. In Aquinas, if the common good relates to the greater good (the divine good) in a means-ends relationship, in Suárez, this relation is only of subordination. The prohibitions, commandments, and permissions from Human Laws do not necessarily coincide with the prohibitions, commandments, and permissions from Natural Law. Immanence has its own logic.

3.2.4 Other Requisites and the Definition of Law

I have analyzed the most important elements of the law in Suárez. Now, we are very close to framing a definition thereof. But a few concepts still require explanation.

The law consists of a common precept. In the previous item, I discussed one of the meanings of common. There are still two meanings left. In the first meaning, common equals public. The will of a public authority creates law. This meaning is the theme of another chapter, in which I shall discuss the origin of public power. For the moment, it is worth pointing out that Suárez equated both terms because, for him, authority (except the divine one) has a conventional origin. Common means the same as public because the law "is created by **common agreement** or authority."[100]

Lastly, the law is a common precept because it aims at regulating a community, not an individual. It seems a bit obvious for contemporary scholars, but Suárez is referring to one of the most important aspects of the law: generality and abstraction.

> The law is, therefore, like a rule establishing or showing through its subject matter or the work through which it is enforced, how one rightfully and correctly acts. Well, this rule is, by itself, universal and refers, proportionally, to everyone. Hence, the law is general in itself.[101]

When one states that law rules a community, not an individual, the notion that it entails general and abstract obligations is implicit. The law does not constitute a rule of individual conduct, although there are individual precepts in other juridical precepts such as awards and agreements. This notion dates back to Aristotle's work: because of its generality and abstraction, the law is insufficient to regulate all aspects of social life. Then, it is necessary to resort to another virtue: equity.

Even the so-called "private laws," which establish privileges, do not invalidate this understanding. Suárez explains that, when you establish a privilege or an advantage in behalf of individuals, these rules still refer to the entire community for two reasons. First, because these advantages are often transferable to successors (as is the case of nobility titles) and, thus, these laws are not limited to the life of that

[100]"(...) *quia communi consensu seu auctoritate lata est*" (**DL**. I, 6, 5).

[101]"*Est ergo lex quase regula constituens vel ostendens in sua materia seu operatione circa quam versatur, medium servandum ad recte convenienterque operandum. Haec autem regula de se universalis est, ad omnes cum proportione pertinens. Ergo lex de se est generalis.*" (**DL**. I, 6, 12).

single person. Second, because the granting of a privilege constitutes an immediate gain for the person receiving it as well as an eventual benefit for the entire community.[102] For example, when a judge is elected among his peers, being granted with a position, everyone else also benefits from that privilege. On the other hand, if the rest of the community does not benefit from a privilege in behalf of a particular someone, then the act through which such privilege is granted would not be a true law. As discussed, the law must uphold the natural criterion of justice.

Another quality of law that comes to some extent with its generality and abstraction is perpetuity. According to Suárez, laws tend to perpetuity. There are two evidences thereof: one towards the beginning and another towards the end. Only Eternal Law is perpetual towards the beginning, since just like God it does not have a beginning. The other laws are perpetual towards the end: they are created at a specific moment in time and remain in force indefinitely.[103] Though it participates in Eternal Law, even Natural Law has a beginning. As it is embedded in rational creatures, it comes into existence with they were created.

Suárez is aware that laws do not last forever. It is not quite that what he means by perpetuity.

> [The] perpetuity to which we refer concerns a certain stability of the law, which means having a life and value of its own and being enforceable by the strength of its origin and constitution, in such a firm and permanent manner that by itself lasts forever or indefinitely.[104]

It is not difficult to substitute the word "perpetuity" for "validity." Valid laws are laws that have certain stability, with power to enforce and to produce juridical effects indefinitely. Compliance thereto does not end with one applicable concrete case. For example, the duty not to kill does not end when a person abides by (or even disobeys) this law. This duty remains throughout a series of situations alike. This stability is what differentiates the law from a specific precept that applies to a single case and, once such a case no longer exists, the precept ceases to exist as well. The law remains indefinitely applicable to subsequent cases.

Suárez distinguishes the positive perpetuity from the negative perpetuity. The positive perpetuity, which is characteristic of Eternal and Natural law, lasts forever and is never revoked. Human Laws, which exist in a secular, unique, and inconsistent reality, are only perpetual in a negative sense: they are gifted with generality and abstraction and thus enjoy an indefinite validity; however, they can be revoked or suppressed by external causes, such as the enactment of a new law. Nonetheless, should they be left to their own fate, Human Laws last indefinitely.[105]

---

[102] **DL**. I, 6, 14 and 15.

[103] **DL**. I, 10, 1.

[104] "(...) *perpetuitas de qua tractamus, solum est quaedam legis stabilitas ad quam spectat ut habeat suum esse cum valore ac efficacia obligandi ita fixum et permanens, quantum est ex vi suae originis et constituitionis, ut de se duret semper aut per indefinitum vel diuturnum tempus*." (**DL**. I, 10, 1).

[105] **DL**. I, 10, 1.

Since Aristotle, Human Laws were regarded as varying from place to place, ever changeable and inconsistent. Suárez allots some measure of stability to them. Human Law does not loose its validity due to its inconsistency. Facts evidence this stability—which Suárez calls "moral perpetuity." There are three distinct evidences thereof:

> The first one refers to those who edict the law, since the law is not eliminated when such individuals are removed from power or die. The second one refers to the subjects to whom the law applies, since not only those who were present, were born and resided in the area in which the law was enacted, but also their successors and those who come to reside in that area afterwards must all be considered equally subject to that law. Thirdly, the law itself, once enacted, lasts until it is revoked or until its content is found to be unjust.[106]

There is no doubt that perpetuity exists in its purest form in the laws established by God. Human Law does not share this divine substance, contrary to what Aquinas may state; that is why such a law reflects the imperfection of its legislator. Despite its differences, the immanence simulates the transcendence and thus Human Laws possess some form of perpetuity, even if they do not last as long as divine laws. The perpetuity in Human Law is what the contemporary lawyer calls "validity."

Suárez fully understands the imperfection of this perpetuity. Civil Laws are only as perpetual as the communities where they exist are.[107] States and human sovereignty last indefinitely, but, as any human construction, they shall disappear eventually. Human Laws do aspire stability; stability is a feature of any law. However, their intermittence is a result of their legislative source.

This close relation with the community that creates the law has another consequence: the law may or may not apply to a person depending on whether he or she belongs to that community. Again, this is no news for a contemporary scholar. But in Suárez's time, this was a Modern trend. The Medieval method of Jurisprudence (science of the law) called *mos italicus* because of the influence of the Italian jurists, such as Baldo, Paulo Castrensis and Bártolo de Sassoferrato, consisted of writing long treatises on everything that there was to know about Law. The first textbooks only resurrected Roman Law (that was considered the pinnacle of perfection by jurists), until eventually the Roman legacy was combined with German institutions. There was a considerable universal aspect to these textbooks (even if the "universal" characteristic was actually European) and only gradually did some books on the Civil Law proper to a certain people began to appear. These works used *topói* and had as their point of reference questions posed by the scholars that had already written on the matter. Slowly, treatises began to focus on specific juridical themes, although they partly conserved the traditional approach. Several works began to

---

106 "*Prima est ex parte ferentis, quia non amovetur illo amoto, nec moritur illo mortuo. Secunda est ex parte subditorum ad quos fertur, quia non tantum obligat praesentes qui vel nati sunt vel territorium incolunt cum lex fertur, sed etiam eorum sucessores postea natos vel denuo ibi habitantes. Tertia ex parte ipsius legis, quia semel lata semper durat, donec vel revocetur vel materia eius aut causa ita mutetur ut iusta esse desinat.*" (**DL**. I, 10, 7).

107 **DL**. I, 10, 14.

arise on the issues covered by the Law of Nations, such as essays on the law of embassies and Just War.[108]

Due to a universal trend of the textbooks and to a "conceptual absolutism" of Roman Law (that offered solutions to every problem), it was not clear that Human Laws limited themselves to the kingdoms and republics that enacted them. What Hans Kelsen terms the "spatial sphere of validity of the norm" in the **Pure Theory** was a confusing and scattered notion in the legal systems of the time. Clearly, a monarch would hardly be able to demand of someone who was not his subject the fulfillment of an obligation set forth by his laws, but he would not consider this idea entirely illegitimate. For different reasons, the idea that the perpetuity of laws could be "imperfect" was something new for both traditional Theology and Jurisprudence.

A more restrict and national concept of Civil Law (in opposition to a more universal and cosmopolitan notion) leads Suárez to consider, as a requisite for law in general that it must be adequately edicted.[109] Only after the legitimate legislative authority enacts the law can it produce effects. The idea that the enactment consists of a requisite for validity inexorably binds the law to the authority that created it and to the extension of such authority. The law is valid because it was enacted by the ruler and it applies to those whom the ruler enacted it for.

The proper enactment of the law is such an important requisite for Suárez that the ignorance of the law, caused by a flaw in this process, may exempt the subject from his legal obligation.[110] This is the issue of sufficient enactment. For that reason, although not necessary, it is advisable that Human Laws should be written. There can be no doubt concerning the publicity of the law. An oral law may exist, but "only if the voice of the one who is disseminating it is sufficiently public and, after that, if it remains in the memory of men and in their traditions."[111] The enactment is one of the main differences between law and customs, a nonlegal kind of Law that possesses certain autonomy concerning the figure of authority. Yet regarding the laws, the most discernable aspect of the connection between the law and the authority is the enactment itself.

Oral or written publicity solves the problem of enactment for Human Laws, but the issue remains for the laws that come from God. In Natural Laws, the enactment stems from nature itself. Through reason, the rational creature (men and the angels) is able to grasp the precepts of the law. This perception is equivalent to a public statement, because "even if the enactment takes place within every men, it is not a private statement, but the common voice of all of nature or yet, of its Author who, by speaking to each individual, speaks as a public person, because he speaks as the

[108] Wijffels (1995–1996), p. 39.

[109] **DL**. I, 11, 1.

[110] **DL**. I, 11, 6.

[111] "(...) *si voce praeconis sufficienter publicetur et postea maneat in memoriis hominum et per traditionem conservetur* (...)" (**DL**. I, 11, 9).

author of nature."[112] Each man perceives right and wrong individually, but everyone possesses the ability to make this differentiation, since it derives from human nature.

But Eternal Law presents serious difficulties regarding this topic. While the enactment consists of an action that is external to the mind of the legislator, Eternal Law lies within God's mind. Moreover, Eternal Law is perpetual ab initio. In this sense, there can be no external sign evidencing that it came into force at a particular moment in time. All seems to indicate that Eternal Law evades the need for enactment.

However, Suárez formulates an answer to that problem. Eternal Law is enforceable from inside the Maker's mind, but its perpetuity toward the beginning is not able to create a valid obligation since the beginning of times. In order to be enforceable, its subjects must undoubtedly exist. Only after creation does Eternal Law become obligatory outside the boundaries of God's mind. "Eternal Law is in place since the beginning of time. But it is not enforceable since the beginning of times, if not within the limits of time."[113] Enforcement implies a relation between the law and its subjects, the creatures that already exist.

Therefore, the enactment (understood as an external act) is an act circumscribed to Creation. Eternal Law is enacted when another law, which fulfills it, is also enacted. Suárez refers to Aquinas' thesis that all laws, in one way or another, are part of Eternal Law. Every law (especially Divine Positive Law) takes its justice from Eternal Law. In Suárez, though, this has a different meaning: it is not so much a reflection of Eternal Law in multiple levels of reality, but rather an inspiration. Eternal Law is the source of justice, which is one of the requisites of laws in general, even Human Laws. Hence, it is enacted when other legislators (not God)—nature or man—enact their own laws. Eternal law is enforceable through other laws that emanate from it. Suárez makes this perfectly clear by quoting Proverbs, 8: 15: "'Through Me, the kings rule', referring to power, 'and legislators declare the just things,' according to reason."[114]

In Suárez, the authority of the legislator is that which distinguishes the law from other prescriptions that derive from reason. The purpose of an advice, a request or a demand may coincide with that of the law: to direct someone's behavior according to someone else's reasoning. However, only law proceeds from a superior being to his subjects.[115] Therefore, the law holds greater power or normative efficacy than other prescriptions derived from reason. This strength comes from the enactment, a

---

[112] "(…) *ideo licet promulgatio fiat in singulis, non censetur esse propositio particularis sed communis vox totius naturae vel potius auctoris eius, quia licet loquatur ad singulos, loquitur ut persona publica quia loquitur ut auctor ipsius naturae* (…)" (**DL**. I, 11, 4).

[113] "(…) *lex aeterna aba eterno ponitur, non tamen aba eterno obligat sed in tempore*" (**DL**. II, 4, 2).

[114] "*'Per me reges regnant', utique quantum ad potestatem, 'et legum conditores iusta dicernunt', videlicet quoad rectam rationem.*" (**DL**. II, 4, 5).

[115] **DL**. I, 12, 4.

proper declaration of the will of the ruler, a quality that distinguishes law from advices, requests and demands.

Finally, it is possible to present a concept of law. All elements are accounted for in the Suarezian definition: common precept, reason, stability, and enactment. Hence, the law is an ordering principle, with an ethical and valid content, which emanates from a legitimate authority. In his words: "The law is a general, just and stable precept, sufficiently enacted."[116]

Though inspired by Thomism, this concept is essentially different from that of Aquinas. Suárez's elements of law refer to a secular reality; even the requisite of justice conforms to a more immanent domain. More than an abstract ordering design, in Suárez, the law exists to oblige.

This obligation is not abstract: it is enforced by coercion. Suárez considers punishment to be one of the four-deontic variations, together with permission, prohibition and command. Though Suárez well knows that punishment is not always applied, the law is capable of warranting it: "In connection thereto, I say, in few words, that deserving a punishment or being guilty is not the same as actually applying the punishment."[117] One thing is to state that the offender deserves to be punished, but actually punishing him is another.

It should come as no surprise that in Suárez all species of law may lead to punishments. Human Laws, even the Church's, achieve this by sanctioning an unwanted conduct. Even God's Eternal Law may also punish, but the punishment will only take place in another life. A secular law sets forth a secular sanction, just as a transcendental law sets forth a transcendental sanction. However, there exists a law enacted by God (and so of a Metaphysical origin) that applies sanction over the immanence: Natural Law. In order to solve this puzzle, Suárez subtly argues that Natural Law may also punish, but the designation of the applicable sanction is left to Eternal or Positive Law: "because even if Natural Law makes or considers an action to be bad, it does not set forth the nature or the extent of the sanction, as it is purely natural."[118] This kind of law does not establish the punishment, but it may determine who deserves it.

The insertion of punishment as a deontic variation may seem out of place, but it is in accordance with a definition of law in which power stems from so many of its elements, such as enactment, will, and authority. But this should not be exaggerated. Placing Suárez among political philosophers who presuppose that coercive enforcement is fundamental to law is an anachronic task. His notion of law does not necessarily refer to coercion. Coercion is not in the essence of law, but is an effect thereof. Accepting punishment as a legal element means that law **may** impose coercion. Coercion is one of the four possible manifestations of the law. This means

[116]"*Lex est commune praeceptum, iustum ac stabile, sufficienter promulgatum.*" (**DL**. I, 12, 5).

[117]"*Ad quod breviter dico aliud esse loqui de dignitate seu reatu poenae, aliud de actuali inflictione poenae* (…)" (**DL**. I, 15, 13).

[118]"(…) *quod lex naturalis licet faciat vel ostendat actum esse malum, tamen ut est mere naturalis non taxat modum vel quantitatem poenae* (…)" (**DL**. I, 15, 13).

that Suárez would not reject the coercive thesis, were he confronted with it "by an impossible chance," but he believes the law does much more than coerce.

3.3 From the Laws of God to the Laws of Men

As discussed in the second chapter, the *jus gentium* was a law between Natural and Civil Law. In Suárez, despite clearly being part of Positive Law, this idea of a middle term remained. The jus gentium lies between Natural and Civil Law. Suárez describes a downward motion towards a greater concreteness in law: the means by which divine precepts apply to men. It is a matter of deducting specific principles from universal ones, concrete norms from abstract precepts, the contingent from the eternal, the circumstantial from the immutable, the secular from the divine: Eternal, Natural, and Civil Law (and other Positive Laws, such as the law of nations). The law of nations is the link between Natural and Civil Law. These two branches are in two different sides concerning their changeability and spatial validity. Another law is necessary to assist in the transition between these two.

This scenario illustrates the difficulties in classifying the branches of Law and in dealing with the changes in Natural Law. So far, the expressions "divine law" and "human law" were used somewhat freely. Suárez himself, before presenting his classification, used these expressions in such a manner. Until now, by divine law, Suárez meant either God's Eternal Law, or Natural and Eternal Law both, as in these two cases the legislator is divine. On the other hand, Human Law was a synonym for Positive Law, but there are divine laws that are also positive. Thus, it is necessary to apply more rigor and precision to the use of these expressions.

First, Suárez divides the laws into Temporal Laws and Eternal Laws. Eternal Law derives directly from God and governs all creation (bearing in mind the issue of their enactment). Temporal Law differs from Eternal Law as the creatures that were created differ from those that were not and as such exist outside God's mind (as they are found in the creation).[119] This dichotomy reinforces the differences between transcendence and immanence. It is a radical, if not absolute, distinction. God never stops caring about his work, but He grants it with autonomy so it can move by itself.

Then, Suárez divides Temporal Laws into Natural and Positive Law. Natural Law consists of a natural inclination. The word "natural" here is in opposition to "supernatural," which means events that take place outside of nature, in a miraculous way. Natural is also opposed to "free" not because it must happen, "like the realization of natural inclinations happens to irrational animals or inanimate beings, but because that law is like a feature of nature and because God Himself inserted it

[119] **DL**. I, 3, 6.

in the nature of things."[120] The law does not address inanimate beings or those deprived of free will. The freedom to which this Natural Law is opposed is much more radical than the notion of free will; it is a freedom in regard to the essence of things. Men can act against the nature of things, but they cannot alter it. Men can do evil, but cannot turn evil into good. This law is engraved in every rational mind and serves to distinguish the honest from the vile. In this sense, Suárez agrees with Aquinas when he affirms: "Natural Law is the Eternal Law's participation in the rational creature." Albeit temporal, this law also stems from God.

Suárez also divides Natural Laws into two. One comes from pure nature, from the substance of the rational soul and the other from the divine and supernatural shine of faith.[121] The first is Natural Law per se. The second corresponds to the Grace of God and is thus examined in the **Treatise of Grace**.

Positive Law "was established beyond them [nature and grace] by an external principle with such power; that is why it is called positive, because it was added to Natural Law, not necessarily deriving from it."[122] Here, the legislator is free: in the domain of indifferent actions, Positive Laws institute the good, when they prescribe, and the evil, when they prohibit. The word that best describes Positive Law is "institution." Suárez concedes that some authors (among them, Connan, a French jurist who influenced Grotius) call this law an "instituted law." Institution refers to a construction and, in this sense, is opposed to nature.

Suárez does not establish a necessary correlation between Positive and Human Law. After all, Positive Law is wider in scope than human life. There is Positive Divine Law (or simply Divine Law) and Positive Human Law (or Human Law). Regardless of deriving from Eternal Law, this Divine Law was created by God Himself in a special manner. This law is temporal because it does not order towards a supernatural purpose (God's love). It came into existence when the Church (a community of people organized around the true faith) was established to reprimand men, because of their blindness and moral depravity and to lead them to perfection and sainthood. It consists of the divine precepts set forth in the Bible known simply as "law." The Scriptures are divided into old and new law, in accordance to the Old and New Testaments.[123]

Lastly, there are the positive Human Laws. The adjective "human" does not refer to the fact that they apply to men neither does it relate to their content (earthly and human issues). Human Laws are "human" because of their legislator. "Thus, it is called Human Law because it was, by proximity, created and established by men. And I say **by proximity**, because, in some sense, all Human Laws derive from

[120]"(...) *sicut executio naturalis inclinationis est in brutis vel rebus inanimis, sed quia lex illa est veluti proprietas quaedam naturae et quia Deus ipse illam naturae inseruit*" (**DL**. I, 3, 9).

[121]**DL**. I, 3, 11.

[122]"(...) *sed ultra illas ab aliquo principio extrinseco habente potestatem posita est; inde enim positiva dicta est quase addita naturali legi, non ex illa necessario manans*" (**DL**. I, 3, 13).

[123]**DL**. I, 3, 15 and 16.

Eternal Law"[124] (marked in the original). Since all power comes from God, even human Positive Law takes its force from the Maker. Nonetheless, God remains as its remote cause of origin, while its immediate cause is man itself. This note wraps Suárez's understanding of the relation between immanence and transcendence, between the temporal and the eternal. Although autonomous, the earthly realm is subject to the divine.

Human Laws can still be divided between Civil Laws, which aim at governing the city and ecclesiastical canonical laws, which govern the Church. Ecclesiastical canonical laws are also Human Laws: the ministers of the Church and the pope are men. The special origin of the pope's power does not change that. Human Laws are needed because divine Positive Laws can only prescribe some fundamental and generic issues of the spiritual republic; they cannot govern all possible circumstances.[125]

It is worth noting that Suárez did not mention the Law of Nations when he set forth these divisions of Human Positive Law. Suárez's *jus gentium* does not fit in a stricter concept of law. Only in a broader sense, in which *lex* coincides with *jus*, is it possible to insert the Law of Nations within the notion of Human Positive Law. As it will be seen, the *jus gentium* is an extralegal law; its precepts are of a customary nature.

Suárez's classification traces back to Aristotle's **Nicomachean Ethics**. However, unlike him, Aristotle proposed a binary classification. "Of political justice, one part is natural and the other is legal: the natural part has the same force everywhere and does not exist because men think in any specific manner; whilst the legal part is initially indifferent but once established ceases to be."[126] The legal and the natural justice differ by contradiction: the presence of a feature in one implies its absence in the other. The fact that Suárez's classification has more divisions leads to some problems concerning its accuracy.

Aristotle's dichotomy is a reaction against the sophists' questionings regarding the variability of the laws. The sophists argued that, in Politics, there was only one type of justice, the legal one (*díkaion nomikón*). Aristotle introduced the expression natural justice (*díkaion physikón*). The word "nature" (*phýsis*) is present in nearly all of his treatises and has a connotation more of a principle than that of a definition. Nature is a "principle (*arché*) and cause (*aitía*) of everything that exists; better yet, it is the beginning and the end of movement, and does not seek movement outside of itself."[127]

Hence, natural justice exists by itself and does not depend on an external principle. But it does not refer to an immutable justice: the movement exists.

---

[124]"*Dicitur ergo humana lex, quia proxime ab hominibus inventa et posita est. Dico autem* ***proxime****, quia primordialiter omnis lex humana derivatur aliquo modo a lege aeterna* (…)" (**DL**. I, 3, 17).

[125]**DL**. I, 3, 20.

[126]Aristóteles (1973), p. 331.

[127]Bittar (1999), p. 121.

Aristotle's teleological reasoning foresaw that everything flowed towards their perfection (*agathós*). This movement corresponds only to the update of a being's potential, such as the seed that has, in itself, all the possibilities to become a tree, if all goes well. This movement does not depend on human interference. Nature existed before men—what is called ontological precedence. Man builds the legal justice above and from the natural justice.

Natural justice, deriving from the *phýsis*, is characterized by its precedence and unity. It stems from the nature of things. Yet legal justice is voluntary, because it can only be found in the *nomós*, in convention. It derives from will. It varies according to the variation of customs. Customs are conventions designed so that a specific principle may function; they are not based in truths, but in opinions, in the *doxa*. Legal justice is not only mutable but also fleeting. Thus, the dichotomy is set: on the side of natural justice, there are unity, truth, longevity, universality, essentiality, and autonomous existence; on the side of legal justice, there are multiplicity, opinion, contingency, relativity, will, and positivity.

It seems logical that such opposition cannot take place in a classification comprising more than two divisions. The problem here is that despite this inconsistency, Aristotle remained as a veiled frame of reference for Suárez, leading the inattentive student to incur in error. In Aquinas' division of laws (from which Suárez's division directly descends), the Law of Nations is considered "positive" but derives from Natural Law. As discussed in the first chapter, the word "positive" has here a different meaning (a broader scope, if compared to Aristotle's use of the word). Aquinas meant only that such law is human in nature. Though it derive from Natural Law, these principles of nature rely on human intervention (however feeble it may be) in order to be understood.

Similarly, those opposing ideas (natural-positive, divine-human, essence-will, universal-relative, and truth-opinion) lose their purpose in Suárez's classification. Both the will and the nature of things play a role in the formulation of Natural Law. Moreover, one cannot state that Divine Law, since it is positive, entails the attributes of being multiple, temporary and opinion-based. This law reflects God's Eternal Law; thus, it is true, one and permanent.

Furthermore, this classification makes Suárez's Naturalism unique among both Medieval Theologians and Modern philosophers. Among the former, Suárez has a special place because he separated Natural and Divine Law from Ecclesiastic Law. No Theologian had ever argued so vehemently for the human nature of the Canonical Law, even though it was possible, at the time, to envisage this. The relation between that law and God was always seen as very close. Suárez goes against that idea and states that it is Human Law, despite deriving from divine precepts. This understanding irremediably inserts Canonical Law into the sphere of immanence. In fact, Canonical Law should aim at the common good, which is not necessarily the same as moral honesty.

Among Modern philosophers, Suárez is unique because for him Natural Law (just like Aristotle's natural justice) is not immutable despite being universal, nor is it indivisible. Modern philosophers are more in line with Kant's understanding of

Natural Law: universal, static, and immutable. Under no circumstance may the precepts of Natural Law be softened. But Suárez is not Kant.

3.3.1 The Unity of Natural Law

The issue of unity and immutability of Suárez's Natural Law is, in the words of Recásens Siches, one of "the brightest moments" of Legal Philosophy. Although a bit long, the compliment is worth transcribing:

> I believe that, in comparison to his predecessors, Suárez makes considerable progress on this issue, for the sharpness and precision with which he establishes the problem and for the mental rigor which he deals with and solves it. Compared to the Natural Law of Grotius, Tomasius and Puffendorf, Suárez's doctrine is much more forward thinking. Moreover, in the context of legal philosophy throughout the ages, his doctrine is one of the deepest studies regarding one of the most debated issues of all times: the width of Natural Law, its rigor or flexibility and its relation to empirical contents of History. I see Suárez's solution as one of the better ones, among those human thought conceived on the conflict between pure Reason and History.[128]

At the beginning of the 8th chapter of book II, Suárez raises three questions regarding the possibility of softening natural precepts: "First, whether Natural Law is one for every man. Second, whether it is the same for all men and at all places. Third, whether it is the same at all times and under any state of human nature."[129] The first question refers to the indivisibility of Natural Law, the second to its universality and the third to not being circumstantial.

The Grenadian Theologian answers the first question in the affirmative. Although there are several precepts thereof, there is only one Natural Law that applies to all men and leads them towards one purpose only: human perfection and happiness. That is how Suárez ensures the unity of the natural-moral obligation.

However, he later moderates his opinion by stating that it is possible to categorize these precepts in relation to men's understanding of them. Natural Law is one, but not indivisible. Some precepts are quite obvious to all men, such as "do

---

[128]"*Creo que con relación a sus predecessores, Suárez representa en este punto un considerable progreso, por la agudeza y precisión con que plantea el problema, y por el rigor mental con que lo trata y resuelve. Comparada su doctrina con el Derecho natural que profesaron Grocio, Tomasio y Puffendorf, significa una etapa mucho más adelantada de la que representan estos tratadistas posteriores. Y en general, dentro de todo el panorama que la Filosofía jurídica ofrece a través de los siglos, la doctrina de Suárez debe figurar como uno de los estudios de mayor profundidad en torno al más discutido de todos los problemas: el que versa sobre la amplitud del Derecho natural, su rigidez o flexibilidad, y la relación que guarda con los contenidos empíricos de la Historia. Yo estimo que la solución de Suárez constituye una de las más felices entre todas las que el pensamiento há producido con respecto al conflicto entre Razón pura e Historia.*" (Recásens Siches 1947, p. 149).

[129]"*Primum, an in uno homine una sit. Secundum, an in omnibus hominibus et ubique una sit. Tertium, an in omnibus temporibus et in omni statu humanae naturae una etiam sit.*" (**DL.** II, 8, 1).

good and not evil" and "do not harm the others." Others are also evident, but not all men can perceive them, only the wise, such as "justice should be respected," "God should be worshipped" and "living in moderation is essential." A third set of precepts calls for reasoning and logical deduction. Often, arduous research is necessary to reach and understand them. They are still part of Natural Law, but they are not evident. If the nature of the first set of precepts is not questioned, neither should the conclusions drawn from them be. Besides, "Natural Law applies more to immediate conclusions than to universal principles, since the law is an immediate rule of conduct. General principles are not rules as long as the specific precepts not apply them for each class of act and virtue."[130] This third set is closer to the existing reality; it is where the specific precepts are found.

However, due to a growing difficulty in their perception, some nations may enact laws or abide by customs that violate precepts of Natural Law. The substantial difference of customs amongst peoples corresponds to one of the foremost objections to the existence of Natural Law. Nevertheless, one must be able to distinguish Natural Law itself from the knowledge that men possess of it. Suárez argues that these laws are human, not natural precepts. There is no excuse for ignoring the first set of precepts and the second set may not be disregarded for a prolonged period of time without any guilt. Yet, regarding the third set, there may exist an invincible ignorance.[131] In this case, until ignorance is purged, such laws are valid and legitimate.

Suárez also answers the last question in the affirmative. Natural Law is the same at all times. This is because this law does not stem from any given state of human nature, but from nature itself. Suárez rejects the notion found in the **Digest** and the **Institutas** of the succession of a golden age, when nature was pure, by an iron age, when nature decayed and became corrupted.[132] According to Suárez, the examples offered in these works (seizures, servitude, and private property) are institutions of the Law of Nations, a Positive Law. What the historical circumstances may bring is the greater application of a specific secondary or tertiary precept and the non-application of other prescriptions. As time changes, some rules become more necessary than others, but they do not lose their validity just because they are not being applied.

According to Truyol y Serra, the issue of the Natural Law's unity in Suárez relates to the knowledge of both its universality and immutability.[133] So far, only the first element was discussed, and the answer was in the affirmative—though

---

[130]"(...) *magis exercetur legis naturalis in his principiis vel conclusionibus proximis, quam in illis principiis universalibus; quia lex est proxima regula operationis*" (**DL**. II, 7, 7). It is important to take into account the author's statement that those that are more intelligent are able to notice the second set of precepts. Contrary to Modern philosophers, for Suárez and the Scholastic movement, reason is not an abstract, universal and common entity, in which all men take part. Natural Law is accessible to men, not to Man. Therefore, it is no surprise that Suárez discusses the issue of ignorance of Natural Law.

[131]**DL**. II, 8, 7.

[132]**DL**. II, 8, 8.

[133]Truyol y Serra (1952), p. 5.

somewhat mitigated. Whether Suárez's Natural Law is immutable remains in the open.

In Aquinas, Natural Law can change by addition or subtraction. A change by addition would take place every time a new human need arises, which led to the enactment of new rules. On the other hand, a change by subtraction takes place when one of those needs disappears. This kind of change could not happen to the first set of precepts, which were more broad and principle-based. The ones in the second set could suffer transformations, as long as they remained true and fair in the universality of cases.[134] This is the classic case of returning a gun to a friend who is under a great deal of stress. The precept that orders the handover of objects left in consignment is still valid and applicable to most cases. However, in this instance, the need for the weapon is subtracted.

Suárez perfects this idea. Change by addition does not constitute a mutation per se. It is an improvement, since the previous law remained whole. The law was improved in order to be of better use to human needs. Yet, change by subtraction is an "authentic" form of transformation, because the law loses its mandatory nature. It can happen by one of the following: by a change of circumstances that ends up distorting the content of the law, or by a change that is external to the law and was introduced by the legislator. In effect, the content of the law can, in time, become harmful and unreasonable, instead of useful and reasonable. In addition, the legislator frequently revokes laws that until then were effective. This happens especially with Positive Laws. Both of these changes may be total, called "derogation," or partial, which is a "discharge" or specific exemption.[135]

Since the Natural Law legislator is God (who establishes such law in accordance with human nature that is both rational and social), there can be no discharge or derogation by an external action. Previously, I have discussed the impossibility of existing two opposing divine decrees. Therefore, Natural Law cannot change in the divine mind. Neither can there be a mutation thereof. Although human nature is not the same in all men (some men may be more rational than others), it is invariable. Some men may be farther from the path, but the direction of the road is still the same to all. If there is any change in their substance, men are no longer human beings (*zoón politikón*) and there should be no more Natural Law.[136]

Nonetheless, the content of the law is quite dynamic: human nature is invariable, but not the circumstances thereof. The content of the law may depend on ties that may be undone. A father will no longer be a father if his son dies and, hence, if there is a law applicable only to fathers, it will cease to apply in his case. What happens here is a change in the content of the law. But the law itself remains mandatory. Furthermore, "as it is not written in boards or paper, but in the minds, [Natural Law] is not always articulated in our conscience with the general and

[134]**ST**. 1-2 q. 94 a. 5.

[135]**DL**. II, 13, 1.

[136]**DL**. II, 13, 2.

undefined terms that we use when putting it into writing."[137] For example, the rule of giving back a thing in consignment is not as absolute as usually expressed. It allows for some limitations and reservations. Reason tells us to return those goods as long as there is no legitimate reason for defending oneself or a third party thereof. Similarly, the precept "thou shall not kill" is not so absolute as to not allow for self defense.

The law was not changed. The precept itself comprises its own exceptions but men often do not realize this. This kind of mutation takes place in the content of the law and results, as Suárez calls it, in an "improper and external" change in law. The first set of precepts, those that are more generic (such as, for example, "thou shall do no harm") leaves no room for any sort of change or limitation. However, those precepts that are inferred from the first set and that are much closer to concrete cases may allow for this sort of improper change. In addition, since they are formulated in a general and abstract manner and their articulation in writing is not always done with enough accuracy, they do allow for exceptions in order to accommodate to the many subtleties of the cases.

Suárez offers a much more realistic and malleable concept of Natural Law than Modern thinkers do. "As seen, Suárez sketches the classical theory of the *rebus sic stantibus* clause (…)." He does not repel the universal concept of Natural Law, but he opens reasonable room for it to be circumstantial. Suárez's Natural Law is immutable and universal, but not non-circumstantial. "The timelessness of the norm matches its unity, the *Einmaligkeist* of the historical, without the second element overpowering the first."[138]

Human Law may alter some institutes that derive from nature, such as the communion of goods (e.g., communal property of goods, in opposition to private property) and the effects of a contract. Such changes, however, consist of permissions of Natural Law. Natural Law does not demand that everything remains permanently the same. Man can change such institutes according to the demands of reason, of time, and of the society in which he wishes to implement them. They are natural precepts whose implementation relies on human action. In the specific example of the communal property, Suárez does not accept a necessary association between that and the state of primordial innocence. In such a state, communal property prevailed because it seemed more convenient and practical to man. This kind of choice leads to curious effects. Natural Law forbids theft, but theft may only take place in a society that has instituted private property, not in a communal society. Suárez terms "Dominative Natural Law" this aspect of Natural Law whose enactment relies on men's freewill, in opposition to the Preceptive Natural Law.[139]

Suárez extracts all possible consequences of his propositions, even when they do not serve his purpose. Some Theologians believed that men could not alter natural

---

[137] "(…) *cum* per se *non sit scripta in tabulis vel membranis sed in mentibus, non semper dictari in mente illis verbis generalibus vel indefinitis quibus a nobis ore profetur vel scribitur*" (**DL**. II, 13, 6).

[138] "*Como se ve, Suárez esboza aquí la teoría de la cláusula* rebus sic stantibus (…)" and "*La intemporalidade de la norma se concilia con la unicidad, la* Einmaligkeist *de lo histórico, sin que la segunda signifique mengua de la primera*" (Truyol y Serrra 1952, p. 9).

[139] **DL**. II, 14, 13.

precepts, but did not include the St. Peter's successor among them, since he represented Jesus Christ himself. That line of thought granted Popes with an outsized authority, including the ability to pardon criminals found guilty under Civil Law and to interfere in the governing of sovereign States. This came to be known as the pope's power of direct interference. Suárez rejects this thesis. If God Himself may not exempt a precept of Natural Law (as seen in the discussion regarding the "impious hypothesis") a human authority, even the pope, certainly could not do it either. There are four reasons for this: man cannot alter the nature of things; an inferior authority cannot modify his superior's rule; Human Law stems from Natural Law and, hence, cannot contradict it; and, since Human Law cannot remove Natural Law's validity, derogation would imply the creation of an unjust law. Yet, if this power were left in men's hands, temporal rulers would also possess it, not only the pope.[140]

Since Aristotle, the virtue of equity softens the precepts of law, to which Suárez refers by its Greek term, *epikéia*. Equity corrects the law in a particular case to prevent injustice. Since the law only speaks in general and abstract terms, it is necessary to adjust it to the case at hand. Often, unforeseen circumstances arise and the application of the law in these cases may lead to an injustice. Thus, justice should prevail over the letter of the law. One should choose the "spirit" of the law, the will of the legislator, in lieu of a literal interpretation thereof.

This duality between law and equity does not exist in Suárez's Natural Law. According to the author, Natural Law is the most pure expression of justice and needs no corrections. What may lack in Natural Law is a matter of interpretation, since such law is divided into three different types of precepts.

> Firstly, I state: many natural prescriptions need further declarations and interpretations so that their true and authentic meaning can be established. (…) the killing of a man does not always constitute homicide, which Natural Law forbids, but only when it is done by its own authority and aggression. It is not homicide when one kills on behalf of a legitimate authority or in self-defense.[141]

And here the intermediate role of the Law of Nations can be comprehended. Positive Law can be used to expand the normative framework, which is constrained, in Natural Law, to those actions that are intrinsically moral. Besides supplementing Natural Law, Positive Law can also introduce some changes thereto in the case of permissible precepts. For example, freedom is a natural instinct, but Human Law can obstruct it due to a criminal sanction. As noted in Suárez's theory of law,

---

[140]**DL**. II, 14, 8 and II, 14, 10.

[141]"*Dico ergo primo: multa praecepta naturalia indingent multa declaratione et interpretatione ad verum sensum uniuscuiusque statuendum. (…) non quaelibet occisio hominis est homicidum prohibitum lege naturali, sed illa quae fit privata auctoritate et* per se *seu ex instituto aut per modum aggressionis; non vero quae fit legitima auctoritate vel per modum causae defensionis*" (**DL**. II, 16, 6).

Positive Law may even allow evil, because the permission to do bad things is not evil itself. Positive Law exists to modify Natural Law.

In a binary classification, such as Aristotle's, there is no bridge between natural justice and legal justice, between the eternal and the temporary, the immutable (even if nature is not that immutable for him) and the variable. On the one hand, there are invariable precepts and, on the other, rules that vary from place to place. The lack of a bridge between these two poles leads Aristotle to appeal to a virtue other than justice, the *epikéia*. However, the same does not happen in a classification bearing more than two categories. In it, there are kinds of law that, by their own essence, possess elements of both poles. In Suárez, the issue of changeability occupies such a prominent place that although Natural Law is invariable, it is not non-circumstantial nor it is timeless. Nevertheless, there are limits and this law cannot change like Civil Law does. That is why the *jus gentium* serves, in Suárez, a purpose similar to that of *epikéia* in Aristotle: the *jus gentium* "softens" the rigor of Natural Law, but without falling into Positive Law's flexibility.

As discussed in the second chapter, the Law of Nations has always been an important link between Natural and Civil Law. In Aquinas, it was a positive (human) interpretation of Natural Law. Suárez recognizes the closeness between these two species of law. From a formal perspective, if the *jus gentium* is a Positive Human Law, since it stems from the will of nations, from a material standpoint, it is "a group of conclusions, generally derived from Natural Law, which includes institutions and norms of universal use to all men."[142] While its form brings it closer to Positive Law, its content is clearly natural. After all, even with all its flexibility, Natural Law cannot descend to a level of greater concreteness. The *jus gentium* is necessary in light of the *jus naturae*'s immutability.

3.4 Summary

It is difficult (maybe even impossible) to say a final and definitive word regarding the basis of Law for Francisco Suárez. Indeed, he is an author of many subtleties. His thinking is rich in distinctions and quite different from both the Medieval theory of law professed by his predecessors and the Modern Philosophy of Law developed by his successors.

However, it may be possible to make this safe assumption: Suárez's Theology gave birth to an original Legal Philosophy. Despite considering himself a Theologian, Suárez is of great importance for jurists. He justifies his incursions into other fields of knowledge by expanding his own dominions. The study of the laws leads him to the supreme legislator, God. Law is nothing more than the Maker's

[142]"(...) *conjunto de conclusiones, derivadas de manera más amplia del derecho natural, que comprenden instituciones y normas de utilidad universal para todos los hombres*" (Pereña 1973, p. xxxviii).

tool to admonish men and to lead them on the path toward honesty and justice. The Philosophy of Law is but a chapter in a larger treatise on God. It so happens that, in Suárez, this chapter stands autonomously.

This autonomy is a result of the fact that Suárez strays from the traditional Thomism. As contradicting as it may seem, he who better summarizes the Scholastic movement is also one of its most "unfaithful" successors. The structure of Suárez's work is parallel to Aquinas. However, the similarities halt there. From a Metaphysical standpoint, their disagreement is even more discernible. In Aquinas, the universal concepts, which really exist, are the basis of his knowledge and the lens through which it becomes possible to observe individual phenomena. By flipping this logic, Suárez discovers, according to some,[143] the modern process of individuation before Descartes himself. Although not the focus of this oeuvre, it is worth noting that the very existence of a controversy regarding the *status* of the founder of Modernity evidences the relevance and originality of Suárez's ideas.

This Gnosiologic difference undeniably distinguishes Suárez's understanding of the laws and of justice from the treaties on law and on justice written by Aquinas and his most faithful followers. The very reunion of both treatises in one single book denotes this *démarche*. Even if the terminology is the same, the meaning of "law" differs. In Aquinas, all kinds of law are reason-based designs, and the greater reason is the Divine Law; therefore, the most perfect and universal law is Eternal Law. All other laws are a part of such law, in one way or another: they are Eternal Law itself materialized in different levels of reality. Since Eternal Law is consubstantial to God, all laws (even positive Human Laws) constitute a transcendental reality. Because of that, all laws represent principles that are extrinsic to men.

Nevertheless, the Conimbrigan Jurist takes the type of law that was closest to his eyes (the positive Human Law) and universalizes it. This difference in perspective averts the understanding that all kinds of laws are transcendental and extrinsic to men. In his Theology, Suárez found a space for immanence.

Also in result of this ontological preference for the individual, Suárez promotes the identity between the Laws (*lex*) and the Law (*jus*). But this identity is not absolute; the Laws are only one of several species of the Law. However, when they coincide, Suárez anticipates (if not introduces) the notion of subjective right. He reinterprets the classic definition of *jus* as "giving to each his own," as a quality that stems from the individual himself. According to Michel Villey, the previous interpretation consisted of reflecting in the individual the set of duties amongst the members of the community. The *jus* for the old thinkers did not always equate power; it often referred to an obligation that befell upon people or things. Despite not extracting deeper consequences thereof, Suárez once again innovated.

Furthermore, both reason and will are present in Suárez's concept of law. He synthesizes two opposing views, Intellectualism and Voluntarism. This choice affects Natural Law greatly. According to Suárez, Natural Law derives from the rational nature (which makes it just) as well as from the divine decree (which makes

[143] Moita (2004), p. 72.

it enforceable). Although Natural Law recognizes honesty and vileness in the actions themselves, Suárez rejects the so-called "impious hypothesis," because God must order what is good and right and He must forbid that which is evil and bad. Suárez's Natural Law lies between Intellectualism and Voluntarism and is able to reaffirm ethical objectivism and to support the imperative nature of the law.

Suárez's immanent conception of the law reaches its climax with the reformulation of Aquinas' concept of common good. In Aquinas, common good is an analogy for a greater good: God. All related goods, including the one that is characteristic of living in society (the common good), consist of means by which the greater good is achieved and are arranged in a hierarchy of sorts (in which the greater good lies at the top). In Suárez, however, only the Human Laws have the common good as their goal. Natural Law, divine in origin, aims at the rectitude and honesty of actions. Even if the notion of a good citizen and that of a good man are similar, they do not match. Civil Law may even allow for evil, because this sphere of freedom may be fruitful to social life. Furthermore, Positive Law demands only an external conformity of behavior, while Natural Law requires good intentions.

Another of Suárez's requisites of the law flows, indirectly, from these aspects. The legislator makes abstract and general laws, by way of a public decree of his will. Thus, in his words, "the law is a general, just and stable precept, sufficiently enacted."

Suárez reveals the full power of his reasoning in his Naturalism. The law remains far from the concrete facts; so, Suárez's Natural Law does not stem from an emotion or another causal reality. Furthermore, his version of Naturalism solves a problem around which his successors struggled: how to adjust Natural Law to History, without tarnishing its immutability. It is precisely why different peoples, with different customs, manage to live together in order. There is a minimum ethical content constraining them all (but respecting their differences) and thus enabling dialogue. It is from these interactions that the *jus gentium* arises, as it will be seen in greater detail in the chapter IV.

Francisco Suárez made quite an impression on Hugo Grotius. His letters attest that. Whether Suárez's fundamental concepts are found in Grotius is to be confirmed. Should that be the case, it is necessary to ascertain whether Grotius merely copied them, or whether he did to Suárez what Suárez did to Aquinas.

References

Alves, Paulo Durão. A Filosofia Política de Suárez. Porto: Livraria Tavares Martins, 1949.

Aquino, Santo Tomás. **Summa contra os Gentios**. Trad. Odilão Moura. ed. bilíngüe. Porto Alegre: PUCRS, 1996.

Aristóteles. **Ética a Nicômaco**. Translation Leonel Vallandro and Gerd Bornheim. São Paulo: Abril Cultural, 1973.

Bastit, Michel. **Naissance de la loi moderne**: la pensée de la loi de saint Thomas à Suarez. Paris: Presses Universitaires de France, 1990.

Bittar, Eduardo. **A Justiça em Aristóteles**. Rio de Janeiro: Forense, 1999.

Carrillo Prieto, Ignácio. **Cuestiones jurídico-políticas en Francisco Suárez**. México: UNAM, Instituto de Investigaciones Jurídicas, 1977.

Cedroni, Lorella. **La Comunitá Perfetta**: il pensero politico di Francisco Suárez. Roma: Studium, 1996.

Chalmeta, Gabriel. **La justicia política em Tomás de Aquino**: uma interpretación del bien común político. Pamplona: Universidad de Navarra, 2002.

Courtine, Jean-François. **Nature et Empire de la Loi**. Études Suaréziennes. Paris: J. Vrin, 1999.

Gilson, Étienne. **L'Être et L'Essence**. 2. ed. Paris: J. Vrin, 1962.

Grotii, Hugonis. Carta a Ioanni Cordesio, Canonico Lemovicensi, n. 329. **Epistolae** Quotquot reperiri potuerunt; In quibus praeter hactenus Editas, plurimae Theologici, Iuridici, Philologici, Historici & Politici argumenti occurrunt. Amstelodami: P. & I. Blaev, 1687.

Haggenmacher, Peter. Grotius and Gentili: a reassessment of Thomas E. Holland's inaugural lecture. In: Bull, Hedley; Kingsbury, Benedict; Roberts, Adam (ed.). **Hugo Grotius and International Relations**. Oxford, New York: Oxford University, Clarendon Press, 2002.

Larrainzar, Carlos. Una introducción a Francisco Suárez. Pamplona: Universidade deNavarra, 1977.

Merêa, Paulo. **Estudos de Filosofia Jurídica e de História das Doutrinas Políticas**. Lisboa: Imprensa Nacional-Casa da Moeda, 2004.

Michel, Suzanne. **La notion thomiste du Bien Commun**. Paris: J. Vrin, 1932.

Moita, Gonçalo. Introdução. In: Suárez, Francisco. **De Legibus**. Livro I. Da Lei em Geral. Trad. Luís Cerqueira. Lisboa: GEOPOLIS-UCP, Tribuna, 2004.

Pace, Paul. Suárez and the Natural Law. In: Salas, Victor; Fastiggi, Robert (ed.). **A Companion to Francisco Suárez**. Leiden, Boston: Brill, 2014.

Pereña, Luciano. Estúdio Preliminar. Suárez, Francisco. **De Legibus**. ed. crítica e bilíngue por Luciano Pereña. Madrid: Consejo Superior de Investigaciones Cientificas, 1971. t. I, (*Corpus Hispanorum de Pace*, v. XI).

Pereña, Luciano. Génesis suareciana del ius gentium. In: Suárez, Francisco. **De Legibus**. ed. crítica e bilíngüe por Luciano Pereña. Madrid: Consejo Superior de Investigaciones Cientificas, 1973. (*Corpus Hispanorum de Pace*, v. XIV).

Recasens Siches, Luis. **La Filosofía del Derecho de Francisco Suarez**. 2.ed. Madrid: Editorial Jus, 1947.

Schneewind, J. B. **A invenção da autonomia**: uma história da filosofia moral moderna. Trad. Magda França Lopes. São Leopoldo: UNISINOS, 2001.

Sciacca, Michele. **Perspectiva de la metafisica en Sto. Tomas**. Madrid: Speiro, 1976.

Suárez, Francisco (S. I.). **Commentaria una cum quaestionibus in libros Aristotelis "De Anima"**. Madrid: Labor Sociedad de estudios y publicaciones, 1978.

Suárez, Francisco. **De Legibus**. Livro I. Da Lei em Geral. Trad. Luís Cerqueira. Lisboa: GEOPOLIS-UCP, Tribuna, 2004.

Suárez, Francisco. **De Legibus**. ed. crítica e bilíngüe por Luciano Pereña. Madrid: Consejo Superior de Investigaciones Cientificas, 1971–1977 (*Corpus Hispanorum de Pace*, v. XI–XVII).

Suarez, Francisci. **Tratactus de legibus, ac Deo Legislatore in decem Librus distributus**. *Venetiis: Sebastianum Coleti*. 1740.

Suñer, Pedro. Teocentrismo de la Ley Natural. In: Suárez, Francisco. **De Legibus**. ed. crítica e bilíngüe por Luciano Pereña. Madrid: Consejo Superior de Investigaciones Cientificas, 1974. (*Corpus Hispanorum de Pace*, v. XIII).

Tierney, Brian. **The Idea of Natural Rights**. Cambridge (UK), Michigan (USA): Wm B. Eerdsman Publishing Co., 2001.

Truyol y Serra, Antonio. Lo mutable y lo inmutable en la moral y el Derecho segun Francisco Suarez. **Boletim da Faculdade de Direito de Coimbra**, separata, v. XXVII, 1952.

Utz, Arthur Fridolin. **Ética Social**. Barcelona: Herder, 1961. t. 1.

Villey, Michel. **Le Droit et le droit de l'Homme**. 2.ed. Paris: Presses Universitaires de France, 1990.

Villey, Michel. **Leçons d'Histoire de la Philosophie du Droit**. Paris: Dalloz, 1962.

Vitoria, Francisco de. **Obras de Francisco de Vitória**. *Relecciones Teologicas. De potestate civili*. Editadas por Teofilo Urdanoz. Madrid: Biblioteca de Autores Cristianos, 1960.

Wijffels, Alain. Early-Modern Literature on International Law and the Usus Modernus. **Grotiana**, v. 16–17, 1995–1996.

Chapter 4
The Foundations of Law in Hugo Grotius

Hugo Grotius read Francisco Suárez. There are four passages in the **De Jure Belli ac Pacis** in which he expressly refers to the **De Legibus**.[1] In addition, in an above-mentioned letter, we know that the Jurist from Delft admired the Jurist from Coimbra. This fact might go unnoticed in the midst of countless references that Grotius makes in his work.[2] In fact, those quotations are marginal both to Natural Law and to the Law of Nations and their suppression would not compromise the understanding thereof. At first glance, these authors do not have much in common; although contemporaneous, they lived worlds apart: one a Catholic Theologian, the other a Calvinist Lawyer.

Each religion symbolizes an intellectual universe of its own. For Reformed thinkers, there was a true hiatus between the Maker and the creature, which made it impossible to conceive human morality as Godly and rational at the same time. Only faith (which is that leap in the dark not explained by reason) could connect man to God. Yet Catholic thinkers believed that God had not abandoned His creatures: the Grace and the different kinds of law were instruments through which Divine Providence intervenes on human life. As a result, Reformers preferred Voluntarism (which, at its most radical form, had been condemned at the Council of Trent) as a way of explaining the origins of Natural Law, since they did not find objective values in nature other than God's will.

Even their professions distanced both authors. When studying the laws, Theologians commented on Aquinas' **Summa** and regarded Natural Law as a Christian update on Aristotle's notion of natural justice. However, jurists from the

---

[1]They are as follow **DJBP**. I, 4, 15, 1; II, 4, 5, 2; II, 14, 5; II, 23, 13, 2. They refer to: the duty to oblige the orders of an usurper monarch; the length of time of a custom in Civil Law; the non-applicability of Civil Law to the conventions of kings, and the impossibility of bilateral justice in war. The last two passages refer to the Law of Nations, while the rest deal with other issues. However, even in those, Suárez is presented as just another scholar who addressed the subject.

[2]In the following editions of **DJBP**, Grotius inserted more and more references, until the posthumous edition of 1646 (which essentially corresponds to the 1642 edition, except for some corrections, but no additions). See Reeves, 1925 p. 255. However, even in the first edition, that of Nicolas Buon, there are four references to Suárez. This means that during the initial phase of his work, Grotius already knew Suárez's work and so these references were part of his original intent.

P.E. Vauthier Borges de Macedo, *Catholic and Reformed Traditions in International Law*, Studies in the History of Law and Justice 9,
DOI 10.1007/978-3-319-59403-3_4

end of the sixteenth century and the beginning of the 17th, even if influenced by a Bártolo de Sassoferrato or a Pierino Belli, felt no need to follow pre-established canons, resting their conclusions on Roman sources only. As a result, the Natural Law in those jurists kept some Stoic remnants.

These differences will become clearer in the following pages. For now, it suffices to say that they instigated the animosity and jealousy of an Alberico Gentili towards a Francisco de Vitória, as evidenced in the second chapter. Suárez and Grotius lived in two different, however, not completely separate, realities, which explains the references made by the latter to the former. Yet, their realities were sufficiently distinct for Suárez not to have exerted a substantial influence on Grotius. Grotius himself seems to acknowledge this. In the *prolegomenon* 38, Grotius names, among his predecessors, only Balthazar Ayala and Alberico Gentili; Suárez was not worthy of any mention therein and he is set among the authors that Grotius criticizes for lacking "historical light."

But appearances can be deceiving. At least that was the conclusion that the revisionist literature of the end of the nineteenth century and the beginning of the twentieth century reached regarding the paternity of International Law. When it became known that the Spaniards had already addressed the issue of the *jus gentium*, Francisco de Vitória was considered a pioneer, but it was Suárez who above all robbed Grotius of his originality. Little by little, from "forerunner," Suárez became known as one of the biggest influences on Grotius. For instance, Jan Kosters argued that the **De Jure Praedae Commentarius**, written in 1604–5, already conveyed the notion of *jus gentium* found in **De Legibus** (1612). Far from absurd, the thesis uncovers the accession of new pages to the manuscript, indicating a subsequent revision of the original writing. A *nova declaratio* regarding the Secondary Law of Nations was introduced at a later and unclear moment, the contents thereof bearing a striking resemblance to Suárez's famous distinction between *jus intra gentes* and *jus inter gentes* (which will be discussed in the next chapter).[3] Although very respectful of Grotius, James Brown Scott subtly criticizes him by considering Vitória the initial exhibitor of International Law and Suárez its philosopher, relegating Grotius to the role of mere organizer. In that very same paragraph, he considers the Dutch a disciple of the Spanish School of International Law.[4] Paulo Merêa scathingly argues that

> There is no essential distinction between Suárez's and Grotius' doctrines; on the contrary, it is beyond doubt that the former inspired the Dutch jurist to the point of leading him to repeat some of Suárez's doctrine most important elements. (…) The comparison is not favorable to Grotius (…) and only highlights his inferiority. (…) Grotius' influence was, outside Catholic circles, considerably larger than Suárez's, but this is more due to his ability to expose his thinking in such a manner that was more appealing to the rationalist tendencies of his time, than to the inner merits of his thinking.[5]

---

[3]Kosters (1925), pp. 39–43.

[4]Scott (1934), p. 184.

[5]Merêa (2004), pp. 178–179 and 181.

To some, Suárez's work becomes so relevant for Grotius that, even when it does not influence him directly, it becomes a secondary source for other past references.[6]

Generally, the specialized literature justifies the lack of substantial references to Suárez in Grotius' oeuvres in two ways. First, as a good Humanist, Grotius favored referring to classical scholars in lieu of contemporaneous ones. If Richard Tuck's view on the issue is correct, Grotius had done so to many others: he referred to Carneades, an ancient skeptical, instead of Charron and Montaigne (as will be discussed later). Voltaire even accused him of being conceited because of the large number of references to ancient scholars. However, this criticism is anachronic if one considers the prominence these references had in books prior to 1650. At the time, classical works seemed to provide all key arguments for any serious discussion. They enjoyed an authoritarian standing even higher that the Scriptures in certain circles.[7] But, in principle, to Modern writers, too many references represent a fallacy of authority. To Grotius, they constituted evidence.

Second, as will be discussed in the following chapter, Francisco Suárez became involved in a controversy against Anglicanism, developed a doctrine of regicide, and had his works banished from England and France. In these countries, it was not suitable to quote Suárez. One should not forget that Grotius wrote the **De Jure Belli ac Pacis** in French soil and dedicated it to King Louis XIII, to whom he owed gratitude for being welcomed after exile and granted a pension. Even before that, when he got involved in the political and religious disputes in the Netherlands, he sought to maintain a strategic friendship to King James I of England. Therefore, he had many reasons to conceal his true admiration towards Suárez.

Notwhistanding, it does not seem easy to prove the hypothesis that Suárez had exerted a substantial influence over Grotius. The three main arguments for this (the four references in **De Jure Belli**, the *nova declaratio* and the embargo on Suárez) are not definitive. Neither is it possible to reject them entirely. They reveal that Grotius knew of Suárez, but not that he was dependent on his doctrine or, at the very least, on his theory of *jus gentium*. If there is a simpler explanation, the principle of Ockam's razor (*entia non sunt multiplicanda praeter necessitatem*) must prevail. And there is one: coincidence. The internal dynamics of Grotius' reasoning reflected the state of the art that Suárez reached a few years earlier. Furthermore, the revisionist literature has never exposed the doctrine of both authors for what they really are, without the deformities that accompany a reading devoted to comparison. If that were to be done, as I propose, it will be possible to identify significant differences between the two, especially on the issues that could make of one or the other the "true father" of International Law.

---

[6]That is James St. Leger's opinion on the origins of Grotius' impious hypothesis: he would have acknowledge it through Gabriel Vasquez's take on Suárez's work. See Leger, 1962, p. 132.

[7]Roelofsen, 1983, p 74.

The purpose of this chapter is to respond to the various interpretations of Grotius, by searching in the Dutch his stand on issues that were important to the Spaniard. Hence, it becomes necessary to prove that Grotius dedicated himself to the study of Theology and that it influences his works on Law. In addition, it is worth emphasizing that despite being a Calvinist, Grotius defended many a Scholastic and Catholic conception. Subsequently, I will present Grotius's method, which is one of the most, if not the most, important arguments in favor of his Modernity. After that, as was done for Suárez, I will display the Grotian theory of law and discuss the differences and similarities regarding his and Suárez definitions of subjective rights. Then, I shall analyze the several theses on the origins of sociability in Grotius, in the attempt to establish (or not) his proximity to the Scholasticism. I shall also discuss the impious hypothesis and its insertion on the debate between Intellectualists and Voluntarists. Lastly, I will demonstrate that Grotius' classification of laws unveils the influence of the Scholastic movement on his thinking, even though such classification seems different and serves to another purpose.

4.1 The Approach of a Jurist-Theologian

Although he was very influential in the field of Philosophy of Law, Suárez considered himself a Theologian. His perceptions and concerns were those of a Theologian, and he only ventured into the dominions of Law because of his overestimated conception of Theology. Yet, he did that with exceptional ability, due to his creative genius and legal knowledge. In the **De Legibus**, Suárez did not neglect the Roman sources nor the Medieval scholars. That is why Suárez is not your typical Theologian. But Grotius is not your typical jurist either.

It is said that on his last breath Grotius showed signs of frustration with his life: "By undertaking many things I have accomplished nothing."[8] No one has ever been so wrong over his own legacy. In the second chapter of this book, I listed all the titles that were bestowed upon him over the years. The **De Jure Belli ac Pacis** was reprinted about 48 times in Latin and translated into more than 26 languages. While he was alive, he amassed enormous prestige, even before the publication of his *opus magna*. However, Grotius never recovered from his forced exile and, for more than 10 years, tried (in vain) to return to the Netherlands. France took him in well and on many occasions, he received job offers from other States. He finally accepted Oxtierna's invitation to become Sweden's ambassador, a position he always took pride on. The **Mare Liberum** was one of the most read and controversial works of all times. Grotius always enjoyed the reputation of a good jurist. What could explain that last display of regret?

[8]See Knight (1925), p. 289. Thomas (1999), p. 61 argues that Grotius considered his works on Theology to be the most important ones.

Grotius wrote more than sixty books, most of which do not refer to legal matters. His most published work, reprinted more than 150 times, was not the **De Jure Belli ac Pacis**, but the apologetic **De veritate religionis christianae**. If one measures the relevance of something by his willingness to sacrifice his freedom and his life in the name thereof, then religion was of utmost importance for Grotius. For defending Arminianism, he gave up his political aspirations, was arrested, sentenced to life imprisonment and exiled.

It is true that Grotius valued his Theological works the most. However, his ideas on this field conflicted with the political and religious movements of his time, and as history would prove, of the next centuries as well. He defended the reunification of the Church, supported Erasthian thesis and even attempted, in the **Meletius sive de iis quae inter christianos conveniunt epistola**, **Ordinum pietas** and the **De veritate religionis christianae** to abridge the Christian doctrine to a rational minimum. By reducing the number of dogmas to those that were rational and evident, he aimed at ridding Christianity of its schisms and making it accessible to every man. This was no new project: several thinkers had attempted it before, including Erasmus. However, Grotius took this task the farthest. The remaining dogmas were only those regarding the existence of a single God (a God that was good, omnipotent, perfect, eternal, omniscient, and the Creator of all things), the Divine Providence and its extent over all men, the final judgment, the brotherhood among all men and, thus, the obligation to love one another.[9] These dogmas are consistent with the Classical Philosophers (and this coherence was important to the Christian Humanist ideal: Antiquity would have prepared the world for revelation) and would have promoted peace (internal and political), which is the very purpose of religion.

However, none of these ideas was successful. The Trinity, Christ and other dogmas remained the essence of Christianity and their absence only served to discredit Grotius' project. The Calvinists did not approve of Arminianism. The reunification of Catholics and Reformers would never happen. The submission of the Church to the stewardship of civil powers, put forth in the book **De Imperium Summarum Potestatum circa sacra**, was one of the most sensitive and polemic issues of the beginning of the seventeenth century.[10] In fact, if his religious convictions had meant that much to Grotius, then he truly died a frustrated man.

---

[9]Grotius (1728). III, 13, p. 202.

[10]Edwin Rabbie emphazises this "sensitivity of the century" with a curious story. In 1617, Petrus Cunaeus, a professor at Leyden University, published a book entitled **De republica Hebraeorum**. Purposefully, he avoided taking sides in the controversy. Nonetheless, the page in which the title of the book is found, in one of the exquisite pocket editions that made Elsevier publisher famous, also contains a drawing—in conformity with the purpose of the book, it must be said—of the two founders of the Jewish State: Moses and Abraham. At first glance, there is no problem there; it just so happens that among orthodox Calvinists, both characters were measured and Moses turned out to be a few millimeters taller than Abraham. The inevitable conclusion was that Moses represented the State and Abraham, the Church; therefore, the author wanted to infer the superiority of the former over the latter! (Rabbie, 1995–1996, pp. 97–98). Even King James I considered exaggerated the kind of subordination of the Church to the State demanded by Grotius.

Religion influenced even Grotius' legal works. When writing about Law, Grotius did not set Theology aside. His Philosophy of Law relied on Aquinas. After all, he set the distinction between human mutable law, Natural immutable Law and Divine Positive Law that man could not alter and did not rest on the *doxa*. The Divine Law aims at a degree of moral perfection even higher than Natural Law does. Grotius also argues for this dissociation: "there are those who argue that ancient law is Natural Law itself, but this is undoubtedly wrong. Many of these rules come, in fact, from God's free will (…)." Moreover, he affirms that Divine Law is a voluntary (positive) law: "It has been already remarked, that there is another kind of law, which is the voluntary law, deriving its origin from the will, and is either human or divine."[11] This categorization is more flexible in terms of defining the contents of Natural Law because it allows for a situation where not all rules provided for in the Bible should derive from nature. This feature is worth mentioning because it does not appear in all jurists, much less in a Reformed jurist, for whom Natural Law also stems from God's will. For example, as seen in the second chapter, Gentili mistook Natural Law and the Law of Nations. He also considered the latter a divine law: "a small part of the Divine Law is the Law of Nations, which God left for us after the original sin."[12] This distinction is a subtlety proper to Theologians—to Scholastic Theologians.

Jeremy Thomas measures the significance of the Divine Law to Grotius by the extent of its incorporation into the law of war. In the first book of **De Jure Belli ac Pacis**, Grotius examines the legality of war and whether it conflicted with Natural Law, the Law of Nations and Divine Law. He dedicates 33 pages to the latter, leaving only 6 pages to address the incompatibility of war to the Law of Nations and to Natural Law both.[13]

Yet, Grotius could have behaved in his juridical books like a jurist that made use of the Legal Philosophy of the Theologians to perfect his own. He would just be careful not to ignore their subtleties and would write more profound legal texts, but not Theological ones. So, unlike the traditional Thomists, Grotius does not present Eternal Law in his classification of the laws. Of all categories, this is the one that would least serve a jurist, since it guides the universe as a whole. However, there would be greater consequences: Eternal Law is consubstantial to God and for a Thomist Theologian all other kinds of law are mere reflections of Eternal Law on different levels of reality. Without it, there would be no *analogia entis*. The absence of an Eternal Law in the thinking of a scholar who is aware of such concept means

---

[11] "*Antiquam legem sunt que urgent pro ipso iure naturae: haud dubie mendose; multa enim eius veniunt ex Dei voluntate libera* (…)" and "*Alteram iuris speciem esse diximus ius voluntarium, quod ex voluntate originem ducit: estque vel humanum vel divinum.*" (**DJBP**. *prolegomenon* 48 and I, 1, 13).

[12] "*Et quamquam ius gentium particula est divini iuris, quam Deus nobis post peccatum reliquam fecit*" (**DIB**. I, 1, 4).

[13] Thomas (1999), p. 85.

that he either does not believe in God (nor he believes that man was made in His image) or that he simply does not realize how His existence may affect his doctrine.

One must dismiss the first alternative because Grotius was not an atheist. Pursuant to the second alternative, if the other kinds of law were not based in Eternal Law, then they would have to rely on another source—the will, both human and divine. Even Natural Law should stem from God's will and there would be no objective morality. For Scholastic authors, all kinds of laws derive, in one way or the other, from Eternal Law (the Maker's own rational design); thus, God leaves trails so that man may find the rules and values that are intrinsic to creation itself. However, Voluntarism and Nominalism were widespread among Reformers. It is worth noting that this viewpoint is only one step away from secularism (another label often attributed to Grotius): besides faith, there is nothing leading man to the Maker. Without faith, there is no transcendence. If a person believes in God, all morality depends on His will and it is impossible to separate Ethics from religion. But if the person is not a believer, he needs to find values looking at man himself or to accept the ethical skepticism. Calvinists were believers without any doubt and their morality was religious. Modern thinkers are known for their struggle against relativism and for their effort to figure out an Ethics that stems from man himself.[14]

However, a closer look at Grotius' writings tells a different story. Leonard Besselink stresses the presence of the expression "Eternal Law" in Grotius' Theological works, like the poem **Adamus Exul**.[15] As it occurs in the Scholastic authors, Eternal Law fulfills in Grotius the role of *analogia entis*. In a letter to his brother, Grotius affirms, "this law, according to which we must abide by our promises, is derived from Eternal Law, that is, from God's nature, according to the image that inspired man's creation."[16]

Albeit discreetly, Eternal Law also appears in a legal text written by Grotius. In the **De Jure Praedae**, while sketching the *regula* I "*quod Deus se velle significarit, id jus est*" ("that which God has shown to be his will is law"), the Primary Natural Law, he writes in the margin of the page a reference to the **Summa Theologiae**, 1-2 q. 93 a 1. However, in Aquinas, this issue corresponds to Eternal Law: "*utrum lex aeterna sit summa ratio in Deo existens*" ("Eternal Law is the ultimate reason that lies in God"). In fact, in Grotius, the Primary Natural Law seems to guide all things, animated or not, gifted with reason or not (that is, after all, closer to the definition of

[14]The idea that Modern Ethics arose from the struggle against relativism is Richard Tuck's classic thesis on Grotius, Carneades and Hobbes (1983, pp. 43–63). An evidence of that is that Grotius disagreed with Carneades in the existence of a Natural Law. In his later works, Tuck softened his view, but the idea remains in the essence of his thesis.

[15]See Besselink (1988), p. 86.

[16]"*Unde apparet ius hoc quo ad implenda promissa obstringimur ex aeterna lege, hoc est ipsius Dei natura, proficisci, ad cuius imaginem homo est conditus.*" (Grotii, 1928, p. 500).

Eternal than of Natural Law). In addition, even in that earlier work on Law, the idea of *analogia entis* is present: he once again refers to the **Summa**, 1-2 q. 93 a. 3, when discussing the Secondary Natural Law, or the Primary Law of Nations. This item aims at demonstrating "*utrum omnis lex a lege aeterna derivetur*" ("if all laws derive from Eternal Law"). Grotius does not label the Primary Natural Law as "Eternal Law," most likely to avoid any reminiscence to Ulpian's Natural Law, which applies to all living beings and evokes the more rudimentary drives.

Furthermore, Grotius' legal writings address human-related issues only. Therefore, as seen in the previous chapter, pursuant to the idea of ranking different kinds of law according to their levels of existence, there are laws much closer to human reality for one to address than Eternal Law. Despite all their similarities, Grotius does not belong to Scholasticism and his study on Law is not part of a greater effort to further develop and comment on Aquinas' work.

In other Grotian legal texts, the behavior of men and the practice of States may also manifest the author's concern with religion. They are a means of proving the existence of human law and *a posteriori* demonstration of Natural Law. As a good Humanist, Grotius pursues historical examples from the Classical Antiquity, which he deems the most perfect. Often, he uses the Bible as a source. That means he believes that the Holy Book carries historical truths and that the examples therein are reliable.

> Much better and more reliable is the method chosen by those who choose to decide these issues based on the Holy Scripture (…). This is especially true when compared to the material collected by nations everywhere, which bear little to none importance in offering a solution, since, as a rule, the worst option is usually chosen.[17]

Many commentators underestimate the religious references in Grotius's works, as they consider them alien to the Grotian conceptual structure. However, this means neglecting the very purpose of his writings. Grotius relies on Classical and Biblical references to universalize his work. Christianism enables this universalization perfectly, while imposing to Christians a standard of conduct higher than that of other peoples. When he states that "[t]hroughout the Christian world I observed a lack of restraint in relation to war, such as even barbarous races should be ashamed of," this highly quoted sentence was considered nothing more than a demonstration of pacifism. However, he continues: "I observed that men rush to arms for slight causes, or no cause at all, and that when arms have once been taken up there is no longer any respect for law, **divine** or **human**."[18] Since religion aims at peace, Christians are bound by an ethical standard higher than the pagans

[17]"*Melius aliquanto illi et certius, qui ex sacis litteris ista malunt disceptari (…). Nam quae passim ex omnium gentium annalibus alii collegerunt, ut ad rem illustrandam plurimum, ita ad dijudicandum aut nihil aut parum valent, cum fere idem saepius fiat, quod male fit.*" (**DJPC**, p. 6. The number of the page refers to Hamaker's edition).

[18]"*Videbam per Christianum orbem vel barbaris gentibus pudendam bellandi licentiam: levibus aut nullis de causis ad arma procurri, quibus semel sumtis nullam iam divini, nullam humani iuris reverentiam (…).*" (**DJBP**. *prolegomenon* 28).

(barbarous races). Nevertheless, peace is also possible to barbarians, because there is a sort of a "legal bound" among nations (Eternal, Natural law, and the *jus gentium*). Christianism (assisted by the Scholastic apparatus) is responsible for unveiling this common law. The **De Jure Belli ac Pacis** is much more than a book on the Law of Nations.

4.1.1 *Consonance and Dissonance from Scholasticism, Stoicism, and Modernity: Grotius' Eclecticism*

Commentators have always overstated Grotius' legacy. For a long time, Grotius enjoyed a completely Modern *status*. As well as being the father of International Law and secularizing Natural Law, Van Eikema Hommes also attributes to him the reading of Descartes while working on **De Jure Belli ac Pacis**.[19] However, the **Discourse on the Method** only came to light in 1637 and the **Meditations** in 1641! After that, Grotius was placed among the Spanish Scholastics, and the fact that he was neither Catholic nor Spanish mattered little. Meanwhile, severe criticisms also spread. Professor Vollenhoven states that in every language there have been written works pointing out the faults on his methods and objectives and in which authors have not sought to indicate what he **should** have written in order to produce a more satisfactory book on International Law.[20] It seems that Grotius suffers from the curse of being read not in view of the issues that he faced and the goals he wanted to achieve, but taking into account his readers' own bias. Lastly, there are those (such as Matija Berljak) who offer a third interpretation of Grotius by asserting a Stoic influence on Grotius' writings[21] as an independent approach.

In truth, Grotius was an eclectic. Even though he took part in heated debates on the freedom of the seas and on the Christian unity among Catholic and Reformers and gained bitter enemies across Europe and a life sentence in the Netherlands, Grotius struck a conciliatory tone in his writings. He attempted to bring together different and often contradictory trends and doctrines. A study of his sources evidences these ideals.

In the **De Jure Belli ac Pacis**, Grotius refers to over 120 Classical scholars, covering all the tenets demanded by Humanism. Among the authors he read, it is possible to find Greek philosophers, jurists, Roman orators and historians, ancient poets, Medieval theologians, and jurists, as well as a few contemporary theologians and jurists, besides the Bible. References to the Bible served more the purpose of providing historical evidence of State practice (of legal practices common to all nations) than appealing to authority. Most of all, it serves to corroborate the

---

[19]Eikema Hommes (1983), p. 64.

[20]Vollenhoven (1925), p. 1.

[21]Berljak (1978).

principles of natural justice. Grotius preferred to rely on the Bible, rather than on Roman jurists for historical examples.[22]

The second largest group of Classical references is that of historians, such as Diodorus Siculus, Demostenes, Livy, Plutarcus, Polibius, Tacitus, Tucidides, and Xenophon. There are only three scarce mentions to Herodotus, which signals the distrust that Grotius felt regarding the accuracy of the information provided by the Greek historian. This suggests that Grotius does not use his sources simply as an appeal to authority. Among Classical authors, there are several references to the Roman orators, such as Pliny, Quintilian, Seneca, and Cicero. The latter is the most frequently quoted ancient author, with over 80 references.[23] This is no coincidence.

Next in line are the Greek philosophers, especially Aristotle and Plato. Nonetheless, contrary to the Scholastics (that followed Aristotle by heart), there are serious doubts whether Grotius accepted the Aristotelism. In the *prolegomenon* 42, he expressly states that Aristotle is superior to all other philosophers. Nevertheless, his admiration seems to be far lesser than the one Scholastics fostered for the Greek philosopher, given that Grotius criticized the "tyranny" with which Scholasticism imposed Aristotle's authority. In the following lines, he rejects and seeks to refute the doctrine of the middle term. Grotius considers it deceitful to alway place virtue between two opposing extremes, because this opposition is often only apparent and, eventually, virtue lies in one of the extremes. It is not possible to sin, *e.g.*, by loving God too much. On another occasion, when Grotius defines *jus*, he once again rejects some Aristotelian notions, although here Barbeyrac suggests that Grotius did not fully understand Aristotle[24] (which I will discuss in a more appropriate moment). For now, it suffices to say that Grotius had a dubious relationship with Aristotle. In any case, it seems right to consider that he rejected the preeminence that Scholasticism placed on the Greek philosopher, for that compromised the scientific enterprise. In Richard Tuck's opinion, Grotius saw himself a follower of Aristotle, without actually being one.[25]

Another group of Classical authors constantly referred to by Grotius is that of poets and writers of epic sagas, tragedies, and drama (especially, Eurípedes, Homer and Virgil).[26] Grotius valued this kind of source because he himself wrote poems. It may seem odd for an author to rely on this genre to write a scientific work. However, such a criticism is anachronic, for it presumes that the contemporary *modus faciendi* of scientific investigation, according to which sources are only good for the collection of data, was applied in the past. For the Dutch, "the thoughts of poets and orators do not carry much weight. They are often referred to not with the goal of providing a basis for our opinions, but because, from their writings, it is

[22]Bederman (1996), p. 4.
[23]Bederman (1996), p. 5.
[24]Barbeyrac (1724), pp. 43–46.
[25]Tuck (1979), p. 63.
[26]Bederman (1996), p. 5.

possible to take out adornments, which are helpful at making our points."[27] All Humanist writers (Suárez, included) exaggerated in the use of ancient references, but Grotius' vast erudition stands out. He employed a number of texts solely for embellishment purposes.

So far, I have examined Grotius' classical sources only. As a good Humanist, he ascribes a significant weight to them in structuring his arguments. Grotius' commentators often undervalue other sources, for they spread across his work and are hard to assort. Nonetheless, if one could assemble all Patristic, Medieval Canonist and Scholastic texts, they would constitute a relevant group of reference. What criterion might one employ for grouping such different works, written over such a long period? After emphasizing the relevance of the Synod tenets, Grotius himself seems to indicate this:

> The Scholastics that followed them showed many times the greatness of their work, but they lived in centuries unfortunate and ignorant of the liberal arts. That is why we should not be surprised if, among noteworthy subjects, some questionable stances are found. **When they agree on moral matters, however, they are rarely wrong**, proving to be astute at what can be perceived from the writings of others.[28]

Therefore, in moral issues the Scholastics are irreprehensible. In Grotius' time, there was no definitive separation between Law and Ethics, even though it was already possible to sketch areas where these domains did not coincide. But jurists did not consider themselves moralists. In his quarrel with the Scholastics, even before telling them to remain silent on legal issues, Alberico Gentili states in the opening of his book that a moralist could say nothing on the law of war.[29] Then why did Grotius chose to use their work, instead of rejecting the Scholastics altogether as Gentili did? He knew Gentili's **De Jure Belli** and, if Haggenmacher is right, that book served as a model for the **De Jure Belli ac Pacis**.[30]

The answer to that question lies in the very purpose of Grotius' work. Contrary to what has been said about Grotius, he knew that he was not writing about an original issue. He did not intend to write a book on International Law; if he ended up sketching a concept of *jus gentium* that surpassed the Roman's orbit, he did so incidentally, almost by accident. He acknowledges that many before him had already addressed the issue. However, (and this may come as shock for a Humanist)

---

[27] "*Poetarum et oratorum sententiae non tantum habet pondus: et nos saepe iis urimur non tam ut inde adstruamus sidem, quam ut his quae dicere voluimus ab ipsorum dictis aliquid ornamenti accedat.*" (**DJBP**. *prolegomenon* 47).

[28] "*Quibis successerunt quantum ingenio valeant saepe ostendunt: sed in infelicia et artium bonarum ignara saecula inciderunt: quominus mirum si inter multa laudanda aliqua et condonanda sunt. Tamen ubi in re morum consentiunt, vix est ut errent: quippe perspicaces admodum ad ea videnda quae in aliorum dictis reprehendi possunt*" (**DJBP**. *prolegomenon* 52).

[29] **DIB**. I, 1, 1.

[30] Haggenmacher (2002), pp. 146–149.

Greek philosophers, the first Christians and ancient Romans were not among them.[31] Classical scholars did not discuss the subject of Grotius' research. By writing a book on the law of war, Grotius placed himself in a Medieval tradition. In his own words, he is amongst Francisco de Vitória, Henry Gorcus, William Mattheus, Johannes Lupus, Francisco Arius, Johannes de Lignano and Martinus Laudensis. This is why the authors most heavily quoted by Grotius (moralists, Scholastics, theologians, Medieval jurists, and canonists) can all be assembled under the label "sources of the Doctrine of Just War."

Grotius perceives his theme in midst of the Medieval tradition of the law of war. Alberico Gentili and Balthazar Ayala had also addressed this issue and had not fallen short on the "light of history." But Grotius believed himself to be different from them because of his unique moral judgment. In the *prolegomenon* 38, he notes that Ayala did not even mention the causes of justice or injustice in war. As to Gentili, Grotius acknowledges that he is in his debt and praises his thoroughness, but criticizes the fact that Gentili relies on too few examples and agrees with the opinions of contemporaneous jurists, the largest part of which "were written with the private interest of the consultants in mind and did not follow the rules of justice and honesty."[32] For the Theologian of Delft, the problem of these scholars lied thus in the absence of a moral judgment. Moralists are essential to the law of war. This means that Grotius interprets this issue according to what Alfred Vanderpol called "the Scholastic Doctrine of Just War." This is why Alberico Gentili does not take part in this tradition, as noted in the second chapter.

Alone, each scholar of the Just War Doctrine means little in the midst of the copious references that Grotius makes. However, taken together, they represent a substantial source. The Dutch took on to write a treatise on the law of war, not on the Law of Nations. Albeit through other paths, this is the conclusion that Haggenmacher reaches in his doctoral thesis **Grotius et la Doctrine de la Guerre Juste**. The concept of *jus gentium* is incidental to his original goal. In the **De Jure Belli ac Pacis**, Grotius aims at uncovering the causes that generate justice in a war and how and what is allowed in an armed conflict. The book he wrote earlier in life, **De Jure Praedae Commentarius** is a preliminary version of his *opus magna*; the actions allowed in times of war encompass the rights of prize and booty. Grotius has always been interested in the law that rules violent interchanges among human beings—which does not necessarily relate to International Law. It is an issue that permeates all political communities, but belongs to various species of law, such as the Law of Nations, Natural Law, the divine voluntary law and a domestic law common to many nations.

One of the most important commentators of Grotius' work, Roelofsen, has quite a cynical opinion regarding his sources. According to him, the primary source for Grotius is his own experience with international relations and the broad knowledge

[31]**DJBP**. *prolegomenon* 36.

[32]"*(...) auctoritatem novorum Iurisconsultorum in responsis, quorum non pauca ad gratiam consulentium, nona d aequi bonique natura sunt composita*" (**DJBP**. *prolegomenon* 38).

he possessed on diplomatic history. Among other examples, the right to passage for warring parties (**DJBP**. II, 2, 10) would refer to the Dutch enterprises in the German Reno; the severe disapproval of rebellions, along with the contradictory recognition of an unlimited right of resistance in specific cases, would resemble the conservative-revolutionary stance adopted by the General States in favor of the rebellion in the Netherlands; the *status* of non-Christian rulers and the binding force of treaties signed between them and Christian kings or between Reformers and Catholics (**DJBP**. II, 15, 8) would also conform to Dutch practices; the emphasis on the Church reunification, more than a theological imperative, resembles the foreign policy set forth by his mentor, Oldenbarnevelt.[33] As a result, Grotius' criticism of Gentili seems somewhat hypocritical.

This hypothesis is neither impossible nor unlikely. Grotius wrote the **De Jure Pradea** because of the seizing of the **Santa Catarina**, a Portuguese vessel, by a ship from the Dutch East India Company. The book aimed at justifying the legitimacy and justice of the action to the troubled consciences of the Mennonite shareholders of the company. As it will be seen in the last chapter, this engendered the defense of private wars, making Grotius' approach unique among scholars of the Just War doctrine. Nevertheless, is not possible to ascertain whether Grotius really believed in all these assimilations made by Roelofsen or whether he simply wanted to justify them; it seems impossible to know if he shared these opinions before or after deciding to defend the Dutch East India Company. The human behavior is not only influenced by the immediate interests of practice, but also by one's intellectual upbringing (that may even condition the perception of these very interests). Furthermore, this theory does not aid my search for the origins of specific institutes or concepts found in Grotius' work. In result thereof, for the purposes of this book, the criticism to Gentili still remains, morality, according to Grotius, is an indispensable element in the study of the law of war and thus the Scholastic sources of the just war doctrine do matter.

Notwithstanding, one should not assume that Grotius was a faithfull follower of the Scholastic movement. He proclaims to be independent of his sources.

> As for me, here and elsewhere I share the freedom of the Christians of the past who did not commit themselves to any school of thought, not because they agreed with those who said that nothing can be understood through knowledge – which is absurd –, but because they believed that there was no school which had uncovered the truth in its entirety, none which had perceived more than a fragment of the truth. For that reason, they considered that assembling the truths uncovered by several philosophers and disseminated among several schools to from a true Christian teaching.[34]

---

[33]Roelofsen (1983), p. 79.

[34]"*Ego et hic et álibi veterum Christianorum sequor libertatem qui in nullius philosophorum iuraverant, non quod eis assentirentur qui nihil percipi posse dicebant, quo nihil est stultius; sed quod nullam esse sectam putarent quae omne verum vidisset, et nulla quae non aliquid ex vero. Itaque veritatem sparsam per singulos, sectasque diffusam, in corpus colligere, id vero existimabant nihil esse aliud quam vere Christianam tradere disciplinam.*" (**DJBP**. *prolegomenon* 42).

A stronger defense of eclecticism is hard to find. The great range of quotations made by the author makes it impossible to classify him as a disciple of a single philosopher. For an eclectic thinker like Grotius, it is not enough to pinpoint Stoic and Scholastic influences. It is necessary to identify in each element of his theory the origins thereof. Most importantly, it is essential to analyze how Grotius assembles all these elements into something that makes sense.

Such eclecticism may pass as originality: mixing old notions and concepts into a new arrangement may lead to the creation of a new way of thinking. That seems to be why several scholars claim Grotius is among the most important (if not the most important) authors of the Modern revolution. In fact, it is not easy to discern whether Grotius did create something new and coherent or if he simply assembled different concepts that do not mix. The choice between one and the other is subtle and often relative. Regardless, beyond the elements of Stoicism and Scholasticism, it is important to find out what brings Grotius closer to Modernity.

4.2 The Method

The emphasis on the method is a distinctive feature of Modernity. Philosophers such as Hobbes believed that the only sciences to have evolved enough "to radically change our understanding of the universe were those which had applied the rigorous demonstrative proceedings of Geometry."[35] The perceived underdevelopment of human and social sciences was largely due to a defect in the applied method. Aristotle thus became the main target of Modern thinkers' criticism for two reasons. The first reason has to do with the authority that his books gained over the Middle Ages, which meant that their reading often lacked judgment and called for no proof. As seen, Grotius shares that opinion. Moreover, Modern writers thought of Aristotle's epistemological realism as being naïve, since it did not question the existence of beings external to our subjectivity. Skeptics such as Pierre Charron argued that it was impossible to erect a safe knowledge in Physics because human perception may be an illusion, nor was it possible in Ethics due to the plurality of customs, beliefs, and behaviors in different places. By the end of the sixteenth century, the Skeptics' assault on Aristotle's work seemed definitive. However, they had merely eroded a paradigm, providing no alternative thereto and thus leaving the task to Modernity.[36]

The Scholastics' (including Suárez's) concern with method had no epistemological basis. The so-called "Scholastic method" was nothing more than a highly

[35]Bobbio, 1991, p. 28. By the age of 40, Hobbes accidently came across Euclid's **Elements of Geometry**. He opened the book on the 47th proposition, and considered it absurd. However, the demonstration thereof referred to the previous proposition, which, in turn, referred to the one before, and so on up to the very first axiom, which was evident and uncontestable. Thanks to that, he fell in love with Geometry (Aubrey 1982, p. 152).

[36]Tuck (1983), p. 45.

didactic exposition of complex issues, the reason why they applied it only to the works designed for their students. Compared to pre-Modern jurists, the Scholastics created a more complex and precise knowledge, and that is attributable to the employment of Aristotle's logic, in lieu of rhetoric. Despite not abandoning rhetoric, Grotius addresses the issue of method as a Modern author.

The debate on method was dear not only to Philosophy; it soon became necessary for Jurisprudence as well. The *mos italicus*, the Medieval manner of making science of Law, was already displaying signs of exhaustion. As previously discussed, it consisted of employing rhetoric in the writing of extensive textbooks on everything that could possibly exist in Law, which was conditioned by the Roman institutions. Gradually, works dealing with specific issues, such as the law of embassies, arose. In result thereof, scholars began thinking of news ways to systematize Law other than the *Codex Iustinianus*. The problem was finding a defining criterion. A *ratione materiae* categorization did not seem obvious enough and a system based on the Roman *actio* was still tempting.[37]

The Medieval tradition still dominated the study of Civil Law in Italy and in several German States, besides prevailing in Canon Law as well; however, in France, Humanism created a new trend, the *mos gallicus*, the French way of making science of Law. Jurists, such as Ulrich Zasius, Guillaume Budé and Andreas Alciatus, were responsible for spreading this new method. Connan, Le Douaren and Doneau stood out as representatives of the *mos gallicus* in the study of the law of war. This trend spread within the University of Bourges, but it was also well received in the Netherlands, especially in Louvain and, later, in Leiden. It is worth point out that Grotius studied at the University of Leiden and received his doctorate in Orleans. The *mos gallicus* is composed of two strands: one, dominated by History and Philology, and the other by a more dogmatic, systematic and methodological reflection. These two strands sometimes met, as is the case with Grotius, whose effort to systematize Law did not preclude the introduction of History and Philology into the study of Law. And there was no blatant opposition to the *mos italicus*: the *mos gallicus* consisted more of an enlargement and transformation than a rupture and rejection.[38]

While comparing Gentili's *opus magna* to Grotius', Peter Haggenmacher remarks to the many similarities between the two: the same subject, similar structure, and topics, among others. Yet, there is a fundamental difference between them. For Gentili, "what may at times look like a system is hardly more than a skilful, often quite elegant, discussion of topical questions as raised and formulated by successive generations of lawyers and theologians in the particular field of the law of war."[39] His method is subject to casuistry and to the listing of *topoi*, finding itself squarely within the Medieval tradition of the *disputatio*. Gentili studied in Perugia and was a follower of the Bartolist movement, the Medieval school of case

[37]Wijffels (1995–1996), pp. 38–39.

[38]Haggenmacher (1983), pp. 47–48.

[39]Haggenmacher (2002), pp. 160–161.

law. He consciously affiliated himself to that school of thought, rejecting the French legal Humanism. But Grotius, although acquainted with the Italian scholars, clearly preferred the *mos gallicus*. "What the French systematizers did for Roman Civil Law—an orderly reconstruction of the subjects listed in the *Corpus Juris Civilis*—he was to accomplish for the whole field beyond the ken of Civil Law, that is, the *jus belli ac pacis* (…)."[40]

The work in which Grotius discusses his own method to a deeper extent is the **De Jure Praedae**. His organization is admirably clear; especially due to the division of the work into three parts: a discussion on the theme from the perspective of Justice (from chapter II to XIII), then a discussion from the perspective of Honesty and, lastly, from the perspective of Utility (which correspond, almost like an appendix, to chapters XIV and XV). The analysis of the Just dominates the entire work and is subdivided into three parts: the *Dogmatica* (II through X), which lays down the general principles thereof, the *Historica* (XI), which present the facts, and the *Examen* (XII and XIII), which corresponds to a practical application of the principles to the facts and thus to Grotius' defense of the seizing of the **Santa Catarina**. It is a well-organized construction. In the second chapter, when Grotius begins the *Dogmatica*, he lays down all his premises in the form of nine definitions (*regulae*), which represent different kinds of *jus* organized in accordance with the hierarchy of their respective legislators. From the *regulae*, thirteen prescriptions follow (*leges*), from which Grotius derives several propositions (*conclusiones* and *corollaria*) in the following chapters.

The title of the first chapter states the purpose of the entire work: *Exordium, Argumentum, Distributio, Methodus, Ordo Operis*. In *Exordium*, for his Mennonite audience, Grotius indicates that the discussion surrounding the incident essentialy results from the idea of justice. Law was still associated with the ancient virtue of being just. Then he explains what kind of legal study he is undertaking: the rights of prize and booty are part of the law of war. Even in his early work, the issue that Grotius dealt was already the *jus belli.*[41] In the *Argumentum*, he describes the incident with the **Santa Catarina** and foretells his general conclusion: the legitimacy of the Dutch admiral's actions. In the *Distributio*, Grotius explains the organization of his work (the Just, the Honest and the Useful) and sketches an interesting rhetoric parallel. He consistently evokes "the help of the three most important oratory genres mentioned by Cicero and Quintilian—*iudicium, laudatio* and *deliberatio*—which preside over the discussions of the *Iustum*, the *Honestum* and the *Utile*."[42] This is what we may call an "eclectic coincidence."

But Grotius distinguishes *Methodus* from *Ordo*: the latter refers to the general order of the elements of demonstration, while the former refers to the proceedings

---

[40]Haggenmacher (2002), p. 161.

[41]**DJPC**. pp. 1–4.

[42]"(…) *l'aide des troix principaux genres oratoires mentionnés par Cicerón et Quintilien*—iudicium, laudatio *et* deliberatio—*et qui président respectivement aux troix discussions du* Iustum, *du* Honestum *et de l'*Utile." (Haggenmacher 1983, p. 57).

of the demonstration itself. Italian logicians, mostly from the Paduan School, had a great influence over this distinction. Jacobus Zabarella (Galileo's older classmate from the University of Padua), under the influence of Aristotle, Euclid and Averrois, began the studies that would lead to the Modern method. He foresaw it as a *regressus*: in order to reach the exact knowledge of an unknown phenomenon, one should study the causes thereof and only after carefully considering these causes and their possible effects *in abstractu*, should one return to the initial phenomenon.[43]

There is a great deal of uncertainty regarding the names and types of methods developed by this school. It is possible to call it the geometric method because Euclid's **Elements** represented the paradigm of scientific demonstration. It is also possible to call it mathematical method, since geometry is part of mathematics. But there is a subtle difference between both conceptions. The geometric method comes from Euclid, while the mathematical method (used by Galileo and Newton) coincides with that used by Modern Physics. One is concerned with explaining axioms, with the certainty of concepts and with demonstrative rigor. The other attends to observation and experimentation, to the measuring of data in mathematical language.[44] As it shall be seen, in the **De Jure Praedae**, Grotius compares his way of doing research to that of the mathematicians.

In Alfred Dufuor's opinion, in the history of Modernity, this subtle distinction led to the creation of two important different methods. Descartes employed geometric method and it became known as the "resolutive-compositive" method. Pursuant to this method, the investigator first decomposes (or resolutes) the phenomenon that he seeks to explain into its simpler elements, in order to identify the relations that govern them (velocity, time, space). Afterwards, the investigator proceeds with the reconstitution (or composition) of the phenomenon, in order to formulate a principle or general law to which this phenomenon belongs. Hobbes employed this method. However, the mathematic metod was originated directly from the Paduan School and focuses on demonstration rather than on innovation. Zabarella created the method, but Galileo brought it to light when he discovered the law of falling bodies. Pursuant to this method, demonstration is a twofold phenomenon composed by analysis and synthesis. The analysis will reveal how a particular thing is assembled and how the effects thereof depend on its causes. The synthesis will unveil the causes through their effects, contemplate the truth in its conclusions and propose definitions, axioms, and theorems. By doing so, it is possible to ascertain how the consequences are part of their anteceding propositions.[45]

---

[43]Haggenmacher (1983), p. 68. Grotius sent a letter to Galileo, claiming to admire his work. (See Grotii, Hugonis. **Epistolae**. Carta a D. Galilaeo Galilaei. n. 654, p. 266). However, Galileo's works, **The Assayer** (1623), **Dialogue Concerning the Two Chief World Systems** (1632) and **Discourses and Mathematical Demonstrations Relating to Two New Sciences** (1638) were written after the **De Jure Praedae**. Therefore, it is likely that Grotius, although interested, only partly followed the Modern revolution in the method.

[44]Dufour, 1980, p. 37.

[45]Dufour (1980), pp. 38–39.

Albeit similar, these methods are not to be mistaken, given that the mathematic method assumes the existence of a conceptual scheme into which the scientist may apply a hypothesis, such as the absolute vacuum in the free fall example. The geometric method assumes the existence of an axiom from which the scientist extracts theorems. Nevertheless, these methods share one important similarity: they are both entirely rational and abstract; there is no room for empiricism. The only experimentation that may take place is an abstract mathematic and conceptual confirmation. This means that these methods incorporate the skeptics' distrust of the human senses.

Yet, Modernity knew other methods as well. Since the hypothetical-deductive method of Modern Physics (which still is the paradigm for every science) directly descends from both described methods, at times, other methods not so averse to our senses are dismissed. The work of the English empiricists, such as Bacon, Locke, and Hume are worth remembering. Of course, a young Grotius could have never read their works, but they are important to point out that there is Modernity outside Galileo and Descartes. By the end of the sixteenth century, the method was of general concern.

Back to the structure of the **De Jure Praedae**, in *Methodus*, Grotius resorts to two types of procedures in order to prove his claims: the *ractio naturalis* and the *auctoritates*. He is not defying Aristotle here, but rather the traditional method employed by jurists who carelessly apply rules and principles of Civil and Canon Law to a theme (law of war) where they lose their validity. As will be discussed, the international aspect does not define this field of law, but the lack of judicial authority does. Thus, without being able to resort to it, the institutions of a hierarchical legal system such as Civil and Canon Law (hence, the Roman *action*) are simply not applicable. Grotius finds an interesting solution to this conundrum: "(…) 'nothing written is valid among enemies; however, customs are followed by all, even when the extreme of hatred has been reached'. The term 'customs' corresponds to Cicero's concept in the statement 'unwritten law, which arises from nature' (…)."[46] The parties should appeal to an unwritten law, indicated by the agreement of several nations, which is nothing more than a manifestation of natural reason. Only this *jus* is valid among enemies. Given that Natural Law, together with Divine Law and the Law of Nations, is one of the sources for the law of war (yet not the only source, and here may lie a flaw in the author's method), it is necessary to conceive a manner of discovering it. Moreover, since Natural Law is rational, it can be demonstrated *a priori*. The *a posteriori* method, which consists of the testimonies of the Scriptures and of human authorities, is only good to confirm what reason has already unveiled: when everyone agrees on a particular consequence, it is probable that it has a common cause. The length that Grotius dedicates in the

[46]"(…) '*Eorum sane quae scripta sunt nihil inter hostes valet; mores autem servantur ab omnibus, etiam cum ad extremum odii processerint.*' *Ubi mores idem sunt, quod apud Tullium* '*non scripta sed nata lex*' (…)" (**DJPC**, p. 6).

book to explain the role of authority (less than a sentence) suggests that this method played a much smaller role than the *ractio naturalis* did.

None of these methods shares any resemblance to those already described that are responsible for the Modern revolution. Yet, the axiomatic–deductive structure of Grotius' work seems to indicate that he was inspired by the mathematical method. However, the argument that explains that influence is found not in the *Methodus*, but in the *Ordo*.

> For the rest, it is expedient for our purposes to order the discussion as follows: first, let us see what is trully universal, as a general proposition; then, let us gradually narrow this generalization, adapting it to the special nature of the case under consideration. Just as the mathematicians customarily prefix to any concrete demonstration a preliminary statement of certain broad axioms on which all persons easily agreed, in order that there may be some fixed point from which to trace the proof of what follows, so shall we point out certain rules and laws of the most general nature, presenting them as preliminary assumptions which need to be recalled rather than learned for the first time, with the purpose of laying a foundation upon which our other conclusions may safely rest.[47]

It seems only a Modern writer would conceive such a description of the method. In the following paragraph, Grotius apologizes to his readers for any mistakes he may have eventually made due to the originality of his intention. Truthfully, if he actually aimed at transposing the method of the demonstrative sciences into moral philosophy, he was thirty years ahead of the **Discourse on Method**.

Notwithstanding, this idea that Grotius developed a Modern reflection on method needs to overcome a considerable obstacle: the reference to the mathematicians' work is found in the *Ordo*, not in the *Methodus*. That is important. For Modern thinkers, this was an issue of method, not simply of organization. But Grotius employed two methods: the derivation of *ractione naturalis* and the confirmation through *auctoritates*. The mathematicians only inspired his order—he searched for an original, and certainly, more "organized" way of exposing ancient content; as a good lawyer, he searched for a better way to present his arguments in a didactic and convincing manner. The allusion to the mathematicians' work represents a mere comparison, not the transposition of the method of another science into the domain of Law. According to Haggenmacher, the fact the Grotius' idea of "proceeding like the mathematicians" lies in the *Ordo* and not in the *Methodus* means that, despite appearances, the method in itself was not the subject of an autonomous reflection. The method, the order and the anticipated apologies to the readers are all in the same level of abstraction; they are directed at the *prolegomena*, the second chapter of the book, and do not cope the main subject of the book, the

---

[47]"*Ordo autem instituto hic convenit, ut initio quid universim atque in genere verum sit videamus, idque ipsum contrahamus paulatim ad propositam facti speciem. Sed quemadmodum mathematici, priusquam ipsas demonstrationes aggrediantur, communes quasdam solent notiones, de quibus inter omnes facile constat praescribere, ut fixum aliquid sit, in quo retro desinat sequentium probatio, ita nos quo fundamentum positum habeamus, cui tuto superstruantur caetera, regulas quasdam et leges maxime generales indicabimus, velut anticipationes, quas non tam discere aliquis, quam reminisci debeat.*" (**DJPC**, p. 6).

materia belli. There is no doubt that the structure of the **De Jure Praedae** is innovative if compared to previous works on the law of war. However, while the manner of exposition thereof may be comparable to the labor of the mathematicians, it is not to be confused with their science.[48]

Furthermore, albeit of less importance, the use of the authorities (which is vehemently despised by Modern writers) persists as a matter of evidence in Grotius. Besides, in the following chapters, he intermingles the two sources of evidence that he tried so hard to distinguish.

On the one hand, if the use of an axiomatic–deductive structure in the *prolegomena* brings Grotius closer to the Modern scholars; on the other, the actual weight he gives to this element significantly separates him from them. The vague reference to the mathematicians proves that Grotius did not actually come into direct contact with the debates of the Paduan School, despite being privy to the discussions on method of his time. According to Vermeulen, it seems more likely that the source of this mathematic method/comparison was his proximity to the Physic Simon Stevin, a close friend of his family, and not Galileo or Zabarella.[49]

The attention that Grotius grants to the method in his early work is a mere reminiscence in the **De Jure Belli ac Pacis**; there are only a few references thereto in the *prolegomena*. Grotius begins discussing his goal by stating that, concerning the Law of Nations, "few scholars have tried addressing this domain, and none have done it to write a complete and methodic treatise."[50] This statement may seem self-congratulatory and even misplaced, since he was perfectly aware of the lack of originality in his intent. However, it is important to perceive the use of the words "complete" and "methodic." In paragraphs 36 and 37 of the *prolegomena*, he resumes this idea and expressly states that the authors that came before him, though in his opinion they "have **said next to nothing** new upon a fertile subject; most have done their work **without any system**, and in such a way as to intermingle and utterly confuse what belongs to the Law of Nature, to the Law of Nations, to Civil Law and to the body of laws which is found in the canons."[51] Grotius considers himself different from the others because of the way he addresses his subject; compared to his predecessors, his treatise is complete and well organized.

Although both the **De Jure Praedae Commentarius** and the **De Jure Belli ac Pacis** discuss the *materia belli*, the difference in their purposes is evident. In the latter, Grotius aims at thoroughness, which could not have been what he intended twenty years earlier, given that the **De Jure Praedae** is the work of a lawyer

[48]Haggenmacher (1983), p. 69.

[49]Vermeulen, 1983, p. 64.

[50]"*(…) attigeunt pauci, universum ac certo ordinem tractavit hactenus nemo* (…)" (**DJBP**. *prolegomenon* 1).

[51]"*(…) sed ni omnes de uberrimo argumento paucissima dixerunt, et ita plerique ut sine ordine quae naturalis sunt iuris, quae divini, quae gentium, quae civilis, quae ex canonibus veniunt, permiscerent atque confunderent*" (**DJBP**. *prolegomenon* 37).

defending his cause, not the work of a philosopher. It is significant that Grotius should appeal to God to lift his nation up and to frustrate the enemy's plans in the epilogue of the **De Jure Praedae Commentarius**, while in the last paragraph of the other book, his appeal to God is that He intervenes in favor of Mankind.[52]

This scientific commitment makes the **De Jure Belli ac Pacis** a purely theoretical work. It is in view thereof that one should interpret this new reference to the mathematicians:

> If anyone thinks that I have had in view any controversies of our own times, either those that have arisen or those which can be foreseen as likely to arise, he will do me an injustice. With all truthfulness, I state that, just as mathematicians treat their figures as abstracted from bodies, so in treating law have I withdrawn my mind from every particular fact.[53]

The work he composed in his mature days is theoretical in nature, with no practical goal whatsoever and distant from real events. He treated the law like a mathematician that dissociates abstract geometrical figures from real bodies. The methodological purpose of this comparison (if such exists) is much simpler than one would imagine it to be: it aims at justifying the absence of contemporary historical facts. By comparing his work with Geometry, Grotius does not employ the mathematical (or geometrical) method, not even a mathematical order, as was the case in the **De Jure Praedae**.

The systematization effort found in his earlier works takes on a new meaning in the **De Jure Belli ac Pacis**. The axiomatic–deductive structure, present in the second chapter of the **De Jure Praedae**, is no longer referred to. Instead,

> In my work as a whole I have, above all else, aimed at three things: to make the reasons for my conclusions as evident as possible; to set forth in a definite order the matters which needed to be treated; and to distinguish clearly between things which seemed to be the same and were not.[54]

Therefore, Grotius pursues three methodological rules in the course of the **De Jure Belli ac Pacis**: to base the institutes of the Law of War in strict evidence as much as possible; to organize the subject matters carefully; and to precisely distinguish similar, yet different institutes. Haggenmacher remarks that this methodological proposal refers to the classification of the sources of Law (Natural and

[52]**DJPC**, p. 341 and **DJBP**. III, 25, 8.

[53]"*Iniuriam mihi faciet si quis me ad ullas nostri saeculi controversias, aut natas, aut quae nasciturae praevideri possunt, respexisse arbitratur. Vere enim profiteor, sicut mathematici figuras à corporibus semotas considerant, ita me in iure tractando ab omni singulare facto abduxisse animum.*" (**DJBP**. *prolegomenon* 58).

[54]"*In toto opere tria maxime mihi proposui, ut definiendi rationes redderem quam maxime evidentes, et ut quae erant tractanda ordine certo disponerem, et ut quae cadem inter se videri poterant necerant, perspicue distinguerem* (**DJBP**. *prolegomenon* 56).

Voluntary Law, Divine and Civil Law, the Law of Nations and the "smaller than Civil" Law) that Grotius presents in the first chapter.[55]

He seems to ground the sources of law in principles and notions so essential as to make them irrefutable. In the case of Natural Law, this becomes emblematic. He bases Natural Law in "fundamental conceptions which are beyond question, so that no one can deny them without doing violence to himself. For the principles of that law, if only you pay strict heed to them, are in themselves manifest and clear, almost as evident as are those things which we perceive by the external senses."[56] Apparently, evidence in this form of *jus* is due to its rational essence. This may be accurate but is still incomplete. In Grotius' opinion, "evidence" is not simply a rational, abstract, and intellectual deduction; it is also a perception through our senses. What we perceive is evidence. That is why Natural Law (which is based in reason) is as evident as Civil Law because the latter may be written in a legal *codex* or heard through the mouth of a legislator and as such perceptible.

The Law of Nations is equally evident. To prove the existence thereof (and as an auxiliary proof of Natural Law), Grotius uses the testimony of the ancient authorities (philosophers, historians, poets, and orators). He does not trust them blindly (since they have the habit of distorting the truth to please the interests of their own school of thought), but when so many individuals, of such different times and places, agree on something, it can only mean that this something derives from the same cause. That cause may result from natural principles or from consensus. The former reveals Natural Law and the latter reveals the *jus gentium*.[57]

This notion of evidence encompasses empirical data, which means that Grotius would disagree with Charron's assaults on Aristotle's epistemological realism or was simply not familiar with it. In either case, it is evident that Grotius did not know of Descartes and Galileo's aprioristic conceptions.

On the other hand, given its recurrence, the theme of the *Ordo* is almost an imperative for Grotius. In the **De Jure Praedae**, he aims at being as orderly as mathematicians are and, in this latter book, in *prolegomenon* 37, he criticized his predecessors for their lack of thoroughness and order. The reason why he insists on this point is that he intended to write a complete and systematic text on the Law of War, accompanied by an adequate categorization of the sources of *jus belli*, right from the start. This classification enables him to separate what exactly in the Law of War stems from Natural Law from that which stems from Divine Law and from the Law of Nations. His predecessors "have said next to nothing new upon a fertile subject; most have done their work without any system, and in such a way as to intermingle and utterly **confuse what belongs to the Law of Nature, to the Law of**

[55]Haggenmacher (1983), p. 452.

[56]"*(...) notiones quasdam tam certas ut eas nemo negare possit, nisi sibi vim inferat. Principia enim eius iuris* per se *patent atque evidentia sunt, multo magis quam quae sensibus externis percibimus* (...)" (**DJBP**. *prolegomenon* 39).

[57]**DJBP**. *prolegomenon* 40.

Nations, to Civil Law and to the body of laws which is found in the canons."[58] This reference to the lack of organization of past writers of the Just War tradition is found in the same context as his criticism on their confusion of the sources of *jus belli*. Here lies the importance of the *Ordo* for Grotius' system: through the *Ordo*, Grotius manages to escape the Roman sphere of *jus gentium*.

The third methodological rule, the distinction between heterogeneous things, refers to the categorization of sources once again. Besides distinguishing *jus gentium* from Natural Law (there existed a persistent conceptual indefiniteness hovering over these terms, as we have seen in the first chapter), Grotius also distinguishes Natural from Voluntary Law. This differentiation corresponds to the first and main distinction introduced by the author when discussing the sources of law.[59] Voluntarism dominated the Reformed cultural universe to the point that Natural Law itself was voluntary. Nevertheless, this generated an enormous confusion regarding Positive Law. According to Grotius and even Suárez, voluntarism is the main feature of Positive Law, not the fact that it is in written (for that would also exclude the customs from Positive Law). The duality between Natural and Voluntary Law plays a key role in the development of the **De Jure Belli ac Pacis** (as it does in the **De Legibus**). If Natural and Voluntary Law are not distinguished one from the other, the task of making a science of the Law is likely to fail.

> Many heretofore have purposed to give to this subject [the law of war] a well-ordered presentation; no one has succeeded. And in fact such a result cannot be accomplished unless – a point which until now has not been sufficiently kept in view – those elements which come from Positive Law are properly separated from those which arise from Nature. For the principles of the Law of Nature, since they are always the same, can easily be brought into a systematic form; but the elements of Positive Law, since they often undergo change and are different in different places, are outside the domain of systematic treatment, just as other notions of singular things are.[60]

Grotius intended to write a theoretical text, reason why it was necessary to keep track of the regularity and steadiness of the phenomena that was his subject of study. However, only Natural Law is invariable and universal; Positive Law is changeable and based in the opinion, in the *doxa*. Grotius' predecessors could not write a theoretical work because they mistook positive elements for natural ones, and vice versa.

Therefore, the three methodological rules do not relate to either the geometrical or the mathematical methods. They refer to the thoroughness and systematization

---

58"*(...) sed ni omnes de uberrimo argumento paucissima dixerunt, et ita plerique ut sine ordine quae naturalis sunt iuris, quae divini, quae gentium, quae civilis, quae ex canonibus veniunt, permiscerent atque confunderent*" (**DJBP**. *prolegomenon* 37).

59**DJBP**. I, 1, 9.

60"*Artis formam ei imponere multi ante hac destinarunt: perfecit nemo: neque vero fieri potest nisi, quod non fatis curatum est hactenus, ea quae ex constituto veniunt a naturalibus recte separentur. nam naturalia cum semper eadem sint facille possunt in artem colligi: illa autem quae ex constituto veniunt, cum et mutentur saepe et alibi alia sint, extra artem posita sunt, ut aliae rerum singularium perceptiones.*" (**DJBP**. *prolegomenon* 30).

that he ambitioned in writing the **De Jure Belli ac Pacis**. There is no doubt that they are methodological concerns—but nothing like Descartes' or Galileo's. They resemble the efforts at systematizing the study of Law endeavored by the French jurists in the *mos gallicus*. Their attention to method was consistent with the spirit of their time, but it never reached the level of concern or the sophistication of the Paduan School.

Lastly, that which Grotius considered method in the **De Jure Praedae** reappears as a means of evidence twenty years later. He verifies Natural Law *a priori* by the conformity of the thing to its rational and social nature and *a posteriori* by the agreement among all nations (or at least the most "civilized" ones)[61] in respect thereto. The opinions found in ancient texts, in the Bible and in the good scholars also provide "historical evidence." In the **De Jure Belli ac Pacis**, Grotius gives more weight to the *a priori* evidence, employing the *a posteriori* evidence solely for confirmation purposes. Nonetheless, the relevance of the *a posteriori* evidence should not be dismissed, since it is thereby that the Law of Nations is "evidenced."

The criticism that Grotius directs at his predecessors in *prolegomenon* 38 concerning their lack of "historical light" is actually a disapproval of their methodological choices: they did not possess enough evidence to base their arguments on. Thence, they compensated by elevating Aristotle's thought to the degree of absolute truth, which Grotius found to be detrimental, albeit his own style seemed a bit too ornamental. He used those authorities to provide himself with historical certainty. However, Grotius' use of history is in no way similar to that of a contemporary historian; he simply referred to events that took place in Antiquity—the older the examples, the stronger they were. In addition, his references were always indirect, made through the Bible or through Classical scholars. The employment of history in the study of law represents for Grotius a methodological concern.

The methodological concern that Grotius experienced in his time was widespread and can be seen as a reaction to the Medieval tradition. Some of those efforts became what we term Modernity, while others were left behind. However, in general, the study of method did not take up as much space for Grotius as it did for Descartes and his followers. According to Haggenmacher, Grotius' epistemology is still somewhat "naïve," typical of the pre-Modern cultural universe.[62] However, agreeing on what constitutes a Modern method is an important task in this context. If Descartes' and Galileo's methods are to be considered the only Modern methods, then Grotius is nothing more than a representative of the *mos gallicus* in the law of war. But this opinion leaves even the English Empiricists out of Modernity.

---

[61]**DJBP**. I, 1, 12.

[62]Haggenmacher (1983), p. 69.

4.3 The Theory of Law

The fact that Grotius uses the word *jus* more often than *lex* is telling. He knew that the latter corresponded only to one type of the former. As I have displayed, the Medieval Theologians and the Spanish Scholastics knew and employed this idea since Isidore of Seville. Yet, they all engendered one theory of Laws and another of Law, because both that was how Aquinas had organized the **Summa** and law, in a broad meaning, transcended justice itself (which was the subject of the Laws) and represented God's orderly design for all creation. However, this idea (of the *lex aeterna*) is not actually useful in a legal work that did not intend to comment the **Summa**. And thus, for Grotius, the theory of the Law includes the theory of the Laws.

Nonetheless, the distinction of these two realities is not always clear in Grotius' work. Despite its axiomatic–deductive structure, in the **De Jure Praedae**, the *jus* expressly appears as a command, as an obligation. Soon after enunciating the first law of nature, Grotius affirms "Indeed, it would seem that the very term *ius* [right] is derived from *Iovis* [Jove] and that the same process of derivation holds good for *iurare* [to swear] and *iusiurandum* [an oath] or *Iovisiurandum* [an oath in the name of Jove]. Alternatively, one might trace the development of these terms to the fact that the ancients designated as *iusa*—that is to say *iussa* [things commanded]—those precepts which we designate as *iura* [rights]. In any case, the act of commanding is a function of power."[63] Therefore, the law means *lex*. However, Haggenmacher seems to have found two different hidden meanings.[64]

> We have seen what constitutes *jus* [rights]: and from it, we derive also the definition of wrong or injury (*iniuria*) guided by the basic belief that this term refers to whatever is done in opposition to the law. Accordingly, **an action is just whereby the various rules and laws grant a right to someone**, whereas actions of a contrary nature are unjust.[65]

When confronting these four notions (*ius* and *iniura*, just and unjust action), the initial concept of *jus* as law seems to change. One should note that *ius* and *iniura*, although perfect opposites, are not in the same level of abstraction: by defining the last term as *quidquid non iure fiat*, Grotius introduces the adverbial ablative *iure*, which presupposes a relation of convenience or inconvenience. Thus, "injury" does not refer to that which does not follow a command or a law, but to that which does not conform to justice.

In his work of maturity, the three concepts (the explicit concept and the two hidden ones) are well distinguished and explained. Right after defining war, Grotius turns his attention to the law. He relates the first meaning of the term to the title of

---

[63]"(...) *jus a Jove dictum, unde et jurare et jusjurandum, Jovisjurandum: aut quia vetere que nos jura dicimus, jusa, hoc est jussa dixerunt. Jubere autem potestatis est.*" (**DJPC**, p. 8).

[64]Haggenmacher (1983), p. 61.

[65]"*Quid jus sit vidimus: unde iniuria etiam noscitur, generali scilicet notione, ut id significet quidquid non jure fiat. Qua igitur actione jus ad eum, cui secundum regulas ac leges competit, perducitur, haec justa est: quae secus, injusta.*" (**DJPC**, p. 30).

his treatise, **De Jure Belli**: he intends to research whether there can be a just war and if so what would be just about it. In this regard, *ius* is synonym of *iustum*, in a more negative sense: that which is not just. And: "what disgusts the nature of rational beings is unjust."[66] The just corresponds to a relation between two individuals, to a fair state of things. To a certain extent, this meaning of "just" relates to Aristotle's *dikaion*, but it differs from the Aristotelian concept due to its Stoic origins, in the clear quotations of Cicero, Florentin, and Seneca. The reference to the three Roman philosophers explains his penchant for a negative definition, for they focused on violations of the social interactions and their consequences: the equation focuses on the unjust and not on the just. For this reason, this meaning of just is not exactly precise.

However, in the following paragraph, Grotius trims the edges of the definition and demonstrates his eclecticism. He separates this *jus* (or justice) according to two social relations. Between equals (brothers, citizens, friends, and allies) the *jus aequatorium* rules; and between non-equals (father and son, lord and slave, king and subjects, God and men) the *jus rectorium* (ruling) reigns. Not without problems, this definition dates back to Aristotle's opposition between justice properly termed and domestic justice, which governs the relations, on the one side, between the man of the household and his wife, and on the other side, between him and his children and slaves—the Scholastics have always developed this antagonism. Grotius specifically refers to Aristotle when he introduces this definition. Therefore, those[67] who argued that Grotius distanced himself from the theological tradition of the just war, according to which "just" were only those actions positively sanctioned by God, are proven wrong. In this point, as in so many others, Grotius unites the Stoic doctrine and Aristotelian-Thomism.

As a result, pursuant to this first meaning, Law equals the virtue of justice. On the other hand, justice refers to everything that is not unjust. Lastly, unjust is everything that is loathed by rational nature. It seems tempting to establish a link between this notion of *jus* and Natural Law. However, there is no identity between these two notions, as I shall explain later on. For now, suffice it to say that, not unlike Suárez, Grotius considers that there is a component of will in the formation of Natural Law.

Next, Grotius introduces another meaning of Law, one that derives from the previous sense, but refers to the individual. It is "a moral quality inherent to a person, making it possible to have or to do something lawfully."[68] Pursuant to this second meaning, a person is entitled to a consideration from another person (*jus in personas*) or to a thing (*jus in rem*). He explains that this right is always attached to the person even if it on occasion follows the thing, as is the case in *in rem* rights. In this case, the *jus* does not stem from the thing, as Romans would have it, but from

---

[66]"*Est autem iniustum quod naturae societatis ratione utentium repugnat.*" (**DJBP**. I, 1, 3, 1).

[67]Tadashi (1993), p. 33.

[68]"*Qualitas moralis personae competens ad aliquid iuste habendum vel agendum.*" (**DJBP**. I, 1, 4).

the individual himself; the individual, and only the individual, has power over that thing.

Michel Villey considered this the first definition of subjective right.[69] However, as I have presented in the previous chapter, Francisco Suárez had already come up with a similar definition: "moral power each one has over what is his or over what it is owed to him."[70] The resemblance is clear. Although there are no references to the **De Legibus**, it seems likely that Grotius found inspiration in Suárez's work.

It is possible to divide the *jus* into faculty, when perfect, as being equivalent to an action, and aptitude, when imperfect, which is equivalent to a possibility (*potentia*). This division corresponds to Aristotle's distinction between actuality and potentiality. The faculty is the right itself, the *suum*, and denotes that its holder may demand the fulfillment thereof; it designates a power-obligation, and Grotius associates it with the expletive justice. The faculty unfolds as power (*potestas*), property (*dominium*) and credit rights (*credita*). The faculty of *potestas* encompasses the power over oneself or freedom (*libertas*), the power over one's own household (*potestas patria*) or over one's slaves (*potestas domenica*). By its turn, property encompasses the usufruct (*usufructus*), the pledge (*jus pignoris*) and, when absolute, the domain (*dominium plenum*). To credit corresponds only debit (*debitum*). Based on another criterion, faculty may be popular (*vulgaris*) or superior (*eminens*). The former takes place between private citizens, while the community exercises the latter over its members and their property for the common good. Therefore, concerning the people, the king has the same powers that a father has over his children or a lord has over his slaves. The ruler also possesses eminent domain (*dominium eminens*) over all the belongings of his subjects, overruling private property (*dominium privatum*).[71]

It is worth mentioning that the Modern notion of subjective right derives from Grotius' "faculty," albeit these ideas are not truly identical. In fact, Grotius' concept seems broader than today's. In addition to the individual rights of private persons, the concept encompasses public powers as well (which stems from the superior faculty). Here, Grotius distances himself from the Scholastic tradition: there is equivalence between individual and collective rights (powers and freedoms). The State is entitled to the same rights that an individual is. The dissonance between Grotius and Scholasticism will become clearer in the following chapters.

On the other hand, aptitude refers to the distributive justice and stems from a person's merit. It is not exactly a right: the fact that something seems adequate for someone does not entitle said person to a legitimate claim over said something. The purpose of the aptitude is to distribute goods such as freedom, forgiveness, and good government.[72] The infringement of a faculty (and not of an aptitude) constitutes cause for a just war.

---

[69]Villey (1962), p. 221.

[70]"*(…) ius vocari facultas quaedam moralis, quam unusquisque habet vel circa rem suam vela d rem sibi debitam*" (**DL**. I, 2, 5).

[71]**DJBP**. I, 1, 4-6.

[72]**DJBP**. I, 1, 4 and 7.

Grotius associates the faculty with the expletive (or commutative) justice, but it also encompasses the relations between unequal people, as is the case of superior faculty (*eminens*), which is traditionally associated with distributive justice. During the Middle Ages, the notions of distributive and commutative justice were the subject of successive reinterpretations based on several aspects inherent to each of them. The commutative justice may involve a relation between equals or a correction: the return of something to his rightful owner. Differently, the distributive justice may involve not only an unequal relationship but also the distribution of public goods, based on merit, need, or any other universal criterion previously chosen. Traditionally, these functions were combined, which does not entail that they were logically inseparable. Richard Tuck argues that Grotius was simply freely interpreting Aristotle's work, since he rejected the Greek philosopher's criterion of distinction between geometrical and arithmetical proportions.[73] However, the basis of the Grotian association lies in the categorization idealized by Suárez, for whom faculty also relates to commutative justice, while *fas* is the subject matter of distributive justice. Just like Grotius' notion of "aptitude," *fas* is not a full right. It takes place amongst non-equal persons, but Suárez conceived a greater inequality, that between man and God: the creature could never sufficiently repay its Maker. Thus, the importance of the *fas* lies in the impossibility of equitable retribution, rather than purporting to some sort of hierarchy.

There are many similarities between Grotius and Suárez's notions of subjective rights—but Grotius designed an entirely new conceptual system of it. In the **De Jure Praedae**, he does not discuss the definition of *jus* as *facultas*, but introduces four rights as belonging (as a faculty does) to the individual: self-defense, vindication of an *in rem* right, the claim of an *in personam* right and the punishment for a violation.[74] Grotius envisaged these rights *a contrario* sensu, not as the *jus*, but as the *iniuria* capable of legitimizing a war. The *iniuria* was an all-encompassing category closely linked to the axiomatic–deductive structure of the second chapter of his book. Self-defense descends from the first law ("it shall be permissible to defend [one's own] life and to shun that which threatens to prove injurious"); the right to property descends from the second law ("it shall be permissible to acquire for oneself, and to retain, those things which are useful for life"); the private right to credit descends from the sixth ("good deeds must be recompensed"); and the right to sanction wrongdoings from the fifth ("evil deeds must be corrected").[75] Subjective rights occupy a relevant place in Grotius' work: the violation of any of these rights represents a material cause for war in **De Jure Praedae**.

There is a distinctive similarity between the *facultas* of twenty years later and these subjective rights. Self-defense belongs in *potestas* (*libertas*), the claim of an *in*

---

[73]Tuck (1979), p. 75.

[74]**DJPC**, pp. 67–68.

[75]**DJPC**, pp. 10 and 15.

rem right belongs in *dominium*; the pursuit of an *in personam* right belongs in *creditum* and the right to punish is the means by which one ensures the faithfull compliance to the *facultas* as a whole. As will be seen, faculty plays in the **De Jure Belli ac Pacis** a role similar to the subjective rights system of the **De Jure Praedae**. In addition, as Grotius does not distinguish individual from State rights (they are all "subjective rights"), he will accept the legitimacy of private wars.

In its third and last meaning, *jus* becomes a synonym of *lex*. However, a word of caution is due: the term *lex* is used here in a very broad and not technical sense: law refers to all rules that are mandatory not only from the perspective of justice, but also from the perspective of other virtues. It is a "rule of moral action which forces those who are honest."[76] The object of these norms is the honest (*rectum*), not the *iustum*, which provides an understanding much broader than its legal meaning. Haggenmacher points out that Grotius employs Cicero's terminology (the *rectum*), whilst referring to Aristotle's idea of justice as a general virtue. This concept of law excludes advice and all other precepts that are not mandatory. For the author, the permission is not a valid manifestation of law, it is rather its mere absence. Everything not forbidden by law is permitted.

Therefore, Grotius does not separate Law from justice and takes part in a tradition tracing back to Aristotle. In spite of recognizing the three meanings of *jus,* Grotius does not attempt to draft a radical distinction between them and considers them all as a whole. Thus, one can read the title of his work **The Law of War and Peace** in three different senses: the justice of war (or just war), the right to war (when possible to exercise this right) and the laws of war.

As well put by a commentator,[77] Grotius does not distinguish Natural Law from natural rights. This distinction will come up in Modern scholars, and the Modern theory on natural rights would provide the basis for the classical liberal revolutions. In this matter, Grotius places himself firmly in the Medieval line of reasoning. However, Suárez and he are at the outer edges of the Middle Ages signalizing what was to come. Benefiting from this privileged position, they enjoyed the virtues of the old and of the new, without incurring in their vices. Unlike the Medieval scholars in general, the jurists of Delft and Coimbra did not consider the law to be a mere list of obligations, but rather understood it as something that emanated fom rational people. The law would also closely relate to justice. For Hobbes, once the State is formed, it is up to the ruler alone to enunciate the laws and to interpret Natural Law as he pleases. The other side of Modernity preaches ethical voluntarism. Before I discuss the categorization of the laws in Grotius, it is important to examine his thoughts on skepticism and relativism, which presupposes the theme of the natural sociability of men.

[76]"*Regula actuum moralium obligans ad id quod rectum est*" (**DJBP**. I, 1 9, 1).

[77]Tadashi (1993), pp. 35–36.

4.3.1 Grotius' Sociability and Modernity: Between Aristotle and the Stoics

Grotius marks a milestone between the Medieval theory of law and the Modern theory of law. He seals the progressive immanence of the law set off by Suárez. He separated the concepts of *lex* and *jus*, if only for didactic purposes. A treatise on the law of war is not equivalent to a book on Theology; despite its intrinsic morality, there is no transcendence in its object. That is why many scholars believe that Grotius did not have the concept of *lex aeterna*: there was no need to refer to this kind of law in a legal text.

Law, rights, and justice are realities that only ideally differ from each other. Thus, Grotius finds himself at the same level of Suárez: The law (in a broad sense, encompassing the notion of rights) is humanized, but does not lose its ethical purpose. Neither Suárez nor Grotius exhausts the progressive immanence of the legal phenomenon—the next step would bring along the secularization and, unfortunately, the disbelief in absolute values. There would be no other criterion with which to analyze the legitimacy of a law other than the will of the ruler. To avoid authoritarian regimes, the criteria employed today are merely formal and, although grounded on immanence, this conception of universal justice would be lost in the corners of history.

According to Grotius, law and justice are inseparable ideas. This is not merely a personal opinion: as Grotius relied on Natural Law to build his theory of law, this proposition is the very basis thereof. As a result, Grotius' first task is to disprove everyone that disagrees with him on this. He was well aware that the arguments to the contrary carried the weight of tradition. There were always those, such as Euphemus, quoted by Thucydides, who argued that nothing that is useful for a sovereign could be unjust.[78] It is a recurring conception of (in)justice, found in all traditions of political realism and immortalized in the words of Thrasymachus against Socrates in the dialogue **The Republic**: "justice is nothing but the advantage of the strongest."[79]

There were other arguments besides the one above that could erode the foundations of Grotius' system. Hence, Grotius chooses someone who embodies all the

[78]**DJBP**. *prolegomenon* 3.

[79]"Because you fancy that the shepherd or neatherd fattens or tends the sheep or oxen with a view to their own good and not to the good of himself or his master; and you further imagine that the rulers of states, if they are true rulers, never think of their subjects as sheep, and that they are not studying their own advantage day and night. Oh, no; and so entirely astray are you in your ideas about the just and unjust as not even to know that justice and the just are in reality another's good; that is to say, the interest of the ruler and stronger, and the loss of the subject and servant; and injustice the opposite; for the unjust is lord over the truly simple and just: he is the stronger, and his subjects do what is for his interest, and minister to his happiness, which is very far from being their own." (Platão. 1976, p. 65).

main arguments against justice: the ancient skeptic Carneades, who became famous for demeaning the Stoics' Natural Law. Carneades raised three objections to the idea of justice:

> [1] men imposed upon themselves laws, which vary according to customs, and among the same peoples often undergo changes as times change; [2] moreover that there is no Law of Nature, because all creatures, men as well as animals, are impelled by nature toward ends advantageous to themselves; [3] that, consequently, there is no justice, or, if such there be, it is supreme folly, since one does violence to his own interests if he consults the advantage of others.[80]

In the seventeenth century, new skeptics such as Charron and Montagine attacked not only Aristotle's epistemology, but also his Ethics, for the sake of cultural relativism. Richard Tuck could not help but notice this coincidence and concluded that Grotius actually intended to refute contemporary skeptics,[81] but directed his attacks at Carneades in the name of a Humanist elegance.

This it is not a hollow analogy: based on this argument, Tuck defends Grotius' Modernity. Modern scholars intended to rebuild human knowledge beyond the Medieval Theocentricism. When it is no longer possible to resort to God to justify morality, there are only two options left: to adopt a skeptical and relativist posture or to attempt to base morality on men themselves.

Hobbes and other Modern scholars preferred the latter. According to Hobbes, "A Law of Nature (*lex naturalis*) is a command or a general rule, **established by reason**, which forbids a man to do anything that is destructive of his life or takes away his means for preserving his life, and forbids him to omit anything by which he thinks his life can best be preserved."[82] Human reason is not only in charge of perceiving Natural Law; it creates it. Other Modern scholars tend to share this view and to ascribe to reason a legislative role.

Yet, Hobbes is known for becoming one of the most ardent opponents of the Aristotelian idea of natural sociability or, at least, of the Scholastics' version thereof. Thence, sociability is not a natural instinct: by nature, man is not a *zoon politikón*; on the contrary, in his natural state, he leans toward degradation. Man's only natural impulse is the accomplishment of his egotistical desires. Man is a passionate being, with intense desires that impel him towards constant dissatisfaction. In the state of nature, man faces some conditions that are out of his hands and that puts him in a greater conflict: the natural equality, the lack of goods and the rights that everyone is entitled to (and which derive from the same Natural Law that

---

[80]"(...) *iura sibi homines pro utilitate sanxisse varia pro moribus, et apud eosdem pro temporibus saepe mutata: ius autem naturale esse nullum: omnes enim et homines et alias animantes ad utilitates suas natura ducente ferri: proinde aut nullam esse iustitiam; quoniam sibi noceat alienis commodis consulens.*" (**DJBP**. *prolegomenon* 5).

[81]Tuck (1983), p. 44.

[82]Hobbes (1983), Chapter XIV, p. 78.

compels him to seek his self-preservation) over all things (*jus in omnia*). This scenario fuels competition, mutual distrust and the search for glory.[83] That is why, in nature, instead of the Scholastic tendency to live in community and to search for God, man finds himself in a state of war against everyone.

Notwithstanding, reason may save this miserable man. Afraid of a violent death, each person acknowledges the advantage (and, for Hobbes, the usefulness is equivalent to Law) of seeking peace and renouncing the *jus in omnia*—these calculations refer to the first and second Natural Law. Nonetheless, obeying these laws would be pointless and even dangerous if not everyone else followed suit. Thus, the need for a third law: the *pacta sunt servanda.*[84] This is the basis of the Hobbesian social contract theory; the State is built at the same that social life is created. These Natural Laws are nothing more than mere rational and utilitarian calculations derived from one principle: self-preservation. It is undoubtedly an objective morality, because every man fears death and yet it provides an answer to skeptical relativism. However, Hobbes made virtue out of selfishness and accepted Carneades second thesis: all beings move according to their own utilities. He did not declare the end of Natural Law only because he changed what was usually ascribed to it.

Grotius' position on this issue is full of nuances. A cursory reading of the **De Jure Belli ac Pacis** may lead one to believe that Grotius sticks to Aristotle and Aquinas" teachings, given the express references to natural sociability. Man is an animal, but a "naturally superior" animal, significantly different from all other species. Among other things unique to man is the need for society, an *appetites societatis.*

This interpretation (which follows the traditional way of studying Grotius' work) associates Grotius with the Aristotle's thesis of man being a *zoon politikón*, a political, social and rational animal. It is thanks to that interpretation that Grotius was considered the father of Modern legal philosophy. Grotius' response to skeptical relativism no longer consists of basing morality in God: he considered morality a human quality. This is why this sociability is not a thoughtless tendency, but a "conscientious inclination, which assumes the consideration of relevant motives, rational preference for order, among other possible orders."[85] Man does not seek to live simply; he wants to live well. And he employs reason for that end:

> (…) together with an impelling desire for society, for the gratification of which he alone among animals possesses a special instrument, speech. He has also been endowed with the faculty of knowing and of acting in accordance with general principles. Whatever accords with that faculty is not common to all animals, but peculiar to the nature of man.[86]

---

[83]Hobbes (1983), pp. 74–78.

[84]Hobbes (1983), pp. 78, 79, 86.

[85]"(…) *inclinação consciente, que pressupõe a apreciação de motivos determinantes, a preferência racional por uma ordem dentre as muitas ordens possíveis*" (Reale 2000, p. 105).

[86]"*Homini vero perfectae aetatis, cum circa similia similiter, agere norit, cum societatis appetitu excellente, cujus peculiare solus inter animantes instrumentum habet sermonem, inesse etiam facultatem sciendi agendique, secundum generalia praecepta, par este intelligi, cui quae conveniunt ea jam sunt non omnium quidem animantibum, sed humanae naturae congruentia.*" (**DJBP**. *prolegomenon* 7).

Man is not gregarious the way bees are. His choosing to live in society is a rational decision. Sociability is inherently human to the extent that reason is in man's nature. Reason and *appetitus societatis* are both natural, but the latter only exists because of the former. The ground for Natural Law lies in this conscientious and well thought sociability. In effect, the *jus* proceeds from the human natural sociability, a secular, not a divine fact. Therefore, both Grotius' and Hobbes's Natural Law are rational, and reason plays an important role not only in unveiling, but also in creating it. The difference between the two is the initial impulse: for Hobbes, it is self-preservation, for Grotius, sociability.

I shall discuss Grotius's impious hypothesis at the appropriate moment. For now, it is worth pointing out that the traditional interpretation of Grotius considers the impious hypothesis a demonstration of his secularism, which adjusts well to the idea that Grotius would be a Modern scholar. That is how the impious hypothesis arises upon the controversy with Carneades: Natural Law emanates from man himself, from a human phenomenon (sociability), not from the divine. Grotius would thus forever bury the idea of the Godly origin of law.

However, this could not be a hastier reading. Even those who support Grotius' Modernity, such as Tuck, consider this interpretation misleading. Grotius natural sociability is not the same as Aristotle's: Grotius' man is not a *zoon politikón*. There is a greater dose of selfishness in him, although not to the point of Hobbes' *homo homini lupus*. Before his death, Grotius read the **De Cive** and, in a letter to his brother, showed his disagreement with Hobbes's anthropology: "I read the **De Cive**. And I was very pleased about what he had to say about the kings. I cannot, however, agree with the points on which his argument lies. He argues that, naturally, there is a war between men, among other ideas I do not agree with."[87] Between Hobbes' selfish man and the naturally social man of Aristotle and of the Scholastics, there are several levels of sociability and selfishness.

In the **De Jure Praedae**, Grotius does not seem to place sociability at the center. On the contrary, the drive for self-preservation is. The first rule (that which God showed to be His will is law) establishes a primary Natural Law, and the first two Natural Laws refer to self-preservation: "it shall be permissible to defend [one's own] life and to shun that which threatens to prove injurious" and "it shall be permissible to acquire for oneself, and to retain, those things which are useful for life."[88]

---

[87]"*Librum de* Cive *vidi. Placent que pro Regibus dicit. Fundamenta tamen quibus suas sententias superstruit, probare non possum. Putat inter homines a natura esse bellum et alia quaedam habet nostris non congruentia*" (Grotii, Hugonis. Letter to Willem de Groot of April 1643. **Briefwisseling XIV**, p. 199).

[88]"*Vitam tueri et declinare nocitura liceat*" and "*Adjungere sibi quae ad vivendum sunt utilia eaque retinere liceat*" (**DJPC**, p. 10).

Divine will instills into each individual part of the Creation certain "natural properties," which, by nature, seek their own preservation and well fare. This comes from a passage, quoted by Tuck to prove Grotius' proximity to Modern scholars, in which he expressly concurs with Hobbes' reasoning in the **De Cive** and **Leviathan**:

> Therefore, since God fashioned creation and willed its existence, every individual part thereof has received from Him certain natural properties whereby that existence may be preserved and each part may be guided for its own good, in conformity, one might say, with the fundamental law inherent in its origin. From this fact the old poets and philosophers have rightly deduced that love, whose primary force and action are directed to self-interest, is the first principle of the whole natural order. Consequently, Horace should not be censured for saying, in imitation of the Academics, that expediency might perhaps be called the mother of justice and equity.[89]

Hobbes himself could not have said it better. The first and foremost impulse in any living being is to ensure its own survival, which does not encompass self-defense only, but everything that is needed for life. By establishing this as law, Grotius created an important connection between justice and utility. But if this interpretation is true, then why would Grotius criticize Hobbes' anthropology?

Such criticism results from the fact that Grotius does not stop at self-preservation; in addition to the love for oneself, the divine will instills in its creatures (especially in rational beings) the love for others.

> But God judged that there would be insufficient provision for the preservation of His works, if He commended to each individual's care only the safety of that particular individual, without also willing that one created being should have regard for the welfare of his fellow beings, in such a way that all might be linked in mutual harmony as if by an everlasting covenant. Seneca has said: "You must live for others, if you would live for yourself." Love, then, is twofold: love for oneself, and love for others. In the former aspect, it is known as "desire"; in the latter, as "friendliness."[90]

Grotius even refers to Aquinas in this passage. The original sin marred this love for others, but not enough to block the divine light. There is an agreement among all men over what is right and true: a universal agreement derived from a common cause. That is the secondary Natural Law or the primary Law of Nations: that which the agreement of all of humanity has proven to be the will of everyone is the law (second rule).[91]

---

[89] "*Cum igitur res conditas Deus esse fecerit et esse voluerit, proprietates quasdam naturales singulis indidit, quibus ipsum illud esse conservaretur et quibus ad bonum suum unumquodque, velut ex prima originis lege, duceretur. Unde principium totius naturalis ordinis recte poetae et philosophi veteres amorem statuerunt, cujus prima vis primaque actio reciproca est in se ipsum. Qua ratione culpandum non est quod secutus Academicos Horatius utilitatem justi et aequi prope matrem dixit.*" (**DJPC**, p. 9 and Tuck 1983, p. 52).

[90] "*At vero non satis conservationi operum suorum provisum Deus credidit, si suam duntaxat incolumitatem cuique commendaret, nisi et rem alteram alterius commodis vellet consulere, ut cuncta inter se velut aeterno foedere consentirent. Seneca: 'alteri vivas oportet, si vis tibis vivere'. Duplex itaque est amor, sui et alterius, quorum ille cupidinis, hic amicitiae dicitur.*" (**DJPC**, p. 11).

[91] **DJPC**, p. 12.

Grotius unites Hobbes's instinct of self-preservation and the Scholastics' sociability under one system. Both inclinations constitute sources of Natural Law: the former is the source of the primary Natural Law and the latter is the source of the secondary Natural Law. Nonetheless, this association does not express Grotius' eclecticism. In this, he found inspiration in the authors most frequently referred to in his work: the Stoic scholars.

The Stoic scholars associated love for oneself with the love for others in a simple manner. Zeno and Chrysippus did accept Epicureanism's claim that the search for pleasure and aversion to pain were the first impulses. The most basic inclinations, the *oikeiosis*, followed the nature established by the law of the divine One, which governs all human laws. Thus, the *oikeiosis* refers to all innate drives of beings, the most important of which is survival. The principle of pain and pleasure could apply here, but with caution, for the concern with survival transcends the individual to reach the species. Love for others is also a primary instinct. In its most intense manifestation (which the care for one's own offspring), this drive is capable of overpowering even the concern for oneself and self-preservation. As kinship weakens, so does the love for others. However, due to the consanguinity of all men, this love for others remains a reminiscent that compels them towards unity. For Stoicism, especially for its Roman version, bonds of blood unite men. There exists a natural equality among all, simply because we are all human beings and mankind takes part in the divine essence. Man, because he is man, is a citizen of the world. Grotius, in the *prolegomenon* 24 of the **De Jure Belli ac Pacis**, quotes one of Marcus Aurelius' phrases from **Meditations**: *civita set patria mihi ut Antonio Roma, ut homini mundus.*[92]

As one can already envisage, the Stoic influence on Grotius would play a relevant role in the very conception of *jus gentium*, for there is a natural brotherhood among all men. The idea of a universal human society densely permeates Cicero's writings. For example, he affirms "those who are only concerned with the citizens, but not with the foreigners break the common social bond of the human genus [*communem humani generis societatem*]."[93] Several centuries later, Grotius would share this very understanding without hiding its Stoic origins:

> Seneca has said: "Just as all the bodily members function in mutual harmony because it is to the advantage of the whole that the individual parts be preserved, even so mankind will show forbearance toward individuals because we are born for a life of fellowship. Society, too, can be kept safe from harm only by love and watchful care for its component." Elsewhere, he declares that, "Security must be obtained by offering security in exchange." Herein lies that brotherhood of man, that world state, commended to us so frequently and so enthusiastically by the ancient philosophers and particularly by the Stoics, whose view Cicero adopts. This view is also the basis of the statement made by Florentinus, namely,

[92]Berljak (1978), pp. 47–57.

[93]**De Officiis**. III, vi, 28.

that because of a certain kinship established among us by nature, it is sinful that man should lie in ambush for his fellow man, a precept which Cicero very properly ascribes to the Law of Nations.[94]

The reference to the human body serves to illustrate the communion efforts among men, the need for interaction. It does not refer to a collectivity above human beings. Free from this *avant la letter* organicism, the Stoic understanding of natural sociability is far more elusive than Aristotle's, at least according to the Scholastic version thereof. Richard Tuck warns that every time Cicero attempts to explain human sociability, he ends up emphasizing its debility.[95] For instance, in **De Amicitia**, he distinguishes *amicitia* (friendship) and *benevolentia* (benevolence) from *propinquitas*, which can be better translated into a relationship.[96]

This thin notion of *propinquitas* differs from that of friendship, which is more intimate and close. According to Tuck, Cicero had the former notion in mind when, in **De Inventione**, he described the life of a natural man without laws, wild and free across the fields, in which man knows nothing of marriage or legitimate children.[97] In the natural society, the quest of each man for his own interests does not bode well for all; there are always those who end up far worst than they started. Natural man may be a little naïve, but never benevolent.

Epicurus' philosophy has always been presumed contrary to natural sociability. The fact that Hobbes was accused of espousing an Epicurist doctrine comes as no surprise. The passage above illustrating natural life was considered inspired by Epicurus and could also be found in Lucretius' work; however, the words are actually Cicero's. Cicero was the one to establish severe limitations to natural sociability: "mankind's common sociability" would mean little more than the mutual reconnaissance between men, although distinct from the relations men establish with the rest of nature. It is about appreciating the benefits of living together, without demanding the sacrifices that the social life of the Scholastics requires. The more distanced someone is, less is owed to him.[98]

---

[94]"*Seneca: 'ut omnia inter se membra consentiunt, quia singula servari totius interest, ita homines singulis parcent, quia ad coetum geniti sunus. Salva autem esse societas, nisi amore et custodia partium non potest.' Idem álibi: 'Securitas securitate mutua paciscenda est.' Haec est illa hominum inter se cognatio, illa mundi civitas, quam tot tantisque praeconiis veteres philosophi nobis commendat, praesertim Stoici, quorum sententiam etiam Cicero exsequitur: ex qua et illud est Florentini: 'cum cognationem quandam inter nos natura constituerit, consequens esse ut hominem homini insidiari nefas sit; quod ille optime ad jus gentium refert.'*" (**DJPC**, p. 13).

[95]Tuck (1999), p. 36.

[96]**De Amicitia**, 20 (Portuguese translation, s/d, p. 112).

[97]Tuck (1999), p. 37. Also **De Inventione**. I. 2, 2.

[98]**De Officiis**. I. 16, 51–52. Evidently, Cicero emphasizes the fact there are obligations between strangers. Nonetheless, the examples he gives (giving water, sharing fire, giving good advices) are much simpler duties than the ones among friends.

Seneca himself, a more orthodox Stoic than Cicero, concedes that the obligations that men have towards global society are more negative than positive. Instead of helping each other and caring for the good of others, men must simply avoid harming each other. "It is terrible to damage both the nation and its citizens (the parts are sacred if the whole must be worshipped). Similarly, one should not harm the other, for he may be a fellow citizen in a greater city. Do the hands wish to do harm to the feet and the eyes to the hands?"[99]

In **De Jure Praedae**, despite some references to Aquinas, the love for others is also feeble. Much like Seneca, the third and fourth laws (which derive from the second rule, the primary Law of Nations or the secondary Natural Law) prescribe negative obligations: "let no one inflict injury upon his fellow" and "let no one seize possession of that which has been taken into the possession of another. The former is the law of inoffensiveness; the latter is the law of abstinence. As a result of the Third Law, life is rendered secure; as a result of the Fourth Law, distinctions of ownership arise, together with the well-known concept of Mine and Thine."[100] The natural instinct of sociability does not create an obligation to help others, but only to avoid harming them. This negative obligation is enough to enable individual survival; by reducing the possibility of violent death and allowing for the existence of external demonstrations of property, the concept contributes to a better quality of life.

Grotius' anthropology is based thus on two principles: love for oneself and love for others. However, it appears that the latter does not play as a big a role as the former. This is how Grotius proves himself similar to Hobbes. Richard Tuck developed this idea in the 1980s and has maintained it ever since. He argues that Grotius developed the natural sociability in a "minimalist" fashion and, to a certain extent, has based altruism in selfishness. The Dutch Jurist apparently asserts this in the following excerpt:

> Accordingly, although the order of presentation of the first set of laws and of those following immediately thereafter has indicated that one's own good takes precedence over the good of another persona — or, let us say, it indicates that by nature's ordinance each individual should be desirous of his own good fortune in preference to that of another, which is the purport of the proverbs, "I myself am my own closest neighbour," and "My tunic is closer than my cloak"

Love for others exists only so that one can perfect the love for oneself, to the extent that the love for oneself contemplates and transcends the love for others. In matters where "there is a comparison between the good of one and the good of all— both could be counted as one, for the word all also refers to a type of unity—, the most general concept should prevail, because it includes the welfare of all

[99]"*Nefas est nocere patriae: ergo cive quoque, nam hic pars patriae est (sanctae partes sunt si universum venerabile est) ergo et homini, nam hic in maiore tibi urbe civis est. Quid si nocere velint manus pedibus, manibus oculi?*" (*De Ira*. II. 31, 7).

[100]"*Ne quis alterum laedat*" and "*Ne quis occupet alteri occupata. Haec lex abstinentiae, illa innocentiae est: inde vitae securitas oritur, hinc dominiorum distinctio, celeberrimumque illud Meum et Teum*" (**DJPC**, pp. 13–14).

individuals."[101] Grotius does not anticipate a possible conflict between the individual and the collective, because he sees them as part and whole, respectively. In this sense, to care for the interests of the whole is to care for the interests of the parts and to take them further beyond. There is a degree of originality in Grotius' understanding as he bases the collective on the individual, and not the other way around, as totalitarian interpretations were prone to do.

Tuck's thesis advocating the existing of fewer differences between Grotius and Hobbes was strongly disputed. For instance, Robert Shaver listed several arguments that evidence the profund differences between the English Philosopher and the Dutch Ambassador,[102] and they are all in **De Jure Belli ac Pacis**. The discussion regarding the relevance of the principle of self-preservation for Grotius is, actually, a dispute on whether the author is Modern or not. Twenty years later, in response to these attacks, Tuck wrote a text in which he attempts to point out the differences between Grotius and the Scholastic Theologians. One of his most interesting ideas is that the first edition of **De Jure Belli ac Pacis** of 1625 is much more similar to **De Jure Praedae** than the following editions are. With each revision, Grotius made the book more palatable to his European audience (especially to the Aristotle's Calvinist followers in the Netherlands), which may confuse readers about where he really stood on Scholasticism and sociability.[103] Although Grotius did not change his original thoughts, the series of successive amendments to this first edition "muddled" the text.

Nevertheless, this hypothesis seems strange once we consider that, according to Laurens Winkel, Grotius inserted more and more notes in each new edition explaining Stoicism. After 1625, the author seems to resume his studies on Stoicism.[104] If Grotius' understanding of sociability comes from the work of Stoic scholars, and if Grotius' sociability is feebler than Aristotle's and Aquinas', the last editions of **De Jure Belli ac Pacis** should further distance Grotius' work from Scholasticism, not the contrary. As a result, it is essential to focus the analysis on Grotius himself.

So, the Jurist from Delft needed to respond to the three objections raised by Carneades against the idea of justice:

> [1] men imposed upon themselves laws, which vary according to customs, and among the same peoples often undergo changes as times change; [2] moreover that there is no law of nature, because all creatures, men as well as animals, are impelled by nature toward ends advantageous to themselves; [3] that, consequently, there is no justice, or, if such there be,

---

[101]"(…) *ordo legum primo loco et deinceps positarum ostenderit bonum suum prius esse alieno, (…) sibi ut quisque melius esse velit quam alteri, quo et illa spectant, 'Proximus egomet mihi, tunica pallio propior'*" and "(…) *tamen ubi quaeritur de bono singulorum et de bono omnium, quorum utrumque recte bonum suum dicitur, si quidem et omnes unum sunt aliquid, bonum illud omnium potius esse debet, quatenus ei scilicet et bonum inest singulorum*" (**DJPC**, p. 21).

[102]Shaver (1993), pp. 63–83.

[103]Tuck (1999), p. 100.

[104]Winkel (2000), p. 395.

it is supreme folly, since one does violence to his own interests if he consults the advantage of others.

These arguments respectively refer to moral diversity, selfishness and the futility of justice (because, if justice exists, it would be detrimental to individual interests). These were, in sum, the objections raised by the ancient skeptic; however, not all skeptics offered these arguments. Some, such as Charron, focused solely on relativism. The second objection was not even exclusive of the skeptics: Hobbes adopted it and made it a central piece of his Ethics. In addition, if Tuck's hypothesis were correct, Grotius would never attempt to reject it. In effect, if Grotius simply wanted to respond the skeptics of his time, he made a bigger enemy than he needed to.

Tuck's idea assumes that no one before the Modern scholars opposed the arguments of the skeptics: the Scholastics either avoided them or responded to them naively. But it is from Lactantius' **Divinarum Institutionum** that Grotius quoted Carneades. Another important source to Grotius was Cicero himself, which also attempted to refute the Greek Skeptic. In the Middle Ages, Lactantius represented the most immediate reference to Cicero's ideas.[105] The Medieval authors could even ignore Sextus Empiricus' philosophy professed by the likes of Montaigne and Charron, but it is extreme to argue that they did not know the quote from Carneades that Grotius transcribes in the *prolegomenon* 5. In addition, as will be discussed, Thomists did not simply resort to tenets of faith when replying to the Ancient Skeptic, but rather defended morality on grounds that were autonomous from God. Thus, even before Modern scholars came about, there was no ignorance or naïveté regarding the skeptics. Thence, Grotius' opposition to Carneades could truly be an opposition against Carneades.

Grotius' responses call for careful examination. With regard to the first objection, he does not reject relativism in its entirety: he knows for a fact that Civil Law varies from place to place. Nonetheless, justice derives from the nature of things. Still not referring to Natural Law, Grotius simply aims at proving that justice conforms to the rational nature. The difference between rational nature and Natural Law will be discussed further below. For now, it is important to note that Grotius is not directly against the idea that the law varies from place to place, according to local customs.[106] He rejects the idea that men would have no judgment of justice besides utility itself. So, his response to the first objection also applies to the second one. By proving that there exists justice out of the rational nature, he rejects selfishness and moral diversity in one strike—since men remain men everywhere. He does not accept the notion that self-preservation is the only natural impulse that man has. In the 1625 edition, he rules out Carneades' standpoint because

[105]Korkman, 1999/2000, p. 83.

[106]Grotius does oppose to that notion. When resorting to cultural diversity, Carneades seems to consider Natural and Civil Law only and not the *jus gentium*. (**DJBP**, *prolegomenon* 17). However, Grotius does not elaborate this law more than these few words in the *prolegomena*. This is not out of contempt: once he distinguishes the Law of Nations from Natural Law and thus leaves the Roman orbit behind, Grotius chooses to study this source of the law of war throughout the rest of the book.

> Man is, to be sure, an animal, but an animal of a superior kind, much farther removed from all other animals than the different kinds of animals are from one another; evidence on this point may be found in the many traits peculiar to the human species. But among the traits characteristic of man is an impelling desire for society [*appetitus societatis*], that is, for the social life-not of any and every sort, but peaceful, and organized according to the measure of his intelligence.[107]

This excerpt was modified in subsequent editions of the book. Grotius notes that this peaceful and rational order corresponds to what the "Stoics call 'domestic state' [*oikeiosis*]." The Dutch Ambassador need not even explain the Stoic origins of this notion. Cicero offers an expression similar to *appetitus societatis*: "man is the only animal that, by his own nature, acts according to a sense of honor and moderation, which refers to a desire of connecting to human society (…)."[108] Thus, as in **De Jure Praedae**, in **De Jure Belli ac Pacis** the Grotian idea of sociability would descend from the Stoics, not from Aristotle.

Nevertheless, the following passage, which would roughly refer to *prolegomena* 6 and 7, suffered extensive changes. In the original version, Grotius states that

> When one states that nature impels animals to seek their own good, this is true for all animals, including man, up until the moment uses that which is peculiar to him. Some of the other animals, in fact, do in a way restrain the appetency for that which is good for themselves alone, to the advantage, now of their offspring, now of other animals of the same species. This aspect of their behavior has its origin, we believe, in some extrinsic intelligent principle, because with regard to other actions, which involve no more difficulty than those referred to, a like degree of intelligence is not manifest in them. In the case of men, however, on they behave in this fashion [rationally], it is reasonable to guess that this comes from an internal principle, which would be associated to qualities that do not belong to all animals, but only human nature.[109]

The beginning of this passage serves as basis for Richard Tuck's thesis on the proximity between **De Jure Praedae** and the 1625 edition of **De Jure Belli ac Pacis**, in which Grotius affirms that animals are compelled to seek their own good

---

107"*(…) nam homo animans quidem est, sed eximium animans, multoque longius distans a caeteris omnibus quam caeterorum genera inter se distant: cui rei testitmonium perhibent multae actionis humani generis propriae. Inter haec autem quae homini sunt propria, est appetitus societatis, id est communitatis, non qualiscunque, sed tranquillae et pro sui intellectus modo ordinatae cum his qui sui sunt generis*." (**DJBP** 1625. which would be a part of *prolegomenon* 6).

108"*(…) quodque hoc solum animal natum est pudoris ac verecundiae particeps appetensque convictum hominum ac societatem* (…)" (**De Finnibus**, IV, 18. In the English translation Cicero, 2001, p. 96).

109"*Quod ergo dicitur natura quodque animal ad suas tantum utilitates ferri, verum esto de caeteris animantibus et de homine antequam ad usum eius quod homini proprium est, pervenerit: quanquam et de animantibus caeteris haec addenda est exceptio, quod quaedam utilitatum suarum studium, partim foetuum suorum, partim aliorum sibi congenerum respectu aliquatenus temperant: quod in illis quidem procedere credimus ex principio aliquo intelligente extrinseco, quia circa actus alios istis neuriquam difficitores par intelligentia in illis non apparet: Homini autem, cum circa similia similiter agat, messe principium quoddam internum par est intelligi, cui quae conveniunt ea sunt non omnium quidem animantium, sed humanae naturae congruentia*." (**DJBP** 1625. Part of *prolegomenon* 6 and all of 7).

and that this would also apply to men, if they do not make use of what is special about them (reason).[110] Tuck sees in this passage the principle of self-preservation, an instinct very dear to the Stoic literature.

However, even in the 1625 text, Grotius does not seem to emphasize the love for oneself. The reference to some species of animals that sacrifice themselves for the good of their offspring and of others of their kind indicates that, contrary to Tuck's view on this matter, Grotius wants to limit the role of self-preservation: even some animals (which, unlike men, are not rational) temper their primal instinct of survival. This idea was already present in the Stoic scholars, but in **De Jure Praedae** we find an Epicurist interpretation of the Stoicism: the emphasis of *oikeiosis* is on the love for oneself; the love for others is built upon that. Twenty years later, the tone seems to change.

The expression *appetitus societatis* appears only twice in **De Jure Belli ac Pacis**, but Grotius evokes it using other words on several occasions, such as the *prolegomenon* 16: "for the very human nature is the mother of Natural Law, because even when there is no scarcity, it **drives us to common society**."[111] This persistence denotes the relevance of this idea for the Grotian system. Yet, it seems strange that there are so few references to the first element of the Stoic *oikeiosis* binomial: the instinct of self-preservation.

In fact, Grotius mitigates the extent of the principle of self-preservation in several passages of the book. For instance, Grotius is more reluctant than Hobbes in accepting civil disobedience, even in cases of extreme necessity. Resistance should only be allowed provided that it causes no serious disturbance to the State and no death of innocents. Resistance may not damage the common good.[112] Even criminals sentenced to death should refrain from resisting. In the name of the common good, there is often an actual duty not to resist.

By mitigating the emphasis on the love for oneself, Grotius does not intend to conclude that man behave altruistically. His goal is to prove that the source of justice, and hence, morality, is the love for others, not the love for oneself—which effectively distances him from Hobbes. Post-1625 changes do indeed point to an intellectual *démarche*. In the subsequent editions of the work, Grotius extends the passage that would constitute *prolegomenon* 7 and elaborates his analysis of sociability.

> Some of the other [irrational] animals, in fact, do in a way restrain the appetency for that which is good for themselves alone, to the advantage, now of their offspring, now of other animals of the same species. This aspect of their behavior has its origin, we believe, in some extrinsic intelligent principle, because with regard to other actions, which involve no more difficulty than those referred to, a like degree of intelligence is not manifest in them. The same thing must be said of children. In children, even before their training has begun, some disposition to do good to others appears, as Plutarch sagely observed; thus sympathy for

---

[110] Tuck (1999), p. 97.

[111] "(…) *nam naturalis iuris mater est ipsa humana natura quae nos etiamsi re nulla indigerimus ad societatem mutuam appetendam ferret*" (**DJBP**. *prolegomenon* 16).

[112] **DJBP**. I, 4, 7, 2 and 4 and II, 1, 18, 1.

> others comes out spontaneously at that age. The mature man in fact has knowledge which prompts him to similar actions under similar conditions, together with an impelling desire for society [*societas appetitus excellente*], for the gratification of which he alone among animals possesses a special instrument, speech. He has also been endowed with the faculty of knowing and of acting in accordance with general principles. Whatever accords with that faculty is not common to all animals, but peculiar to the nature of man.[113]

In fact, if the tone of his argument in the 1625 edition lies on sociability, then later changes were not meant to "confuse" the reader or to "hide" his "true intention," but actually to better explain what he meant by this social appetite. Grotius compares children (who do not fully make use of reason) to animals who tame their selfish instincts in favor of their offspring and the good of other members of their species. This comparison is relevant because, for both animals and children, sociability is not a rational and thought out tendency. Still, it exists. To refute Carneades, Grotius aims at proving that the love for others is so natural that does not depend solely on reason.

Therefore, in a grown man who makes full use of reason the social inclination is much more complex. He has two resources that animals lack: language and the ability to perceive general principles that are evident (and to act accordingly). These tools show how developed human sociability is. When Aristotle states that man is a "political" animal, he takes advantage of the multiple meanings of this word: the word alludes to both sociability and rationality in men. Thus, human sociability does not represent a mere irrational instinct (as it does in some gregarious animal, such as bees), but a drive enhanced by the employment of rational tools, such as language. The human sociability develops communication and unites human beings, while animals depend on a "coincidental instinct."

Grotius also seems to resort to Aristotle regarding this second tool: the ability to know in accordance with general principles. As previously discussed, according to the Greek Philosopher, all things lean towards their own good, towards their *telos*. However, due to reason man is moved by a special kind of purpose: he searches for abstract knowledge. The Scholastics understood that to mean the knowledge of God and the quest for eternal truths. That interpretation is not present in Grotius' work, but that does not mean that Aristotle's influence is not there.

Although one may find only implied references to Aristotle in the amended passage, Grotius is clearer when it comes to explaining the Stoics. Despite having already explained the origins of the expression *appetitus societatis* as a variation of

---

[113] "*Nam et caeterarum animantium quaedam utilitatum suarum studium, partim foetum suorum, partim aliorum sibi congenerum respectu e aliquatenus temperant quod in illis quidem procedere credimus ex principio aliquo intelligente extrinseco, quia circa actus alios, istis neutiquam difficiliores, par intelligentia in illis non apparet. Idemque de infantibus dicendum, in quibus ante omnem disciplinam ostendit se ad bene aliis faciendum propensio quaedam, prudenter a Plutarcho observata: sicut et in ea aetate misericordia sponte prorumpit. Homini vero perfectae aetatis, cum circa similia similiter, agere norit, cum societatis appetitu excellente, cujus peculiare solus inter animantes instrumentum habet sermonem, inesse etiam facultatem sciendi agendique, secundum generalia praecepta, par este intelligi, cui quae conveniunt ea jam sunt non omnium quidem animantibum, sed humanae naturae congruentia.*" (**DJBP**. *prolegomenon* 7).

"dominant drive towards sociability," the author does not want to leave room for doubt. Therefore, right after employing this expression, he inserts a footnote in which he quotes Marcus Aurelius (for whom "man was born to do good to others") as well as Nicetas, Choniates and Augustine. They all appear as arguments of authority to prove the existence of this social appetite. Grotius also mentions Plutharc as a source of the doctrine on *oikeiosis*.[114] However, if the references to Stoic authors became more frequent in the later editions of **De Jure Belli ac Pacis**, then why did the work took up a final form that was so different from **De Jure Praedae**—a work in which, according to Tuck, Stoic influences are abundant?

The answer to that question seems paradoxical: the **De Jure Belli ac Pacis** became so different from **De Jure Praedae** because Grotius studied the Stoics better. According to Laurel Winkel, by 1625 Grotius did not know enough about classical literature to place the notion of *appetitus societatis* within the Greek Stoic tradition. Until that time, he was familiar with Cicero and Seneca's work—the latter through Justus Lipsius, to whom Grotius dedicated several poems. If one considers the timing of these amendments, it appears that Grotius studied the Stoics more and more on his own between the end of the 1620 s and the publishing of the 1642 edition of **De Jure Belli ac Pacis**.[115]

In his earlier work, Grotius betrays his confusion with the Stoic and the Epicureanism's ideals in a passage: "Consequently, Horace should not be censured for saying, in imitation of the Academics [Stoics], that expediency might perhaps be called the mother of justice and equity."[116] For a Stoic scholar, utility could never be the basis for justice—at least not in an isolated manner, not even in Cicero's eclectic version. In general, Humanists of that time could not exactly pinpoint the difference between Stoicism and Epicureanism beyond common sense.

It is worth noting that Grotius inserts this argument (of utility as the origin of *jus*) in Carneades' mouth and makes a concerted effort to refute it. By further studying the Stoics, Grotius was able to better unravel the Epicurist traces of his doctrine. For that reason, even in its first printing, the **De Jure Belli ac Pacis** places more emphasis on sociability than on the love of oneself and thus distances itself from **De Jure Praedae**. That distinction was often attributed to a Scholastic influence, but sociability kept its Stoic origins even in his work of maturity—Grotius only studied these philosophers in depth. This is evident when, quoting Lactantius, Grotius refutes the Epicurist principle of seeking pleasure and averting pain: "But man, because he has knowledge of good and evil, refrains from doing harm to another, even with disadvantage to himself."[117] If the Stoicism and Epicureanism appear intermingled in his earlier work, in his treatise on war and peace they are well distinguished.

---

[114]Winkel (2000), p. 398.

[115]Winkel (2000), p. 395 and 401.

[116]"*Qua ratione culpandum non est quod secutus Academicos Horatius utilitatem justi et aequi prope matrem dixit.*" (**DJPC**, p. 9).

[117]"*Homo vero, quia scientiam boni et mali habet, abstinet se a nocendo etiam cum incommodo suo.*" (**DJBP**. I, 1, 11, 1).

Thus, Grotius rejects the skeptic notion that law is born out of selfish interests. But he is not done; he must respond to Carneades' third and final objection: although justice is not based on utility, it is also not useless. "The Law of Nature nevertheless has the reinforcement of expediency; for the Author of nature willed that as individuals we should be weak, and should lack many things needed in order to live properly, to the end that we might be the more constrained to cultivate the social life."[118] A well-organized society according to Law and Justice brings peace and security for all—an argument that even Hobbes would agree to. This reasoning applies to international relations. There is no State so strong as to not need the help of others. That is why rulers are frequently searching for alliances, proving that law does not end at the boundaries of a nation. "The truth is that, when treaties are broken, all things become uncertain."[119]

In **De Jure Belli ac Pacis**, Grotius places emphasis on the sociability and the instinct of self-preservation loses its status. At times, Grotius' sociability surpasses the Stoic conception of social appetite. Even when not demanded by law, some obligations must be upheld for the common good. By demanding that an innocent subject surrender himself to the enemy to avoid greater destruction, Grotius recognizes the existence of a charitable obligation, not a juridical duty per se. As noted by Shaver,[120] Grotius recognizes Charity to have a supplemental role to law and justice in several passages of his book (DJBP. III, 2, 6; III, 11, 2; III, 18, 2, 1; III, 18, 4; III, 20, 43, 2). As I will discuss in the next chapter, the idea that Charity constitutes an order that imposes extra and ultra-juridical social obligations belongs to Scholasticism.

Grotius does not hide the religious base of Charity: when investigating what is allowed during a war, after analyzing the issue through the lens of Natural and Civil Law and of the Law of Nations, he wonders what is allowed according to the law of Charity, and even adds the adjective "Christian" after the term.[121] The Jurist-Theologian once again displays his eclecticism. There is no doubt that Grotius' sociability stems from Stoicism. In his earlier work, he presents a rather Epicureanist understanding of those philosophers, but, as time passed, he studied more and purified his understanding. As seen, the Epicurist sociability is more tenuous than the Aristotle's: instead of demanding mutual assistance, it imposes obligations of abstention. However, by adding the law of Charity, Grotius expands the reach of the social appetite up to Scholastic standards. Originally, Grotius' sociability is not Scholastic, but it ends up producing the same effects as if it were.

---

[118]"*Sed naturali juri utilitas accedit: voluit enim naturae Auctor nos singulos et infirmos esse, et multarum rerum ad vitam recte ducendam egentes, quo magis ad colendam societatem raperemur.*" (**DJBP**. *prolegomenon* 16).

[119]"*Verissimum illud, omnia incerta esse simul a iure recessum est.*" (**DJBP**. *prolegomenon* 22).

[120]Shaver (1993), p. 73. He even mentions the passage **DJBP**. III, 10, 1; however, in this instance, Grotius is not referring to Charity, but to honor and honesty, principles that are found in both Epicureanism and Stoicism. For that reason, all the writers that he mentions are not religious men.

[121]**DJBP**. III, 18, 4.

4.3.2 Voluntarism and Intellectualism: The Objectivity of Values

By seeking to refute Carneades in response to the argument that there is no nature-based justice, Grotius professes the words that would immortalize him: "What we have been saying would have a degree of validity even if we should concede that which cannot be conceded without the utmost wickedness, that there is no God, or that the affairs of men are of no concern to Him."[122] That is Grotius' famous impious hypothesis. It corresponds to the most debated passage of his work. Grotius surely did not give much importance to it, but his commentators did. It is worth mentioning that this sentence is in the first edition of **De Jure Belli ac Pacis** —meaning it was part of his original intent.

Much like the Scholastics, Grotius does not accept the hypothesis: God exists and He cares about men. This "truth" is embedded in all of us, partly by reason and partly by an "eternal tradition," confirmed by several evidences and miracles across the centuries. Grotius is not an atheist. His God is the Christian one: He is infinitely kind and loving; He would never abandon men, his main creation. He is always present and watches over men through his Divine Providence. Men know all of this because some of it is perceptible through reason (which coincides with the author's purpose of elaborating a treatise on natural religion) and because God Himself revealed this and His word was passed along through generations, through tradition.

Since Grotius' death, the *etiamsi daremus non esse Deum* has been interpreted over and over and is still a matter of controversy. There are at least three different understandings of this passage. The most traditional reading suggests that this hypothesis is an example of secularism: Natural Law would exist even if God did not exist. Grotius would have purged the Natural Law doctrine of the Middle Ages of all its theological elements in order to reestablish it on rational grounds. For that reason, Grotius would belong to Modernity and **De Jure Belli ac Pacis** would be the first work on Modern legal philosophy.

This thesis is so widely spread that it is difficult to trace back its origins. Jules Basdevant sealed it in Antoine Pillet's classic oeuvre **Les Fontateurs de Droit International**. In his comments to the impious hypothesis, Basdevant affirms: "through this understanding, (…) Grotius distinguished Natural Law from Theology and Metaphysics. He made it an object of scientific study grounded on man's social nature. He can be considered the father of Natural Law because he focused on this conception and spread it through the spirits."[123] A good part of the textbooks on International Law and other widely disseminated works reiterate this

[122]"*Et haec quidem quae im diximus, locum haberent etiamsi daremus, quod sine summo scelere dari nequit, non esse Deum, aut non curari ab eo negotia humana*" (**DJBP**. *prolegomenon* 11).

[123]"*Par cette conception, (…) Grotius degage le droit naturel de la théologie et de la métaphysique. In en fait matière à une étude scientifique portent sur la nature sociable de l'homme. C'est parce qu'il s'est attaché à cette conception el l'à repandue dans les esprits qu'il a pu ètre considéré comme le père du droit naturel.*" (Basdevant, 1904, p. 233).

interpretation to the point that it became ordinary. In one of the most quoted textbooks, Arthur Nussbaum repeats the idea that Grotius secularized Natural Law in the *prolegomenon* 11.[124]

The idea of a purely rational basis for something previously explained in reference to God was immensely attractive in the following century. The hypothesis seemed to forestall a perfect Anthropologic paradigm for Natural Law. The project of an objective and secular morality conformed to the Modern scholars' mathematic ideal of investigation.[125]

Despite all the controversies that surround the hypothesis, some aspects of it are certain. In addition to being anachronic, this interpretation ignores how Grotius' writings on Law are impregnated with Theology. Grotius believes in God and many of his legal institutions depend on Him, as seen in the beginning of this chapter. His reasoning could never forsake God. Grotius constantly refers to the Bible as a source of history. By taking the Old and the New Testaments as precise historical accounts, Grotius was indirectly accepting God's existence and the fact that He intervened in human affairs.[126]

Contrary to this understanding, Grotius' hypothesis is not original. Several authors before him presented different versions of it: Anselm of Canterbury, Hugh of Saint Victor, Duns Scotus, Gregory of Rimini, Gabriel Biel, Francisco de Vitória, Domingos de Soto, Gabriel Vázquez, Roberto Bellarmino, Francisco Suárez and Luís de Molina. If one is willing to go beyond Christian authors, Plato's **Eutyphro** and Marcus Aurelius' **Meditations** are also worth mentioning. The direct source of Grotius' hypothesis remains unidentified.

The second meaning of the famous passage considers that Grotius would have taken his hypothesis from the Scholastics and thus would have taken part in the debate between Voluntarism and Intellectualism. Despite initially favoring the more traditional interpretation, Giorgio Del Vecchio changed his stance and was one of the first to support the Scholastic origin of the hypothesis. He even lists Gregory of Rimini and Francisco Suárez as scholars who discussed the issue before Grotius ever did. Notwithstanding, Del Vecchio did not entirely discard the traditional interpretation and still considered the impious hypothesis as an effort to remove theological elements from scientific works.

> The tendency to render scientific and political treatises (including those on law and politics) independent of theological premises had already been prevalent for at least two centuries, representing as it did a characteristic trait of that general upsetting of traditional thinking which we refer as the Renaissance. Grotius, hence, did not initiate, but merely confirmed that tendency.[127]

[124]Nussbaum (1953), p. 113.

[125]Crowe (1993), pp. 32–34.

[126]Chipman (1983), p. 71.

[127]Vecchio (1962), p. 262.

This second understanding gained strength with James St. Leger's thesis, **The "Etiamsi Daremus" of Hugo Grotius**. The author claims that the key subject in Legal Philosophy is the debate between Voluntarism and Intellectualism. "Like the goddess of Justice, the historian of the Philosophy of Law holds high in his hand a set of balanced scales. When the role and importance of the intellect tips the balance in the doctrine of a philosopher, he is said to be an intellectualist. When the role of will predominates, he is called a voluntarist."[128] St. Leger elaborates a "Philosophy of the History of Legal Philosophy" based on this dichotomy, and travels from the Greeks to Grotius in search of the hypothesis. His conclusion is that Grotius took the formula from Suárez's **De Legibus**, but he would not have adhered to the Suarezian syncretic proposal. Grotius would have opted for a more purely intellectual version, such as Gabriel Vázquez's, and used the work of Suárez merely as a research tool, due to the abundance of references and the summary of the Scholastic school.[129]

In order to prove his thesis, St. Leger must overcome two obstacles. The first refers to the small number of references to Suárez in **De Jure Belli ac Pacis**. On the other hand, Grotius frequently quotes other Scholastics, such as Vitória and Molina, who wrote different versions of the hypothesis. St. Leger shares Jan Kosters' opinion that Suárez conception of *jus gentium* had a great influence over Grotius even before the publishing of his *opus magna*. I shall discuss this idea in depth in the fifth chapter; for now, it is worth mentioning that for these two commentators, Grotius could not openly refer to Suárez because of the community where he lived. The **Defensio Fidei Catholicae adversus anglicanae sectae errors** caused so much controversy that it was forbidden and burnt in France and the United Kingdom. For this reason, despite the profound impact that Suárez may have had on Grotius, the latter could not make this publicly known.[130]

The other obstacle that St. Leger must overcome refers to Grotius' clear voluntarist position in **De Jure Praedae**. There are countless of references to the will as a legislative source in this book: all rules from which the laws derive illustrate this inclination. As a Reformer, voluntarism is the school of thought that would come naturally for Grotius. However, according to St. Leger, from 1605 to 1625, Grotius would have gradually changed his standpoint toward the extreme intellectualism of **De Jure Belli ac Pacis**. The change would be a consequence of the contact that Grotius had with Gabriel Vázquez's work, probably through Suárez's books. By 1609, the transformation would become complete. In the **Mare Liberum**'s written dedication, Grotius states that the just and the unjust exist "for their very nature [*suapte natura*]."[131] The expression *suapte natura* appears six

[128]Leger (1962), p. 61.

[129]Leger (1962), p. 132.

[130]Leger (1962), pp. 98–110.

[131]"*Error est non minus vetus quam pestilens, quo multi mortales, ii autem maxime, qui plurimum vi ataque opibus valent, persuadent sibi, aut, quod verius puto, persuadere conantur, justum atque injustum non suapte natura, sed hominum inani quadam opinione, atque consuetudine distingui.*" (GROTIUS, Hugo. **The Freedom of the Seas, or the right which belongs to the Dutch to take**

times in the third chapter of Vázquez's **Commentariorum ac Disputationum in Primam Secundae Sancti Thomae**—a fact that, according to St. Leger, was no mere coincidence. As a Calvinist voluntarist, Grotius would have converted to the Scholastic intellectualism thanks to Vázquez, through Suárez's works.[132] Therefore, Suárez became a major influence on Grotius even outside the scope of the doctrine on *jus gentium*.

Despite the flaws in St. Leger's thesis, Grotius' Natural Law theory does have several features (besides the intellectualism) that bring it closer to the Catholic Scholasticism and further away from Calvinism. Calvin and his followers found two limitations in Natural Law. First, the corrupt nature of the human being: the original sin separated man from God and obfuscated man's rational abilities. As a result, man can shut his mind to Natural Law and devise different versions of it (that all distance him from the Truth). Second, Natural Law is too generic. For Calvin, it is left for the States to determine how best to implement it. For instance, Natural Law forbids theft; however, as some societies have more trouble with this type of criminal behavior than others do, State should decide on the penalty for this crime.[133]

Grotius rejects the first limitation and puts the second one in another perspective. The Grotian Natural Law is perceptible as an evidence (as seen) and is realized through human practice in history. Calvin would never accept that. All men are tempted by evil, which is irresistible to human will. First, men might even discover what is right, but they would refuse to observe it. In time, this ability to distinguish good from evil would be compromised.

In addition, in his definition of Natural Law, Grotius provides a criterion out of which an entire system is built. "The Law of Nature is a dictate of right reason, which points out that an action, whether it conforms or not to the rational nature, is affected by a moral deformity or a moral necessity; and that, in consequence, such an act is either forbidden or enjoined by the author of nature, God."[134] Each action must be examined in light of the rational nature: if there is a moral necessity compelling the action, then such action will conform to Natural Law; should the action result of a moral deformity, then that action is contrary to it. There is no room for mistakes because Natural Law is evident. By confronting it with rational nature, it seems possible to determine the justice or the injustice of any human action. With that case-by-case criterion, Grotius lessens the vagueness of Calvin's Natural Law.

(Footnote 131 continued)

part in the East Indian Trade. Trad. Ralph van Deman Magoffin. Introduction by James Brown Scott. New York: Oxford University Press, 1916. p. 1. Henceforth, ML).

[132] Leger (1962), pp. 141–142.

[133] Thomas (1999), p. 72.

[134] "*Ius naturalis est dictatum rectae rationi,s indicans actui aliqui, ex eius convenientia aut disconvenientia cum ipsa natura rationali, inesse moralem turpitudinem, aut necessitatem moralem, ac consequenter ab auctore natura Deo talem actum aut vetari aut praecipi.*" (**DJBP**. I, 1, 10, 1).

Indeed, it does not settle the issue of determining the penalty; however, it leaves no room for uncertainty in terms of what is forbidden, demanded, and allowed.

Therefore, Grotius did come up with a very Catholic understanding of Natural Law. However, even within the Scholastic tradition there were disagreements and the so-called adoption by Grotius of Gabriel Vázquez's pure intellectualism calls for a further analysis. St. Leger focused too much on the impious hypothesis and neglected other passages in which Grotius refers to Natural Law. Much like Suárez, Grotius opted for a synthesis between voluntarism and intellectualism to explain the foundation of Natural Law.

In **De Jure Praedae**, except for the last rule, all others refer to the will as a legislative source. In **De Jure Belli ac Pacis**, Grotius does not accept all the premises of the hypothesis, but seems to agree with the conclusion thereof, denoting a pure version of intellectualism. However, the *prolegomena* of his mature book (in which the impious hypothesis appear) do not have the same introductory purpose as the prolegomena of his 1605 work. According to Haggenmacher, the former seem to have been written at the end, for they offer a retrospective look of the entire text. In fact, the introduction to **De Jure Belli ac Pacis** corresponds to **De Jure Praedae** to the very short first chapter, where the most important concepts upon which the law of war is built can be found.[135]

The way that Grotius organized his work may confuse readers, because many issues that he carefully examines later in the book are described briefly in the *prolegomena*. However, the first chapter adequately covers important issues such as the concepts of *jus*, war, and Natural Law. That is why Grotius offers right in the first chapter a complete concept of Natural Law. As mentioned, it is "dictate of right reason, which points out that an action, whether it conforms or not to the rational nature, is affected by a moral deformity or a moral necessity; and that, in consequence, such an act is either forbidden or enjoined by the author of nature, God." There we find the two main aspects of the Suarezian Natural Law: the right reason leads us towards the action, but God commands it. Both reason and will are part of Grotius' Natural Law: the first indicates what is right and the second makes it mandatory.

Grotius more aptly establishes the relation between the reason and the will in the **Inleiding**: "Law (which is also sometimes called Right because it determines what is right) is a product of reason ordaining for the common good what is honorable, established and published by one who has authority over a community of men."[136] It is worth mentioning that this concept applies to law in general, not only to Natural Law. As in Suárez, all laws seek justice, but they only become binding after an act of will, the promulgation thereof by a competent authority. This notion corresponds to the one found in his *opus magna*, since Grotius wrote the **Inleiding** while in prison in Loevenstein (which lasted from June 6, 1619 to March 22, 1621), a period also dedicated to the writing of **De Jure Belli ac Pacis**. The prisoner had

[135]Haggenmacher (1983), p. 449.

[136]Grotius (1953), v. 1. I, 2, 1, p. 5.

no intention of publishing it (which is why he wrote it in Dutch), but after some copies with errors became public, Grotius found himself obligated to authorize the publication of an official version in 1631.

Grotius does dedicate most attention in **De Jure Belli ac Pacis** to the elements of intellectualism in Natural Law. For that reason, he distinguishes Natural from human and voluntary Divine Law, since they neither prescribe nor forbid obligatory and lawful actions in themselves; on the contrary, they make them unlawful by forbidding them and mandatory by commanding them.[137] The impious hypothesis found in the *prolegomena* has the same level of abstraction that the following passage of the first chapter: "Just as even God cannot cause that two times two should not make four, so He cannot cause that which is intrinsically evil be not evil."[138] As God cannot change the rules of logic and Math, He cannot change the essence of an action. For all the power He possesses, there is a limit: the very order that He Himself created. God cannot contradict Himself.

Despite carefully considering the role of the intellect in the makings of the law, the will is also present. As in Suárez, God cannot refuse to forbid that which is intrinsically bad, nor can he omit from commanding the doing of good. According to Haggenmacher, this idea corresponds to the meanings of the adverbs *consequenter* and *necessario* in the definition of Natural Law, as employed by Grotius in regard to the divine sanction: the divine sanction is a mandatory and constitutive aspect of the norm.[139]

Furthermore, it seems possible to conclude that in Grotius the naturally just is not mistaken for Natural Law. The author argues that some actions are improperly attributed to Natural Law while being mere behaviors devoid of injustice.[140] This natural justice, apart from Natural Law, corresponds to the first understanding of *jus*: the *dikaión* of Stoic heritage. A moral judgment capable of perceiving what is unjust derives from man's social nature. It is not Natural Law itself, as it is nothing more than a negative judgment: human beings only see the just as a reflection of the unjust. Man often associates everything that is repulsive to him not only with law, but with honesty as well. Therefore, the contrary of the unjust (which is forbidden) is not necessarily the mandatory but also the allowed. The difference between the naturally unjust and the unjust action forbidden by Natural Law lies in the fact that the former contradicts human sociability, while the latter also offends his rational nature. The idea of natural justice is a reminiscence of that feeble Stoic sociability (the Epicureanism's version of it), while Grotius' mature Natural Law resembles the Scholastic's Law of Nature. This means that the philosophical sin is present in Grotius' thought and encompasses a much wider range of actions than Natural Law does.

---

[137]**DJBP**. I, 1, 10, 2.

[138]"*Sicut ergo ut bis duo non sint quator nie a Deo quidem potest essiei, ita ne hoc quidem, ut quod intriseca ratione malum est malum non sit.*" (**DJBP**. I, 1, 10, 5).

[139]Haggenmacher (1983), p. 504.

[140]**DJBP**. I, 1, 10, 3.

The concept of Natural Law in **De Jure Belli ac Pacis** may induce a purely intellectualist reading, because it emphasizes the rational elements whilst, in Suárez, the emphasis of Natural Law lies in the will. The origin of this difference is the cultural environment that each author belonged to. Suárez lived in a Catholic and Thomist world: reason requires no explanation, but the will does. But Grotius comes from a Protestant environment, so the element of will is more common.

Haggenmacher even softens the alleged "conversion" of Grotius to intellectualism. There exist traces of it in **De Jure Praedae**: the idea that Natural Law is not only revealed by oracles and miracles, but that in creation itself there are natural properties that compel things to their own good.[141] Grotius was well aware of the debate between voluntarists and intellectualists and his work does not reject the idea that there exists in creation an essence that may not be altered, not even by divine will. Nonetheless, the book as a whole seems to favor voluntarism because of its audience (the Mennonite). Grotius initial position was already syncretic and, in time, he only became more aware of it. And reading Suárez's work did play a key role in that.[142]

It is a matter of utmost importance: the similarities between Grotius' and Suárez's Natural Law. They will be the subject of further examination in a more appropriate moment. For now, it is important to point out that in spite of the similarities it is not possible to prove that Suarez's impious hypothesis served as inspiration for Grotius, as St. Leger claims. In fact, the odds are against this thesis. There are several other Scholastic writers who could have influenced Grotius—for instance, there was a copy of Domingos de Soto's **De Iustita et De Iure** in his personal library.[143] In addition, if on the one hand, Grotius refers to Suárez four times in **De Jure Belli ac Pacis**, Vitória is mentioned forty four times.

The Theologian of Salamanca is emblematic because he introduces not just one, but two variations of the hypothesis: "That is confirmed, since, if by an impossible chance, there were no God, there would be no obligations to do anything."[144] In this passage, Vitória explains that if God did not exist, there would be no laws and thus there would be no sins. He seems to employ the hypothesis to prove the exact contrary of what Grotius intended. However, the hypothesis did not always serve the debate between intellectualism and voluntarism. The schools of thought debated whether God played the role of legislator of Natural Law, but they both agreed that He is its Creator. The key point of contention is whether God is the immediate cause of the law, for there was no doubt among religious men that He is its remote cause. In the passage, Vitória aims at showing the autonomy between morality and God. He was concerned with establishing whether morality depended on God as Maker, not as legislator.

---

[141]**DJPC**, pp. 8–9.

[142]Haggenmacher (1983), pp. 496–523.

[143]Negro, 1998, p. 17.

[144]"*Et confirmatur, quia se per impossible non esset Deum, nullius obligaretur.*" (**De eo ad quod tenetur homo cum primum venit ad usum rationis**, 1960, p. 1347. *Segunda pars relectionis*. 8).

However, a few pages later, Vitória immerses himself in the controversy between intellectualism and voluntarism:

> Regarding the contrary reasons, Gregory of Rimini, in 3 d.34, argues two ideas: First, even if by an impossible chance, God did not exist, there would still be sin and bad morals. Secondly, even if there were no forbidding Divine Law, there would still be sin. From that, we conclude: there are many sins with so much wickedness in them that they are not crimes because they are forbidden by Divine Law; their fundamental basis is that for someone to do evil, he must only go against right reason, human or angelic.[145]

Despite his more orthodox adherence to Aquinas' teachings, Vitória disagrees with the pure intellectualism of this proposition and states that he does not understand how something can cease being a sin in the absence of the divine authority. For Vitória, nature is not capable of distinguishing between the severity of the crime of patricide and that of a wolf killing his mother, for example. Although Vitória's proposition is not as clear as Suárez's, it shows how Grotius had other available options at his disposal to inspire him.

The hypothesis did not always served the debate between reason and will in the formation of law. Gregory of Rimini was popular among neo-Scholastics as an example of pure intellectualism. However, according to Besselink, his version of the hypothesis referred to quite something else entirely. De Rimini defines sin as something against the right reason. He employs the hypothesis when wondering about why he should not use the expression "divine reason." He compared divine reason, perfect and sufficient, to right reason, a mere reflection of the former, infused into men and angels. The hypothesis does not oppose reason to will, but rather divinity to humanity as basis for moral values. He also uses the same distinction made by Suárez on the indicative and prescriptive elements of the law. If, by an impossible chance, there were no God in charge, it would still be possible to perceive the commitment of a crime.[146]

Therefore, St. Leger's "Philosophy of the History of Legal Philosophy" incurs in a crucial error: the debate between intellectualism and voluntarism in itself is not sufficient to define the two sides of a long lasting debate on the constitution of Natural Law. At least, the impious hypothesis does not serve this purpose. In truth, the impious hypothesis indicates a far more generic debate (of which intellectualism and voluntarism are only a part) that will be presented shortly.

Still within this second understanding on Grotius' famous passage, Javier Hervada proposes a very original point of view. For him, the impious hypothesis was commonplace in the Scholasticism and Grotius did take it from there, but he

---

[145]"*Ad rationes autem in contrarium, Gregorius quidem Ariminensis in 3 d.34 tenet duo. Primum, dato per impossible quod non esset Deus, adhuc esset peccatum et malum morale. Secundum, dato quod nulla esset lex prohibitive divina, adhuc essent peccata. Infert corollarium, quod multa sunt peccata ita secundum se mala, quod non sunt mala, quia prohibita etiam lege divina. Fundamentum eius potissimum est, quia* ad hoc *quod quis male agat, satis est quod agat contra rectam rationem, sive humanam sive angelicam.*" (*De eo ad quod tenetur homo cum primum venit ad usum rationis. Segunda pars relectionis*. 9, p. 1353).

[146]Besselink (1988), pp. 102–103.

gave it a new meaning. Hervada considers Grotius to be purely voluntarist, without any trace of intellectualism; Grotius was just an ordinary Reformer who did not accept the *analogia entis*. Therefore, there would be no ontological necessity between God and human nature: human nature behaves the way it does pursuant to the free will of the Maker, not because it is a reflection of His divine reason. Man is the way he is because God intended him to be, not because he infused him with His own reason. As seen, a voluntarist scholar would not consider the hypothesis impossible, merely false. God exists and concerns Himself with human affairs; He is, thence, the source of Natural Law. A typical Medieval voluntarist thinker would never extract Natural Law from human nature, only from divine will. For that reason, there would be no Natural Law without God. However, according to Hervada, Grotius innovates in relation to his voluntarist predecessors because he considers the hypothesis valid: if it is not possible to extract law from divine will, then law can only derive from human reason (which does not mirror divine reason). Albeit associated with voluntarism, Grotius came up with a conception of Natural Law intelligible in itself, without the need of any references to God. Hervada thus suggests that Grotius' hypothesis is a manifestation of secularism.[147]

This opinion has two *ab initio* flaws: in Grotius there is the *analogia entis* and, like Suárez, he believes the law encompasses both will and reason. Even if that were not true, there is still a structural mistake in Hervada's reasoning. Grotius does not accept the validity of the hypothesis: he completes the paragraph of that passage insisting that God exists and that He cares about human affairs. Hervada regards this as an unnecessary effort that no Scholastic scholar would put himself through, because God would become superfluous due to the absence of the *analogia entis* in Grotius's system and of God's will in the formation of Natural Law (as a result of accepting the hypothesis). Since Grotius was no atheist, he felt obliged to justify His existence. Here lies a mistake: since Grotius does not truly accept the hypothesis, Natural Law could only come from God's will if he were a voluntarist. He would have to accept the hypothesis (which he does not) in order for Hervada's assumptions to be correct.

Furthermore, one cannot forget that Grotius clearly distinguishes between Natural and voluntary Law (and the latter between human and divine).[148] Therefore, Natural Law does not (only) stems from God's will. In the most varying degrees of intellectualism, as there is no need to resort directly to God to justify Natural Law, it is somewhat autonomous from Him. This same idea is present in other conceptions of secularism: that is why it is so tempting to associate the impious hypothesis with secularism.

Finally, with regard to the third understanding of the famous passage, the formulation goes back to Marcus Aurelius, who did not discuss Natural Law or its basis, but the behavior of man towards his own life and death, if he wished to live philosophically (in the ancient meaning of wisdom). If the gods existed, then the

[147]Hervada (1983), pp. 18–21.

[148]**DJBP**. I, 1, 9 and I, 1, 13.

wise man did not need to fear death, but if they did not (which was a lie), why would that man want to live in meaningless world? In both cases, death should not be feared.[149]

Marcus Aurelius' hypothesis shows signs of a nonchalant behavior towards life. According to Berljak, this would lead to objective values; morality forgoes God in binding men.[150] If that holds true, it would seem to bode well with the meaning and intent of Grotius' hypothesis: he introduces the *etiamsi daremus* to refute Carneades and reject the argument that nature cannot tell the difference between right and wrong. Grotius does not analyze the formation of Natural Law in the *prolegomena*. As a result, the second interpretation implies a change in focus, as the Jurist from Delft would not have employed the hypothesis for the purposes of the debate between intellectualism and voluntarism.

In the *prolegomenon* 11 (where the impious hypothesis is found), Grotius does not quote the Roman Emperor. Nevertheless, there are good arguments to support the idea that the Roman was actually the source of Grotius' inspiration, besides the similarities in their formula. In the following *prolegomenon*, Grotius refers to the **Meditations**—which, according to the imprecise quotation technique of the time, suggests he had his attention focused on Marcus Aurelius. Besides, Pufendorf himself, the first great commentator of Grotius' work, defended that the hypothesis originated in Marcus Aurelius' work.[151]

However, Haggenmacher raises a serious objection to this interpretation: Grotius only inserted the footnote referring to Marcus Aurelio in the 1642 edition, two decades after the original writing of the *prolegomena* (and of the impious hypothesis). If the origin thereof really were the Roman Emperor's work, it would be strange for Grotius not to quote him in 1625, seeing that this kind of source was one of the most valued for the author. Further, in the following paragraph, the reference to the **Meditations** does not coincide with the passage regarding the impious hypothesis. The most likely scenario is that Grotius knew the formula from reading the Scholastic scholars (since it was commonplace for them to use it) and only inserted Marcus Aurelius after studying his work better, in order to adjust the hypothesis to the Stoic context to comply with Humanist standards. Once again, Grotius faces an "eclectic coincidence."[152]

The theses regarding the Stoic sources of Grotius' thinking are recurrent and, largely, true. However, they tend to downplay the Scholastic influence on Grotius, as if Stoicism and Scholasticism were completely antagonistic schools of thought. In fact, there is nothing closer to Stoicism than Christianism. Christianism, still in its earlier stages, incorporated the Stoic philosophy in order to pass along Christ's messages. The *jus naturae* of the monk Gratian is closer to the Stoic *lex naturalis* than to Aristotle's natural justice. St. Ambrose was an avid reader of Cicero.

---

[149]Antonino, 1986, p. 268. Book II, 11.

[150]Berljak (1978), pp. 94–99.

[151]Pufendorf (1703), II, 3, 19, p. 112.

[152]Haggenmacher (1983), p. 501.

Actually, it seems likely that the Scholastic writers themselves took the idea for the impious hypothesis from Marcus Aurelius. There would not even be a slight change in its meaning. The debate between intellectualism and voluntarism relates not only to the elements that take part in the constitution of the law, but also to the autonomy of values before the God Maker of all things. On the one hand, when a voluntarist states that Natural Law is the product of God's free will, he intends to prove that God created this *jus* directly. On the other hand, when an intellectualist argues that Natural law can be deduced by the right reason, he intends to diminish divine interference in nature, because God acts more through nature than through miracles. This position reveals the existence of absolute values, which depend on no-one's will (or whims), not even God's.

Aquinas, a "pure" intellectualist, never mentioned the hypothesis, but he supports the idea of an objective morality. While analyzing if the Eternal Law coincides with the ultimate reason that lies in God, Aquinas needs to overcome a serious obstacle: the Eternal Law is one, but the reasons behind things in the divine mind are multiple. Since the Eternal Law corresponds to the ordering of the entire creation, should it be plural then God would be able to alter things after they were created. The laws of logic could change and two and two could no longer be four. Aquinas' response is that, like in any artist, preexists in God the design according to which the craft is made in such a way that his creation is bound to such reason.[153] Creation was not a random act by God. He conceived it as it should be and subjected all of His subsequent acts to that standard. Perhaps the rhetoric of the impious hypothesis would not be pleasing to Aquinas, but he expressed this same idea in other words.

4.4 From the Laws of God to the Laws of Men

In **De Jure Praedae**, Grotius introduces a sophisticated system of analysis of *jus*, based in nine *regulae* and thirteen *leges*. The former roughly designate the sources of the law in a formal sense: they correspond to the different types of law. The latter are rules of conduct that derive from the *regulae*.

Here, *jus* means objective law or *lex*. Yet, the *leges* do not coincide with the species of law of the Scholastic school (which, in fact, generally, refer to the *regulae*). This occurs because Grotius employed the axiomatic–deductive structure of the *prolegomena* to explain the law of war, which only applies to the violent dealings between nations and lacks a judicial organism above the States. Thus, each type of law (Natural, Divine, of Nations and Civil) is a source for the law of war.

The first axiom is "What God has shown to be His will that is law."[154] Divine will is revealed not only through supernatural means, but also because God infused

[153]**ST**. 1-2 q. 93 a.1.

[154]"*Quod Deus se velle significarit, id jus est.*" (**DJPC**, p. 8).

it in His creation. The first law of nature derives from this *telos* of all things. In spite of its name, as seen, Grotius relates the first law of nature to Aquinas' Eternal Law. As exposed in the first chapter, the idea of separating Natural Law in line with a genetic-chronologic criterion dates back to the time of the glossators. And the first impulse that all individual parts of the creation express relates to their own survival. Grotius' first Natural Law accomplishes the most primary of the Stoic-Epicureanist instincts: the love for oneself. From this rule, two laws derive: "It shall be permissible to defend [one's own] life and to shun that which threatens to prove injurious" and "It shall be permissible to acquire for oneself, and to retain, those things which are useful for life."[155]

But God deemed that the instinct of self-preservation would be insufficient to preserve his creation and so He bestowed men with the love for others, which is the second Stoic inclination. Although this drive is also present in other animals and even in inanimate objects, it is inherent to the rational spirit. God imprinted upon man the image of His own mind.[156] It is a rational faculty. Sins may darken man's perception, but never entirely, so that all men can distinguish good from evil. The universal consent can only come from a common cause, and this is the second law of nature or the first law of nations: "What the common consent of mankind has shown to be the will of all, that is law."[157] Each name focuses on one aspect of this law: it is natural, since it comes from reason; and it is *jus gentium* since all peoples are able to reach the same conclusion regarding its precepts.

This rule drives all men toward a certain kind of sociability; not the Aristotle's, but the Stoic's sociability. Grotius even quotes Seneca's analogy between the human body and humanity: just as all parts of the organism must work harmoniously, each individual should work for the good of mankind.[158] Therefore, while the first and second laws arise for the benefit of the individual, the third and the fourth laws limit them: "Let no one inflict injury upon his fellow" and "Let no one seize possession of that which has been taken into the possession of another."[159] Yet they would be inadequate if no penalties were prescribed. That is why the fifth and sixth rules exist to ensure compliance thereto: "Evil deeds must be corrected" and "Good deeds must be recompensed."[160]

However rudimentary they may be, a society built upon these laws already allows the individuals to provide for their basic needs. But this society fails, for there is no stability in relations; human interests are fleeting and do not permit the development of institutions. It is necessary to advance on this "legal–civilizational"

---

[155]"*Vitam tueri et declinare nocitura liceat*" and "*Adjungere sibi quae ad vivendum sunt utilia eaque retinere liceat*" (**DJPC**, p. 10).

[156]**DJPC**, p. 12. This passage proves that, when writing **De Jure Praedae**, Grotius already knew and accepted the *analogia entis*.

[157]"*Quod consensus hominum velle cunctus significaverit, id jus est*" (**DJPC**, p. 12).

[158]**DJPC**, p. 13.

[159]"*Ne quis alterum laedat*" and "*Ne quis occupet alteri occupata*" (**DJPC**, pp. 13–14).

[160]"*Malefacta corrigenda*" and "*Benefacta repensanda.*" (**DJPC**, p. 15).

process. In addition, once men are born free, their will is enough to bind them and thus the good faith rule emerges: "What each individual has indicated to be his will that is law with respect to him."[161] Through this axiom, it is possible to bind man to himself (promise) and to other (pacts).

Because of the stability of agreements, men were able to gather in kingdoms and States, congregations far larger than families and clans. In order for these large societies to function "individual citizens should not only refrain from injuring other citizens, but should furthermore protect them, both as a whole and as individuals" (seventh law). Besides, "citizens should not only refrain from seizing one another's possessions, whether these be held privately or in common, but should furthermore contribute individually both that which is necessary to other individuals and that which is necessary to the whole"[162] (eighth law). These *leges* direct the love for others towards the good of each individual and the common good.

For Grotius, common good must always prevail. For that reason, there exists the fourth rule: "whatever the commonwealth has indicated to be its will, that is law in regard to the whole body of citizens."[163] This principle is the source of Positive Law, of the *jus civile*. The will of the State may be general or private. When directed at an individual, it is called a judgment. Thus, the fifth rule derives from the previous one: "whatever the commonwealth has indicated to be its will that is law for the individual citizens in their mutual relations." Consequently, an individual cannot pursue justice on his own. From that notion, the ninth law is drawn: "no citizen shall seek to enforce his own right against a fellow citizen, save by judicial procedure."[164]

In order for the Legislative and the Judiciary branches of power to be reliable and legitimate, both judges and legislators must undertake several obligations. The tenth and eleventh rules supplement the previous one: "The magistrate shall act in all matters for the good of the state" and "The state shall uphold as valid every act of the magistrate."[165] By "magistrate," Grotius refers to all people to whom the public *munus* befalls (which encompass both legislators and judges). After all, the will of these people is also a source of law. The sixth and seventh rule prescribe: "What the magistrate [legislator] has indicated to be his will, that is law in regard to the whole body of citizens" and "what the magistrate has indicated to be his will, that is law in regard to the citizens as individuals."[166]

---

[161] "*Quod se quisque velle significaverit, id in eum jus est*" (**DJPC**, p. 18).

[162] "*Ut singuli civis caeteros tum universos, tum singulos non modo non laederent, verum etiam tuerentur*" and "*Ut cives non modo alter alteri privatim aut in commune possessa non eriperent, verum etiam singuli tum quae singulis, tum quae universis necessaria conferrent*" (**DJPC**, p. 21).

[163] "*Quidquid respublica se velle significaverit, id in cives universos jus est*" (**DJPC**, p. 23).

[164] "*Quidquid respublica se velle significaverit, id inter cives singulos jus est*" and "*Ne civis adversum civem jus suum nisi judicio exsequatur*" (**DJPC**, p. 24).

[165] "*Ut magistratus omnia gerat e bono reipublicae*" and "*Ut quidquid magistratus gessit respublica ratum habeat*" (**DJPC**, p. 26).

[166] "*Quod se magistratus velle significavit id in cives universos jus est*" and "*Quod se magistratus velle significavit id in cives singulos jus est*" (**DJPC**, p. 26).

The ninth law plays an essential role in Grotius' thinking. In every well-established State, it is up to public institutions to hand out justice. However, the very absence of these institutions characterizes the law of war. The author then concentrates all his efforts on building a legal system able of functioning despite the precarious effectiveness of the law in international relations. Just like the common good of the people created the *jus civile*, Grotius argues that there is a common good of all nations, which engenders a kind of mixed law, composed of the Civil Law and the primary law of nations. That is the secondary law of nations: "Whatever all states have indicated to be their will, that is law in regard to all of them."[167] (eighth rule). Grotius' *jus gentium* is the subject of the last chapter of this book; for now, it is worth noticing that the idea of a Law of Nations is not fully developed in **de Jure Praedae**. The *jus gentium* represented a mixed law and not a middle ground; it contained norms of Natural and Civil Law.

Therefore, States are forbidden (like the individuals are) from pursuing justice on their own: "Neither the state nor any citizen thereof shall seek to enforce his own right against another state or its citizen, save by judicial procedure."[168] (twelfth law). Here lies the complications in determining which of the conflicting States has jurisdiction to pursue justice, in the absence of an international authority. Grotius suggests a solution for this problem in rule nine: "precedence shall be given to the state which is the defendant, or whose citizen is the defendant; but if the said state proves remiss in the discharge of its judicial duty, then that state shall be the judge, which is itself the plaintiff, or whose citizen is the plaintiff."[169] It may not seem so, but Grotius builds with this rule the theoretical framework that will allow him to settle the issues of the law of war. As will be seen in the last chapter, Grotius associates the just war doctrine with a judicial proceeding.

Those precepts are generic and necessary and can resolve all legal problems that may arise in the absence of a common authority. Nevertheless, they are rules of personal competence and only apply in the case of conflict of jurisdiction. How to settle conflicts between laws? Grotius resolves this with the thirteenth law: "In cases where the laws can be observed simultaneously, let them [all] be observed; when this is impossible, the law of superior rank shall prevail."[170] The law of divine origin should prevail over the Law of Nations and this over Civil Law. The law that generates a greater good overtakes the inferior and private one. In short, the laws deriving from the first axioms and of the first rules of this hierarchical and deductive system should prevail.

Contrary to the Scholastics, Grotius' categorization of law in **De Jure Praedae**, does not aim at the *analogia entis*: the descending process from the law closest to

---

[167]"*Quidquid omnes respublicae significarunt se velle, id in omnes jus est*" (**DJPC**, p. 26).

[168]"*Ne respublica neu civis in alteram rempublicam alteriusve civem jus suum nisi judicio exsequatur*" (**DJPC**, p. 27).

[169]"*In judicando priores sint partes ejus reipublicae, unde cujusve a cive petitur. Quod si hujus officium cesset, tum respublica, quae ipsa cujusve civis petit, eam rem judicet.*" (**DJPC**, p. 28).

[170]"*Ut ubi simul observari possunt observentur: ubi id fieri non potest, tum potior sit quae est dignior*" (**DJPC**, p. 29).

God to the law of men. Albeit known to the author, he does not make use of this notion, for Grotius did not want to write a book on Theology; in spite of all the knowledge he had on the subject, his goal was to write a legal text. Since he did not intend to comment on Aquinas **Summa Theologiae**, Grotius stuck to his subject, the *jus belli*. The purpose of these nine rules and thirteen laws was to unify the case-by-case prescriptions of the Doctrine of Just War under general principles of law and to make them comprehensible.

On the other hand, the system of **De Jure Belli ac Pacis** is much more simple and similar to the Scholastic categorization of laws. The third meaning of law, *lex,* is divided into two categories: Natural and voluntary Law. Grotius does not hide his influence on this division and mentions the Aristotelian distinction between legal justice and natural justice.[171] He uses the word "voluntary" to emphasize the artificiality of this law. The voluntary law is an arbitrary *jus* that actually establishes "right" and "wrong" and not simply recognize them. All the characterization of the last chapter regarding Positive Law applies here.

Voluntary law may be either human or divine. The former may be Civil Law, broader than Civil Law or narrower than Civil Law. Grotius' *jus civile* coincides with Suárez's *jus civile*: both come from a public power (although the notion of State differs greatly between these authors). The law broader than Civil Law corresponds to the *jus gentium* itself. The narrower Civil Law is almost an innovation of Grotius: it is subject to Civil Law and encompasses the order of a father, of a master; it corresponds to the *jus rectorium*, the justice between non-equals of the first definition of *jus*. There, Grotius classified the *jus* in accordance with the idea of justice. Here, Grotius classifies the *jus* according to the legal precept to which it refers. This law corresponds to Aristotle's domestic justice.[172]

Divine Voluntary Law may be either universal or specific. The distinction focuses on the recipient of the obligation: all men or just one people. God gave humanity its law in three different moments: after creating men, when the pact was renovated after the Flood and with Christ's message. The Old and New Testaments, as well as the Ten Commandments are all part of the Divine Voluntary Law. God deigned to grant specific laws solely to the Hebrews and Grotius argues at length that foreigners were never the recipients of this specific divine law. Yet, Christians, as descendents of the Jewish tradition, could make use of this law, as long as they adapt it to the precepts of the Gospels.[173]

---

[171]**DJBP**. I, 1, 9, 2.
[172]**DJBP**. I, 1, 14, 1.
[173]**DJBP**. I, 1, 15-17.

4.4.1 The Unity of Natural Law

Twenty years later and Grotius' Natural Law is finally integrated, abandoning the glossators' genetic habit of separating this law. As discussed, Grotius employed in his youth the two Stoic inclinations, love for oneself and love for others, as criteria to separate Natural Law into primary and secondary Natural Law. However, in his work of maturity, a single Natural Law corresponds to all inclinations of the rational and social human nature. Grotius did not combine these two inclinations into one law; he simply eliminated the primary Natural Law. All references to the origin of that law refer to sociability and there is no mention on self-preservation. The rational and social human nature is the mother of Natural Law.[174] Survival and selfishness can move men, but they do not generate law. Grotius does not seem to distinguish between rationality and sociability, which puts him even closer to the Scholastic concept of Natural Law.

All men are capable of perceiving this law and it applies equally in different places. It is valid even for peoples that do not share the "true" religion.[175] And God cannot change it. Yet, Grotius' Natural Law is not as rigid and immutable as the Natural Law of the Modern scholars who came after him. In fact, it is closer to the flexible Natural Law of the Scholastics: the changes are not in Natural Law itself, but in the human circumstances that influence it.

Less precisely than Suárez, Grotius describes three ways of circumventing the immutability of Natural Law. Firstly, this law does not encompass only things that are beyond the reach of human will; it may govern the consequences of voluntary actions as well. For instance, human action created private property. However, ever since its creation, Natural Law forbids theft.[176] Similarly, Grotius discusses the nature of the *summum imperium* (**DJBP**. II, 4, 13), of the contract (**DJBP**. II, 12, 9) and of the war (**DJBP**. III, 4, 1). They are institutions created by human ingenuity, and it is from the essence thereof that these natural precepts derive.[177] The resemblance to Suárez' Dominative Natural Law is not a coincidence.

The second way of circumventing the immutability of Natural Law refers to the possibility of there being a change in Natural Law. In truth, this law does not change, but human circumstances do. When a creditor pardons a debt, the natural obligation of giving back what belongs to others remains; it simply ceased to apply to the case at hand. Grotius adds another example, which confirms the Scholastic origins of this idea. When God orders the immolation of someone (as He did with Abraham) or the stripping of their assets, the crime of homicide or theft is not being committed, because these actions would have been practiced on His orders, and He is the supreme master of all lives and goods.[178]

---

[174] **DJBP**. *prolegomenon* 16.

[175] **DJBP**. II, 15, 8.

[176] **DJBP**. I, 1, 10, 4.

[177] Tadashi (1993), pp. 41–42.

[178] **DJBP**. I, 1, 10, 6.

Lastly, there are matters that are part of Natural Law because they come from a particular circumstance of things (*pro certo rerum statu*). Before the appearance of private property, the common use of goods was natural; before the appearance of Positive Laws, the defense of goods by force was permissible.[179] This concept is very relevant to the Grotian system since it is by means of this concept that Grotius is able to defend the freedom of the seas and the legitimacy of private wars. As I shall discuss in the last chapter, the sea, which is insusceptible to appropriation, remains in the primitive system of common use. Regarding the law of war, as there is no international judicial body, self-defense is legitimate for anyone (public or private individual) and, hence private wars are not necessarily injust.

4.5 Summary

After all, Hugo Grotius is a very eclectic thinker. It is not possible to say with certainty that he is affiliated to any school of thought, be it Scholasticism, Stoicism, Epicureanism, Juridical Humanism, or even Modernity. His Legal Philosophy depends on Theology, which, in turn, is built on rational grounds. Everything about Grotius is so uncertain, he seems to have been influenced by so many different thinkers, that he might have been yet original.

That is why there are so many different interpretations of his work. A more traditional reading favors Grotius' Modernity and is based on different aspects of his work: his criticism of the Scholastics, for granting too much authority to Aristotle; his considerations on method (similar to the ones developed by Galileo and Descartes) and his impious hypothesis as a clear sign of secularism. However, such reading neglects several other features of the Grotian system that dispute this so-called Modernity. After all, he also appeals to authority (even if said authority is a means of proving historical facts that actually happened); the genesis of the Grotian method (*mos gallicus*) does not correspond to that of the Paduan School and his impious hypothesis already existed in the cultural Scholastic universe.

Because of these criticisms, another reading arose; one that places emphasis on the Scholastic influences in Grotius' work. There are well-reasoned arguments in its support, but some authors overdid their conclusions. According to them, Grotius is but a follower of the Spanish Scholasticism. These scholars interpret Francisco Suárez in such a way as to disqualify Grotius: all the ideas that made him famous (the impious hypothesis as a sign of intellectualism, the *jus gentium*, the subjective right and a flexible Natural Law) would have come from Suárez. The fact that these institutes represented a necessary evolution on Grotius' conceptual system is not even considered. For some, Grotius would have "copied" Suárez; for others, he used **De Legibus** as a book of reference. The fact that there are few explicit quotations to Suárez in Grotius' work matters little; he would still have been one of

[179] **DJBP**. I, 1, 10, 7.

Grotius' most important sources. Grotius simply concealed this source of influence because of the environment he lived in.

And those exaggerations set off a reaction: a third reading, which emphasizes the Stoic influences on Grotius' work. His Modernity is restored, albeit by other means: by refuting an ancient skeptic, Grotius rejects the arguments of a new one and builds an objective morality centered on men. His notion of sociability does not correspond to Aquinas' comprehension of Aristotle and previous interpretations thereof have neglected the role that the principle of self-preservation plays in Grotius' Natural Law. In addition, his impious hypothesis is not about the constitution of the law and thus is not a part of the debate between intellectualism and voluntarism. Marcus Aurelius also introduced his formula and in him, the hypothesis serves the same purpose that it does in Grotius: to emphasize the existence of values, even in the absence of a divinity.

In effect, Grotius reserves to the Stoic authors the largest part of his references, but is difficult to perceive fundamental differences between Stoicism and Christianism. For an author whose Theology plays a direct role on the understanding of his legal institutions, the references to Stoic authors are simply an elegant way (according to a Humanist aesthetics) of relaying the Christian message. It is also likely that the Scholastic's idea of the impious hypothesis came from Marcus Aurelius. The debate between intellectualism and voluntarism is part of a greater discussion, already found in Aquinas' writings, on the moral objectivity in the face of God. Furthermore, the more Grotius studied the Stoics, the less importance he gave to the role of self-preservation in the formation of Natural Law.

Lastly, despite being a Reformer, Grotius' doctrine of Natural Law is quite similar to that of Catholic Scholastics. Even if he did not use the *analogia entis* in his legal writings, he was aware of it and it certainly lived on as reminiscence. Albeit his categorization of laws does not comply with the Scholastic typology, he employs the same division, distinguishing Natural from Voluntary Divine Law. Moreover, Grotius' Natural Law is as immutable and inflexible as Suárez—and quite different from the Modern (and Protestant) scholars who followed him. His Arminianism produced a set of convictions similar to that of Catholicism.

References

Antonino, Marco. Meditações. In: **Antologia de Textos**. Trad. Agostinho da Silva et alii. 2. ed. São Paulo: Abril Cultural, 1986.

Aubrey, John. **Brief Lives**. Edited by Richard Barber. Woodbridge, Suffolk: The Boydell Press, 1982.

Barbeyrac, Jean. Nota de rodapé viii, comentário ao texto. In: Grotius, Hugo. **Le droit de la guerre et de la paix de Hugues Grotius**. Trad. J. Barbeyrac. Amsterdam: Pierre de Coup, 1724.

Basdevant, Jules. Hugo Grotius. In: Pillet, Antoine. **Les Fondateurs du Droit International**. Paris: V. Giard & E. Brière, 1904.

Bederman, David. Reception of the Classical Tradition in International Law: Grotius' *De Jure Belli ac Pacis*. **Emory International Law Review**, n. 10, 1996.

Berljak, Matija. **Il Diritto Naturale e il suo Rapporto con la Divinità in Ugo Grozio**. Roma: Università Gregoriana, 1978.

Besselink, Leonard. **Keeping faith**: a study of Grotius' doctrine of natural law. Florence, European University Institute, 1988. EUI PhD theses; Department of Law.

Bobbio, Norberto. **Thomas Hobbes**. Trad. Carlos Nelson Coutinho. Rio de Janeiro: Campus, 1991.

Chipman, Lauchlan. Grotius and the Derivation of Natural Law. **Australian Society of Legal Philosophy Bulletin**, n. 26, 1983.

Cicero, M. Tullius. De Amicitia. In: Cicero, M. Tullius; Ernesti, J. August. **Opera Omnia**. Oxonium, Collingwood (London), 1810. v. 5. Cícero, Marco Túlio. **Diálogo sobre a Amizade**. Trad. José Perez. São Paulo: Cultura Moderna, s/d.

Cicero, M. Tullius; Stroebel, Eduard. **Rhetorici libri duo qui vocantur de inventione**. In: Aedibus B.G. Teubneri. Lipsiae. 1915.

Cicero, M. Tullius. **De Officiis**. William Heinemann (London) and G. P. Putnam's Sons (New York), 1928.

Cícero, Marco Túlio. **On moral ends**. Trad. Raphael Woolf. Cambridge: Cambridge University Press, 2001.

Crowe, M.B. The "Impious Hypothesis": a paradox in Hugo Grotius? In: Haakonssen, Knud (ed.). **Grotius, Pufendorf and Modern Natural Law**. Dartmouth: Ashgate, 1993.

Dufour, Alfred. L'influence de la méthodologie des sciences physiques et mathématiques sur les Fondateurs de l'École du Droit naturel moderne (Grotius, Hobbes, Pufendorf). **Grotiana**, v. I, 1980.

Eikema Hommes, Hendrik van. Grotius on Natural and International Law. **Netherlands International Law Review**, v. XXX, 1983.

Grotius, Hugo. **De Iure Belli ac Pacis libri tres**. *In quibus ius naturae et Gentium: item iuris publici praecipua explicantur*. Parisiis: Nicolaum Buon, 1625.

Grotius, Hugo. **De Iure Belli ac Pacis libri tres**. *In quibus ius naturae et Gentium: item iuris publici praecipua explicantur*. Amsterdã: I. Blaeu, 1646. Edited by James Brown Scott. Oxford, London: Clarendon Press, Geoffrey Cumberlege, 1925. (The Classics of International Law).

Grotius, Hugo. **De Iure Belli ac Pacis libri tres**. *In quibus ius naturae et Gentium: item iuris publici praecipua explicantur*. Cum Annotationibus Auctoris, ejusdemque Dissertatione de *Mari Libero*; Ac Libello singulari *De Aequitate, Indulgentia et Facilitate*: Nec non Joann. Frid. Gronovii Notis in totum opus de Jure Belli ac Pacis, Ex altera recensione Joannis Barbeyracii. Amsterdã: apud Janssonio-Waesbergios, 1735.

Grotius, Hugo. **De Jure Praedae Commentarius**. La Haye: Hamaker, Nijhoff, 1868.

Grotius, Hugo. **De Jure Praedae Commentarius**. I: Trad. Gwladys Williams e Walter Zeidel. II: **The Collotype Reproduction of the Original Manuscript of 1604 in the Handwriting of Grotius**. Edited by James Brown Scott. Oxford, London: Clarendon Press, Geoffrey Cumberlege, 1950. 2 v. (The Classics of International Law).

Grotius, Hugo. **Traité de la Verité de la Religion Chrétienne**. Trad. P. le Jeune. Amsterdam: Ledet, 1728.

Grotius, Hugo. **The Freedom of the Seas, or the right which belongs to the Dutch to take part in the East Indian Trade**. Translated by Ralph van Deman Magoffin. Introduction by James Brown Scott. New York: Oxford University Press, 1916. (The Classics of International Law).

Grotius, Hugo. **The Jurisprudence of Holland**. Trans. R.W. Lee, D.C.L., F.B.A. 2. ed. Dutch-English bilingual edition. Oxford: Clarendon Press, 1953.

Grotii, Hugonis. Letter to Willem de Groot February, 1616, n. 450. **Briefwisseling I**. edited by Molhuysen, Meulenbroek and Witkam. The Hague: Martinus Nijhoff, 1928.

Haggenmacher, Peter. **Grotius et la doctrine de la guerre juste**. Genève, Paris: Heige, Presses Universitaires de France, 1983.

Haggenmacher, Peter. Grotius and Gentili: a reassessment of Thomas E. Holland's inaugural lecture. In: Bull, Hedley; Kingsbury, Benedict; Roberts, Adam (ed.). **Hugo Grotius and International Relations**. Oxford, New York: Oxford University, Clarendon Press, 2002.

Hervada, Javier. The Old and the New in the Hypothesis "Etiamsi daremus" of Grotius. **Grotiana**, v. 4, 1983.

Hobbes, Thomas. **Leviatã**. Trad. João Paulo Monteiro e Maria Beatriz Nizza da Silva. 3. ed. São Paulo: Abril Cultural, 1983.

Knight, William S.M. **The Life and Works of Hugo Grotius**. Londres: Sweet & Maxwell, 1925.

Korkman, Peter. Barbeyrac on Scpeticism and on Grotian Modernity. **Grotiana**, v. 20/21, 1999/2000.

Kosters, Jan. **Les Fondements du Droit des Gens**. Contribution à la théorie générale du droit des gens. Haia: Lugduno-Batavae, 1925.

Leger, James St. **The "Etiamsi Daremus" of Hugo Grotius**: a study in the origins of international law. Roma: *Pontificium Athenaeum "Angelicum" de Urbe*, 1962.

Merêa, Paulo. A Origem do Poder Civil em Suárez e em Puffendorf (Escolástica e Jusnaturalismo). **Estudos de Filosofia Jurídica e de História das Doutrinas Políticas**. Lisboa: Imprensa Nacional-Casa da Moeda, 2004.

Negro, Paola. A *Topos* in Hugo Grotius: "*Etiamsi daremus non esse Deum.*" **Grotiana**, v. 19, 1998.

Nussbaum, Arthur. **Historia del Derecho Internacional**. Trad. Francisco Javier Osset. Madrid: Revista de Derecho Privado, 1953.

Platão. **A República**. Trad. Carlos Alberto Nunes. Belém: Globo, 1976.

Pufendorf, Samuel. **Of the Law of Nature and Nations**. Trad. Basil Kennett. Oxford: Lichfield, 1703.

Rabbie, Edwin. L'Eglise el l'Etat dans la pensée de Hugo Grotius. **Grotiana**, v. 16/17, 1995–1996.

Reale, Miguel. **Horizontes do Direito e da História**. 3. ed. São Paulo: Saraiva, 2000.

Reeves, Jesse. Grotius, De Jure Belli ac Pacis: a bibliographical account. **The American Journal of International Law**, v. 19, n. 2, pp. 251–262, April 1925.

Roelofsen, C.G. Some Remarks on the "Sources" of the Grotian System of International Law. **Netherlands International Law Review**, v. XXX, 1983.

Scott, J. B. **The Catholic Conception of International Law**. Washington D.C.: Georgetown University Press, 1934.

Sénèque. **Dialogues**. Trad. A. Bourgery. Edição bilingüe. Paris: Les Belles-Lettres, 1951. *De Ira*.

Shaver, Robert. Grotius on Scepticism and Self-Interest. In: Haakonssen, Knud (ed.). **Grotius, Pufendorf and Modern Natural Law**. Dartmouth: Ashgate, 1993.

Tadashi, Tanaka. Grotius' concept of law. In: Yasuaki, Onuma (org.). **A Normative Approach to War**: peace, war and justice in Hugo Grotius. Oxford: Clarendom Press, 1993.

Thomas, Jeremy. The Intertwining of Law and Theology in the Writings of Grotius. **Journal of the History of International Law**, n. 1, 1999.

Tuck, Richard. Grotius, Carneades e Hobbes. **Grotiana**, v. 4, pp. 43–63, 1983.

Tuck, Richard. **Natural Rights Theories**: their origin and development. New York: Cambridge University Press, 1979.

Tuck, Richard. **The Rights of War and Peace**: political thought and the international order from Grotius to Kant. New York: Oxford University Press, 1999.

Vecchio, Giorgio del. Grotius and the Foundation of International Law. **New York University Law Review**, v. 37, n. 260, pp. 260–266, April 1962.

Vermeulen, Ben. Simon Stevin and the Geometrical Method in De jure praedae. **Grotiana**, v. 4, 1983.

Villey, Michel. **Leçons d'Histoire de la Philosophie du Droit**. Paris: Dalloz, 1962.

Vitoria, Francisco de. *De eo ad quod tenetur homo cum primum venit ad usum rationis*. **Obras de Francisco de Vitória**. *Relecciones Teologicas*. Edited by Teofilo Urdanoz. Madrid: Biblioteca de Autores Cristianos, 1960.

Vollenhoven, Cornelius van. Grotius and the Study of Law. **AJIL**, v. 19, n. 1, January 1925.

Wijffels, Alain. Early-Modern Literature on International Law and the Usus Modernus. **Grotiana**, v. 16–17, pp. 35–54, 1995–1996.

Winkel, Laurens. Les Origines Antiques de l'Appetitus Societatis de Grotius. **The Legal History Review**, v. 68, n. 3, pp. 393–403, March 2000.

Chapter 5
The Law of Nations in Francisco Suárez

The Suarezian *jus gentium* differs in essence from that of his predecessors, but tradition remains a constraining force. It should come as no surprise that the author addresses the *jus gentium* right after discussing Natural Law in book II, chapter XVII onward of the **De Legibus**, and before investigating Positive Law. As seen in chapter II, the authors before Vitória and Suárez mistook this branch for the *jus naturae*. Suárez's first task was to find a new distinctive criterion for the *jus gentium*.

Suárez did not reject tradition entirely. The Jurist from Coimbra will reject the ancient authors: Gaius, Ulpian, Isidore of Seville (to some extent) and even Aquinas (although he was always cautious of it, especially concerning Aquinas). This scenario changes completely in relation to Francisco de Vitória. Vitória's legacy was carefully and meticously assembled and developed by several Spanish professors up to Suárez.

> The university teaching is the most important source [of Suarezian thinking about *jus gentium*]. Since the Chairs of Theology, Canon Law and Laws, the Spanish maestros, through Salamanca, Coimbra, Évora and Alcalá Universities, mainly, have been gradually creating national awareness of human coexistence. This period is historically set since Francisco de Vitória pronounces his first lecture on political power (1528) until it culminates in Francisco Suárez with the publication of his treatise **De Legibus** in 1612.[1]

To affirm that Vitória influenced Suárez is correct, but not complete. The Spanish *maestros* were united by scientific solidarity. They borrowed each other's class manuscripts and passed them along hand to hand. Vitória's **Relecciones** were published ten years after his death and thirty years after he lectured on the first. Soon after, copies thereof reached the most distinctive universities of Spain. It is

[1]"*El magisterio universitario constituye la fuente más importante. Desde las Cátedras de Teología, Derecho Canónico y Leyes los maestros españoles, a través de las Universidades de Salamanca, Coimbra, Evora y Alcalá principalmente, fueron creando, progresivamente, una conciencia nacional de convivencia humana. Este período comprende históricamente desde que Francisco de Vitória pronuncia su primera relección sobre el poder político (1528) hasta que culmina en Francisco Suárez con la publicación de su tratado De Legibus, en 1612.*" (Pereña, 1973, p. xix).

P.E. Vauthier Borges de Macedo, *Catholic and Reformed Traditions in International Law*, Studies in the History of Law and Justice 9,
DOI 10.1007/978-3-319-59403-3_5

known that Melchior Cano in Alcalá and Martin de Ledesma in Coimbra made use of Vitória's copies in their teachings. In Salamanca, Soto, Cano, Chaves, Barrón, Cuevas and Covarrubias used them as well. One of the greatest theologians of the second generation of the Spanish Scholasticism, Luis de Molina, taught the **Relecciones** in Évora. Many other authors, specially, Melchior Cano, Domingos de Soto, Pedro de Sotomaior, Juan de la Penha, Mancio de Corpus Christi, Juan de Guevara, Friar Luís de Lion, Bartolomeu de Medina, Pedro de Aragón and Domingo Bañez not only repeated Vitória's lessons, but also made some valuable additions thereto. In his introductory study to the book II of **De Legibus**, Luciano Pereña wrote a short but interesting comment on the concept of *jus gentium* in each of these authors and others that came before Suárez.[2]

The problem for all those authors was to find a legal basis for peace in this amazing new world, since the legal Medieval structure of the *orbis christianus* had lost its validity. The idea of the universal empire was a distant reality, Christian Europe faced new and unknown spaces and peoples, the world became bigger and Canon Law was no longer able to unite everyone.

Suárez inherits a pressing and much disputed issue from the historical circumstances of his time: a legal bond for all mankind. Given the extent of the controversy, Suárez did not always offer a full explanation. On the contrary, he went through many phases until he was able to present the definite text of **De Legibus**. The first phase corresponds to the manuscripts **Quaestio 90 of De Legibus**, **Quaestiones de iustitia et iure**, and especially the last *disputatio* in **De Bello**, inserted in the Treaty of Charity. Therefore, Suárez at first surrenders to the old inclination of addressing certain topics of the *jus gentium* (wars, embassies, trade, slavery) instead of the *jus gentium* as a whole. However, writing about the law of war meant addressing an issue that is far older than the notion of *jus gentium* as a Positive Law among peoples. In order to write about the law of war, the author returns to the very origins of Western Civilization, to the Just War Tradition.

---

[2]Pereña (1973), p. xx et seq. The extent of this cooperation between the Spanish maestros is very controversial. In the first half of the Twentieth Century, the very existence of a Spanish School of International Law was questioned. The American internationalist J. Scott Brown was the first to support this idea in his acclaimed work **Origen Español del Derecho Internacional Moderno,** 1928. He argued that the Spanish school began with Victoria and ended with a Dutch of Iberian thought, Hugo Grotius. This position received an attack and a defense. J.T. Delos published in 1929 **La Société Internationale et les Principes de Droit Public** in which he defended the theory that Vitoria's *jus gentium*, which is based in an objective and institutional axiological order, would not have exercised immediate influence; on the contrary, Suárez would have corrupted the concept with voluntarist and subjectivist elements, which would result in a voluntarist and statist view of International Law. Then, in 1932, Miaja de la Muela, a professor inValladolid, wrote a text on Fernando Vazquez de Menchaca in support of the Salamanca School, pursuant to the following assumptions that were supposedly shared by all lawyers-theologians: the existence of a Natural Law whose principles influenced international relations; these relations are not the result of chance, but a requirement of human nature; people do not live isolated, but among them there are links arising out of convenience and common humanity; the theologians were committed only to the truth and to the enthusiasm of their own opinions. (Scott 1928; Delos 1950; Miaja de la Muela 1932; For an overview of this debate, see Barcia Trelles, 1933, pp. 389–396).

In this chapter, I will first examine the concept of *jus gentium* and, in particular of the law of war, developed by Suárez in his youth. I will demonstrate that it corresponds to an ideology in defense of civility. Then, when describing Suárez's final notion, I shall display the arguments he raised against the traditional concepts of *jus gentium* that muddled it with Natural Law. There is no doubt that these two branches of law stand close one to another, as evidenced in the study on the possibility of there being changes to the Law of Nations. However, according to Suárez, the Law of Nations belongs to Positive Law. Also, I will present the foundations of this law in Suárez. In order to do so, I will describe Suárez's theory of the State, which shall enlighten his understanding on the State and on the popular origin of sovereignty. Then, I shall demonstrate that Suárez chose custom as a formal source of the Law of Nations to avoid the requirement of a global legislator. Finally, I shall prove that Suárez was not theorizing about international relations, but about the international society itself.

5.1 The Law of War in Suárez

Given that Aquinas elaborates the classical formulation of the Just War Doctrine that all subsequent scholars (including Suárez) would pursue, one must begin by Aquinas. His investigation on war is encapsulated in *Quaestio* 40 of the *secunda secundae* of the Treaty of Charity, and it sums up four articles. The first article questions whether wars are licit; the second article questions whether it would be legitimate for clerics to wage war; the third article questions whether the use of stratagems and fighting on festive days should be licit. However, the key aspect of Aquina's formulation lies in the requirements for a war to be just, which are set forth in the first article:

> First, the authority of the sovereign by whose command the war is to be waged. Private persons should not declare war, because they can present their right before a higher court. (...)
>
> Secondly, a just cause is required, namely that those who are attacked, should be attacked because they deserve it on account of some fault. (...)
>
> Thirdly, it is necessary that the belligerents should have a rightful intention, so that they intend the advancement of good, or the avoidance of evil.[3]

Although the "law" of war (a *jus*) is the issue, its study is inserted in the Treaty of Charity. A contemporary reader may find it strange for a book on one of the three theological virtues to examine a branch of Law. However, for Suárez, that was

[3]"*Primo quidem, auctoritas principis, cuius mandato bello est gerendum. Non enim pertinet ad personam privatam bellum movere: quia potest ius suum in iudicio superioris prosequi.* (...) *Secundo, requiritur causa iusta: ut scilicet illi qui impugnantur propter aliquam culpam impugnationem mereantur.* (...) *Tertio, requiritur ut sit intentio bellantium recta: qua scillicet intenditur vel ut bonum promoveatur, vel ut malum vitetur.* (**ST**. 2-2 q. 40 a.1).

ordinary: only charity can surpass the limits of justice and Law. Even if one seeks only to establish justice, war is a reality that transcends this dominion to another more noble.

There were questions to which law provided no answer. In Antiquity, the skeptic Carneades attacked the doctrine of Natural Law held by the Stoics. He gained fame, with his method of demonstrating pros and cons, by ridiculing the notion of justice. One of his most celebrated arguments was the thought experiment known as the "plank of Carneades". In a shipwreck, two persons swim up to a plank to save themselves from drowning, but the plank can only hold one. In this case, who has the right to the plank? According to the skeptic, in an extreme case of need and self-preservation, the answer would be both and neither. Today, legal systems recognize the "state of necessity" in situations like this one and any of the castaways would be entitled to take the board without facing responsibility for the other person's drowning. But this answer would not satisfy an Ancient thinker, because it was believed that justice could only be on one side of things. Rommen[4] asserts that, seventeen centuries later, Suárez would provide one correct answer. Law cannot function in situations marked by extreme scarcity or absolute abundance, because it presupposes some criteria of distribution. In the aforementioned example, the order of Justice and Law should end and the reign of Charity begin.

In Aquinas, peace corresponds to an internal effect of charity. In turn, war (together with hatred, acedias, envy, discord, strife, schism, baiting, sedition and scandal) is a vice that is contrary to charity. For a theologian, evaluating justice in war is important not so much in determining an injury, but rather because it constitutes a sin against one of the Three Theological Virtues. The investigation of justice or injustice in war is a means to ensure the fulfillment of a much more important theological end. An unjust war, in addition to harming Law, harms Charity. Francisco Suárez repeats this same disposition and does not cover the law of war in his treaty on Law and Justice, the **De Legibus**, but rather in the last *disputatio* of the Treaty of Faith, Hope and Charity. First and foremost, he is a theologian.

This first phase of Suarezian thought regarding the issue of the law of war begins with his teachings at the Roman College (1580–1585). Paradoxically, his Treaty of War corresponds to Suarez's intellectual youth and maturity both. It was mostly thought out and written in 1584, but it was revised and published only in 1621. This time lapse ensured that that his message did not stray from that of the Treatises of Laws.

In his concrete, specific dispositions on the law of war, the author does not demonstrate much originality; his text summarizes all of the work of the Second Scholastic on just war. This was his merit and his intention. The work was, most importantly, a Catholic and Spanish conception. Even so, surprising was the fact that, since Francisco de Vitória, the Spanish maestros preached a high tolerance for other peoples and religions (particularly the Islam) and reproached the fervor of the

---

[4]Rommen (1998), p. 18.

Iberian conquest. For example, Suárez did not hesitate in admitting the possibility of justice in a war waged by a non-Christian sovereign against a Christian prince. And according to Vitória, given that authority does not result from religion, but rather nature, all peoples, even infidels, are able to hold dominium. Therefore, the Indians also exercise sovereignty and live in a "pacific dominium of public and private property. Thus (excluding any impeding obstacle), they should be considered true owners and, in these circumstances, they cannot be removed from their territory".[5] Therefore, the Spanish Scholastic law of war obstructs the titles of property held by the Spanish in America and takes the monopoly of justice away from Catholic monarchs.

Indeed, at first glance, the "Spanish school of peace" (a term employed by Luciano Pereña) seems hardly Spanish and Catholic. However, its "Spanishness" and "Catholicness" represents much more than a mere defense of a state policy or an outdated conception of the world. The grand dilemma of the sixteenth century was the inexorable dissociation between the two cities: the earthly city and the city of God. Suárez employed all his intellectual force to fight Machiavelli on his own terms. The idea of empire had lost its glimmer in historic years, and there were as many sovereignties as there were States. For the author, Spain was the key to the crisis and the last hope for the reconstruction of a Christian Europe. The country was to convert itself into an empire at the service of religion, justice and civilization. All Catholic princes, as an imperative of their Faith, could protect the Church. Yet, only a State with the size and strength of Spain could intervene in the schism of the earth and save the Christian civilization.[6]

As a truly civilizing mission (an undertaking that had to be both Catholic and Spanish), Suárez conceived the **De Bello**. If this work seemed hardly Catholic and Spanish, it is because it must be read in the light of chapter eighteen of the Treaty of Faith, which Luciano Pereña named the "Treaty of Intervention". This work deals with the just means of coercion for the conversion of infidels, and its main message sums up to the duty of pagans to hear and tolerate the Christian faith.[7] This is not an obligation to convert (which presupposes free adherence) but to support evangelization. The Catholic Religion contained the Truth, and so none could stop its disclosure. In order to guarantee the preaching of religion, the Pope may commission the Catholic princes to intervene and promote war. In the end, the project of the Second Scholastic truly justified the Spanish imperial policy in the conquest of both America and Asia.

Even so, this represented a considerable advancement over the previous conception of "the barbarians encircling the Christian and European empire." Sovereignty and titles of domain held by infidels were no less important than those

---

[5]"*(...) in pacifica possessione rerum et publice et privatim. Ergo omnino (nisi contrarium constet) habendi sunt pro dominis. Neque in dicta causa possessione deturbandi*" (**De Indis**, *Relectio* 1, 5, p. 651).

[6]Pereña (1956), p. 19 et seq.

[7]Pereña (1956), p. 19 et seq., as well as the entire second part thereof, entitled **El Derecho de Intervención**.

held by Christians. The politics of pagan peoples held the same importance as those held by peoples that preached the true faith. The lesson of the separation of the two cities was well learned. However, Suárez knew very well that without the action of Justice (as well as Charity), this dissociation would lead to ethical relativism and a lack of religion. If the defense of Christian Europe could no longer be conducted in the old ways, then neither could civilization (and all those centuries of culture centered on reason and the emancipation of man) have no shelter. So, the law of war and the *jus gentium* in general were valuable instruments in the civilization's struggle against the barbarian relativism.

Thus, **De Bello** was a book for moralists and aimed at expanding their consciences. Hence, this was the motive of the casuistic character of the study and its inclusion in the Treaty of Charity. The tone and audience were a response to Alberico Gentili, to whom the study of war was not a part of the theologians' business.[8] In another passage, while trampling over all subtleties of the Scholastics, Gentili had said that justice in war has no relation to religion, as if the Scholastics had espoused such a rudimentary opinion. Gentili ends this passage with the famous warning: "Theologians, keep silence about matters outside your province!"[9] This is a clear attack to Vitória's hipertrofied view of Theology. There is no doubt that Francisco Suárez would reaffirm the Spanish Scholastic conception in the face of such a rude attack from the Italian Jurist from Oxford. The Scholastic law of war was not a mere pamphlet in the defense of Catholicism. It was a sophisticated theoretical *corpus* abounding with nuance and which identified justice in war not with religion, but with civility among peoples. The greatest subtlety, which is difficult to perceive, is the fact that the identifying character of the civilizing project was the monotheistic religion and, especially, Christianity.

This requires an explanation. To regulate the phenomenon of war, one does not rely solely on the principles resulting from nature. Although a fair portion of the law of war was based on Natural Law, some practices fell outside nature's domain. Cavalry codes and military honor, as well as certain procedures regarding spoils and the capture of nobles were positive binding norms. Writing on the existence of a legal system with precepts applicable to all peoples is equivalent to accept the validity of Natural Law. However, demonstrating the validity of a legal *corpus* with fairly precise and concrete norms, particularly in a situation so extreme as that of war, meant defending a common Positive Law. Furthermore, Medieval Roman Law could no longer serve this purpose: the decadence of the Roman Law and the discovery of non-European peoples (who never knew of the law in question) prevented this.

Although many institutes of the Medieval Law of War were part of Positive Law (and thus its domain surpassed the limits of national law) this did not imply

[8] **DIB**. I, 1, 1.

[9] "Silete theologi in munere alieno!" (DIB. I, 12, 4).

universal validity. The thirteenth century knew four types of war, each governed by a different set of rules, according to its nature and its enemy.[10] Due to the division of the Church (Catholic and Reformed) and the discovery of American peoples, the law of war was at risk of never becoming universal. At this point, the different types of war could continue to exist, each with its own standards, in accordance with those waging the war. Not all of the precepts of this field were moral; therefore, they were not Natural Law, which is universal *par excellence*. Spanish Theologians managed to make this law universal by finding rational rules that would lead to peace. The law of war in the Second Scholastic could be understood as a justification of both Spanish foreign policy and the expansion of Christianity. Nevertheless, it is possible to understand this issue as an effort to propagate civilization. Given that religion could no longer become universal, then civilization should. It is important here to note that the civilization in question at the time was the fruit of Christian and European values. But this was the only alternative to relativism.

It is clear that the *Eximius Doctor* does not explicitly mention the terms "civilization" or "civility"; however, they correspond to the general meaning of all of his casuistic prescriptions for the law of war. It is the author's choice of a point of view that exceeds the realm of Law and enters Charity that allowed for the universalization of ideas that were not of moral origin. In order to provide for a better perception of this fact, those precepts must be the subject of a closer examination. So, Suárez begins his work by providing a quite operational concept of war: "the exterior conflict that opposes exterior peace is duly known as war when entered into by two sovereigns and two States."[11] As will be seen later, the Grotian conception is quite more sophisticated, resembling the current legal theories on the subject. However, Suárez did not seek to address the issue on legal grounds. While very short, this definition reveals certain fundamental ideas for those that study war through the lens of Charity. The fact that war is an exterior conflict that opposes exterior peace is in clear opposition to the disturbances of the soul, which are internal to the hearts of men. War is a social vice, not an individual one, and this sets it apart from other corruptions of peace. Furthermore, in its characteristic as a struggle between States, war is different from sedition (combat between a sovereign and his people) or from a rift or duel (between individuals).

---

[10]Among them: the *guerre mortelle*, also called "Roman war" in which there were no prisoners and there was no rescue. They took place against non-Christians. The *bellum hostile* was the war among Christians and it provided for many rules of civility: limits to abuse, ransom of noble prisoners, etc. The *guerre couverte* took place between two vassals who pledged to the same lord. There were no restrictions regarding the death of the enemy, but the property should be safeguarded. Besides these three forms, there was also the siege, which was subject to its own set of precepts. Stacey (1994), pp. 32–39.

[11]"*Pugna exterior, quae exteriori paci repugnat, tunc proprie bellum dicitur, quando est inter duos principes, vel duas respublicas*" (Suárez, R. P. Francisci. **Opera Omnia**. *Editio Nova. Parisiis: Ludovicum Vivès*, 1858. *Tomus* XII. **De Fide, Spe et Charitate**. *Tratactus de Charitate. Disputatio* XIII. **De Bello**, *Proemium*. Henceforth, **DB**).

The first problem that Suárez deals with refers to the idea that war could be intrinsically evil. This could destroy the entire notion of just war. Linked to this question, he had to cope with the obstacle of whether any moral decree would impede a Christian from waging war. Then the Grenadian Theologian had to determine if war was contrary first to human nature and second to the Christian religion. Suárez called upon a number of biblical excerpts, already found in the **Gratian Decree** to prove that God never prohibited war. As for those passages in which God seems to condemn it, Suárez is able to prove that they were critical of other circumstances, not of war itself.[12]

In addition to being permitted, there are situations in which war is mandatory, through the lens of Charity. In defensive wars, any and all who are fit to fight have a duty to defend their homeland. In addition, aggressive war is not evil in itself either. In Suárez's understanding, this form of war is not the same as an imperialist expansion. The difference between defensive war and aggressive war is injury. When war is waged, the opposing State's actions characterize a defensive war; once conditions have improved, their actions may come to characterize an offensive war.[13] Thus, no war, either defensive or aggressive, is an affront to nature or the Gospel.

As it had to be, Suárez called upon the three conditions of justice in war laid out by Aquinas: "firstly, legitimate power to wage war. Secondly, a just cause or legal title. Thirdly, that the initiation of hostilities be dignified and fair, as well as the fighting and after the victory."[14] Outside of these requirements, war should be condemned, even though it is not an evil in itself, but because it brings evils to bear. Death and destruction caused by all wars must be justified by a greater good. This is not an application of the maxim "the ends justify the means"; however, some ends do justify certain means. The purpose of the remainder of his work will be to examine which ends and means may be used as justification. It becomes clear that the author modified, to the slightest degree, Aquinas's last condition of "good intent." Given that war corresponds external actions, good intent may only be perceived in the behavior of the parties during hostilities.

Suárez then went on to analyze the first condition. As Natural Law authorizes anyone to defend themselves, legitimate authority is not an issue for defensive wars, only for aggressive wars. He who holds sovereignty holds authority. If the sovereign fails to act, the decision then befalls to the people.[15] This will become clearer later on Suárez's theory of the State. For now, it is enough to say that sovereignty to Suárez represents the supreme power of a unappellable decision. The Roman-German Emperor no longer embodies the legitimate authority. There will be many sovereignties as the number of kingdoms and republics.

---

[12]**DB**. 1, 2.

[13]**DB**. 1, 3-5.

[14]"*Primum, ut sit a legitima potestate. Secundum, ut justa causa, et titulus. Tertium, ut se vetur debitus modus, et aequalitas in illius initio, prosecutione, et victoria*" (**DB**. 1, 7).

[15]**DB**. 2, 1.

The reasons behind this first condition is of great interest to this book. According to Suárez, a sovereign declares war first because it is his duty to defend the State. Second, because this ability (to declare war) is a power of jurisdiction. The exercising of this ability is tied to the vindictive justice, "of the highest need in a republic to punish wrongdoers. Such as a head of State can punish his own subjects when they harm one another, so he may also take revenge on another sovereign whose State became subject to the former through an offense."[16] The jurisdiction of the sovereign falls on its subjects, because they integrate its people, but extends to a third State because of an offense. This is a criminal concept of war: war is a form of criminal sanction. Since there are no judges with the ability to rule on a dispute between two princes, if the offending party offers no reparation, war becomes the only means possible of delivering justice.

In a primitive legal system, self-defense seems to be the only manner of safeguarding justice. This is indeed a defective, yet possible measure. "What else did the jurists and theologians of the sixteenth century do other than accommodate the immutable and eternal laws of justice and Natural Law within a historic circumstance?"[17] Natural Law grants all individuals with the right to defend themselves, but does not grant the right of jurisdiction. It is for this reason that individuals may defend themselves, but not declare a war. Within Suárez, there is no possible analogy between war and a private raid.

A just cause for a war is always a serious injury that cannot be avenged or repaired in any other way. In principle, self-preservation and the preservation of one's rights may justify combat. However, the offense must be quite serious: the causes that pagans point out (ambition, avarice, conceit and ostentation) are unacceptable, since any State could invoke them, leading to the absurdity of a just war for the both sides involved.[18] There are three classes of serious injuries. The first occurs when a prince takes control of the property of another; second, when the sacred rights of *jus gentium* are denied, such as the right to transit over a public route or international exchange; and third, when an injustice is an insult to one's reputation or honor (moral damages). These injuries constitute cause for war when effected on a sovereign, his people or even an ally. In the latter case, in addition to the right, the sovereign must manifest the will to react through war. The reparation of an injury is applicable up to the limit of indemnification for the damage, as well as punishment of the guilty party.[19] As seen in chapter III, punishment is one of the deontic variations of law and thus can be justly undertaken only by the offended State.

---

[16]"*(...) quae maxime necessaria est in republica ad coercendum malefactores; unde sicut supremus princeps potest punire sibi súbditos quando aliis nocent, ita potest se vindicare de alio principe, vel republica, quae ratione delicti ei subditur*" (**DB**. 2, 1).

[17]"*Qué hacían los juristas y teólogos del siglo XVI sino acomodar a una circunstância histórica los principios inmutables y eternos de la justicia y el derecho natural?*" (Pereña, 1956, p. 46).

[18]**DB**. 4, 1.

[19]**DB**. 4, 3-4.

Since his work expounds on two virtues (justice and charity), an interesting situation could arise: the cause may be just, but nonetheless, contrary to Charity. Suárez affirms that one should consider, when facing a war, the damage of the State against which war will be undertaken, the damage to the State waging war and the damage that could be done to the Church. In this case, there is a clear dissociation of Charity and Justice. Even though a Christian king may have a just cause, in the establishment of his rights, he may weaken another Christian sovereign that is fighting off the advances of the enemies of faith. In this case, the Pope may use his indirect power of intervention to prevent war. Regarding the first of the three offenses, there is no obligation to restore, given that they were provoked by the (bad) will of the offending State to offer satisfaction. However, if after the victory the offended party demands an indemnification that is not required, and that the aggressor cannot meet without great inconvenience, the former has sinned against Charity. In the second case, if the offended sovereign goes to war without considering the damage he may suffer, he is working against both the charity and justice he owes to his people. He will open up his kingdom to a destruction that far outweighs the offense.[20]

That is a very interesting situation, as it represents a true concession by the doctrine of just war in favor of political realism. A sovereign should not undertake (even if justice is on his side, in principle) foolhardy adventures that could endanger his reign. Suárez justifies his position by that fact that the prince must protect the common good and, in this case, the medicine could kill the patient. Moreover, he observes that this condition only applies to aggressive war, because in a defensive war, there is no alternative to combat. Suárez added that this criterion refers to a probability of victory, rather than certainty. Not rarely, victory cannot be revealed before the dispute. Often, it is not even in the common good to wait for a degree of absolute certainty. And if certainty should be required, a weaker sovereign would never declare war against a stronger opponent.[21] In collective actions, there are no certainties, only probabilities and hope.

Then, Suárez analyzes whether Christian princes hold any other right to war, aside from those prescribed by Natural Law. He sought to discover if professing the true faith grants an advantage that pagans do not have, if war is "more just" for Christians than for other peoples. In principle, Suárez did not find this to be so. Unbelief was no cause for war, since conversion implies an internal devotion and cannot be achieved through force. As a result, idolatry is not a legitimate cause for war either. "God did not give all men the power to avenge injuries against Him, because He could easily do so if He so desired."[22]

Nonetheless, if a head of State mandates by force his subjects to practice idolatry, this would provide for a just right to intervention by another Christian

[20]**DB**. 4, 6.

[21]**DB**. 4, 7-8.

[22]"*Deus enim non dedit omnibus hominibus potestatem vindicandi suas ipsius injurias, quia ipse facile id potest*" (**DB**. 5, 1).

prince. In this case, the offense is not against God Himself, but against the innocents that desire to profess the true faith. At this moment, Suárez and all of the other Spanish *maestros*, the thoughts of which he summarized, reveal the core aspect of the Spanish School of Peace. This title is not "exclusive to Christians, but is common to all infidels that worship a single God."[23] Monotheism, not the Christian religion, is found to represent civilization, and it is easy to understand why. The polytheism known to Europeans was ancient paganism and a few scant notices of African religions, all of which contained the idea of human sacrifice and cannibalism, which were already considered barbarian. Furthermore, both Islam and Judaism, the other two great monotheistic religions, preached mutual love and respect, teachings that Christians could easily relate to. Beyond the revealed religions, civilization was far from certain.

The proof that Suárez's argument centers on civilization, rather than religion, is the fact that he futhers this line of reasoning. So, Christian princes may intervene in non-Christian States to defend the people from their sovereign's idolatry. They may also intervene in Christian States, if the prince has converted to paganism and has forced the conversion upon his people. But Muslim kings may do the same with other Muslim sovereigns that have strayed from the path and even with Christian princes as well. In the name of monotheism and civilization, Suárez allows non-Christian sovereigns to intervene in Christian States.[24]

Since Vitória, Scholasticism had known that Indians had a just right to property and dominium of their lands. Suárez pondered on the Aristotelian concept of natural slavery, but did not accept a general application of the thesis, because "there are many infidels that are better endowed than many Christians and often more disposed for the political life."[25] Therefore, it is impossible to take away the lands or government of an infidel in a just manner. For this to be possible, it would not be enough that a certain people be less intelligent. It would be necessary that they proved themselves to be so backwards that

> they live more like beasts than man (...) [a people lacking any framework of political organization, the members of which live] completely naked, eat human flesh, etc. If this class of man does exist, they may be made subject through a war not to destroy them, but to organize them in a humane manner to allow for their governance with justice. But this right should rarely or never be admitted, except in the death of innocents and other similar crimes. Therefore, this right is best adapted to the idea of defensive rather than aggressive war.[26]

---

[23]"(...) *non proprius Christianorum est, sed communis cum iis infidelibus, qui unum tantum Deum colerent*" (**DB**. 5, 3).

[24]**DB**. 5, 3.

[25]"(...) *multos esse infideles ingeniosiores fidelibus, et aptiores ad res políticas*" (**DB**. 5, 5).

[26]"(...) *potius ferarum more quam hominum vivat, (...) nudi prorsus incedunt, carnibus vescuntur humanis,* etc. *Et si qui tales sunt, debellari poterunt, non ut interficiantur, sed ut humano modo instituantur, et juste regantur. Raro tamen aut nunquam admittendus est talis titulus, nisi ubi intercedunt occisiones hominum innocentum, et símiles injuriae: quare potius titulus hic revocatur ab bellum defensivum, quam aggressivum*" (**DB**. 5, 5).

Should this right exist, it extends to all kings that seek to defend civilization, not merely the Christian kings. There are (without any doubt) limitations to this religious tolerance. If a non-Christian State wishes to submit itself to the laws of Christ, but the government prevents this act, then Christian sovereigns may defend the innocent. Nevertheless, if the civilization is not in danger, the same right does not assist other monotheistic religions. If this same State wishes to receive the religion of Mohammad and its sovereign forbids this, if no barbarian practices such as cannibalism or human sacrifice are committed, Turkish sovereigns would have no right to intervene.[27] Civilization is identified with monotheism, but only Christianity holds the Truth. Hence, the Truth may only be defended by those that know it, and them alone.

Another obstacle in the study of just causes that the creators of the Just War Doctrine faced was the bilateral nature of justice in a war. If two sovereigns have equal rights to the same good, both would possess a just title. That said, a theologian would be unable to accept this, as it would imply that the will of God is not unequivocal, or that His creations are imperfect. The Spanish *maestros* resolved this problem by appealing to a dimension that Suárez would discover in his **Metaphysical Disputations**: subjectivity. From an objective point of view, Justice would remain united, and only one side would in fact hold the just title; however, if faced with unsurpassable ignorance, or an excusable error, then subjectively Justice would become bilateral.

In this situation, both parties would be obligated to avoid error to the best of their ability. Suárez, for one, accepted this duty. On each warring side, he contends that there are three classes of persons involved: the prince, other politicians and the military heads (which are responsible for strategy), and the soldiers. It seems logical to suppose that these classes have a decreasing degree of responsibility to diligently investigate the justice of war. The sovereign must always act with the greatest of care. Politicians and military leaders must proceed with the same care should their opinion be requested; otherwise, they should behave as soldiers. And, in general, soldiers must obey the commands of their superiors, unless the injustice thereof is evident.[28] Strict compliance with legal duty serves as an important excuse, but does not absolve them from every moral judgement.

Of these classes, the greatest responsibility falls on the prince. Suárez then teaches a number of rules to prevent error. If both sides have the right to the same thing, the sovereign should act as a judge and thus rule as to which of the two parties probability favors. Once again, the author compares war to a legal proceeding. If the destruction of war merits a penal sanction, this procedure for investigation and attribution of rights corresponds to an "act of distributive justice through which the most deserving party should be favored."[29] If probability is equal or there is a great deal of uncertainty, the item should remain in the possession of

[27]**DB**. 5, 7.

[28]**DB**. 6, 1-7.

[29]"(…) *ille est actus justitiaedistributivae, in qua dignior est praeferendus*" (**DB**. 6, 2).

the current owner, in accordance with the effective legal standards of the time. If the doubt precedes ownership by either party, the later owner should give the other party satisfaction proportional to the doubt. Only in the hypothesis of equal doubt (and neither party owning the item) does Suárez accept the bilateral nature of justice. This is the unsurpassable ignorance. Even so, the two kings should avoid war, dividing the item or seeking out another procedure for the attribution of the item, such as arbitration. In this situation, there is no risk of injustice; therefore, arbitration is the best means for resolving the issue. Only if one of the two parties refuse any of the solutions shall war be allowed, and it will be just (subjectively) for both parties.[30]

Regarding the final condition (dignified conduct before, during and after hostilities) Suárez also identified different obligations for each varying class of persons involved. Here, the Jurist from Coimbra catalogues a number of different hypotheses for *jus in bello*; including a number of separate prescriptions that are difficult to group. He sought to answer the following questions: what are you allowed to do to your enemies?; how should a king behave regarding his soldiers, and vice versa?; how should each class treat those that house them during military expeditions? The author came to very humane conclusions, given the standard of violence prevalent at the time. He discovered that reparations should be accepted, even after war has started, as long as it is not inexorably biased towards one of the two sides. This satisfaction of demands includes the restitution of the item in question, indemnification for damages and the punishment of the guilty, but should be prudent enough not to impede future peace. Suárez distinguished between combatants (all of those who are effectively involved in hostilities and those who could become involved) and non-combatants (women, children and the elderly). He also argues that the life of the innocent should be protected. Furthermore, he demonstrated that, after the war, when the victor demands indemnification and punishment of the guilty parties, he may take the goods of the innocent, but never their lives. Even regarding the goods, he recommends moderation.[31]

Then, Suárez analyses the so-called "mixed wars" and "private wars," in which one or both parties are not public and thus illegitimate authorities. The first of these, sedition, is not always unjust. When a prince comes to rule without regard for the common good, but with regard to his own good, he becomes a tyrant and a people's war against his government is permitted.[32] The author studies this issue at length in the **Defensio Fidei**, as will be seen later. In turn, the private war *par excellence* is the duel, which is equivalent to the private strife that sometimes occurs under certain public conditions. However, there is another war fought in the shadows: the fracas. In both wars, killing someone under private authority proves to be unfair.[33]

---

[30]**DB**. 6, 2-5.

[31]**DB**. 7. *in totum*.

[32]**DB**. 8, 2.

[33]**DB**. 9, 2.

The Scholastic Law of War did not reflect the standards for war common at the time. *Los maestros* in Spain chose certain rules that were part of common practice, but recommended others that, while not always flowing from Natural Law, represented precepts that humanized the act of war and made it more difficult an endeavor. They did not seek to end war, given the fact that without a universal judge, wars did serve an important function in distributive justice. However, they sought to make peace the final goal of war. War is not a fact of life, but rather a ruthless realization of law in the service of international peace.

Even so, the Scholastic Just War represented more than just a right. If it was merely a *jus*, this theoretical construction would be limited to a given continent and time period. Justice, in and of itself, is not enough to serve as a basis for war. Since this field presents a number of positive precepts, the justice thereof cannot be universal. Therefore, the *Eximius Doctor* employed another virtue that, while religious in origin, is common to all people that reach a certain level of spiritual progress: charity. This allowed the law of war to become more than a law from a particular nation.

Whereas Christianity was no longer universal because of the Reformation, since the law of war transcends *jus* and moves into the dominion of charity, ethical relativism is replaced by an objective order of values. Thus, this order is foreasble and identifiable beforehand, even if the study thereof results in a casuistic work. The singular rules of this treaty, while difficult to unite, are not based in religion, but civility.

For this reason, Francisco Suárez was always able to conceive war through the lens of peace. The laws of war include standards that seek to protect peaceful coexistence and a harmonious future among the peoples. In the eleventh disputation of the Treaty of Charity, the author characterized two aspects of peace: the positive aspect, the harmony of wills and unity of criteria, ends and words, and the negative, the renunciation of all actions that could be detrimental to this harmony. Luciano Pereña translates these two elements as justice (that which lends order and meaning to the actions of man and peoples) and the principle of humanity (that which moderates the former to promote deeper ties between men, relations of love and of friendship).[34] Only justice and harmony, together, as Law and Charity, can prescribe universal rules of civility. In the absence of a religion that is valid for all peoples, it is civilization that serves as basis for International Law.

5.2 The Final Formulation

By the time he began teaching in Coimbra (1596–1608), Suárez became truly interested in the *jus gentium* itself, not in just one of its topics. Suárez's rudimentary thoughts on the subject is found in **De iustitia Dei** (1598), **De opere sex dierum**

---

[34]Pereña (1956), p. 36.

(1600), in the preliminary versions of **De legibus** (1601–1603), in **De inmunitate** (1607) and **De statu religionis** (1608). It is already clear by these texts that this branch of law in question belongs to Positive Law.[35]

However, the *jus gentium* would receive a special, more systematic and organic treatment in Suárez's work of 1612. Suárez uses the Scholastic method to build its notion and to define its contours. First, he critically examines all the different criteria employed in European legal thought in the interpretation of the *jus gentium*. Afterwards, he presents his own conception thereof. Finally, he attempts to classifies all institutions traditionally deemed to be the Law of Nations compiled by Isidore of Seville.

Suárez examines the Law of Nations soon after addressing the immutability of Natural Law, and just before dealing with Civil Law. This order is not random and the author justifies his methodological choice: "Because it keeps great affinity with the Natural Laws to the extent that many confuse it or consider it part of it. Moreover, because even in the sense in which they differ, they are very close, as if it were an intermediate step between Natural and human law."[36] The analysis of the Law of Nations serves as a bridge to the study of Civil Law.

This way, Suárez attempted to accommodate his understanding of the *jus gentium* to tradition. The choice of *locus* indicated both familiarity with the past and a desire to expand from it. But it was not an easy task. Despite the explanation in the *relecciones*, the meaning of the term remained blurred and Vitória's work did not enjoy the same authority as the **Digest**, the **Gratian Decree** and the **Summa Theologiae**. Suárez had to redo all the work. As always, he would not be satisfied with the mere reproduction of previous works, he would try to leave his distinctive mark. With the exception of Aquinas, Suárez seems to lose the almost dogmatic respect for Jurisprudence and for the Medieval authors in his study of the Law of Nations.

As seen in the second chapter, these three texts offer very different conceptions of the tradition of *jus gentium*. There were two major definitions in the **Digest**: one of Gaius and another of Ulpian. Like Aristotle, Gaius proposed a twofold classification of the branches of Law and identified the Law of Nations with Natural Law. Apart from the issue of terminology, his definition brought no major problems. However, the same could not be said of Ulpian's division: Civil, Natural Law and Law of Nations. Despite all the rejection it suffered in the Middle Ages, his tripartition proved that there was indeed a difference between Natural Law and the Law of Nations; the former derives from nature and is proper to the animals; while also part of Natural Law, the latter was particular of men.

In turn, the **Gratian Decree** resumes the listing of all institutes of the Law of Nations, as promoted by Isidore of Seville: occupation, building, fortification, the

---

[35]Pereña (1973), p. xxxvi–xli.

[36]"*Tum quia magnam habet cum iure naturali affinitatem, ita ut a multis cum illo confundatur vel pars quaedam eius esse censeatur. Tum etiam quia, eo modo quo ab illo distinguitur, est illi proprinquissimum et quasi medium inter naturale ius et humanum* (…)" (DL. II, 17, 1).

captives of war, slavery, *postliminium*, peace agreements, truces, the inviolability of embassies and the prohibition of marriage between foreigners. He adds that the *jus gentium* has an "almost" universal spectrum. There is no definition of the *jus gentium*, but it is already clear that this branch belongs, without doubt, to Positive Law.

Finally, by seeking to incorporate all the literature that preceded him, Thomas Aquinas promotes a fusion between the concepts of Ulpian and Isidore. This is only possible because Aquinas' definition of law is broad enough to apply to all creation, even creatures devoid of reason. According to the author, Natural Law produces three inclinations in man: the pursuit of everything that matters to the preservation of life, the instinctive impulse toward the union of the sexes, to the rearing of children, etc., and a natural inclination to know the divine truths and to live in society. Man shares with other animals the first two inclinations, and they create the Natural Law itself. The third inclination, which is characteristic of human beings, creates the *jus gentium*. So far, Aquinas seems to recreate Ulpian's definition.

However, while Natural Law directly stems from the first two inclinations, the Law of Nations derives from the third inclination *per conclusionem*; that is, it requires a "positive" interpretation. Man needs to intervene and carry out a series of deductive procedures, such as conclusions are extracted out of a theorem, in order to draw out the Law of Nations from this natural inclination. Thus, it is disclosed as a type of Natural Law that requires human intervention. As seen, the term "positive" does not refer to the positivity of this law, but to the positive effort of deduction that man must employ. When it comes to Aquinas, Suárez will try his best to diminish the friction, but he cannot accept his view, because Aquinas' *jus gentium* corresponds to what he termed Dominative Natural Law.

The problem that Francisco Suárez had before him was as follows: he had to reject a conflicting tradition without making *tabula rasa* of it, especially with regard to Aquinas, and without being able to choose from any of the three interpretations. With the manuscripts of the Spanish *maestros* in hand, he had to develop his own notion of *jus gentium*. The Grenadian Theologian was quite conservative when it came to using arguments of authority (if compared to its peers) since he preferred to rely on the strength of his own arguments. However, to have the support of the thinkers of the past fulfilled his purpose to continue and develop the tradition. In addition to not being able to use this artifice, the authorities from the past seemed to conspire against Suárez in this matter.

In order to reveal Suárez's concept of *jus gentium* in all its nuances and contours, reach and limitations, I shall present his work through an exegetical lens.

After affirming the affinity of this branch with Natural Law, Suárez reaffirms its existence. Given the inconsistency of the tradition in the treatment of this matter, Suárez had to find the only certainty shared by all the writers of the past: the existence of the *jus gentium*.[37] This law existed and was not to be confused with Natural or Civil Law: it was autonomous and required further explanation.

---

[37]**DL**. II, 17, 1.

Suárez then submits the most supported definitions of the *jus gentium* to a critical examination. According to the definition of the Roman jurists, this law would correspond to the Natural Law that was prone to human beings. Suárez argues that nothing in this tripartite classification differs from the Aristotelian bipartite division, because in both cases the *jus gentium* would remain being part of a whole, of Natural Law. The mere "coincidence with the irrational animals in the materiality of these actions has nothing to do with the distinction of law or the legal rule".[38] The fact that the animal instincts of reproduction, conservation of the species and education of the offspring share an identity with a rule of Natural Law does not alter their legislative substance. The fact that the command is directed at two different types of living beings does not change the origin of the law.

Moreover, the idea that Natural Law applies to animals as well is false. As seen, Suárez rejects the idea that irrational and inanimate beings may be the subjects of law. Only the creature that is free to disobey a precept of law may be the recipient thereof. Even when Natural Law commands certain behavior of a sensitive nature, there is always a trace of rationality. The rules of marriage between men and women differ greatly from those that command a certain animal instinct. The same occurs in other examples such as the children's education, the preservation of life and species, etc. Moreover, Natural Law sometimes prohibits an action that the instinct itself allows. Such is the case of incest.[39]

In addition, Suárez does not accept the idea that the Law of Nations presupposes an intrinsic need of its own and neither that it only differs from Natural Law to the extent that the latter requires no discursive process or complicated deductions. According to Suárez, Aquinas may seem to be the author of this theory, but that was a misinterpretation. Domingos de Soto and other Thomists, such as Manuel Soares, Bartolomé de Medina and Fernando de Mendoza would have been the ones responsible for the development of this criterion.[40] Suárez then swiftly avoids clashing with Aquinas directly.

The author rejects this view because many of the institutions traditionally comprehended as part of the Law of Nations (the ones catalogued by Isidore de Seville, to whom Aquinas expressly refers) such as private property and slavery, simply have no intrinsic necessity. They could not belong to Natural but human Law. Furthermore, Suárez resumes his idea that Natural Law encompasses the first more general precepts as well as those logically deducted therefrom.[41]

Suárez avoids this first confrontation with Aquinas because he found less formidable contenders. The problem is that the Thomistic conception is broader than Suárez's, and it was not always possible to appoint a commentator to excuse the master. There is thus a point of view which all agree was firmly defended by

---

[38]"(...) *communitas cum brutis in materiali opere nihil refert ad distinctionem iuris vel legis*" (**DL**. II, 17, 5).

[39]**DL**. II, 17, 6.

[40]**DL**. II, 17, 8.

[41]**DL**. II, 17, 8.

Aquinas that Suárez simply disagrees with: the notion that the *jus gentium* consists of conclusions necessarily derived from natural principles, but not completely so, because these conclusions presuppose human society and take into account certain circumstances that are essential for the preservation of that society. This is what Suárez had previously called Dominative Natural Law. If the deductive process develops without mistakes, both the principle and the conclusion thereof belong to Natural Law, in spite of their human condition. For example, the *pacta sunt servanda* is a natural precept, but it only comes into effect once a promise or a contract is entered into in accordance with human laws.[42]

For Suárez, the contents of the *jus gentium* do not proceed from nature. The Law of Nations does not prohibit anything that is essentially evil, nor does it command the righteousness of conduct, whether we are to presuppose a human circumstance or not. This time, Suárez retraces Vitória's path: the denial of the naturalness of the *jus gentium*. The *jus gentium*, by its content, may be closer to Natural than to Civil Law, but the fact that it consists of a Positive Law means that the purpose thereof is not to regulate honesty or moral turpitude. The common good sought by the *jus gentium* may exceed the boundaries of a kingdom, but it is still human and earthly.

Suárez then examines the thesis of Francisco Connan and Gabriel Vázquez, for whom the Law of Nations did not include precepts or prohibitions, only permissions. The first two deontic variations could only exist by virtue of reason itself or by the human will of an authority. Therefore, only Natural and Civil Law could ordain or prohibit. The *jus gentium* would consist of institutions that would promote the common good and, to that extent, these institutions would be legitimate in and of themselves. However, they would not be essential to ensure moral rectitude, nor would Positive Law prescribe them. According to these authors, the Law of Nations was a kind of "secondary natural law", because, as the previous notion entailed, it did not apply to men unconditionally but only as long as they lived in society.[43]

Suárez ironically criticizes their point of view: "To be honest, I cannot understand this thesis".[44] He found that the theory made no sense because it did not use the term *jus* accurately, unless it did not accept that definition of *jus* that equaled *lex*. But if that were the case, the theory would still make no sense, for it would not be possible to classify the *jus gentium* as one of the branches of law. This theory converts the *jus gentium* into a subjective right only, into a mere *facultas utendi vel non utendi*, disregarding that other notion of *jus* as an objective law.

Even if, *ad argumentando*, one were to leave this misunderstanding aside, this notion does not consider that there is in fact a Natural Law of a concessive nature, as the precept of marrying. Natural Law does not dictate this behavior, only allows it. If that possibility is not legislated by men, it is a *jus naturae*. Moreover, it is not possible to separate the concessive from the prohibitive or mandatory law. As seen in chapter III regarding both meanings of the term *jus*, the objectivity and

---

[42]**DL**. II, 17, 9.

[43]**DL**. II, 18, 1 and 3.

[44]"*Hanc vero setentiam, ut verum fatear, non satis intelligo.*" (**DL**. II, 18, 2).

subjectivity of law represent two aspects of the same reality. For instance, for the one who receives it, privilege is a concession, but for everyone else, it establishes a prohibition of not preventing its exercise. Suárez thus begins to demonstrate in the institutes that were commonly accepted as part of the Law of Nations that there exists, in each one, a concessive element followed by a preceptive one.[45]

Some institutes are worth mentioning. In the specific case of capture and slavery, the correct interpretation considers these institutes a sort of punishment against those who waged an unjust war. Suárez considers punishment a deontic variation of Law. However, as seen in chapter III, although Natural Law may dictate the punishment, the assessment of the corresponding penalty is something for Positive Law to address. And here the penalty consists of the very capture and slavery; therefore, this institute can only belong in Positive Law. The case of marriage between people of different cultures and faiths clearly denotes prohibition. This prohibition represented a particular custom of the faithful people, of both the Old and New Testaments. Thus, because it lacked universality, it seemed to correspond more to a divine or canonical institution rather than to the Law of Nations.[46]

So far, Suárez has only criticized the different explanations of the *jus gentium*. He did not make any comments on Isidore's thesis; at least, not yet. He has silenced not because he considered it true, but incomplete. The mere listing of institutes did not contribute to solving the issue at hand. Nevertheless, the other two traditions were not spared. All his arguments come logically from his less ancient and more modern theory of Law. Suárez directly confronted even Aquinas whom he ought to revere by professional and religious duty. What bothers Suárez is the fact that one way or another the foundations of which the Law of Nations sprang kept pulling it back to Natural Law. When making his critics, he did not fail to show his preference that this branch should lie on positive bases.

In effect, the *jus gentium* and *jus naturae* had much in common. Francisco Suárez himself makes this statement in the beginning of his oeuvre. In addition to being directed at human beings and prescribing concessions, prohibitions and precepts, they are both common to all men.[47] However, common does not mean universal. As seen in the second chapter, Aristotle used this term to explain the coincidence of several positive standards from different communities, without appealing to Natural Law. In Rome, the merger of the *jus proprium* applied to the Romans and the *jus gentium* of foreigners created the notion of a *jus commune* extended to all free men, regardless of their nationalities. At the time of the High Scholastic, a common law,[48] which stem from the Roman Law, ruled mainly because of its decisive influence on Canon Law (*vivit ecclesia iure romano*). The Christian world, which was guided by the rules of the Ancient Roman Empire, was

[45]**DL**. II, 18, 2 to 5.

[46]**DL**. II, 18, 8 and 9.

[47]**DL**. II, 19, 1.

[48]Although very closely related, the term "common law" here refers to the *droit commune* of Medieval continental Europe, not to the British common law.

an immense community of men who were subject to this law. The common law legitimized imperial monism and opposed national sovereigns. In this sense, the idea of a common law is somewhat incompatible with a *jus gentium* that regulates the relations between different States. It even opposes the classification of the Law in several branches. The common law is a Law in itself, as a whole. It encompasses Public and Private, National and International, Positive and Natural Law.

However, to an Iberian such as Suárez there was nothing more distant than the imperial monism. Although slightly older, he was closer than Grotius was to the notion of a world divided into sovereign States, due to the societies in which they were born and lived. Suárez does not believe in a common law. He does not use the term "common" in lieu of "universal", as he comments on this last feature later. He employs this term with no ignorance of its past, because he expressly mentions the Roman texts. The word appears in a metaphorical sense: common is not the Law itself, but Natural Law and also the Law of Nations. By mentioning these two branches, Suárez does not want to affirm that the Law reveals itself to be common, but that the *jus naturae* and the *jus gentium*, each of them isolated, plays the role that the ancient common law used to play. Law as a whole, with all its institutes, does not apply to all men. Only some goods and some ends, set aside from each other and proper to each branch of Law, do extend to all men. Suárez already draws the limits of the spatial validity of legal orders.

Therefore, Natural Law and the Law of Nations had many features in common. But there is a fundamental distinction between them: the precepts of the Law of Nations do not declare the evilness or goodness of a given behavior. They determine it. Its prohibitions and commandments do not originate from the nature of things and thus are not entirely necessary. Two differences arise out of this distinction. First, the Law of Nations cannot be immutable like Natural Law, because immutability derives from necessity. Second, the necessity in Natural Law implies that it must be complied with in all places by all peoples. Only an error justified an exception thereto. However, as Isidore of Seville once stated, the Law of Nations is almost universal. The word "almost" is important. It means that a given community may fail to comply with one or more of its precepts, without committing an error or an illicit behavior. Therefore, Suárez forecasts the possibility of the total revocation of the Law of Nations or, at least, the exemption or the partial revocation thereof.[49]

And so there is only one possible conclusion: the Law of Nations is human and positive. Since these words also came from Aquinas, they may provoke ambiguity. Once again, Suárez seeks to "save" his master by erecting an original interpretation thereof. A law may be human either by its recipient or by the substance to which it refers. In this last sense, even Natural Law is human, for it intends to regulate men's actions. According to the author, Aristotle himself employed this understanding

[49]**DL**. II, 19, 2.

when referring to Political Law as human law—and Political Law is divided into natural and legal. Aquinas apparently shared this view.[50]

In this case, the Law proves to be human because it prescribes a human substance, regardless of being established in Positive Law or not. Yet, Suárez opts for a more formal and less substantive criterion. Law is a Positive and human Law in virtue of the fact that its legislator is a human being. This formalism in no way resembles that of the German jusphilosophers from the twentieth century. In order to excuse Aquinas and reveal the "true" meaning of his words, Suárez needs to tone down this position. He cannot accept that the substance of the Law of Nations is already in Natural Law nor that the difference between them is merely positivity.

As seen in the second chapter, Aquinas believed that the Law of Nations derives from Natural Law *per conclusionem,* as theorems derive from an axiom, while Civil Law derives per *determinationem*, such as abstract shapes materialize into something particular (e.g., like an architect keeps in his mind the notion of "house" and uses it as a template to build a concrete building). Suárez does not agree with that because the precepts of the *jus gentium* are not established by means of a necessary intellectual effort, but accepts that they are closer to nature than those of the Civil Law are. This closeness is due to impulses of an *instigante natura*, that is, nature incites them. There is no hiatus between Natural Law and the Law of Nations. The human will contributes to the creation of this law only as an efficient cause. On the one hand, if the *jus gentium* governs the relations between nations in a non necessary manner, on the other hand, in addition to being close to the *jus naturae*, the *jus gentium* is quite convenient and beneficial to the **nature** of a humanity divided into different States.[51]

> (…) not because the will [of the prince] is a sufficient reason, but because creation [of that law], which could occur in several ways, is perfectly reasonable [according to the specific form chosen]. Often, there is no reason to have to be done this way and not another; then we say that it was proceeded depending on the will more that reason. Other times, we need to consider a special reason in relation to specific and quasi-material circumstances; then this creation refers more to circumstances than to the substance.[52]

This does not mean that only the Law of Nations regulates relations between peoples. Natural Law also does. The *pacta sunt servanda*, the mutual obligation of the communities to respect their possessions reciprocally, as well as to repair the damage they may cause, and perhaps other provisions, are natural principles that rule the life of the States.[53] Thus, Aquinas' theory indicates the existence of a natural *jus gentium*. Thanks to this, Suárez can unite the Thomistic conception with

---

[50]**DL**. II, 19, 3.

[51]Rommen (1951), p. 476.

[52]"(…) *non quia sola voluntas pro ratione sufficiat, sed quia determinatio illa, diversis modis facta, esset rationabilis, et saepe nulla est ratio ob quam potius hoc modo, quam illo fiat, et ita dicitur fieri voluntate potius quam ratione, vel certe ubi aliqua specialis ratio intercedit, consideratur in ordine ad particulares et quasi materialis circumstantias; atque ita est determinatio magis in circumstantiis quam in substantia*" (**DL**. II, 20, 2).

[53]**DL**. II, 19, 8 and **DB**. 4, 3.

that of lawyers such as Alberto Arias and Bolognetti Pinelo, who divide the Law of Nations into primary and secondary law of nations.[54] The problem would be of terminology only. The primary law of nations corresponds to the Natural Law itself, but receives this name because different peoples may make use of it. However, Suárez warns that the meaning of *jus gentium* that he employs coincides with the secondary law of nations, which is human and positive.

Suárez builds this argument only to show that his theory did not annihilate Aquinas'. Suárez would merely be focusing on another meaning of the *jus gentium*, one that Aquinas would have chosen not to pursue. This terminology may already be found in Hugo Grotius' first great work, the **De Jure Praedae**, which predates the **De Legibus**. However, in **De Jure Belli ac Pacis**, which is subsequent to the Suarezian treaty, Grotius chose to address only the second meaning of *jus gentium*, as the Grenadian Theologian did. In spite of his attempts to preserve the word of his master, the two concepts are so contrasting that Suárez ends up burying the legacy of Thomas Aquinas for the future.

Despite their similarities, Suárez finally differentiates the Law of Nations from Natural Law. By exclusion, the Law of Nations may only be positive. It is thus necessary to distinguish it from Civil Law. This is a seemingly simple task; past traditions never found trouble accomplishing it. So, the author analyzes the most common views on the topic. The first difference leaps to the eye: Civil Law is applied only to a kingdom, while the *jus gentium* is common to all peoples. However, Suárez considers the extent of spatial validity a mere accidental and quantitative feature, which does not encompass the substance of the matter. Moreover, since an act of will creates law, it seems impossible for the Law of Nations to actually rule all peoples, because it would need to be generated by a consensus of all men. "Because it is not frequent that all peoples agree on matters that depend on opinion and free will of men. It is common for men that there are almost as many opinions and inclinations as heads."[55] Thus, either the *jus gentium* does not belong in human law or it cannot be different from Civil Law.

With only one shot, Suárez explains why the extension of the Law of Nations is a mere accident and solves the practical problem of obtaining the consent of all men. "The precepts of the Law of Nations differ from the precepts of Civil Law because they are not formed by written law, but by custom, not of this or that State or province, but of nearly all nations."[56]

---

[54]**DL**. II, 19, 4.

[55]"*Quia in his quae ab opinione et arbitrio hominum pendent, non solent omnes nationes convenire. Nam hoc est hominum ingenium ut quot sut capita, tot fere sint placita et opinions*." (**DL**. II, 19, 5).

[56]*Praecepta iuris gentium in hoc differunt a praeceptis iuris civilis quia non scripto sed moribus, non unius vel alterius civitatis aut provinciae sed omnium vel fere omnium nationum constant*." (**DL**. II, 19, 6).

I shall address further below how custom serves as a source to the *jus gentium*. Suffice to say that this branch emanates from a non-legal and a non-written source, but a human source nonetheless. Customary law was often seen as a proof of the existence of Natural Law or even the concrete manifestation thereof. The reason lies in the fact that its precepts date back to immemorial times, and no one knows for sure how they came into being. Yet, in Suárez, customs correspond to one of the many legal manifestations of a perfect community or a State. It does not stem from a formal act enacted by a sovereign authority and as such is not mistaken for *lex*. But Civil Law expresses itself, by excellence, in the form of *lex* and this expression is the core difference between Civil Law and the Law of Nations according to Suárez. These are two different forms of Law. Customs may also exist inside a kingdom, as long as the sovereign admits it, but it will then exist, without any doubt, as the expression of the will of a single people, not of "almost" all peoples. And so, this "almost" is the accidental difference between the Law of Nations and Civil Law.

Still, the consensus of almost all peoples is more easily obtained by customs rather than by a universal law, which would need to be enacted by an authority above the nations. For Suárez, humanity is divided into several states and kingdoms. The *jus gentium* stems from a sort of tacit pact.[57] It is not a formal or explicit consent. Thus, the simple repetition of the practice allows almost all peoples to agree on certain behaviors and institutes.

In Suárez, the customary manifestation of the *jus gentium* does not exclude the possibility of two peoples entering into a treaty. He expressly states that trade agreements, peace treaties and truces are permissions within the Law of Nations.[58] But the author does not elevate the treaty to a source of the *jus gentium*, probably because he was not familiar with the idea of a multilateral treaty. In Suárez's time, treaties were bilateral and not different from contracts. In his eyes, the only possible way to bind all (or nearly all) peoples was by customs.

Suárez then seeks to demonstrate his theory. First, by exclusion: there is no better way to differentiate the *jus gentium* from the other two branches of Law. He proves this by employing examples: the institute of receiving ambassadors who were entitled to several immunities and commercial contracts and agreements.[59] The first example does not necessarily flow from Natural Law. Should a State refuse to receive or send diplomatic representation, it would not be infringing the rules of moral rectitude. But this refusal is a sign of enmity because of an implied covenant (*pacto subintellecto*) among States. The immunity and the duty to receive ambassadors are institutes of the *jus gentium*, but the obligation to respect the immunity after accepting a diplomatic representation by way of a pact emanates from nature, from the *pacta sunt servanda*.

---

[57] Rommen (1951), p. 475.

[58] **DL**. II, 19, 7 and 8.

[59] **DL**. II, 19, 7.

In the case of agreements, their concrete form belongs to Civil law, their compliance stems from a natural obligation, but the freedom to enter into a commercial agreement with a State that is not an enemy comes from the Law of Nations. Indeed, nothing prevents a nation to live isolated, but this branch of law has established commercial freedom, and it would constitute a violation thereof to prohibit such freedom without good cause. James Brown Scott observes that here Suárez aligns himself with Vitória, for whom trade should be free. However, differently from Suárez, this freedom corresponds to a natural right to Vitória. There should be a penalty in Civil Law for the non-compliance thereof. In its absence, the recalcitrant nation would become liable for damages before a judicial process in the courts of the offended prince.[60]

5.2.1 A Subtle and Important Distinction

Suárez realizes that Roman Law and Isidore of Seville employed the term *jus gentium* in two very similar but different meanings. The first, a *ius gentium propiissime dictum*, addresses almost all nations in their mutual relations, a true *jus inter gentes*, closer to the contemporary Public International Law. The second, a *ius gentium per similitudinem* corresponds to a law that is enacted by a State within its territory and that matches or is comparable to an institute found in other States, a *jus intra gentes* (to use the traditional terminology) a sort of Cosmopolitan Civil Law.[61]

With the exception of Grotius, after Suárez this distinction will again be eclipsed. But the Jurist of Coimbra was not the first to unveil these two meanings. Fernando Vazquez of Menchaca expressly refers to them[62] and some even say that they already underlied Vitória's work. The reason for that lies in the Romans' confusion of the term, since they believed that the law of nations derived from natural reason. For contemporary jurists, it seems an elementary mistake to consider private property and peace treaties institutions of the same body of law. However, in the Ancient world, no political constitution could match the Roman Empire. Thus, to Rome, the entire *jus gentium* corresponded to a *jus intra gentes*. There were no true political communities outside Rome to exist a *jus inter gentes*. In feudal Europe, the Empire subsisted only as an idea. Although the notion of State was still shrouded with uncertainty, in the sixteenth century, the Empire was already a very distant reality. Therefore, the Spanish Theologians were able to perceive that difference in the *jus gentium*.

Suárez then begins to classify each institute of the Isidorian catalog. Those that did not proceed from Civil Law (such as the embassies and trade agreements) belonged to the *jus inter gentes*. The coercive aspect of the law of war also came

---

[60]Scott (1934), p. 177.

[61]**DL**. II, 19, 8.

[62]Barcia Trelles (1933), p. 459.

from this branch. This system of enforcing punishment and ensuring reparation for injustices in the law of war comes from a custom among the peoples. Indeed, it seems very easy to classify the law of war within the *jus gentium*. It surely does not belong to municipal law. And Suárez also warns that it cannot be mistaken for Natural Law because it is not necessary. "Men could have established other system for enforcing punishment or trust that power to a third sovereign who would act as arbitrator, with coercive powers."[63] It is interesting to notice that the idea of an international justice was already present in the mind of one of its visionaries. The same argument is valid for the enslavement of prisoners of war as well as for peace treaties and truces.

If the *jus inter gentes* is indeed a law between political communities, the *jus intra gentes* comprises

> certain precepts, rites and ways of life that by themselves and directly do not refer to all men, nor have as immediate end a progressive association and international collaboration of all peoples. Each State establishes them through legal proceedings and in accordance with their constitutional procedures. But they are of such nature that all nations coincide in the practice of similar uses or laws, which denotes a certain parallelism between generic systems and between concrete rules.[64]

Suárez illustrates this subdivision with some examples extracted from tradition. Justinian mentions religion in the **Digest**: to worship God is a natural obligation. One should not overlook the fact that Suárez is a theologian and that, for him, God created Natural Law. However, the concrete form of worship is a matter of Positive Law, which, in the earthly order, corresponds to Civil Law (to the law of the citizens). Since such an obligation coexists in several peoples, it belongs in the *jus gentium* as an intermediate formula. The offering of sacrifices does not stem from nature, but almost all nations seem to follow this precept. The same applies to the existence of a class of individuals dedicated to the service of the cult, which seems to be shared by almost all peoples.

Suárez includes in Isidore's list of institutes the occupation of territories, the building of houses, the fortification, the use of money (for the same reason he also includes some private contracts such as the purchase and sale) and the *postliminium*. He asks why the prohibition of marriage between individuals of different religions is so widespread. It even seems to go against the exchange and cooperation of mankind. However, if it exists, it would belong to the *jus intra gentes*.[65]

---

[63] "*Potuissent enim homines instituere alium modum vindictae, vel committere illam potestatem alicui tertio principi et quasi arbitro cum potestate coactiva.*" (**DL**. II, 19, 8).

[64] "(...) *quaedam praecepta vel ritus aut modos vivendi qui* per se *et directe non referetur ad universos homines, neque habent veluti pro fine proximo convenientem societatem et communicationem omnium nationum inter se, sed in unaquaque republica, foro suo, conveniente regimine constituuntur. Et nihilominus tales sunt, ut in usu similium rituum aut legum fere omnes nationes inter se conveniant vel similitudinem habeant, interdum genericam, interdum veluti specificam.*" (**DL**. II, 19, 10).

[65] **DL**. II, 19, 10.

5.2.2 The Mutable Nature of the Law of Nations

Francisco Suárez concludes its exhibition of Natural Law by demonstrating its universality and unity. The mutability of its rules is only apparent: the third precepts of Natural Law seem to vary only because they are set out in such general terms that lack precision and rigor. The Jurist of Coimbra thus starts a descending reasoning from Natural to Civil Law, from an absolute and universal law to another of opposite features, contingent and circumstantial. The *jus gentium* is a transition between them. And if the author deems Natural Law immutable, it should not seem strange that he finishes his analysis of the Law of Nations by demonstrating its mutability. In addition, as discussed in chapter III, it is proper of the author's methodology that he should finish his study of each type of law with the theme of *mutatione legum.*

Since the Law of Nations does not cope with good or bad behavior in themselves, it seems logical to assume that it may vary. However, it could vary as Civil Law does, for which a mere act of revocation or waiver by the sovereign suffices. The legislating authority that enacted Civil Law might also change the Law of Nations. If the *jus gentium* belongs to Positive Law, then change is part of its nature; however, Suárez must prove that this is possible still in the absence of a specific legislating world authority.

He begins to solve this problem by presenting how the two kinds of *jus gentium* came about. The *jus inter gentes* "can easily be seen that, by use and historical tradition, was gradually introduced worldwide in a continuous process of expansion and mutual imitation between peoples, without the need of assemblies or concurrent agreements between nations".[66] Although it is not a natural *jus*, it is so intrinsically related to human nature (beyond its obvious utility and convenience in the relations between peoples) that it spread in a "near natural" way throughout mankind. In the same sentence, Suárez confirms the positivity of the *jus inter gentes* (because it springs from the "use and historical tradition") and signals the way by which it can be changed: a new consensus among peoples.

With regard to the *jus intra gentes*, Suárez explains that it represents certain institutes of Civil Law that are similar in many nations. It may thus change as laws do. No two things similar are ever exactly the same, but in some cases, there is such a significant coincidence between rules and institutes that one could question their positivity. Although the precepts of this law are not part of Natural Law, they "are so bound and conformed to nature that each nation alone found itself inclined to accept without difficulty these norms".[67]

---

[66]"*(...) facile constat potuisse, ipso usu et traditione, in universo introduci paulatim et per sucessionem, propagationem et imitationem mutuam populorum, sine speciali conventu vel consensu omnium populorum, uno tempore facto*" (**DL**. II, 20, 1).

[67]"*(...) est tamen adeo propinqua et adeo consentanea vel commoda naturae, ut facile potuerit singulas nationes ad talia iure inclinare*" (**DL**. II, 20, 1).

If one were to imagine a scale of convenience of laws, utility must come after necessity. Utility corresponds to Positive Law while necessity corresponds to Natural Law. The norms of the *jus intra gentes* are not needed, they are only useful. However, they stand at the top of the utility parameter. The author wants to say that this law does not stem from nature, but it is so convenient and so well adjusted to it that it is not surprising that there are so many coincidences among the most divergent peoples. Moreover, historical tradition and reciprocal imitation that contributed to the diffusion of the *jus inter gentes* would also have influenced this second type of *jus gentium*.

Because of this unequivocal proximity to Natural Law, the rules of the *jus gentium* are just. As these rules are almost universal, they take into account not their usefulness to a particular nation, but to all common good of humanity.[68] The common good sought by the *jus gentium* reaches spiritual progress of far higher level than that achieved by the common good of a given community. As seen before, the Suarezian common good was not thought of in the same continuous and levelled way as Aquinas' common good. The differences between the good sought by Natural Law and the good sought by human Positive Law are significant. By the same reasoning, there must be a difference between the common good in Civil Law and the common good in the *jus gentium*. Natural Law seeks the righteousness of conduct, seeks to make man good. Civil Law seeks to make man a good citizen. Since the scope of the *jus gentium* coincides with humanity, it is possible to say that the *jus gentium* seeks to make man a good human being, more solicitous with his brothers and more tolerant of their differences.

Still, one should not forget that the *jus gentium* is Positive Law and therefore may allow evil, since the permission of evil does not offend Natural Law, as seen before. This hypothesis proves true especially in the case of the *jus intra gentes*, which actually corresponds to a part of Civil Law. The tolerance of evil is necessary, for it results from human weakness, and almost all nations seem to respect it. Suárez uses an example that seems to linger in the current days—prostitution.[69]

Taking into account everything that was seen so far, the Law of Nations can indeed change, since it depends on the men's consent. And Suárez does not refer to the changes that are inherent to Natural Law only. He illustrates this rather prosaic type of mutation that the Law of Nations shares with Natural Law: such is the case of the religious man who renounces the possession of earthly goods. This renounciation of a concessive right resembles that of a priest to his (natural) right of marriage. All Positive (whether Civil Law or the Law of Nations) and Natural Law share this kind of mutation.[70]

---

[68]**DL**. II, 20, 2.

[69]**DL**. II, 20, 3.

[70]**DL**. II, 20, 6.

Yet, the change that Suárez has in mind is the one that the Law of Nations shares with Civil Law: a revocation carried out by a sufficient authority. Both kinds of *jus gentium* change in a different way. The *jus intra gentes* is modified just like Civil Law, so that any republic or kingdom can decide for the convenience of its revocation in accordance with its internal procedures and by its sovereign's own authority.[71] This revocation is always partial: each State choses to proceed as it sees fit, but the general rule still remains. In this case, since the *jus gentium* is an internal law, a single act of change cannot modify the content of the entire rule.

Yet, that is exactly what the *jus inter gentes* requires to change: a single (almost) universal act of revocation. It is thus infinitely more difficult to modify this *jus gentium*. "But there is no reason to amend the content [of that law] if all nations consent or gradually introduce and consolidate a contrary custom."[72] Suárez notes that this hypothesis is possible in theory, but does not seem feasible. It is worth mentioning here that this is a limitation of that time that Suárez could not surpass. A similar agreement among almost all nations in the sixteenth century would encounter several practical problems: the difficulty of bringing together the ambassadors of various peoples, insecurity, language barriers, etc. There was also the problem of considering the Indians worthy and equal interlocutors. Half a century before Suárez, when Victoria approached the rights of the Indians in his *relectio*, he was not taking account of a fact, but rather advocating a cause. Little had changed until Suárez.

Therefore, by its nature, if the *jus intra gentes* could not bear a complete change, neither could the *jus inter gentes*, albeit for a different reason: a practical difficulty. However, total revocation was not the only way to change; there was also partial revocation or waiver. A particular community may order the non-fulfillment of a precept of *jus inter gentes* within its territory. Suárez gives the example of enslaving prisoners captured in a just war. In Christian States, this rule was not complied due to an ancient ecclesiastical custom. In this case, there would be a sort of regional International Law. There is then another difference between the *jus gentium* itself and Civil Law: the latter may be revoked or waived, but the former may only be partially revoked. That does not imply that the *jus gentium* is not capable of changing. Both laws address unnecessary matters. However, the difference in their manner of change is a result of a practical unfeasibility.[73]

Civil Law can tolerate a custom contrary to the *jus gentium* if it does not result in damages to other nations. Thus, "in somewhere if it is not permitted the transit on public roads, except under onerous conditions, [this custom] could not be extended to foreigners who, in their land, allow transit without this condition."[74] The

[71]**DL**. II, 20, 7.

[72]"*Nihilominus tamen non repugnat mutatio ex vi materiae, si nationes omnes consentirent vel si paulatim introduceretur consuetudo contraria et praevaleret*." (**DL**. II, 20, 8).

[73]**DL**. II, 20, 8 and 9.

[74]"(…) *si alicubi non concederetur transitus per vias publicas nisi sub aliqua conditione onerosa, non posset extendi ad extraneos qui in suis terris transitum sine tali conditione concedunt*" (Suárez 1973, p. 164).

imposition of a custom or a law that does not observe the *jus gentium* is also against Natural Law, because it deprives people of freedoms by way of a precept to which jurisdiction and authority they are not subject.

In the first example, the change happened for the best: it broadened a human right. In addition, the provision of enslaving a prisoner of war is a capacity, and, as seen, may be modified by Natural Law. In the second example, the extension of a rule contrary to the *jus gentium* to other peoples is prohibited. It is worth analyzing whether Civil Law may discharge its own people not of a capacity, but of a prohibition of the *jus inter gentes* directed. Although Suárez did not give an explicit example of this kind, his words seem to indicate this possibility. He himself said before that he intended to deal with a change other than the waiver of a concessive right. Moreover, by insisting on the fact that the *jus gentium* applies to almost all (but not all) nations, the author wants to say that a particular community may lawfully fail to comply with this law.

When writing on Natural Law (the universal law) Suárez recognizes that some peoples do not comply with their third precepts, but this could only take place for a short period, after which they would be deemed to incur in error. There can be no human revocation of Natural Law, either totally or partially. However, the *jus inter gentes* belongs to Positive Law, and thus may be changed by a legislative authority. The only reason why it cannot be fully revoked is of a practical nature: the necessity of obtaining the consensus of all nations. Since it does not exceed the boundaries of a particular republic or kingdom, in the case of a waiver, the competent authority belongs to the community and thus requires no permission from other States to implement the change.

This means that Civil Law may oppose the *jus gentium*: it may ban a behavior that is permitted or commanded, or even allow or command an act that is prohibited. In this case, there is no doubt that the State would disobey the Law of Nations—or, for a contemporary jurist, this State would incur in international responsibility. But the fact that the *jus gentium* is "almost" universal means that a breach of its provisions does not imply the invalidity of Civil Law. From this assertion, one should not conclude that Suárez advocates a kind of legal dualism *avant la lettre*. For Suárez, as will be seen, the Law of Nations only exists for civilized people.

5.3 The Foundations of the Law of Nations

When Francisco Suárez begins his study of the *jus gentium*, he starts with a certainty: it exists. That was a rhetorical tool, for it was the only common denominator of the three traditions prior to him. He did not want to show his repudiation of the past at once. However, starting with the certainty of its existence meant brushing off all the effort of finding the reasons behind the *jus gentium*. Apparently, this is what happens to Suárez. After criticizing the various theories, by the time he starts to expose his conception thereof, he does not actually explain the basis of this law.

This is indeed a very complex task. To investigate the basis of the Law of Nations implies solving not only one, but several issues, of which three are worth mentioning: "what means 'peoples'", "what is the nature of this law?" and "to what kind of society it applies?" The first question is legitimate because "peoples" are the subject of this branch. The Suarezian theory of the State is the answer thereto. The second question seeks to conform the *jus gentium* to the legal philosophy of the Jurist of Coimbra and it apparently collides with the lack of a world legislative authority. This problem relates to the Suarezian understanding of the customs. Finally, the third question (which presupposes the answers to the previous two) discusses the possibility of the international community to create its own law. It aims to assert the nature of the international or inter-peoples society.

Suárez does not answer them clearly, but he is not a thinker that leaves gaps in his theory. He himself realized the lack of reasoning in his main work and added a chapter (which is part of the version of **De Legibus** of the *Corpus Hispanorum de Pace*) with a very suggestive title: "How the Law of Nations was created." Even so, this chapter is not enough. Since the author is a thinker who forms a system of ideas, this text contains notions and concepts that need to be sought out in the **Defensio Fidei** and in books III and VII of the Treaty of Laws. The theory of State, which is the answer to the first question, is found in the first two documents. Book VII deals with customs as a source of Law. Suárez offers the answer in a few paragraphs in chapter XIX of Book II, the same place where he analyzes the *jus gentium*. However, without the study of the other texts, these small paragraphs cannot unmask all of their content. If it were not for their literary beauty, they might even go unnoticed.

Henceforth the three questions posed by Suárez will be now examined.

5.3.1 The Theory of State

Francisco Suárez reveals all his Modernity in Political Theory. Although his subject of study was still Theology, the author is an exceptional political scientist. In fact, he uncovers ideas that British philosophy would slowly develop only a century later. He deals with issues such as the popular source of sovereignty, the relations between the Church and the State and the right to civil disobedience. However, Suárez had little influence on subsequent generations and the comments to this part of his work are scarce. Even so, the few that exist supply the lack of quantity with quality. Despite the importance of this area, I will limit my analysis to the aspects of his theory that matter to the *jus gentium*.

Suárez's theory of State appears in Book III of **De Legibus** and in the **Defensio Fidei Catholicae adversus anglicanae sectae errores**. The history of this oeuvre is well known. Since 1600, Cardinal Roberto Berlarmino was engaged in the Catholic restoration of England and had put all his hopes in James I, at that time known as James VI of Scotland. But the events of the Gunpowder Conjuration of 1605 resulted in severe frictions between the King and the Catholics, especially the Jesuits. The Provincial Garnet was even executed by a royal order. The response of the monarch did not end with the exemplary punishment. In 1606, persecutory laws were voted based on an oath of allegiance.[75]

It was the third oath that an English Monarch imposed on his Catholic subjects since the Reformation. The first, imposed by Henry VIII only to clerics who could vote in the Parliament received a new formulation by Elisabeth the I that prescribed it to everyone, except the civil authorities. James broadens considerably both the text and the content. English Catholics should declare, and God would be witness, that he was the legitimate king and the supreme lord of the kingdom. The oath adds that no foreign power, especially the Pope, could interfere in his government, and nothing and no one would have the authority to condemn his actions. It remains to the subjects only the duty of obedience even in the face of a sentence of excommunication.[76]

Apparently, the oath had merely a political character and could not attract the attention of the Catholic Church. King James wanted to secure his supremacy and personal security by consolidating the absolute sovereignty over the English State. It was, in principle, a manifestation of the absolutism current at that period. It should be noticed that the last political oaths had occurred in the High Middle Ages to sanctify mutual obligations that bound lords and their vassals. At that time, there was no need to seduce the commoners; they would follow their leaders by necessity or instinct. The opinion of the mass mattered so little. However, times have changed, and it was necessary to appeal to the individual conscience, which, until then, was a reserved area of a foreign power: the Church. Therefore, the oath of political allegiance also affected relations between the Church and the State.[77]

The absolutism of James I was a true compendium of the Protestant political tradition of the time. Due to Nominalism, Protestantism vouched for legal voluntarism and extolled the omnipotence of the sovereign. King James was convinced of his own superiority.

> He believed in good faith to be a brilliant theologian who brought the truth to those misguided Englishmen. James I considered himself the first theologian of Europe. Proclaimed that he had been personally chosen by God to rule his people, invested with powers directly by God and that he was responsible only to God.[78]

Therefore, King James supported the divine origin of the rights of the kings. Protestants, in general, made a very literal interpretation of the apostle Paul statement "*non est potestas nisi a Deo*". Since Francisco de Vitoria, Catholics exalted

---

[75]Carrillo Prieto (1977), p. 58.

[76]Third oath of alliegence arbitrated and defended by King James I. See Suárez (1978), pp. 22–24.

[77]Elorduy (1965).

[78]"*Creía de buena fe ser un teólogo genial que traía la verdad a los ingleses desorientados. Jacobo I se consideraba el primer teólogo de Europa. Proclamaba que había sido personalmente elegido por Dios para gobernar a su pueblo, investido de sus poderes directamente por Dios y que sólo era responsable ante Dios.*" (Pereña, 1979, p. 16).

the popular origin of sovereignty. In fact, this theory integrated the traditional interpretation of Thomism. Already in the thirteenth century, Pope Innocence IV enunciated in explicit terms that while the Pope's power comes from God (because of the donation made by Jesus Christ Himself to Peter) the power of the Emperor stems from the people.[79]

The statement of Innocence IV seems to, apart from finding the popular basis of the authority, extol the papal power. But it was given at other times, when the notion of imperial monism still hung over the heads of Christendom. And, as will be seen in the words of Suárez, a variant of this monism attributed the title of emperor (and therefore lord of all Christians) to the Pope.

However, the Catholics themselves would recognize a limitation on the authority of the Supreme Pontiff. In 1568, even before the controversy with James I, Cardinal Bellarmine drafted the doctrine of the indirect power, according to which the Pope would be entitled to interfere in temporal affairs whenever spiritually convenient to the Church. His doctrine did not entrust the temporal power to the head of the Church, but admitted the possibility that princes be dethroned in defense of faith. His solution was also advocated by the more moderate supporters of the papacy; however, since it did not praise the pontifical power as the doctrine of direct power did, the Holy See and Gregory XIII were outraged by it. Yet, the theory of the indirect power was more in line with the political conditions of the time, so Bellarmine's book was withdrawn from the Index and rehabilitated before the Catholic opinion.[80]

Therefore, according to the limited interference of the new times, the papal response to the oath of allegiance was a simple condemnation: in a minute, Paul V declared the illegitimacy of the oath. James I answers with the treaty **Apologia pro Iuramento Fidelitatis**. Bellarmine retorts with the first **Responsio**. The King, in turn, ordered a reprint of the **Apologia**, preceded by a **Prefatio Monitoria**. Bellarmine then attempts to put an end to the controversy with a second **Responsio**.[81]

In this context, there were some movements within the Catholic Church so that Francisco Suárez would intervene in the aid of Bellarmine. The Reformation had unleashed its most powerful blow and the Church could only respond by resorting to its most important theologian of the time. Suárez accepts under the condition that the Pope himself ensured the doctrine that he would formulate. With this certainty, albeit averse to controversy, Suárez amiably accepts the task. However, instead of writing a pamphlet, he elevates the discussion and writes a scientific tome of over eight hundred pages.

King James I did not dare to answer to Suárez' **Defensio Fidei**. Instead, he comfortably commanded the doctors of Oxford to rejected Suárez and Bellarmine in a public act. In addition, he ordered the burning of the book in London and

[79]Merêa (2004), p. 119.

[80]Merêa (2004), p. 125.

[81]Carrillo Prieto (1977), p. 58.

forbade its reading across England, under severe penalties. In France, the work was burned in the courtyard of the Parliament, because it advocated the doctrine of tyrannicide. Since this was a Catholic kingdom, the Council of Louis XIII answered to the pope; however, so that the Parliament would not be offended, the ban on the book was preserved long enough until Suárez became undesired.[82]

5.3.1.1 The Origin of the Power

In Political Theory, Francisco Suárez once more innovates in relation to the traditional Thomism. The issue is quite carefully examined. Suárez had already addressed this subject, although very incipiently, in a work of his youth, **De Opere Sex Dierum**. It is possible to consider Political Theory as a recurring theme in Suárez' life. Still, the author is not a political scientist and his political thought is always guided by Theology.

It should come as no surprise that the first question proposed by Suárez in the first chapter of Book III of **De Legibus** is whether man has power, as well as legitimacy to legislate. The main political problem, to Suárez, is in the binomial obedience-freedom: did God grant power to some men (or to a man in particular) over others? Based on the equality of men established by their divine paternity, how can a man come before another? This issue traces back to the Bishop of Hippo's denying a natural basis for the State. When transcribing a passage of the Genesis, Augustine says that God created man to have dominion over the fish of the sea, the birds and the land animals, but not to overpower their similar. A whole stream of writers inferred from this statement an unnatural character of power; power would originate from sin and human corruption.[83]

Suárez does not share this view. The author begins with Aristotle's conception of man as a social animal. Man may only dismiss political power if he were to live alone or only with his family, but life in society is natural. And "if there was no form of power, each would act according to their particular interests, considering that the particular interest does not coincide with the common good and many times is opposed to it".[84] Even a society of angels presupposes some form of power, so that order exists within the group. The directive principle of power is natural; only the coercive portion thereof results from human recalcitrance and sin.

The word "society" is in itself ambiguous. Like Aquinas, Suárez distinguishes the perfect or civil society from the imperfect or domestic one. The family corresponds to the more "natural" or "purely natural" society and is a result of the relations between husband and wife, parents and children and even between slaves

---

[82]Elorduy (1965), pp. XXV–XXX.

[83]Calafate (2001), p. 576.

[84]Calafate (2001), p. 577.

and masters. It consists of the natural society by excellence, depending directly on the natural instinct inherent to men. Therefore, the family already existed in the state of innocence—albeit without some institutes such as slavery and domestic service, which were developed after the original sin. Nevertheless, this first human community is imperfect in relation to the political community because it is not enough in itself. Men cannot satisfy all their interests and aspirations through the family. Even the satisfaction of the natural needs, like procreation, is limited.[85]

Like many Modern political writers, Suárez recognizes a moment prior to the formation of the State as the "state of innocence". The Portuguese Jurist Diogo Fretas do Amaral compares his and Hobbes' state of nature and points out three interesting similarities: the natural freedom, the absence of political power and the necessity of a voluntary act for the constitution of the civil State.[86] But his comparison errs in a core issue: there is no correspondence between them since they fulfill different roles. The Suarezian state of innocence performs a function quite diverse from that of the Hobbesian state of nature. It does not seem possible to properly compare them; at best, an analogy is possible. The state of innocence does not constitute a historical situation, or an ideal moment prior to the State, but a state that precedes the original sin. It is not opposed to the "civil state", as the state of nature is, but rather to the "state of corruption". The state of innocence represents an idyllic time, in which men lived as animals: only to satisfy their basic instincts. It precedes both the original sin and the subsequent redemption by the infusion of the divine grace. There is no State because there is no coercive power since there is no sin. In addition, the state of innocence is a social State. In Suárez, there was never a pre-social moment, in which men lived as isolated individuals. Man is born and, by his own nature, lives among his similars.

In the state of innocence, man realizes his sociability only within the family. After corruption, slavery and servitude join the structure of the family. Thus, there are three relations now: those of husband and wife, of father and son and of master and slaves. The first two correspond to natural necessities: procreation, survival and also the education of the offspring. After sin, slavery and servile work are added to assist in the domestic economy. Hence, sin itself does nothing to improve the social relations beyond the family.

However, the family does not contain in itself all the necessary services and crafts for human life to flourish. Nor does it allow man to pursue his own and rational purpose: to know God. It is necessary that many families gather in at least one city or in a larger grouping, such as a kingdom. Moreover, if all families were

---

[85]**DL**. III, 1, 3.

[86]Amaral, 1994, p. 13. Although I disagree with the **correspondence** between the two terms, it seems possible that Hobbes himself wished to make an **analogy** with the Scholastic political categories. The fine irony of the Philosopher of Malmesbury is famous. Also, the author's allusions to the Bible, like the monster Leviathan, and to Theology are various. It is noteworthy that, although the state of nature does not cease with the advent of the divine grace, it ends with another divine epiphany, but from a "mortal god", the State.

kept separate, peace would be preserved among men, but it would not be possible to ward off or punish injustices in an orderly fashion.[87]

For this reason, the political and perfect community is also a natural need, albeit exclusive of the rational being. If men had remained in the state of innocence, they would still gather in perfect communities, despite not using coercive power. In other words, the State is a precept of Natural Law.[88]

Until this moment, Suárez remains loyal to Aristotle's legacy: the *appetitus societatis* of man propel him toward forming a State. The author does not accept the idea of a state of nature in which men live *more bestiarum,* nor does it pleases him to explain the creation of social life by the degeneration of human qualities and a consequent need to remediate our indigence. Suárez is not Hobbes' precursor. Before the formation of political communities, there was a transitional state where only families existed. However, even if man had not known sin, the family societies should still assemble into perfect political groups. With the exception to its coercive power, the State

> does not represent a remedy to the corrupt nature of men, a process that to him was not the resource to defend himself of the primitive dangers of the state of nature, but an eminently natural state, that is necessary to man in any circumstances and is an indispensable condition of perfectibility.[89]

This idea of political authority and law as a natural necessity of man is an outrage to the Reformers' political ideas. For Reformers, there was a true gap between God and man. Within this gap, there would be no institute that provides a rational basis for human morality, such as the Eternal and the Natural Law, which in any case ultimately proceed from the Creator. Only faith can cross the abyss between God and man. In turn, Suárez defends a more optimist view. The Catholic God is closer to men. Social life and political authority do not correspond to a means of compensating degeneration; they are rather a step in the journey towards human moral development. The original sin only makes it difficult to achieve perfection in this and other aspects of moral existence.[90] Even in the **De Legibus**, before addressing the controversy with the English King, Suárez exposes a theory that the Reformers would eventually reject.

By demonstrating that the State is a natural precept, Suárez partially answers the first question "whether men have power over other men". This prerogative is legitimate, as it stems from Natural Law. Now, Suárez needs to investigate how that power was constituted; in other words, how it came to be determined who should rule and who should obey. Even if the Scholastics did not believe in a de facto

[87]**DL**. III, 1, 3.

[88]**DL**. III, 1, 12.

[89]"(…) *não representa um remédio para a natureza corrupta do homem, um processo a que este tenha recorrido para se defender dos perigos do primitivo estado de natureza, mas sim um estado eminentemente natural, que convém ao homem em quaisquer circunstâncias e é uma condição imprescindível de sua perfectibilidade.*" (Merêa, 2004, p. 134).

[90]Haakonssen (1996), pp. 18–25.

equality among men in view of their equal divine paternity, they would not accept any substantial inequality either. This is not about legal equality, but theological. Even so, it is disturbing to realize that some men ruled while others obeyed.

Demonstrating the need for the State is not the same as proving its creation. Necessities are not always fulfilled. It is here that Suárez distances himself from tradition. Although the family constituted an indispensable base for the political community, the latter is not an enlargement or a variation of the former. The author rejects the theory of patriarchy: the power of the father differs from the power of the prince, not only in the number of persons who pledge obedience to him, but also in essence. Even Adam, the first man, held only a domestic power, not a political one.[91]

Nature may propel men to create the State, but the immediate cause of it lies in man himself: his will. Men must gather and celebrate a pact. Albeit in a different colouring, in Suárez, there is an outline of the social contract doctrine: "in other way, therefore, the human crowd can be considered: by a specific will or a general **consent**, it congregates in a political body". Or still: "For this reason, it said before that the power of the king is based on a **contract** or **quasi contract**."[92] The word "pact" permeates Book III of **De Legibus** as well the **Defensio Fidei**.

Despite the express references to the term, the Suarezian contratualism is not similar to the Moderns'. In Suárez's conception, there is no space for a Hobbesian or Lockean individualism: freedom of men to autonomously join the social contract is conditioned by a natural necessity. The human will is the immediate cause of the political power, but the decision to form a State is not made without the intervention of any *a priori* impulse. There is no moral anarchy in need of a purely rational redemption. In Suárez, the human reason ratifies the drive of moral natural structures that compel human beings to form a State. In the pre-political state, man is not considered in abstract, dissociated from his social context. For this reason, Rommen prefers to use the term consensus instead of agreement.[93] The State is a result of the collaboration between nature and freedom.

The jusphilosopher Teresa Rinaldi points out that Vitória already manifested the idea that political power would be formed out of the consensus of men. But the notion of consensus differs in these two authors.[94] Vitória lacks the voluntary dimension of Suárez. In Vitória, the consensus is a natural consequence of life in community. The civil power is constituted in a consuetudinary manner, not by a

---

[91]**DL**. III, 2, 3.

[92]"*Alio ergo modo consideranda est hominum multitudo, quatenus speciali voluntate, seu communi consensu in unum corpus politicum congregatur*" (**DL**. III, 2, 4) and "*Et ideo supra dixi potestatem regiam fundari in contractu vel quasi contractu*" (*R. P. Francisci Suarez. Granatensis è Societate Jesu, Doctoriis Eximi.* **Defensio Fidei Catholicae et Apostolicae adversus Anglicanae sectae errores**, *cum responsione ad Apologiam pro Iuramento Fidelitatis et Praefationem Monitoriam Serenissimi Iacobi Angliae Regis. Conimbricae: Didacum Gomez de Loureyro*, 1613. Book III, chapter 2, item 20. Henceforth, **DF**).

[93]Rommen (1951), p. 114.

[94]Rinaldi (2001), p. 194.

formal bond manifested in a single act, but every day, through little resignations. In Suárez, the authority comes from nature, but the implementation thereof stems from human intelligence. In Vitória, the authority and its implementation share a natural ground.

However, for a contract to be the basis of the sovereign's authority, it should assume a popular, not divine, origin of power. Therefore, Suárez needs to circumvent Paul's assertion in the Roman Epistole (XIII, 1): "there is no authority that does not come from God (*non est enim potestas nisi a Deo*)". The divine origin of power represented a common and unquestionable axiom of the time. But the axiom only answered the origin of power in abstract terms; concretely, it was necessary to determine how power was transferred to secular chiefs. There were two hypotheses that fit the framework of the Christian culture: the power would either be transferred directly by God to the sovereign (as it is read in the Bible in the case of Saul and Dave) or through a mediator.

James I defended the first hypothesis, because it removed him from the temporal and spiritual subordination of the Pope. Suárez accepts the immediate transfer of the power to Saul and Dave, but considers this an extraordinary and supernatural case. Normally, God acts through nature: "according to general and ordinary providence, it is not transmitted this way because in accordance with the natural order of civil things, men are not governed by revelations, but by natural reason". In the **Defensio Fidei**, Suárez even questions the validity of this transfer, because he advocates that God would only chose who should be king, but his appointment to the office is left to the people.[95]

Once this first hypothesis is excluded, all that is left is mediation. As a good religious man, Suárez accepts Paul's statement as true and valid. In abstract, all power comes from God, but He would later have conferred it to men. There are two ways for this transfer to take place, that is, there are two mediators who could make this happen: "First, [God] confers a power that, by essence, is necessarily united to the thing that was created by the same God". Here, the power arises from the thing itself and God presents Himself as the first owner of this power, as he created the thing. God immediately grants the power not by a special action, but as author of nature. It is the case of the authority of the father over the son: the transfer of this power is effected through paternity. The power is granted and the thing is created through one single act. "In other way, God immediately grants by Himself (so to say) and through a special donation, a power that is not necessarily bound to the creation of a being, but God grants such power to a nature or person, in a free or supplementary fashion".[96] It is a direct grant that God performs beyond nature. This

[95]"(...) *iuxta communem autem, et ordinariam providentiam non ita sit, quia homines iuxta naturae ordinem non revelationibus, sed naturali ratione regulatur in his, quae civilia sunt*" (**DL**. III, 4, 2). See also **DF**. III, 3, 5–10.

[96]"*Unus modus est dando potestatem, ut ex natura rei necessario connexam cum aliqua natura quam Deus ipse condit*" and "*Alio modo datur a Deo immediate potestas* per se *(ut ita dicam) et peculiari donatione, non ut necessario connexa cum alicuius rei creatione, sed ut voluntarie a Deo superaddita alicui naturae vel personae.*" (**DF**. III, 2, 3).

was what happened when Jesus Christ entrusted the government of the Church to Peter. In the first manner, power stems from Natural Law; in the second, from Positive Law.

Therefore, the two possible mediators would be the Pope and the community itself. Then, Suárez explains why the successor of Peter should be excluded from this position in the issue at stake. According to the author, political authority was given by God to man in the moment of creation. This is the first transfer; man can do whatever he wants with this power later. However, this power does not lie within each man individually considered. God did not grant authority to anyone in special, but He did not fraction and donated it to each single human being either. Authority only arises when men form a group, not as an inorganic crowd, without physical or moral bonds,

> but in other way, as, it can be considered the human crowd: by a specific will or general consent, it congregates in a political body with a society bond and to help themselves mutually in direction to a political finality, in the same way that they constitute a mystical body that morally can be called *uno* by its nature; its body, in consequence, has the necessity of a head.[97]

Only when men gather in an orderly fashion, with defined (political) purposes, does the authority arise, as a natural predicate. The mystical body is a true organism, not a biological, but a moral one. It is a whole distinct of the sum of its two parts, because it is qualified by the authority. And, in order to achieve its purposes, it needs a head. Once the need to live in society is presumed, the subjecting to political power is a natural corollary thereof.

But nature needs the confluence of human wills. It is in this mystic body that the pact takes place. Since natural freedom is a precept of Dominative Natural Law, it may be alienated by men to one or more individuals. Suárez resumes the traditional tripartition of government forms (monarchy, aristocracy and democracy, in their pure or corrupted forms) and the variations of mixed government. Although he prefers monarchy, he concedes that Natural Law prescribes no special type of government. The choice will fall on the content of the pact; all kinds of government belong to Positive Law.[98]

The only exception is democracy. It may exist without any positive institution, only as a result of men's natural sociability.[99] However, it does not represent a commandment of nature, only a permission. Natural Law does not oblige the community to keep the power with which it was vested in the first place; in view of historical and cultural circumstances, other political orientation may become advisable. Therefore, men are free to choose the form of government they desire.

---

[97]"*Alio ergo modo consideranda est hominum multitudo, quatenus speciali voluntate, seu communi consensu in unum corpus politicum congregatur uno societatis vinculo, et ut mutuo seiuvent in ordine ad unum finem politicum, quomodo efficiunt unum corpus mysticum, quod moraliter dici potest* per se *unum: illudque consequenter indiget uno capite*." (**DL**. III, 2, 4).

[98]**DF**. III, 2, 7.

[99]**DF**. III, 2, 8.

However, unlike Modern political theories, it is the community as whole that alienates its natural rights to a sovereign and not each individual. The authority constitutes a natural predicate of the organized crowd, not of singular men.

As a result of the contract, no regime is essentially bad. In principle, all can be good and useful. It is required only that the holder or the holders of the political power receive such power from the community itself.[100] The legitimacy of the sovereign is subject to the provisions of the agreement. Although it constitutes an act of subjection (the people irrevocably "alienates" the power), the community may insert limits to the authority of the sovereign. Thus, there may be constraints to the power of the sovereign, even of Positive Law.

In Suárez's time, there existed a legal doctrine of political power according to which the power belonged to the person (or persons) of the sovereign, not to the State itself. This doctrine is known as the State-object theory. Therefore, the pact does not correspond to an actual title by means of which the State is formed, rather it reflects the fact that the political authority belongs to a given man or men. Nevertheless, this *potestas* does not bear any resemblance to the institute of ownership in Private Law. "It should be added that the kingdom is not comparable with other goods or the administration of dowry because it is like an office which is assigned to the same person to whom it is conferred, and its purpose is not so much this person, but those who should be ruled".[101] Hence, Suárez adopts a conception that was already widespread in Antiquity and was favorably received by the Church: *regnum non est propter regem, sed rex.* For the author, this is a safe criterion with which to distinguish the true king from a tyrant. The mere fact that the human laws emanate from the sovereign power does not make them legitimate nor respectable. Their intrinsic value should be taken into account: they must comply with Natural Law, to the common good and to the conditions of the pact.[102]

In addition to the contract, there are other legitimate titles of political power. The hereditary succession is a derivative title, since the sovereign's successors receive the power that emanates from the people only indirectly. War and subsequent territorial conquest can also increase the size of a State. In the case of a just war, the title proves to be legitimate *ab initio*; in an unjust war, it may be that the people with the passage of time give their consent and admit the conqueror as their sovereign. Therefore, the time lapse may justify a claim to power.[103]

Suárez is now able to fully answer the initial question (whether men may rule over other men). He answers in the affirmative, because man himself would have agreed to it. Authority in abstract is found in God and in concrete in the people, who can do with it whatever they please.

---

[100] **DL**. III, 4, 1-2.

[101] "*Accedit, quod in hoc non est comparandum regnum cum aliis bonis, seu cum administratione dotis, quia regnum est veluti quodam officium, quod incumbit propriae personae, cui confertur, et non tam est propter ipsam, quam propter eos, qui regen di sunt*" (**DL**. III, 9, 12).

[102] Merêa, 2004, p. 135.

[103] **DL**. III, 4, 3-4 and **DF**. III, 2, 20.

In the beginning, this power may have been shared by all men. However, this was not convenient to the administration of this community. Suárez recalls Aristotle, for whom a very large city would be difficult to govern. Therefore, little "after the creation of the world, men began to divide themselves in different States, and in each one existed such power separately".[104] In this excerpt, Suárez already displays that imperial monism is not desirable. In addition to being a fact, the division of mankind in States (and the consequent possibility of a law between peoples) is the best that could have happened. It is a most desirable fact.

5.3.1.2 The Doctrine of Tyrannicide

The other possible mediator of God's power would be the Supreme Pontiff. Peter received his power directly from Jesus Christ, and his successors (despite being elected by a board) would also receive their authority from God. The human act (the election) is the proximate cause for God (the main cause) to confer His power. While the Church itself is a community, God did not transfer His power to the entity as a whole, but only to its head.[105] Besides commanding the Church, could the Pope govern all kingdoms or at least all Christian kingdoms? There was a widespread theory according to which the Pope would retain the power *in habitu* and the Christian princes would reign as his delegates.

Suárez demonstrates his realism when he affirms that this delegation has never taken place, because it could not be undone. But Suárez's opposition to this theory is even more profound. Such a theory could only be valid if Jesus Christ had wanted to include all kingdoms in the decree of donation to Peter. Suárez remembers that God promised to deliver "the keys to the kingdom of heaven", but said nothing about the kingdoms of the earth. In addition, Christ had always said that his kingdom was not from this world. So, the Pope's jurisdiction was necessarily limited to the Church.[106]

Suárez conceives this limitation to the authority of the Pope and, in result, to the authority of the Church, because he advocates a radical distinction between temporal and spiritual powers. On quoting Pope Nicholas in a letter to the Archbishop Albinus, Suárez reminds that "the Holy Church of God has no sword except the spiritual". He thus concludes that even in Christian States which take part in a single mystical and spiritual body of the Church,

---

[104]"(...) *post mundi creationem coepisse hominis dividi in varias respublicas, et in singulis fuisse hanc potestatem distinctam*" (**DL**. III, 2, 5).

[105]**DF**. III, 3, 13.

[106]**DF**. III, 5, 14-15.

by Natural Law there is no immediate temporal and universal jurisdiction over all Church, as there are as many supreme temporal jurisdictions as the number of political communities that are not part of a kingdom or of a State.[107]

Throughout the **Defensio Fidei**, Suárez clearly says that the spiritual power belongs to the Pope and the temporal power to the prince. The author abandons the idea of the two swords of the Church and, even in the beginning of the seventeenth century, emphasizes the difference between temporal and spiritual jurisdictions. It is not possible to infer from this that Suárez was advocating the separation of powers between the State and the Church, but he did recognize the difference between the political domain, which was essentially human, and the religious domain, divine and supernatural. Although the conception of a laic State was still odd to Suárez, the idea of secularism was not. Suárez seems to agree with the distinction between the temporal and spiritual domains to such an extent that if Christians were subject to a pagan prince, they could not rebel, unless their prince was a tyrant.[108]

There was still the possibility that the Pope would exercise temporal jurisdiction over kingdoms and principalities in the event that the Emperor himself would have granted such power to him. In the first case, Suárez rejected the idea of a decree of donation from the perspective of Positive Divine Law; now, he addresses a problem of Positive human Law. This is a variation of the thesis of imperial monism according to which the pope, and not the emperor, would exert jurisdiction over all Christians. For Suárez, there was nothing more obsolete than this conception.

Then the Roman Empire itself was divided into east and west, and furthermore the Western Empire (which alone remained in power of the Christians after the Eastern had been seized by the pagans), although so far as dignity is concerned it endures in one person, was divided among many princes and kings in regard of its jurisdiction. Although some [peoples] are subjects of the emperor, more are thought to be lawfully exempt due to the right of time lapse, to which one must add the consent of the peoples, or titles of just war. And thus we now suppose that, besides the emperor, there are several temporal kings entirely free from his jurisdiction, such are the Kings of Spain, France and England.[109]

In Suárez's time, the idea of a universal empire no longer made sense. Therefore, the donation of the Kingdom of Rome by the Emperor Constantine to the Pope implied at most jurisdiction over the cities of this legacy, never over all

---

[107]"*Sancta Dei Ecclesia gladium non habet, nisi spiritualem*" (**DF**. III, 8, 9) and "(…) *ex vi iuris naturalis non est in tota communitate Ecclesia immediate uma suprema iurisdictio temporalis et universalis super totam Ecclesia, sed tot sunt iurisdictiones temporales supremae, quot sunt politicae communitates, quae non sunt membra unius regni seu reipublicae civilis*" (**DF**. III, 5, 11).

[108]**DF**. III, 4, 2.

[109]"*Accedit illum ipsum romanum imperium in orientale et occidentale fuisse divisum, et deinde occidentale imperium (quod solum in christianis permansit, orientali a paganis occupato), licet quoad dignitatem in una persona duret, quoad iurisdictionem in multos principes et reges divisum esse. Ex quibus licet aliqui sint imperatori suiecti, plures censentur legitime exempti, iure praescriptionis, accedente simul populorum consensu vel titulo iusti belli. Ac proinde praeter imperatorem plures esse reges temporales ab illus iurisdictione omnino líberos, ut sunt rex Hispaniae, Galliae et Angliae, nunc supponimus.*" (**DF**. III, 5, 7).

Christians.[110] As Rommen observes, the idea of imperial unitarianism on the person of the pope had in itself the seeds of its destruction. By subtracting from the Emperor his autonomy from papacy as well as his divine title over the territorial princes, he lost his political influence. And in times of Reformation, with the creation of national churches, a divine title of legitimacy exclusive of the pope could not be convincing.[111]

So far, Suárez does not seem to contradict the interests of the King of England. On the one hand, his theory prescribes political conformism, since the transfer of power from the people to the king is a pact of subjection: there was a real alienation of power. On the other hand, Suárez removed the temporal power from the Pope, the only figure who could oppose to the pretenses of the English Monarch.

Moreover, the historical and cultural context surrounding Suárez did not seem propitious for developing theories of civil disobedience. During the second half of the sixteenth century (a great part of Suárez's life) the internal war representated the normal state of affairs in countries that experienced the Reformation, mainly France. In times of religious and political tribulations, there came to light a famous literature that praised the rights of the people at the expense of the royal power, even legitimising the deposition and execution of kings. The supporters of these ideas were known as the "*Monarchomachs*" according to the description of their opponent William Barclay. In Spain, however, the conditions were different. The conservative and Christian background of the population, invigorated by the Holy Office, kept the country far from the political turbulence of the time. To the king's strong Catholic faith corresponded the feelings of the nation in unison chorus. So, it seems strange, that the Jesuit Juan de Mariana, a brother of exalted temperament and a little older than Suárez, would formulate the doctrine of tyrannicide in **De Rege**—a work ironically dedicated to the Monarch. As expected, his work was not well received, even by his colleagues at the Company of Jesus.[112] Still, Suárez had knowledge of it and, although it did not apply to the Spanish context, it could certainly be put to use in other places where the sovereign was controversial.

So, the doctrine of tyrannicide was not a novelty, but it seemed rather eccentric to the Suárezian thought. However, even without giving up on the difference between temporal and spiritual power (or perhaps because of it) Suárez was able to introduce this concept. For the author, for one to hold the sovereign authority ("supreme" authority in the original) there can be no higher human authority. This non-submission of the sovereign may be absolute, when it recognizes no higher power in both temporal and spiritual matters, or relative, when limited to temporal matters.[113] The latter corresponds to the degree of temporal sovereignty of princes, since the Pope also exercises spiritual sovereignty.

[110]**DF**. III, 5, 13.

[111]Rommen (1951), p. 394.

[112]Merêa (2004), pp. 120–122.

[113]**DF**. III, 5, 1.

A prince may legislate in spiritual or related matters. In this case, because of the spiritual sovereignty of the pope (as well as the subordination of the temporal and political happiness to the spiritual and eternal happiness), the temporal sovereign is subject to the pope's authority.[114] Suárez's counter-attack to James I begins to take shape; it is the theory of the indirect power of the Pope. And the proof of the validity of this thesis reveals both the realism and the theological coherence of Suárez: if God had conferred authority on political issues to the pope, this power would be imperfect because it is ineffective and nothing imperfect can derive from God.[115]

The papal interference was well defined. It was not up to the Supreme Pontiff to determine the cases in which the sovereign has exceeded the limits of his power. The situations are already established a priori. In order to explain this, Suárez distinguishes two classes of tyrant rulers: tyranny *quoad titulum* and tyranny *quoad administrationem*. In the first class, the tyrant is not the legitimate sovereign, since he usurped the post. In the second, although the prince may rightfully occupy the throne, he reigns in a tyrannical manner. This equals saying that the sovereign exercises the power in his own benefit at the expense of the common good: "[the tyrant] oppresses his subjects unjustly, robbing, killing, perverting and perpetrating against them in public, similar injustices".[116]

Tyranny may take shape first by the breach of the conditions laid down in the pact—which were called "regal law" at the time of Suárez. But these caveats had to be express. And second, by the non-compliance with the precepts of Natural Law (that still subsists in the perfect community). Differently to what happens with the Hobbesian contract, men do not alienate their right to interpret Natural Law. It is rather ironic that in Hobbes, Natural Law remains in force in the civil state, but only the sovereign has the power to interpret it. For example, murder is still forbidden by Natural Law, but it is up to the sovereign to define what is murder.[117] This difference occurs because Hobbes, and other Modern authors in general, base Natural Law on feelings or instincts of man, or (as described in chapter III in the topic about changes in Natural Law) is based on facts, on what is, and not on values, on what should be. But in Suárez, since Natural Law (although unveiled by human reason) derives from both the divine will and the essence of things, it may not be invalidated by any human act. It also has an objective basis, the existence of which is not

---

[114]**DF**. III, 5, 2.

[115]Scott (1934), p. 268.

[116]"(...) *subditos iniuste affligit, spoliando, occidendo, pervertendo vel alia similia publice et frequenter iniuste perpetrando*" (**DF**. VI, 4, 1).

[117]"Theft, Murther, Adultery, and all injuries are forbid by the Laws of nature; but what is to be called. Theft, what Murther, what Adultery, what injury in a Citizen, this is not to be determined by the natural, but by the civil Law: for not every taking away of the thing which another possesseth, but onely another mans goods is theft; but what is ours, and what anothers, is a question belonging to the civil Law. In like manner, not every killing of a man is murther, but onely that which the civil Law forbids; neither is all encounter with women Adultery, but onely that which the civil Law prohibits." (Hobbes, 2002, p. 112).

bound to human interpretation. No facts, not even reason alone, create the law, only the will. And, in regard to Natural Law, it is the most supreme will who creates it.

There exists varying degrees of civil disobedience prior to regicide to cope with tyranny. In principle, the Jurist of Coimbra abhors any form of resistance to a sovereign command. The author is a political conformist. If the injustice on the command is trivial, he still advises compliance for the sake of order and the common good, which could be tainted with the insubordination. However, when common good itself is found at risk because of an unjust law, disobedience becomes even mandatory, since the sovereign's command is not a true law. Yet, so far the action of the people should remain within the sphere of passive resistance.[118]

Everything becomes different in the case of an usurper. Suárez explicitly talks of deposition. In this case, the sovereign is no rightful king, he is an enemy of the kingdom and is virtually at war with it. Any member of the State (and even a stranger) may defend the community until death. But it is necessary that there is no superior authority to whom the people may resort, that the sovereign's title be patently unfair, that there be no other less extreme means to liberate the State, that there be no truce or pact with the people, that the regicide causes no greater evils and that the people (gathered in a perfect society again) does not expressly oppose the deposition.[119]

Between the two classes of tyranny, Suárez prefers to address the tyranny according to which a sovereign, despite holding a just title, becomes unlawful in result of the form he rules, since this class fits the case of the English King. The reasoning seems simple. If the perfect community transferred its power to the king, it was under the condition that he would not govern as a tyrant; therefore, should he becomes one, the community could justly resume its initial authority. By the principle of self-defense, for its own conservation, the people could rise up and depose the tyrant and even condemn him to death if there is no other way to defend itself.

Nonetheless, the author recalls that the Council of Constance condemned those who threaten the life of the tyrant by their own private authority. This council took place in 1415; it predates by over a century Reformation. This condemnation was directed at the doctrine of Wycliffe and John Huss, according to which the masters of the world would lose their domain automatically should they incur in any mortal sin and could be punished by their subjects. This council is not associated with the Protestant Reformation. But Suárez, as a good theologian, cannot defy it. Indeed, no man can take the life of his king for several reasons: first, because punishing and rejecting insults are prerogatives of the one who was entrusted with the common good; second, because the coercive power belongs only to the sovereign; third, because this kind of act may cause an uproar within the State. If an individual cannot kill another individual, even if he has committed a crime, murdering the king, even a tyrant, would be far worse.[120]

---

[118]**DL**. III, 10, 7.

[119]**DF**. VI, 4, 7-11.

[120]**DF**. VI, 4, 3-4.

At the core of the issue is the concept of private authority. No man can, by his own authority, assassinate the tyrant, because the power lies within the people, brought together in a mystical body, not in any individual. When the king becomes a tyrant, the power returns to the community and not to its isolated members. Therefore, the moral body needs to gather again, so that the sentence of the tyrant does not come from one individual, but from a public board of all cities and prosecutors. At this moment, it is possible to resort to the Pope. The State may gather in this kind of public assembly everytime its very existence is put at risk. But, in the special case of unjust laws on spiritual or spiritually related matters, the authority of the Supreme Pontiff can and should be heard.[121] It is the replacement of a public authority (the community) by another (the Pope).

However, Suárez does not go so far as to applaud the attitude of Seneca who, under the orders of a tyrant emperor, agrees to kill himself. The prohibition to commit regicide does not prevent the legitimate defense. But the subject cannot resort to violence if the value at risk is a material good. Only the defense of life justifies the death of the tyrant. Because "the right to protect one's own life is above all and, this time, the need that moves the ruler is not as compelling to the point of forcing the subject to sacrifice his life for him; rather the sovereign places himself at risk".[122]

Even if the pact provides for the absolute submission, without any reservation, including on the right to life, Suárez admits the individual self-defense. Yet corporal punishment and death penalty were very common and considered legitimate in Suárez's time. Suárez is not advocating the abolition of the death penalty. A possible explanation lies in the pact itself: the pact was established by the community as a whole, gathered in a moral body, not by an individual. According to the cultural and historical circumstances, the community decides to accept or not the affliction of corporal punishment and the death penalty in order to maintain domestic peace (which is a requirement for the common good). If there are any reservations, they must be expressly set forth in the pact. However, even in their absence, it was the community, not the individual, who agreed to the death penalty. One person in special, apart from the communal coexistence, has the right to defend his own life.

The right to self-defense proves to be the only exception by means of which someone acting by his own private authority may assassinate the king. Still, Suárez warns that this exception should not be extended to all circumstances. If the death of the sovereign brings disturbances that may harm the common good, then the love for the nation must prevent the individual from killing the prince, even if he places his life at risk. But Suárez notes that this kind of obligation surpasses the scope of Law and falls within the order of Charity.[123]

---

[121]**DF**. VI, 4, 15.

[122]"(...) *ius tuendae vitae est maximum, et tunc princeps non est in necessitate, quae obliget subditum ad vitam pro illo perdendam, sed ipse voluntarie et inique in illo discrimine constituit*" (**DF**. VI, 4, 5).

[123]**DF**. VI, 4, 5.

Civil disobedience (and, in its most extreme form, tyrannicide) is possible only because the first holder of the power is the people (despite having alienated it by the pact) and there are ways for the people to regain back the power. And it is because of this popular source of power that Suárez is able to ground the *jus gentium* in customs.

5.3.2 The Formal Source of the Law of Nations

The Scholastics did not usually concern themselves with Legal Philosophy, opting to develop a Theory of the Laws. Aquinas wrote a Treatise on the Laws, but the rights are the object of the virtue of justice and so they were dealt in another oeuvre, the Treatise of Justice. Among his peers, Suárez is one of the most enthusiastics on the extra-legal forms of Law. As seen in chapter III, he accepts Isidore's thesis that *lex*, together with the mores, the customs and the judicial acts are a species of the genus *jus*.

According to Suárez, the Laws are a common, fair and stable precept, adequately enacted. In general, customs have the same characteristics of the written law, only differing in its exteriorization. Yet, it passes a specific legislative process and constitutes the living proof of the popular origin of sovereignty. Even after transferring the power to their prince, the people still hold some legislative capacity, which is expressed in the form of customs.

Suárez justifies approaching this subject only in book VII, after analyzing the human law, for it coincides with the order of exposition adopted by Gregory IX in **Decretales**. In addition, despite being a highly controversial issue, he believes that laws come first not only on importance, but also on historical precedence.[124]

Even though Suárez accepts the thesis of the Archbishop of Seville according to which the laws and the customs are species of the genus *jus*, he rejects his definition whereby the customs are "a law created by practice, which is considered law when there is no law". Neither did he adopt the Tertulian concept: "customs become the law in civil matters when there is no law".[125] Once again, he disagrees with tradition and there are three reasons for it. First, customs cannot be a law created by practice: it consists of a fact that only later will be recognized as law. Second, the word "practice" (*mores* in Latin) does not seem very adequate. Isidore sometimes affirms that practice is the origin of custom, but at other times he confuses it with custom itself—like in the sentence "practice is the custom that comes from the repetition of acts". Finally, the fact that the custom is considered law is not of its essence, rather an effect thereof.

---

[124]**DL**. VII, *Proemium*.

[125]"(...) *esse ius quodam moribus institutum, quod pro lege suspitur cum deficit lex*", "*consuetudo in civilibus rebus pro lege suspitur cum deficit lex*" and "*mos est consuetudo de tracta tantum*" (**DL**. VII, 1, 1).

A terminological issue here needs solution. There are three similar terms that result from free human acts: use (*usus*), practice (*mos*) and custom (*consuetudo*). In Theology, the use corresponds to every act that the will freely performs towards that which it elects as its purpose. It is an action in itself. However, vulgarly the use refers to a repetition of similar behaviors. In turn, practice relates to similar recurring voluntary behaviors. This conception is not different from the second meaning of the term use. Additionally, practice originates from a natural inclination and creates a habit (*habitus*). Yet the custom refers to the rate of recurrence, not to each particular action itself. Nevertheless, this word is not the synonymous to practice because it can be understood from two different perspectives: the very repetition of acts (*consuetudinem formalem*), which is the external expression of the custom (in this case, the habit constitutes its physical form), or the effects of this frequency, the product thereof. Therefore, the custom may translate a simple repetition of behaviors (a custom in fact) or it may create laws (a custom in law).[126]

Suárez insists on stressing the free and unrestrained character of those actions, regardless of the term he employs. Those three words are limited to human behaviors; brute animals do not possess this capacity. This observation is crucial for the author and points his readers to the role that will plays in the creation of the law. The custom, such as the law, is within the domain of human will. This was a novelty to a current and more ordinary conception that connected the customs with ancient traditions that men observed as if they were a natural, and even instinctive, inclination.

Not all repetition of acts is able to create law. The mere practice may simply result in a custom in fact. It seems like Suárez almost predicted the difference between a fact and a law. James Brown Scott suggests that Suárez would have already foreseen the spiritual element, the *opinius juris*, by which contemporary jurists characterize the international custom.[127] It is an effect of a moral order, a recognition that one must act in a certain way, or a faculty to eliminate previously binding obligations. Therefore, not all customs create law. For instance, bad customs have no legal effect, neither those that come from merely complying with law on a regular basis, because they represent the effects of a law.

Before analyzing the legal custom itself, Suárez affirms that there exists a kind of *usus* of juridical yet no legal consequence. To understand this, it is necessary to resume the two conceptions of *jus*: as a subjective faculty and as a law. Typically, the custom refers to a conduct repeated by an entire perfect community or by most of its members. Individual actions or family actions within an imperfect community do not create law. However, they may induce a right over something or the property of a thing: the acquisitive prescription or usucaption.[128] Every legal system needs to acknowledge some factual realities in order to maintain the stability of social

---

[126] **DL**. VII, 1, 2-4.

[127] Scott (1934), p. 213.

[128] **DL**. VII, 1, 9.

relations. In this case, the frequency refers to the use of a particular good. After a while, this use should result in a right to own this good.

There are three differences between the usucaption and the legal custom. The first lies in the *jus* itself: one creates a right of property, the other a legal rule. Another difference is consent. The legal custom is established with the acceptance of the people and the consent of the sovereign. Since custom is set where there should have be a legal rule, the custom, in a certain manner, is established "against" the prince—the prince is the true legislative authority who should have enacted a legal rule but he did not do so. On the other hand, the usucaption does not require the approval of those against which it is prescribed. Finally, both require a time lapse in order to achieve validity; however, the law itself defines the exact period of time necessary for an acquisitive prescription to take place, while custom is vague, providing only that there must have spent time enough for the consensus among the people and the prince to arise.[129]

When the old definitions ponder that custom came from "the absence of law", they should be understood as saying that custom creates true law, for if such a law were to exist, custom would no longer be required. The custom that produces a legal right is a kind of popular law, opposed to the "legislative law" enacted by the sovereign. And like every law, the custom needs to be voluntary, ordinary, fair, stable and adequately enacted. These elements are certainly present in the custom, albeit in a *suis generis* fashion, quite differently from law.

Because of their increasing order of difficulty, I shall begin this analysis on the characteristics of custom backwards. In the law, the enactment is the manner through which the prince makes his intention known. It makes the law public. On the other hand, custom does not have the benefit of a practical and exterior manifestation of its publicity.[130] It is revealed and publicly "enacted" by its very use.[131] But it is necessary to comprehend the publicity of such use. Suárez cleverly explains his opinion, by saying that the public character of the practice is achieved in two different ways:

- by means of a factual notoriety. Even if only one person or authority carries out the action, as in the usucaption, the action must take place in the presence of all, and not in a secret clandestine way;
- by means of a legal notoriety. It is a sort of a "legal demonstration" of the act. It occurs through an (implied or expressed) acceptance thereof by the sovereign or its recognition by scholars (the opinion of the wise) or by the precedents. While the agreement of the public authority does interfere with the creation of the custom, the role of the doctrine and of the jurisprudence is to only recognize a certain custom, but neither wisemen nor judges can create law. The judge can only declare it valid or not.

[129]**DL**. VII, 1, 12.

[130]**DL**. VII, 9, 1.

[131]**DL**. VII, 11, 5.

A few remarks are needed. The legal custom is a legislative product of the perfect community and of the perfect community only. As seen, the authority lies in the people, not as a crowd, but as a moral group. The members of this group transfer their power to a prince, and he thus enjoys the prerogative of passing laws. Whenever there is a gap in the law, the people (as the initial holder of that power) resumes its original faculty and diffusely works to fill that gap. However, the people still requires the acceptance of the sovereign, since it transferred its authority to him. Therefore, people may create a custom as long as their sovereign approves of it.

Suárez displays all his geniality in this matter. How many individuals and who are necessary to form the will of the people? The law faces no such difficulty, as it requires the will of only one person: the sovereign authority. But in customs, number and capacity matter. First, it is required that this will comes from the majority of the people; and "majority", according to Suárez, is not a quantitative concept. It is necessary that the majority of the people practice the custom so that it acquires notoriety. The author does not elaborate whether he means simple or qualified majority. He just requires that a sufficient number of people practice the action for it to become public. Second, only those who are able to express their consent may count in the formation of such majority. Therefore, the children and the mentally ill are excluded. It is worth remarking that three centuries prior to the beginning of the feminist movement, Suárez does not exclude women (nor minors under twenty-five years old).[132]

> Francisco Suárez is rightly considered as a great theologian and philosopher, and a no less great jurist, and these qualities his various works demonstrate beyond the possibility of successful contradiction, but in the quotation which we have just made of his exact language, Suárez proclaims himself as a feminist in a day when feminism was hardly a dream, let alone a hope.[133]

Therefore, only the people may create a custom. Within a State, individuals and imperfect communities are able to establish an acquisitive prescription, at best. The prince's practice alone is insufficient to create a custom. For the same reason, minor authorities, such as a judge (who cannot legislate) cannot create a custom. The uses of the sovereign and of other authorities may only form what Suárez calls "tradition", devoid of legal power.

Regarding the requirement of stability, Véronique Michel affirms that Suárez established a period of ten years for a custom to consolidate.[134] However, there is no period of time actually set. It is required that a sufficient period of time passes to enable a reasonable quantity of repetitions. The 10-year period in Suárez is only a prudent count. There is no need to obtain an express authorization of the prince acknowledging that sufficient time has passed; ten years is enough time for the

---

[132] **DL**. VII, 9, 14.

[133] Scott (1934), p. 227.

[134] Michel (1997), p. 448.

sovereign to become aware of the practice and to take measures to prohibit it should he wishes.

The use also needs to be fair. Because of that, Suárez does not recognize the legal character of a bad custom. "The customary law cannot be formed without reason."[135] Reason here means the straight natural reason. Consequently, the custom must not oppose Natural Law. However, this idea is not absolute when it comes to Dominative Natural Law, because the custom, like every Positive human Law, does not try to reach the moral honesty, but the common good.

The custom may revoke Civil Law. Although the subjects' consent is no pre-requisite for a law to be deemed valid, the sovereign may not impose laws capriciously.[136] As seen, the Suarezian social contract transfers, rather than delegates, all the authority of the people to the prince. However, this social contract is far from Hobbes' submission pact. It has limits. In Grotius, this phenomenon will be termed "charitable interpretation". Suárez foresees an actual right to disobey civil laws that offend Natural Law. As to civil laws regarding morally indifferent issues, it is possible to say that there is a conditioned right to disobedience. The common desire of the people, by itself, cannot repel Civil Law. However, this recurring practice represents the voice of the people urging the sovereign to cancel the law. The revocation of a law by a custom is subject to the internal rules of each State, but it is justified by the reunion (or even by the pressure) of the people with its legislator. "The role which the prince plays in the matter is, we might say, that of a silent partner who supplies the legal formalities and has the power to tolerate and give consent to the popular will."[137]

The revocation of a law by a custom is an exception while the revocation of a custom by a law is the general rule. Considering where Suárez placed the issue in his Treaty, it is possible to infer that he believes the custom to be a less perfect form of *jus* than the laws. The laws represent the "normal" form of producing human legislation, which involve an act of the directive and coercive authority of the community. The custom consists of a complementary tool designed to fill in some gaps. Hence, the laws still exercise control over the customs of the people; the laws may revoke, prohibit, condemn and oppose to a given recurring practice. Revocation makes a pre-existing custom invalid; prohibition prevents future practices; condemnation applies to those customs which usefulness is still questioned and is the result of a declaratory or annulment law; and opposition occurs when a law punishes a practice that is authorized by a custom.[138]

Due to his work on customs, Francisco Suárez may be considered a supporter of what we today call "legal pluralism": not every Law comes from the State. In the Middle Ages, the pluralism of normative sources was ordinary. Statism is a Modern invention, one that not even the first Modern thinkers thought possible. This culture

---

[135] "*Ius consuetudinis induci non potest sine ratione.*" (**DL**. VII, 12, 5).

[136] **DL**. VII, 13, 3.

[137] Scott (1934), p. 232.

[138] DL. VII, 7, 2 et seq.

reached its climax in the twentieth century, when Kelsen identifies the State with Law itself. What is peculiar in Suárez's theory is not the pluralism itself, but the fact that he thought it subject to the central power of the State. In many aspects, the custom needs the prince: prior to becoming valid, the custom depends on the approval of the prince; then, once it becomes valid, it depends on the prince's continuous agreement not to revoke it. Undoubtedly, there are limits to the interference of the sovereign. A custom may continue in effect even against his legislative will; hence, it is prudent that the king should listen to popular aspirations. Yet, on its own account, the custom cannot revoke a law. Suárez created a legal pluralism that is subject to the monism of the State.

The custom must also be common. As seen in chapter III, in Suárez, there are three meanings for the word "common": "first, because it is produced by a mutual agreement, or authority. Second, because it must be common to everyone. Third, because it must be appropriate to the common good".[139] The first notion confuses itself with the problem of the will, which I shall examine below. The second one relates to the fact that the custom is general and abstract, such as law, so that it may apply to an entire community. Finally, the custom should be guided by the common good.

In addition to the observations applicable to the laws regarding the common good, the custom shows some peculiarities. There is a different custom to each type of community. In an ecclesiastical community (diocese, archdiocese or the entire Church), the custom creates Ecclesiastical Law. On the other hand, nonreligious customs may extend over entire cities, kingdoms or even different nations. The first three correspond to Civil Law and the last to the Law of Nations. Each community searches for a different kind of common good. The common good sought by the *jus gentium* (since it is almost universal) pursues the coexistence of different peoples. The *jus gentium* establishes an ethical minimum that allows the communication among peoples and their peaceful endeavors, whenever possible. Mostly, these are rules grounded either on natural principles such as the good faith and the *pacta sunt servanda*, as well as on useful and practical principles, such as reciprocity or non interference in domestic affairs. In other words, if the *jus gentium* is indeed located between Natural and Civil Law, its common good drifts between nature and society.

Finally, just like the laws, human will creates custom. It is its efficient cause. The repetition of acts itself (the custom in fact) is not enough to create a custom in law. The will must recognize such practice as a mandatory rule. However, differently from the laws, there is no legislative act enacted by a given sovereign authority. Instead, the will appears diluted and dispersed. A myriad of wills take part in the formation of the custom. For didactic reasons, it is possible to distinguish at least two wills: the intention of the people to create a custom and the approval of the prince.

[139]"*Primo, quia communi consensu seu auctoritate lata est. Secundo, quia debet esse communis omnibus. Tertio,quia pro bono communi*" (**DL**. I, 6, 5).

There are four criteria through which one may recognize the intention of the people.[140] First, the custom should be old (meaning older than ten years), manifestly safeguard the common good and impose an obligation. No burden previously accepted by the people (or by the majority thereof) as a legal rule should be tolerated. Second, the opinion of the wise and prudent must be taken into account. If they condemn those who breach a certain practice, then there are strong signs suggesting of the existence of a law. This sort of criterion may seem old nowadays, but one need only to ponder on the value of scholarly works of prominent jurists as a source of International Law to see that the words of this jurist from the sixteenth and seventeenth centuries are still worth reading. Third, the opinion of political authorities also count; especially if they reproach and punish recalcitrant subjects. Finally, if the content of a certain practice has become so beneficial to the community, so it may as well be a legal custom, which creates a binding obligation.

The will of the people does not exactly coincide with the practice. The will of the people to reiterate a behavior dissipates with the act itself, and this is nothing more than a custom in fact. The people's intention to transform the act into a customary law is of a different order. It is qualified by the acceptance that a specific practice constitutes a legal rule. This is the reason why Suárez struggles so much to present ways to identify such an intention.

The will of the people must be free, and freedom means no obstructions and no coercion. Hence, differently from Hobbes, Suárez does not accept that actions motivated by fear can produce legal effects.

> Because external acts are not enough to form the custom, so that it is necessary such practice with the intention of creating a custom, and this intention commonly is more tacit than explicit. So, when acts are practiced just because of fear, in such a way that without it they would not occur, there is no such intention and one cannot suppose its existence, because fear by itself excludes intent. Hence, the frequency of acts practiced just because of fear is never a satisfactory evidence of the public acceptance of the entire people to adopt such custom.[141]

The will of the prince is the substantial cause of the custom's existence, while the will of the people is its proximate cause. The material element and a part of the spiritual element may stem from the people, but the essential portion of the custom comes from the sovereign. Suárez's legal pluralism depends on the State. Yet, the will of the prince takes part in the formation of the custom as the ratification thereof. It is expressed in a personal fashion, when the sovereign (either expressly or tacitly)

---

[140] **DL**. VII, 15, 11 et seq.

[141] "(...) *quia ad consuetudinem, non sufficiunt actus, sed necesse est, ut fiant animo inducendi consuetudin, qui animus ordinarie est potius tacitus, quam expressus. At vero quando actus fiunt ex solo timore, ita ut sine illo non fieret, non est talis animus, nec moraliter praesumi potest, quia merus de se quodammodo illum excludit, et ideo frequentia actuum ex solo mero factorum nunquam est sufficitus signum publici consensus totius populi de consuetudine inducenda*" (**DL**. VII, 12, 11).

personally authorizes the custom; it is also expressed in a legal fashion, when the custom is introduced by force of a law that recognizes its existence.[142]

In the laws, the authority of the prince and the will of the legislator are found in the same person. However, in the custom, the will and the authority are dissociated from its creation. The custom is born from the will of the people; the ruler cannot create this kind of law by himself. And the authority who sanctions the custom, who confers the validity thereof, is not the same who creates it. Conferring validity to the custom is a voluntary act. However, while this action is essential to the "legal character" of the custom, it is irrelevant to its creation. This idea fits perfectly within the Suarezian system. Every Law (with a capital letter) comes from an act of will and it becomes valid through an act of authority. In the laws, these acts are the same; however, Suárez never said that they had to be the same to all *jus*. Moreover, the people transferred its political power to the sovereign: it no longer has legislative authority. Despite being voluntary, a popular practice by itself lacks authority. Therefore, it is necessary that two agents take part in the formation of the custom.

Once the prince "lends" his authority to the custom, it becomes law in the full sense of this word. Thereby, custom also incorporates the four deontic variations of a law including punishment. Suárez expressly states that a custom may create a Criminal Law.[143] The creation of criminal laws through customs is possible because authority (and the human authority as well) is based on two principles: the directive and the coercive principle (this one stems from sin and men's recalcitrance). Albeit less explicit, custom does not lack authority.

It is this dissociation between the legislative authority and the creating will that enables the existence of the *jus gentium* without the need of a global power, since these two elements do not need to be present in same person for the custom to exist as a legal rule. The existence of the international legal custom depends solely on the recognition of a given practice by different peoples and on their princes authorizing the exercise thereof within their kingdoms. Although the sovereigns ratify this behavior and their consent is the most important factor for its validity, the *jus gentium* is still a law of popular origin.

The emphasis that Suárez places on the will in the formation of the custom (and, consequently, of the *jus gentium*) does not result in a voluntarist theory of International Law. The will of the States is not the only creative force at work in the formation of the Law of Nations. According to Suárez, the law is composed by will and intellect. As will be discussed, there is an international objective order beyond the will of the States.

Furthermore, although the Suarezian idea of perfect community resembles the modern notion of State, his *jus gentium* is not a State law. Because of its popular origin and its close relation with ethical precepts, the Law of Nations does not follow a logic of *raison d'état*. National and selfish interests do not take part in its

---

[142]**DL**. VII, 13, 6.

[143]**DL**. VII, 16, 3.

formation. On the contrary, this branch of law searches for a common moral denominator for all peoples. It does not represent a normative system created out of the discretionary will of perfect communities, but rather a system that is born out of the practice of their peoples. Therefore, despite disagreeing with tradition entirely, Suárez preserves the name "Law of Nations". It is thus the law of almost all mankind; a mankind that is divided into sovereign States.

5.3.3 The International Society

Suárez's reasoning is almost complete. So far, it was established that "people" corresponds to the perfect community in Suárez's view. The subject of the *jus gentium* is no longer the individuals in their mutual relations, as in Natural Law, but peoples politically organized in a moral body. "Therefore, one should not confuse the *ius gentium* with *ius naturale*, which also has humanity as a subject, although more directly, without considering its division into States".[144] It was also established that Suárez's concept of *jus gentium* is not linked to a voluntarist theory of law, as the rules of the Law of Nations acquire the form of customs, not of laws. When the legislative authority is lost in ancient times, it is not possible to establish a direct link between its will and the product thereof. Now, it must become clear how the precepts of the *jus gentium* apply not to every perfect community isolated, but to all of them. Just as the authority (and Civil Law) does not proceed from individuals, but from their reunion in society, so does the Law of Nations come from a truly international society, and not from each individual State.

If there is, in Suárez, a foundation for the Law of Nations, it must conform to the rest of the author's theory. For that reason, he needs to answer a very uncomfortable question: why did Suárez decide to think of a *jus gentium*? Since he defined the perfect community as the opposite of an imperfect community, as an arrangement by means of which men are able to fulfill all their needs and accomplish all their aspirations, why isn't the State enough? Suárez's political theory seems to point towards the direction of autocracy, which is incompatible with the idea of a Law of Nations.

This poses a dilemma for anyone, except for a theologian. Some comments are in order. Unlike the formation of the authority inside a kingdom or a republic, the international society is not created by the combination of various States. In Suárez, the international society has an ontological precedence: it already exists autonomously, independent from the association of perfect communities. The international society is humanity itself. So, according to Suárez, the Law of Nations is not the result of inter-state relations, it is not a perfect inter-community law; the Law of

[144]"*Por consiguiente, no debe confundirse el* ius gentium *con el* ius naturale, *que también tiene a la Humanidad como sujeto, pero más directamente, sin tener en cuenta su división en Estados*" (Rommen, 1951, p. 474).

Nations is instilled between the nations (at least the *propriissime dictum*), but does not come from their interactions. It arises out of the dynamics of the life of a legal society far more primitive and fundamental.

In order to understand this, it is necessary to return to the idea of the popular origin of authority. When God created all things, by the same act, he transferred His power to all men, who immediately began to form a kind of universal community. However, this had little use and was inconvenient to the management of resources and goods. In his amendments to the theory of the *jus gentium*, Suárez repeats a well-known section of his study on political power: "Therefore, it seems more likely that a power to all mankind did not exist, but if it has existed, it was for a very short time. Shortly after the world's creation, men began to break up into several States and each held a distinctive power".[145] The author does not care and even denies the historical existence of a moral body of all first humans prior to nations. But this universal community fulfills a very important function as a rational explanation: it was to this universal community that God conferred authority.

In the main body of the **De Legibus**, Suárez reveals with greater eloquence the notion that the *jus gentium* proceeds from all humanity. He does so in only two paragraphs, which lack further explanation on the part of the author, but are nonetheless worth transcribing in full:

> The reason of being of this law is that the human race, although divided into various nations and kingdoms, maintain, at all times, a certain unity, not only specific [that we all belong to the same human species], but almost political and moral, as the natural precept of charity and mercy [solidarity] extends to everyone, including foreigners and to any nation.
>
> So, although a state, a monarchy or a republic, is in itself a perfect community and endowed with constant [perennial] parts, nevertheless, each State is also, in relation to mankind, in a way a member of this universal community. Because each State never enjoy so absolute an autonomy that do not need any help, common association or exchange, sometimes for their greater well-being, progress and development, and others by a real moral necessity and lack of resources, as shown by their experience.[146]

In this text, every element that permeates the Suarezian concept of *jus gentium* is found. Luciano Pereña decomposes the argument into three main ideas: the

---

[145]"*Unde mihi verisimilius est vel nunquam vel brevissimo tempore fuisse hanc potestatem hoc modo in tota hominum collectione, sed paulo post mundi creationem coepisse homines dividi in varias respublicas est in singulis fuisse hanc potestatem distinctam.*" (Suárez, 1973, item 2, p. 154).

[146]"*Ratio autem huius partis et iuris est quia humanum genus, quantumvis in varios populos et regna divisum, semper habet aliquam unitatem, non solum specificam, sed etiam quasi politicam et moralem, quam indicat naturale praeceptum mutui amoris et misericordiae quod ad omnes extenditur, etiam extraneos et cuiuscumque nationis.*

Quapopter, licet unaquaeque civitas perfecta, respublica aut regnum, sit in se communitas perfecta et suis membris constans, nihilominus quaelibet illarum est etiam membrum aliquo modo huius universi, prout ad genus humanum spectat. Numquam enim illae communitates adeo sunt sibi sufficientes sigillatim, quin indigeant aliquo mutuo iuvamine et societate ac communicatione, interdum ad melius esse maioremque utilitatem, interdum vero etiam ob moralem necessitatem et indigentiam, ut ex ipso constat." (DL. II, 19, 9).

sociability of perfect communities, the interdependence of States and a relative concept of sovereignty.[147] Since mankind already existed, the sociability of States is a natural assumption. The principles of solidarity and mutual assistance express nothing more than this first reality. In addition, States cannot live in isolation. They need to cooperate in order to pursue their own national interests. Thus, their association reflects a progressive law of common utility. Finally, States' sociability and interdependence end up limiting their sovereignty. No national community is so perfect that it cannot take advantage of trade and commerce with other communities.

These three aspects spring from the same basis, an extra-legal foundation. In order to grasp this, it is necessary to understand the Suárez's starting point in the section transcribed above. The author affirms something that was discernible already in his time: mankind is divided into different kingdoms and peoples. This was not a premise of faith or an assumption regarding an idyllic period, but a statement concerning the historical reality in which Suárez lived. This statement is close to Machiavelli's opening of **The Prince**: "All States, all powers that have held and hold rule over men have been and are either republics or principalities".[148] Both are factual statements, not judgments. Suárez resorts to realism to bury imperial monism (that was a rather distant ideal) once and for all. Indeed, the human race is politically divided.

Thus, Suárez conceives mankind as a tree that ramifies into several States. However, among them there remains a quasi-political and moral unity, reminiscent of the tree of which States are all branches. And this unity transcends the unity imposed by biology (by the fact that we are all human beings). Suárez illustrates this connection among States with the natural precept of love and solidarity. The rational explanation of the first universal community remains and seems to demand a return to itself. Here, Suárez's final conception on the *jus gentium* fits perfectly with his early writings on the subject when he addressed the doctrine of just war. The basis of the Suarezian Law of Nations lies in the greatest theological virtue: Charity.

It is Charity that makes the sociability among States a fact of nature; Charity promotes the interdependence of autocratic communities that do not need one another; Charity limits sovereignty beyond the provisions of the social contract. One of the most common theological explanations for God (who is sufficient in Himself) creating the world is Charity. God does not feel alone and therefore does not need the world; however, out of love, He wanted to need it. Mature love

---

[147] Pereña (1973), pp. lvii–lx.

[148] Maquiavel (1999), p. 7. It should be pointed out that Suárez read Macchiavelli and disagreed with his position, considering it "false and wrong". However, later, Suárez seems to notice the distinction (better elucidated) between the fact and the rule "(…) *loquor autem de postestate iuris, non facti: nam per erronem saepe Magistratus civilis potest praecipere aliquid iniustum vel illicitum: iure tamen non potest*" (**DL**. III, 12, 4). ("I speak about the factual, but not rightful power, because often a public authority may indeed command an injustice, but he cannot rightfully do so").

between a man and a woman does not presume emotional or psychological dependence between them. They do not need each other to live. However, they wanted to need one another. The peoples do not depend on the others to satisfy their needs, but they wanted to. There is no legal boundary obliging their exchange. Yet, Charity transcends the Law.

Suárez chooses his words carefully. Unity among peoples is not political, but "almost". The precepts that flow therefrom are "solidarity" and "assistance"—"charity" and "mercy" in the original. Because of its "almost" political nature, the international society is not a perfect community of all men, but there are many ties that bring mankind closer to the primordial idea of a perfect community. And these ties (the "solidarity" and the "assistance") have no legal essence. Charity does not necessarily come from nature, but it is very useful in social organization. Charity is the reason why the principles of the *jus gentium*, although rational and very convenient, do not proceed from nature.

There is certain circularity in this reasoning, which should please a theologian. The foundation of Natural Law lies ultimately in obeying God. It flows from Christ's first commandment to men: love God above all things. In turn, Civil Law is earthly and very ordinary: its foundation lies in obeying the sovereign. If the *jus gentium* is placed between Natural and Civil Law, then its foundation must also lie somewhere between the divine and the earthly. The foundation of the Law of Nations is Christ's second commandment to men: love thy neighbor.

Therefore, despite its universal calling, the *jus gentium* extends to almost all peoples. Th Law always produces enforceable obligations but Charity can only bind those more civilized peoples: cultures that do not offer human sacrifice and that do not practice cannibalism; nations that do not incur in serious offenses against Christ's second commandment. The fact that the *jus gentium* is "almost universal" reconciles Suárez's later concept thereof with his first. The Law of Nations applies only to civilized peoples.

To say that Charity, rather than the Law, is the basis of the *jus gentium* does not make it "less legal". The custom remains as the formal source of the Law of Nations, ensuring the "legality" of its rules. Charity corresponds to its material source. As the rational nature of man and the common good provide meaning to Natural and Civil Law, which are enacted by God and the Prince, so does Charity provide the reason why the provisions of the *jus gentium* bind States in a certain way and not another. In fact, there is a common good proper to all mankind. But the virtue that informs such good is Charity, not justice.

Nevertheless, the Law of Nations does not encompass all precepts of Charity. Only few charitable rules qualify, for that seeks solely to create and maintain a harmonious and peaceful living among nations. In any case, the traditional subjects of *jus gentium* (the law of war, the law of embassies, the right of passage, etc.) refer to the principles of peace and harmony among peoples. The Law of Nations does not aim at improving man spiritually nor at organizing a political system. It merely seeks to keep a line of communication open among the peoples so that they may eventually, at a higher stage of moral progress, nurture unity and recognize themselves as children of God. The *jus gentium* only creates the basis, the foundations of a better world, but not this better world itself. Therefore, the *jus gentium* translates an ethical minimum.

In his classic work on the principles of Public Law, Joseph Delos states that Suárez's view of the Law of Nations is a subjective conception.[149] For the author, there would be two opposing views: the one from Vitória, which is organic and institutionalized, for whom the State is a member of an international society that predates it, and another from Suárez, individualist and voluntarist, according to which the State precedes international society, which is formed out of the interaction among the different nations. Hence, the Law of Nations would depend on the will of the peoples and would not have an objective existence. Delos acknowledges that his view is not consistent with Rommen's, one of the greatest interpreters of Suárez, but in the history of Public Law, publicists could only support one of these two streams.

However, as seen, Suárez's voluntarism does not strip the *jus gentium* of its "objectivity". Delos is mistaken in not establishing nuances between these two conceptions. Once one realizes that Suarez's approach is that of a theologian, not of a lawyer, the nuance of his position is better understood. Mankind (that is connected by Charity ties) has ontological precedence over the States, which correspond only to a historical manifestation thereof. By conceiving mankind as a universe divided into States, and the *jus gentium* as the law not of the relations between peoples, but of this humanity itself, Suárez envisages an objective legal order, without needing to resort to the figure of a world federation, as the typically Modern projects for perpetual peace do. In Suarez' conception, there are values that do not depend on the States to be valid. In order to exist, the Law of Nations does not require the will of the States. It exists before their endorsement.

5.4 Summary

Francisco Suárez's theory of the Law of Nations is a typical formulation of a theologian of the late Spanish Scholasticism. Unlike the Reformers' view, there is no great gap between the Catholic God and man that can be overcome only by faith. Suárez's God did not abandon men to themselves by creating a number of institutions, such as the Laws and Grace, to admonish and correct them. Each within its scope and validity, Natural, Civil Law and the Law of Nations are instruments of the divine action. The entire legal philosophy of the author represents forms whereby the divine providence interferes in human life.

Suárez innovates if compared to the traditional Thomism because he discovered an eminently human space in his Theology. It is a separate and autonomous domain, with a dignity of its own. Therefore, the purpose of Natural Law, whose creator is God Himself, is to make men good. Natural Law has a transcendental

[149] Delos (1950), p. 266.

nature, but the purpose of Civil Law, which is enacted by men, is to ensure the common good, reason why it belongs to an immanent space. There needs to be a transition between the divine and the earthly. This task falls to the *jus gentium*. It aims at establishing a minimum of civility among the peoples and organizing their peaceful and harmonious coexistence.

This goal of finding a link between the divine and the earthly expressly appears in Suárez's first writings on the subject. The **De Bello** is part of the Treaty of Charity and Suárez thinks about the war in through the lens of peace. People should engage in wars to promote peace. War and peace are not conflicting ideas; there are indefensible peaceful scenarios that offend justice and thus should be undone even with the use of force. War serves to correct injustice and to avenge injuries. However, since it brings violence and destruction, force should be used very carefully and in moderation. The ones responsible for the decision to engage in a war should keep in mind not only justice, but charity as well. Then, Suárez describes several rules that transform the war into an actual criminal sanction for nations, with the purpose of punishing the transgressors of civilization.

In Suárez's maturity work, the references to Charity and to civility appear somewhat veiled. The *jus gentium* is inexorably part of Suárez' investigation on Law. His first task is to confront the tradition and his Thomist legacy. Since the days of the Romans, the Law of Nations was defined as a type of Natural Law. In order to demonstrate the positive character of the *jus gentium*, Suárez denies all consecrated definitions, including Aquinas'. Yet, there is an undeniable similarity between the *jus gentium* and Natural Law. After clarifying the difference between *jus intra gentes* and *jus inter gentes* (a difference which is hidden in the very name of this law) Suárez explains that, although possible in theory, changes to the Law of Nations itself are impractical, which brings it even closer to Natural Law.

Nevertheless, the grounds on which the Law of Nations stood remained unclear. It could not take the form of *lex*, because that would imply the existence of a global authority over the kingdoms and republics, which simply did not exist. In Suárez's time, imperial monism was a distant idea. Suárez then had to first demonstrate the popular origin of power, since the Law of Nations is not enacted by a sovereign. In certain circumstances, the people could resume their power to enact legal rules.

Afterwards, Suárez had to show which extra-legal form of Law corresponded to the *jus gentium*: the custom. Only the custom enables the emergence of a law among peoples circumventing the notion of a supranational authority. The will of the legislator is still present in the custom, but diluted in an infinity of people and immemorial times.

Finally, after discovering the formal source of the *jus gentium*, Suárez proceeded to uncover its material source. Here, Suárez' maturity and youth conceptions intertwine. The author sees mankind as a tree that ramifies into several States. He is quite incisive. However, his perception that the Law of Nations does not stem from the relations between the States, from the interaction between the many branches of this tree, is subtle. The *jus gentium* is itself a fruit of the tree, of mankind. Despite mankind does not form a perfect community, there are bonds of charity that unite the different peoples. The *jus gentium* is an ethical minimum among civilized nations.

Therefore, Delos' classification of Suárez's theory cannot be accepted; in truth, Suárez's theory stands in opposition to the subjectivist theories. Since the Law of Nations derives from mankind and not from the will of the States, this law reflects an objective order of values. The subjectivist theses, which are proper of voluntarist jurists, advocate that peoples interact as individuals and thus the *jus gentium* is created in the same manner that individuals create the social contract within their States. The problem is that this position leads to an axiological relativism: there is no greater standard of legitimity to international rules than the will of the States. In this scenario, peace and harmonious coexistence are subject to national interests and to the *raison d'état*. Nevertheless, there exists an individualistic conception that does not induce relativism. This is the law of war and peace thought by Hugo Grotius.

References

Amaral, Diogo Freitas do. Francisco Suárez e Thomas Hobbes: uma comparação instrutiva. **Estado e Direito**. Revista Luso-Espanhola de Direito Público, n. 13, pp. 7–24, 1° semester 1994.

Barcia Trelles, Camilo. Francisco Suárez: les théologiens espagnols du XVIe siècle et l'école moderne du Droit International. **Recueil de Cours de l'Académie de Droit International de Le Hague**, n. 1, t. 43, pp. 386–503, 1933.

Calafate, Pedro. A filosofia política em Francisco Suárez. In: ______. (coord.). **História do Pensamento Filosófico Português**. Lisboa: Caminho, 2001. v. II.

Carrillo Prieto, Ignácio. **Cuestiones jurídico-políticas en Francisco Suárez**. México: UNAM, Instituto de Investigaciones Jurídicas, 1977.

Delos, J. T. **La Société Internationale et les Principes de Droit Public**. 2. ed. Paris: Pédone, 1950.

Elorduy, Eleutério, S. J. *La soberanía popular segun Francisco Suárez*. In: Suárez, Francisco. **Principatus Politicus o la Soberania Popular**. Elaborado bajo la dirección de Luciano Pereña. Madrid: Consejo Superior de Investigaciones Cientificas, 1965 (*Corpus Hispanorum de Pace*, v. II).

Haakonssen, Knud. **Natural Law and Moral Philosophy**: from Grotius to the Scottish Enlightenment. New York: Cambridge University Press, 1996.

Hobbes, Thomas. **Do Cidadão**. Trad. Renato Janine Ribeiro. São Paulo: Martins Fontes, 2002.

Maquiavel, Nicolau. **O Príncipe**. Trad. Lívio Xavier. São Paulo: Abril Cultural, 1999.

Merêa, Paulo. **Estudos de Filosofia Jurídica e de História das Doutrinas Políticas**. Lisboa: Imprensa Nacional-Casa da Moeda, 2004.

Miaja de la Muela, A. **Internacionalistas Españoles del Siglo XVI**. Fernando Vazquez de Menchaca. Valladolid: Universidad de Valladolid, Sección de Estudios Americanistas, 1932.

Michel, Verónique. La coutume das le De Legibus ac Deo Legislatore de Francisco Suárez. Archives de Philosophie du Droit. Paris: Sirey, 1997, t. 41.

Pereña, Luciano. *Estudio Preliminar*. In: Suárez, Francisco. **Guerra Intervención Paz Internacional**. Translation by Luciano Pereña. Madrid: Espasa-Calpe, 1956.

Pereña, Luciano. Génesis suareciana del ius gentium. In: Suárez, Francisco. **De Legibus**. ed. crítica e bilíngüe por Luciano Pereña. Madrid: Consejo Superior de Investigaciones Cientificas, 1973. (*Corpus Hispanorum de Pace*, v. XIV).

Pereña, Luciano. *Perspectiva Historica*. In: Suárez, Francisco. **De Iuramento Fidelitatis**. *Estudio Preliminar. Conciencia y Política*. Elaborado bajo la dirección de Luciano Pereña. Madrid: Consejo Superior Superior de Investigaciones Cientificas, Escuela Española de la Paz, 1979. (*Corpus Hispanorum de Pace*, v. XVIII).

Rinaldi, Teresa. Origine e finalità della società politica nel **De Legibus** di Francisco Suárez. **RIFD – Rivista Internazionale di Filosofia del Diritto**. Giuffrè, aprile/giugno 2001, n. 2, serie V, anno LXXVIII.

Rommen, Heinrich. **The Natural Law**. English translation from Thomas Hanley. Indianápolis: Liberty Fund, 1998.

Rommen, Heinrich. **La Teoria del Estado y de la Comunidad Internacional en Francisco Suárez**. Tradução para o espanhol de Valentin Garcia Yebra. Buenos Aires; Madrid: Facultad de Derecho y Ciencias Sociales y Instituto de Derecho Internacional; Instituto Francisco de Vitória y Consejo Superior de Investigaciones Cientificas, 1951. (Colección de Obras Maestras de Derecho Internacional, v. 1).

Scott, J. B. **El Origen Español del Derecho Internacional Moderno**. Valladolid: Universidad de Valladolid, Sección de Estudios Americanistas, 1928.

Scott, J. B. **The Catholic Conception of International Law**. Washington D.C.: Georgetown University Press, 1934.

Stacey, Robert. The Age of Chivalry. In: Howard, Michael; Andreopoulos, George, SHULMAN, Mark (org.). **The Laws of War**: constraints on warfare in the Western World. New Haven, London: Yale University Press, 1994.

Suárez, Francisci. **Defensio Fidei Catholicae et Apostolicae adversus Anglicanae sectae errores, cum responsione ad Apologiam pro Iuramento Fidelitatis et Praefationem Monitoriam Serenissimi Iacobi Angliae Regis**. Conimbricae: Didacum Gomez de Loureyro, 1613.

Suárez, Francisci. **De Iuramento Fidelitatis**. *Documentación Fundamental*. Elaborado bajo la dirección de Luciano Pereña. Madrid: Consejo Superior Superior de Investigaciones Cientificas, Instituto Francisco de Vitória, 1978. (*Corpus Hispanorum de Pace*, v. XIX).

Suárez, Francisco. **De Iuramento Fidelitatis**. Estudio Preliminar. Conciencia y Política. Elaborado bajo da dirección de Luciano Pereña. Madrid: Consejo Superior Superior de Investigaciones Cientificas, Escuela Española de la Paz, 1979. (*Corpus Hispanorum de Pace*, v. XVIII).

Suárez, Francisco. *Iura Gentium Quomodo Introducta Sint. Additiones Suarecii ad Ius Gentium*, n. 11. In: ______. **De Legibus**. Elaborado bajo la dirección de Luciano Pereña. Madrid: Consejo Superior de Investigaciones Cientificas, 1973. t. IV. (*Corpus Hispanorum de Pace*, v. XIV).

Suárez, R. P. Francisci. **De Fide, Spe et Charitate**. *Tratactus de Charitate. Disputatio* XIII. **De Bello**. In: ______. **Opera Omnia**. *Editio Nova. Parisiis: Ludovicum Vivès*, 1858.

Suárez, Francisco. **Principatus Politicus o la Soberania Popular**. Elaborado bajo da dirección de Luciano Pereña. Madrid: Consejo Superior de Investigaciones Cientificas, 1965 (*Corpus Hispanorum de Pace*, v. II).

Suarez, Francisci. **Tratactus de legibus, ac Deo Legislatore in decem Librus distributus**. *Venetiis: Sebastianum Coleti*. 1740.

Vitoria, *Francisco de. De Indis, Relectio 1*. In: **Obras de Francisco de Vitória**. *Relecciones Teologicas*. Elaboradas bajo la dirección de Teofilo Urdanoz. Madrid: Biblioteca de Autores Cristianos, 1960.

Chapter 6
The Law of Nations in Hugo Grotius

I saved the best for this final chapter. Here, I shall analyze Grotius' concept of the Law of Nations and demonstrate how close it is to Suárez's. So far, despite the Scholastic influence on Grotius and the fact that these two authors tackled the notion of subject rights, Suárez and Grotius were kept somewhat separate. In Chap. IV, I presented James St. Leger's thesis and found it inconclusive. After spending most part of the entire last century in disbelief, Grotius is more original than previously thought. Still, Suárez exerted some influence over the Grotian *jus gentium*.

Throughout the centuries, the opinions on the Jurist from Delft were exacerbated and even passionate. He was lauded and despised; he was regarded as either a classical thinker or a mere plagiarist; he became the savior and then the villain. Few are the balanced readings. In an intellectual environment of such extremes, one should be careful not to succumb to radicalism. Given the various interpretations of Grotius, Suárez's presence in his work has been considered either too subtle or exaggerated. Indeed, Suárez's influence does not outshine Grotius' originality (in view of the Roman conception of *jus gentium*), but it is enough to instill more consistency into his own thoughts.

Due to Suárez's influence and the internal dynamics of his own system, Grotius was able to envisage the *jus gentium* as a Positive Law applicable between the peoples. This distinguishes the author from his predecessors (except for Suárez) who did not escape the Roman cultural orbit and thus intertwined the Law of Nations with Natural or with a universal Civil Law. Despite its positive character, this *jus* preserves an ethical content and albeit applicable to political communities, the subjects thereof are human beings, not abstract collectivities. There is no doubt that the author achieves this delicate balance, thanks to the persistence of certain medieval legal–political doctrines that would not be accepted today. Nevertheless, investigating the foundations of a human law that is able to avoid moral relativism seems like a good endeavor.

The success of this undertaking lies in understanding Grotius' basic purpose, to study the law of war. Indeed, Grotius' legal works did not deal with the *jus gentium*

P.E. Vauthier Borges de Macedo, *Catholic and Reformed Traditions in International Law*, Studies in the History of Law and Justice 9,
DOI 10.1007/978-3-319-59403-3_6

itself; they were all about the long tradition of the Just War. All fields of study that made Grotius a celebrated jurist (Legal Philosophy, Natural Law and the Law of Nations) are only ancillary to his main subject of study. Grasping the significance of the Just War tradition for Grotius allows us to research a secondary institute (the *jus gentium*) without resorting to contemporary prejudices.

For the reasons above, I shall examine Grotius' law of war and then the foundation for the Law of Nations. In order to do so, I shall analyze his notion of "people" and make a short incursion into his Political Theory. After that, I will present the positivity of this law and its formal source. Here, Suárez's influence on Grotius will be disclosed. Finally, the contours of an implicit idea in Grotius will become fully unveiled: the idea of a global society.

6.1 The Law of War in Grotius

From everything that was discussed so far, it seems clear that Hugo Grotius was never concerned with writing a work on International Law. Yet, he did not intend to write a treatise on the Law of Nations either. The law of war and the Law of Nations are not synonyms. As seen in the fourth chapter, the *jus gentium* corresponds to one of the sources of the law of war, together with Natural and voluntary Divine Law. "Source" means the formal provenience of these rules and is not synonymous to "branch of law." When the authors divided the Laws into *jus civile, jus naturale*, and *jus gentium*, they did not mean to designate branches or thematic areas (as contemporary jurists do with Criminal, Constitutional and Civil Law), but their legislative origin. The Law remained one (and thus conflict of laws was not even possible), but its legislator had changed. Today, branches of law and sources intermingle ever since the Modern classification endorsed by the School of Natural Law and the Law of Nations.

So, the law of war is not a topic of International Law in Grotius. The study of the law of war undoubtedly enables a greater understanding of his concept of the Law of Nations, but it remains a hybrid institution that permeates other sources of law. Therefore, the purpose of this section is not to perform an exegesis of Grotius' law of war, but to unveil the implications thereof for his concept of *jus gentium.*

The title of Grotius' *opus magna* may induce the reader to an error: there appears to be a law of peace beyond the law of war and thus the oeuvre should cover (however incipiently) the entire body of International Law. However, there is no law of peace, at least not as an institute of *jus gentium* valid outside the boundaries of the state of war. The author himself indicates in *prolegomenon 2* from where he got the idea for the title: in the ***Oratio pro Cornelius Balbus***, 6, 15, Cicero refers to the "science that covers all the laws of war and peace." Grotius had already quoted this same excerpt in his work of youth. "So, from another source other than the body of Roman laws, there must elapse that noble science which comprises, according to Cicero, the alliances, treaties, agreements of people, kings, and foreign nations, in short, the law of war and peace."[1] In the **De Jure Praedae**, Grotius seems to counteract this *jus belli ac pacis* to the *jus civile*, and at first glance, that *jus* seems to correspond to the contemporary International Law. But in the *prolegomenon* 1 of the **De Jure Belli ac Pacis**, the law of war is this "part of the law that, however, intervenes in the relations of many peoples or heads of States, **which precepts are founded on nature itself or established by divine laws or introduced by custom and by tacit agreement**"[2] (emphasis added). Standing in opposition to the *jus civile*, there emerges not the *jus naturale* or the *jus gentium*, but the *jus belli*, a set of rules that derive from nature and the will of God both, as well as from the consent of the peoples.

Therefore, in the course of **De Jure Belli ac Pacis**, Grotius discusses only the law of war. Traditionally, it was believed that the book II dealt with the law of peace. It is the longest book of his work, in which Grotius addresses unrelated topics such as acquisition, ownership, promises, contracts, treaties, embassies, the right of burial and penalties. Some topics even belong to Private domestic law. For this reason, there was a spread belief on the existence of a law of peace in Grotius. But this belief does not take into account the author's own words. In the *prolegomena*, when Grotius sets out to explain the contents of each book, he clearly states that the second book addresses the causes of war.[3] I shall examine further below the reason why this book is so comprehensive. For now, Grotius' words suffice: all these issues are the causes of war.

The Grotian law of peace, which justifies the word *pacis* in the title, is quite different from its contemporary counterpart. To Haggenmacher, Grotius followed the Ciceronian formula and decided to turn himself to peace at the end of the treaty. Thus, chapters XX to XXV of the third book constitute the *jus pacis* of Grotius. The author investigates the validity of the agreements that address armistice, truces, rescue of prisoners, etc., and exhorts peace. The Grotian *pax* is more an action than a state of things: it means, "to make peace." Since Grotius sought to build a systematic and thorough work, he needed to address the ways by which war is interrupted, suspended, and ended.[4] Hence, the Grotian *jus belli ac pacis* is a law on the beginning, the middle, and the end of war, not a work on the whole *jus gentium*.

In Grotius' time, there were no books exclusively dedicated to the *jus gentium*. However, the same cannot be said of certain institutes that are today comprised in International Law: besides the law of war itself, the rights of prisoners, the right of

---

[1]"*Aliunde igitur quam ex legum Romanarum corpore petenda est praestabilis illa scientia, quam Cicero dicit consistere in foederibus, pactionibus, conditionibus populorum regum exterarumque nationum, in omnni denique belli jure ac pacis.*" (**DJPC**, p. 6).

[2]"(…) *aut ius illud, quod inter populos plures aut populorum rectores intercedit, sive ab ipsa natura profectum, aut divinis constitutum legibus, sive moribus et pacto tacito introductum*" (**DJBP**. *prolegomenon* 1).

[3]**DJBP**. *prolegomenon* 34.

[4]Haggenmacher (1983), pp. 564–565.

embassies, etc. The Law of Nations had no autonomy, but the law of war did. As seen in the second chapter, researching the law of war meant delving into a very ancient tradition, the Doctrine of Just War. Due to the prolonged existence of this doctrine, many writers could have inspired Grotius. As seen in the fourth chapter, the author's eclecticism dodges any sort of labeling regarding the foundation of Law. However, not without criticism and hesitation, Grotius' standing in this regard seems to converge with Scholasticism. Likewise, there are several similarities between his law of war and that of the Scholastics.[5]

Grotius interprets the Just War doctrine as a legal and ethical tradition. It is worth mentioning that Grotius held the utmost respect for the Scholastics and deemed them irreproachable on moral matters, despite living in unhappy times and being ignorant of the liberal arts. In order to grasp the full meaning of Grotius' understanding of the law of war, it is necessary to identify against what or whom was Grotius protesting. As Grotius elected Carneades as a villain to explain the grounds of the *jus*, he also assigns two enemies to justify his conception of just war: Thucydides and Erasmus.

The fact that Grotius expressly disputes such contrasting thinkers is revealing. He stands in the middle ground. Grotius attributes to Thucydides the claim that "nothing that is useful is unfair to the kings and sovereign States."[6] He dismisses the Greek Historian together with skepticism because his ideas lead to ethical relativism and even supported Thrasymachus' concept of justice. Thucydides is considered the father of political realism, a school that in the name of abstractions such as "national interest" or *raison d'état*, does not allow any moral judgment of state actions. Armand Jean du Plessis, Cardinal de Richelieu, whom Grotius knew and abhorred, reportedly would have stated that, as the human soul is immortal, the salvation of men transcends this sphere, but the "State has no immortality, its salvation is now or never." The States do not get credit for doing what is right, but are rewarded for having enough power to do what is necessary.[7]

In the Melian Dialogue, which takes place in the sixteenth year of the Peloponnesian War, when the Athenians besieged the small island of Melos and imposed the classic choice of surrender or death, all the characteristic features of political realism are present. Melos sends diplomats to negotiate with the attackers. At first, the Athenians avoid discussing ethical issues:

---

[5]**DJBP**. *prolegomenon* 52.

[6]"(…) *regi aut civitati imperium habenti, nihil iniustum quod utile*" (**DJBP**. *prolegomenon* 3). The author states that this sentence implies a "proposition similar to the one that considers men in the peak of fortune, that bigger or smaller equity depends on bigger or smaller force and it is not possible to rule a State without injustice" ["*cui simile illud, in summa fortuna id aequius quod validius, et rempublicam sine iniuria geri non posse*"]. This corresponds to an opinion that prevents legal and moral judgements on war. Law and War would be antithetical realities.

[7]Kissinger (1994), p. 61. When Pope Urban VIII was informed on Richelieu's death, he would have delivered the following epitaph on his tomb: "if there is a God, the Cardinal de Richelieu will have much to answer for. If not… well, he had a successful life." (p. 58).

> For our part, then, we will not use fine phrases saying that we exercise our right to rule because we defeated the Persians (...) it should be known, as much as we know that Justice, in discussions among men, only prevails when the interests of both sides are consistent, and that the strong exercise power and the weak submit.[8]

The cruelty with which the Athenians set out their claim is almost cynical: "it would be advantageous for you to subject yourselves before you have suffered the most terrible evil, and we would gain by not having to destroy you."[9] The Athenian position to envisage mutual advantages in this situation echoes the conception of justice as the convenience of the strongest. The Melians are reminded that the war was not a struggle between equals; their own salvation was at stake, so there would be no humiliation in submitting to slavery.

Without being able to resort to justice, the Melians turn to hope. They trusted that the Lacedaemonians (Spartans) would not betray their settlers (the Melians themselves). They also relied on the unpredictable nature of war. The emissaries of Athens respond, "Hope is a stimulant to danger (...)"[10] and end the debate in an attempt to make the Melians abandon their *wishful thinking*:

> Judging by the outcome of your deliberations, it seems to us that you are the only ones to consider more certain future events than the present before your eyes; your desires make you see the unreal as if it were already happening. You are risking everything to put your trust in Lacedaemonians, on luck and hope, and you will lose everything.[11]

Melos decides to refuse Athen's "offer." As a result, the Athenians killed all Melians of military age, enslaved their children and women, and established five hundred settlers. This is a cautionary tale, a story that shows the futility of moral principles against power.

Yet, Erasmus of Rotterdam is an advocate of a radical pacifism that repudiates any war. In 1500, he publishes in Paris an annotated collection of eight hundred Greek and Latin proverbs under the title **Adagiorum collectanea**. This work was subject to successive editions, which expanded the number of adages to 4151. The success was immediate. Over time, Erasmus improves and changes one of the adages, the *Dulce bellum*, until publishing it in 1517 under the simple title *Bellum*. And **The Complaint of Peace** is first published in Basel in December 1517. With these two works, Erasmus inaugurates what is called "Irenicism." Irenicism is derived from the Greek word *eirenè* or "peace" and means "the attitude that profess repudiation for all kinds of belligerence and an unlimited confidence in the effectiveness of the dialog and the use of arbitration for the resolution of conflicts that oppose men."[12]

In both texts, Erasmus seeks to characterize war as something unchristian and unnatural. Right at the beginning of **The War**, he affirms that human nature is incompatible with war. Nature has endowed all living creatures with weapons such

[8]Tucídides (2001), p. 348.

[9]Tucídides (2001), p. 349.

[10]Tucídides (2001), p. 351.

[11]Tucídides (2001), p. 353.

[12]Guimarães Pinto (1999), p. 7.

as claws, horns, fangs, venom, etc. However, "only man was created naked, weak, delicate, unarmed, of tender flesh, and thin skin. In his members there is nothing that might seem to have been given to fight or to exercise violence (…)."[13]

Human nature seems prone to peace. As a child, man depends entirely on the protection of others. He does not have a frightening appearance; he can hug, kiss, laugh, and shed tears, "symbols of clemency and mercy." Therefore, nature made man lean toward benevolence, friendship, and love, which are all feelings directed at good harmony.[14]

As if nature was not enough, reason itself brings men closer to peace. For Erasmus, reason is the basic premise of sociality:

> And not satisfied with these things, nature granted only to man the use of language and reason, which indisputably serves to prepare and foster goodwill, so that nothing among men is resolved by force. Nature imbued man with the hate for loneliness and the love for living.[15]

Therefore, if everything in man compels him to peace, war can only represent an unprecedented evil. Indeed, war would be the source of all vices.

> Now, why speak of the ruin of customs, when it is certain that no one ignores that all that is bad in life comes ultimately from the war? From war the hate for pityness is born, as well as the neglect of laws, the willingness to dare any sort of crime. From this source flows an immense crowd of thieves, robbers, profaners and murderers.[16]

If human nature is so contrary to war, then it could only settle in the hearts of men after sin. According to Erasmus, since war is irrational, reason and wisdom must provide the cure. The author then suggests that men must resort to arbitration instead of war.

> The world has so many grave and learned bishops, so many venerable abbots, so many grey-haired noblemen wised by the long experience, so many councils, so many assemblies instituted not in vain by our ancestors. Why should not the childish quarrels of princes be settled through arbitration of these learned men?[17]

Grotius believes that the ferocity of men is the reason why many embrace this sort of disposition, but he considers Irenicism an "exaggeration in the efforts to the contrary." According to Grotius, it would be necessary to return to the just measure and to "remedy these two extremes, so that we are not led to believe that everything is forbidden or that everything is permitted."[18] The Doctrine of Just War presupposes an intermediate route. It rejects both the moral absolutism of an Irenicism, which condemns all wars, and the ethical relativism of political realism, which of

[13]Erasmo de Roterdão (1999), p. 28.

[14]Erasmo de Roterdão (1999), p. 29.

[15]Erasmo de Roterdão (1999), p. 29.

[16]Erasmo de Roterdão (1999), p. 31.

[17]Erasmo de Roterdão (1999), p. 66.

[18]"*Medicina ergo utrisque adhibenda fuit, tum ne nihil, tum ne omnia crederentur licere*" (**DJBP**. *prolegomenon* 29).

the sake of defending the State (to the fullest extent of such a defense) naturally accepts the killing of civilians and innocents and any war waged to expand power. For the Grotian version of the just war, some reasons may be strong enough to call for war (since some unjust orders are intolerable) but there are morally unacceptable behaviors to practice even against the most vile enemy. His version lays down a comparative theory of justice that criticizes human actions even in times of crisis: since war is not conceived as the failure of Law and Morals, there still remains a few valid parameters of judgment.

This conception of the law of war is not necessary and not even natural to Hugo Grotius. In fact, the typical law of war preached by legal Humanism corresponds to that of Alberico Gentili. As seen in the first chapter, the Italian Jurist supported views that would unnerve a Scholastic: the balance of power, the legitimacy of preventive defense, the idea of probable cause (rather than a fair), and the possibility of bilateral justice in war. He addresses all these issues because he fervently disagrees with the Scholastics in a fundamental topic. Like every reformer, Gentili believes that sin has obscured Natural Law from the human mind. Justice may even exist, but it is only clear to God. The realistic approach is just a step away. If human weakness prevents the knowledge of this reality that is so pure, then it would not be possible to produce any coherent thoughts about it. Therefore, man can only investigate a fleeting likelihood, never the perennial truth.[19]

Grotius defends the idea that sin did not obscure the human reason to such an extent that man is no longer able to perceive Natural Law. This is indeed a more Catholic than a Calvinist opinion. Because of this initial disagreement with Gentili, Grotius draws very different conclusions, despite using the Italian Jurist's **De Jure Belli** as a model for his *opus magna*.

6.1.1 The Law of War of 1605: The Initial Aristotelianism

As seen in the third chapter, at the beginning of the **De Jure Praedae**, in the *prolegomena*, Grotius builds an axiomatic–deductive structure of the sources of the law of war, in lieu of the sources of the Law of Nations. According to him, the most striking feature of the law of war is the lack of a common judge. How to solve problems if there is no judicial authority common to and accepted by all? Rather than to International Law, Grotius turns his efforts to an "extra-national" law.

Were the Law not able to rule the phenomenon of war, if it were not possible to reach just outcomes therefrom, then there would be no need to study the law of war. The whole system of nine *regulae* and thirteen *leges* would fall senseless if it were not possible to compare war with a legal proceeding. Thus, after defining *jus*, Grotius aims at conceptualizing *bellum* and establishing some form of correspondence between them.

---

[19]**DIB**, I, 6, 1.

The author begins addressing the concept of war at the end of the second chapter. Some actions that the human mind conceives are not articulated and never leave the sphere of inner desire, but the ones that surpass mere intention become real action through a process that Grotius calls "execution." This is a clear reference to the Aristotelian distinction between act and potency. Since the human body is vulnerable, men use various extra-corporeal instruments, including weapons, to assist them in the execution of their actions. The just man employs weapons to defend himself and to vindicate a right; the unfair man uses them to attack others and to plunder. "War" is the "armed execution of an action against an armed adversary."[20] If war is employed in the execution of a *jus*, it will be a just war; if it is used for the implementation of an *iniuria*, it will be unjust.

It is a simple, yet solid, definition. Since war relates to the execution of acts, it leaves the domain of the intention. This excludes from Grotius' scope of study all those internal disputes that Aquinas addresses as being contrary to peace. Moreover, only after conceptualizing war does Grotius insert the just or the unjust adjective. In itself, war is a neutral event; the legality of a war lies in its scope, whether it is a lawful one or an injustice. Therefore, only the just war (the execution of a right) is equivalent to a lawsuit. It is worth remembering that the Scholastics also did not condemn war in principle. But this cannot be said of Gentili, who inserts the quality "just" into the very definition of war: "War is the just dispute of public weapons."[21] Gentili's law of war leaves no room for moral judgments about war: either a particular conflict is a war (and therefore it is also just) or it is not war at all.

Only after introducing the adjectives of just and unjust does Grotius divide the wars into public and private. This division entails a different classification from that of just and unjust wars; the justice or injustice of a war does not relate to its public or private character. Furthermore, both public and private wars are divided into external or civil wars.[22] By separating the *jus* from the publicity of a war, Grotius succeeds in upholding the justice of some private wars. And since private wars can also be external or civil, the author presents a broader range of validity of private wars, which transcends even the rebellions for the deposition of tyrants—the only form of private war that a theologian such as Suárez would accept. Despite the Scholastic influences, Grotius is a lawyer above all.

Subsequently, Grotius attempts to answer four questions: whether any war is just; whether Christians may engage in wars; whether a war between Christians can be fair, and finally whether a war between Christians can be just according to all the laws. The author responds all these questions in the affirmative. Those who disapprove of all wars base their hatred on the causes or on the effects of a war (which truly must be condemned), but not on war itself. The destruction that wars cause is

---

[20]"*Armata in armatum exsecutio bellum dicitur*" (**DJPC**, p. 30).

[21]"*Bellum est publicorum armorum iusta contentio*" (**DIB**. I, 2, 1).

[22]**DJPC**, p. 30.

indeed an evil, but unavoidable to defend one's own life or rights. Since Natural Law does not prohibit self-defense or the defense of one's belongings and because it applies to all peoples, Christians may wage wars. In addition, Divine Law provides no prohibition to the waging of wars; hence, Christians may fight other Christians, in a just manner. The *jus gentium* also does not forbid wars: it seeks only to moderate their use. No law within this extra-national domain prevents the realization of wars.[23]

In the fourth chapter of his work of youth, Grotius formulates these same four questions, not on war, but on the right to prize. The resemblance to the Scholastic method (the coincidence of the questions and the form of the articles) is a rhetorical tactic. Grotius needed to justify his position before the Mennonite shareholders of the Company of the Western Indies, who would only be appeased with a book that appealed to the laws of men and to the laws of God both. Thus, the author's theological influences on legal thought are crucial to the success of his efforts. Not every jurist could take a case like that; however, educated and wise one might be, should he tell theologians to be quiet, he would simply not deliver.

The basis of the Grotian law of war of the **De Jure Praedae** is in the fifth chapter. Its size may be misleading: the entire chapter has only two pages; however, they fully epitomize the conception of *iustitia belli* of the work. Grotius begins by establishing a correlation between the law of prize and the law of war. Seizure will be lawful if it results from a just war. Thenceforth, the problem is determining the conditions for a war to be just. Grotius criticizes the writers who preceded him for they were satisfied by listing elements without using any scientific criteria. Some list three conditions, others seven, and they all vary. However, if war is an action, then it should be explained based on the four causes: the persons who conduct the war, the reason why and against whom war is made, how the war is led and to what purpose and end.[24]

This classification corresponds to the four Aristotelian causes. The efficient cause is the belligerent; the material cause corresponds to the object—the "cause" for war in the ordinary sense of the term—as well as to the opponent; the formal cause relates to the procedures that govern the manner the conflict begins and is conducted, as well as the limits that belligerents must comply with; and the final cause addresses the purpose of war and the interior disposition with which the just contender must wage it. This four-part division came from Scholasticism and applied to the most different branches of human knowledge. It had been accepted into the study of Law since the time of the Glossators. Concerning the law of war specifically, John Lignano had already applied the four causes[25] in his **Treatise of Reprisals**.

It is true that these four causes stem from Scholasticism. Yet, this association is not absolute, since this system was so popular that even Gentili himself made use of

---

[23]**DJPC**. pp. 31–42.

[24]**DJPC**, p. 59.

[25]Haggenmacher (1983), p. 65.

it,[26] although differently. In fact, the Spanish Scholastics had already largely abandoned the four causes, preferring the tripartite division of Aquinas instead. By employing the Aristotelian causes, Grotius displays his knowledge and his attachment to tradition. And he will stray from the current legal Humanism by reaching conclusions that resemble those of the Scholastics.

Grotius begins the explanation of the efficient cause with the assertion that individuals are responsible for implementing their own rights in the natural state.[27] That means that the *bellandi potestas* of the individual is legitimate according to Natural Law. Only when there is a State does Civil Law ban taking law into one's own hands. But in nature, the only restriction is a proportionate response. The jurisdiction of the individual is originary and independent from any State delegation. Therefore, in areas where Civil Law does not apply, the individual still has the same rights of a State to promote a just war.

This is a key statement to justify the seizure of the ship Santa Catarina, but it is also a major deviation from the Spanish Scholastics, who perceived war as an activity arising out of public jurisdiction. Only in very exceptional cases (those in which there exists a failure on the power of the perfect community, such as in the various forms of tyranny) could the *jus belli* be transferred to the citizens. However, as will be seen later, Grotius believed that the authority to wage war initially rested on the individuals themselves, not on the community. Therefore, both the public power and the individuals had the same right to defend themselves.

In this regard, Haggenmacher softens the idea that Grotius would have departed from the just war tradition. The Middle Ages knew the institute of the *faide*, a state of enmity between individuals, permeated by acts on both sides in the exercise of their own reasons, without any express authorization from the sovereign power. Occasionally, the *faide* was mistaken for blood feud, but in principle, it applied to any *iniuria* and was restricted to noblemen. Indeed, the advancement of the royal power occurred to the detriment of this private war, but, apart from a special legislation, there remained an old and very broad customary law authorizing the *faide* and the blood vengeanceas well. The feudal war (a genus of which *faide* and *bellum* are species) that derived from the Germanic Law applied not only between peoples, but also within the domestic legal order. In the High Middle Ages, the Roman *bellum publicum* no longer clashed with the *bellum privatum*. The requirement of the authority of the prince was fulfilled with a simple permission, even tacit. Only after the thirteenth century did theologians such as Alexander of Hales, Ulrich of Strasbourg, and Thomas Aquinas began to insist on the requirement of the competent authority to distinguish war from other vices contrary to peace: schism, sedition, and strife. Nevertheless, Grotius seems older than Aquinas in this and bases the aptitude of the individual to wage war in the Stoic notion of

[26]**DIB**. I, 7, 3.

[27]**DJPC**, p. 60.

totius humani generis societas. As a good Humanist, the author bases a feudal practice (the (i) legitimacy of which was not very clear) upon an ancient notion.[28]

Traditional or not, this position was quite convenient for Grotius, not only in relation to the seizure of the Catarina ship. Since the *belli gerendi potestas* does not belong exclusively to the person of the sovereign, in a State where the chief magistrate cannot express his position, his authority may be transferred to the next magistrate in the hierarchy.[29] And, because of the authorization of such magistrate (who is a public figure, yet not the supreme one); such a war may become public as well. In addition to legitimizing private wars, Grotius is also able to justify the Netherlands' war of independence against the Spanish King Philip II as a public war, thus fulfilling his patriotic purposes—which were paramount in this period of his life.

The other causes are not significantly different from the Scholastic law of war. The material cause in the Aristotelian thought designates the potential entity over which the efficient cause is exercised. The form defines the matter and they both presuppose an external agent who will shape their features. In the present case, this craftsman is the belligerent, and his actions correspond to an armed execution. The object of this action is the material cause itself and may be a *jus* claimed by an active belligerent, a substantive right (*iusta materia belli circa quam*), or the person who suffers the action, that is, the purpose of the armed execution, the passive belligerent (*iusta materia belli in qua*).[30]

Although Grotius could not have read Suárez's **De Legibus** in 1605, and so become familiar with Suárez's concept of subjective right, all causes of war (the substantive right) resulted from the four *jus* that "belong" to an individual: the self-defense, the claim of a right, the recovery of a credit and the punishment of an injury. Grotius associates these rights with the axiomatic structure of the *prolegomena*; they come from the first ("It shall be permissible to defend [one's own] life and to shun that which threatens to prove injurious"), second ("It shall be permissible to acquire for oneself, and to retain, those things which are useful for life"), sixth ("Good deeds must be recompensed"), and fifth laws ("Evil deeds must be corrected").[31] Therefore, war, the *armata exsecutio*, is nothing more than the violent accomplishment of something that the judicial process is unable to achieve. Given that the Grotian subjective rights can be held by both the State and the individual, all causes of war apply to public and private wars, without any discrimination.

In relation to the opponent (the material cause) a clarification is in order. If the enemy is a plurality of persons, then there are two ways for such enmity to occur: either the enmity is directed at a collective entity (and thus the individual only becomes an enemy to the extent that he is part of such entity) or it is directed at an

---

[28]Haggenmacher (1983), pp. 76–148.

[29]**DJPC**. pp. 63–64.

[30]Haggenmacher (1983), pp. 148–151.

[31]**DJPC**, pp. 67–68.

individual only, who happens to take part in a collective entity. Grotius adopts this second conception, which is reminiscent of the Medieval *faide*, a personal war above all. In the Medieval *faide*, only the masters, the belligerents, are enemies and hate each other.[32]

Grotius employs a very simple criterion to define the combatant in a war: the will. Only those who wish to be are enemies.

> War is just to those who are in it voluntarily, both against individuals and against a republic whose magistrate suffered an injustice. It will also be fair when brought against a State that protects a citizen who is a wrongdoer, or against the allies and subjects – to the extent of their participation – of an opponent who practiced the injustice.[33]

Paradoxically, that is a broad and at the same time restricted notion. The armed execution targets supreme magistrates, officership and soldiers as well as their counterparts in an allied country. However, all those who do not voluntarily take part in the dispute are excluded from war. War is personal: all those involved in both sides of the dispute are enemies. But war does not extend to the whole State; those who do not directly take part in the combat, such as servants, villagers, and peasants, are not targets.

The perception of the conflict varies in accordance with the different persons engaged in it: the sovereign, the officers, and the soldiers. Indeed, the latter are not exactly voluntary agents in a war. Despite being free men, soldiers do not participate in the conflict because they are expressing their willingness thereto, but because they are following orders. The criterion of the will causes a problem well known to the Scholastics: the limits of the obedience of a subordinate to his superiors' commands. In fact, the soldiers not only may but should disobey the command, if it contradicts a higher rule (those above Civil Law in the hierarchy of *prolegomena*: Natural, Divine Law, and the Law of Nations).

Grotius' reasoning begins with the duty to obey, rather than the right of resistance. The author compares the relationship between the soldier and his superior to that of a father and his son, or that of a master and his slave. In principle, a soldier must always carry out his duties. Even a righteous man can serve as a soldier of a tyrant, because the faithful compliance with the tyrant's orders contributes to the common good. However, the duty of obedience does not prevent the soldier from using his mind. He should only comply with an order that he is sure to be consistent with God's law, or at least which inconsistency he is unsure. When in doubt, the soldier should always obey. For Grotius, this rational weighting involves no certainties, but a calculation of probabilities. Therefore, "to the subjects, the cause of

---

[32]Haggenmacher (1983), p. 182.

[33]"(…) *justum est bellum his, qui voluntarie gerunt, in singulos et in rempublicam, quaeve cujusve magistratus injuriam fecerunt et in rempublicam, quae civem injuriae auctorem tuetur inque eorum omnium, qui injuriam faciunt, qua tales sunt, socios et subditos*" (**DJPC**, p. 75).

war is the order of the superior, provided that, after weighting the odds, their reasons are not opposed to it."[34]

The weighting that Grotius mentions does not entail an inaccurate rational judgment: in order to obey, one must calculate the probability of the command being just; yet, in order to disobey, one must be certain of the injustice. This thesis is based on the belief that those who are closest to the center of decision perceive reality better than those further away from it. The mere possibility of an error in such perception introduces a subject that separates the Scholastic Theologians from the Humanist Jurists: the bilaterality of justice in war.

As seen in chapters II and V, for the Scholastics there could be only one possible answer: that justice was all in one side or in the other. The divine justice is always one and indivisible. However, in the wake of other authors of the Legal Humanism such as Alciato and Fulgosa, Gentili does not share these qualms and admits the bilaterality of justice. Despite advocating a "balance of probabilities," Grotius follows the Scholastics on this by dividing the problem according to the individuals under scrutiny. Regarding the leaders, there are simply no concurrent probabilities or obscurities. "With respect to the voluntary agents, there is no just war for both sides."[35] Admitting the contrary would be improper, *per accidens*, for it takes place when the belligerent incurs in an invincible error. War *per se* can never be fair to the two contenders.

But the conclusion differs from the subordinates' perspective, since the information that they have access to is provided by their superiors. They are exempt from complying with their superiors' commands only if they are manifestly illegal. For the nonvoluntary agents, war may sometimes be objectively fair on both sides.[36] If the prince deceives his soldiers and sends them to a war that he knows to be unjust, the soldiers themselves commit no crime and all the blame falls on the sovereign.

Haggenmacher points out that Grotius advances a substantial innovation of Scholasticism, but without changing its essence. Grotius conceives an objectively just war to both sides, not merely more *formaliter* and *quoad opinionem* but also *materialiter* and *quoad veritatem*.[37] However, he does not dilute the concept of justice. Grotius innovates not in distinguishing leaders from subordinates (many Scholastics had done that before) but in stressing the soldiers' duty to obey and the presumption that the commands of their leaders are valid. Grotius draws the bilaterality of justice out of well-known elements with mathematical precision. As a result, the soldier becomes a combatant without guilt.

---

[34]"*Subditis id bellum justam habet causam, quod jubetur a superiore, dum ratio probabilis subditorum non repugnet.*" (**DJPC**, p. 80).

[35]"(…) *eorum qui voluntarie agunt respectu, bellum ex utraque parte justum non datur.*" (**DJPC**, p. 83).

[36]**DJPC**, p. 84.

[37]Haggenmacher (1983), p. 222.

The formal cause refers to the procedures that the active belligerent must follow in the exercise of his *jus*, which are present not only at the beginning of the hostilities, but throughout the whole war. Because of the similarities that Grotius finds between war and the judicial process, the author's position on this issue does not differ much from the Scholastics. Regarding private war, the conflict becomes legitimate only if there is no possibility of appealing to the judicial body.[38] As to public wars, in addition to this requirement, it is necessary that the opponent State refuses to give any satisfaction.[39] During combat, war will remain just to the voluntary agent that remains within the sphere of the right under dispute: he will not be able to recover more than the disputed object nor injure those that have nothing to do with his right.[40] Injuring is only justified if it results from the exercise of a right to punish or if directed at those who, albeit ignorant, were obstructing the execution of justice (the innocent soldiers of the opponent State). Nevertheless, the right of prize and booty is exercised not only against certain individuals, but also against the whole community, up to the total amount due.[41] In what concerns the formal cause of war, the involuntary combatants must refrain from acting beyond the strict performance of their legal duties, so that the war remains just for them.

The transposition of the rules of court proceedings into the domain of the law of war can only be possible if one assumes the existence of a society among peoples, comparable to that which exists within States. In fact, when Grotius introduces the secondary *jus gentium*, he appeals to the idea of a world common good.[42] Such a good is proper of a society that, in the absence of a better name, may be called international, but which is characterized by its inability to appeal to a judicial body. Grotius was most likely thinking of the Ciceronian *magna humani generis societas.*

The discussion of the final cause proves somewhat disappointing not only by the size of the chapter (five pages), but because, at first glance, the debate appears to be limited to the material cause. The author offers two conclusions: "voluntary agents must act with right intention throughout any war that they become involved in order to retrieve a right" and "subjects must conduct themselves with righteous intent in any war that they engage in to carry out the orders of their superiors."[43] However, a careful reading of these two sentences reveals a new element that was not present in the assessment of the material cause: the right intention. This expression comes from "*recta intentio,*" the third requirement of a just war in Aquinas.

Haggemacher says that there was a tendency to mitigate the notion of the *recta intentio* among the authors of the Spanish Scholasticism. As seen, Suárez mentions

---

[38] **DJPC**, p. 95.

[39] **DJPC**, p. 101.

[40] **DJPC**, p. 107.

[41] **DJPC**, p. 115.

[42] **DJPC**, p. 26.

[43] "*Hoc est: hi qui voluntarie agunt justo animo bellum gerunt, quod juris adipiscendi gratia gerunt*" and "*subditi justo animo id bellum gerunt, quod gerunt ut obediant superiori*" (**DJPC**. pp. 125–127).

that the belligerents must carry a "worthy manner" and abide by "equity." Vitória states that war should aim at peace and security, as well as at the tranquility of the State. Similar conceptions appear in Bañez and Molina. Since war is an external vice, Aquinas' idea that the internal disposition of the belligerents (their right intention) consisted of a requirement of war[44] did not convince these authors.

Grotius here adopts a hybrid position. Although he insists on the requirement of the right intention for both the voluntary agent and the subjects of the prince, only the right intention of the voluntary agent would correspond to Aquinas' *recta intentio*. The right intention of the subjects should imply a mere compliance of their behavior to the commands of their superiors. It would mean nothing but an external adhesion to war.

6.1.2 The Law of War of 1625: The Scholastic Reassessment

The law of war does not undergo radical transformations in the **De Jure Belli ac Pacis**; Grotius merely resumes some issues and develops others (and that ends up approximating his work even more to the Spanish Scholasticism). Still, as it is a work of pure theory, certain subjects of the **De Jure Praedae** are left out of it. In addition to the lack of references to contemporary events, Grotius seems to change a few old ideas that were essential in justifying the seizure of the **Santa Catarina**. Moreover, as he no longer needed to address concrete events, he modified the structure of the work, leaving behind his division of the study of the Just into *Dogmatica*, *Historica,* and *Examen*. In addition, the book focuses on the law of war, a *jus*, although some passages are devoted to the Honest and the Useful. Grotius also introduces the notion of *temperamenta*, which aims at softening the rigor of justice. Yet, these deviations do not imply a loss of focus and the author remains within the Scholastic conception of the law of war.

In his work of youth, Grotius sought to defend a cause, but in his work of maturity, he is moved by a higher purpose. He seeks to admonish the desire for war and to restrain the destructive impulses of men in general and of Christians in particular.

> I saw in the Christian university a levity in relation to war that would have shamed the very barbarous nations. For trivial or no reason they turned to arms, and when they already have them in hands, there was no observation of any more respect for the divine law and for the human rights, as if by the force of an edict, the furor had been initiated on all crimes.[45]

This statement not only conveys a typical disapproval of the destructions of war, but also foretells Grotius' main purpose. As seen in the third chapter, the

[44]Haggenmacher (1983), pp. 406–407.

[45]"*Videbam per Christianum orbem vel barbaris gentibus pudendam bellandi licentiam: levibus aut nullis de causis ad arma procurri, quibus semel sumtis nullam iam divini, nullam humani iuris reverentiam, plane quasi uno edicto ad omnia scelera emisso furore.*" (**DJBP**. *prolegomenon* 28).

minimization of violence and the quest for peace are Grotius' theological projects. As a result, Grotius distances himself from the Humanistic law of war praised in Gentili, whose book served as a model for him in several matters.

Grotius' analysis begins with the following definition: "War is the state of those who resolve their disputes by force."[46] As in the **De Jure Praedae**, Grotius conceived a generic term to encompass all kinds of war: the just and the unjust, the private and the public. Despite reading Gentili, for whom war is necessarily just (although this virtue is later softened) or is no war at all, Grotius remains faithful to his conception of youth.

However, by designating the phenomenon as a *status*, the author seems to put aside the notion of war as an *actio*. This definition should not evoke the today's sense of state of war, which implies the establishment of a coherent body of rules, a *jus in bello,* ruling the relations between the belligerents. Still, it implies a certain situation of things opposed to the state of peace.[47] Grotius' classification of truce unveils the reason behind the change from *exsecutio* to *status*. This institute seems to be a middle ground between war and peace. This poses a problem for the author, because he does not accept an intermediate state between peace and war. War and peace are mutually excludent opposites and leave no room for a middle ground, composed of elements from one and the other. Therefore, Grotius inserts the institute of truce in war, not in peace, for war implies a state that exists even without producing external effects.[48] Truce is thus a convention that suspends warlike actions, but without ending war itself.

There is no doubt that Grotius had in mind the Aristotelian division of act and potency. During the state of war, military actions do not always occur. However, in the work of 1605, war as a whole corresponded to an act. Grotius does not reject his previous definition, but he now deems it less comprehensive and impartial. The author tries to build a concept generic enough to encompass all sorts of war and broad enough to include all the moments of the conflict. Before, the impartiality of the formula *armata in armatum exsecutio* seemed obvious: the justice or injustice of war depended on its connection with a *jus* or *iniuria.* However, in itself, the notion of execution is not neutral: in a judicial proceeding, you can only execute a *jus*. Therefore, this change in the definition of war is a result of the development of Grotius' thought toward Scholasticism; more than the previous definition, his new definition distanced him even more from the politically compromised conceptions of Legal Humanism.[49]

After defining war, Grotius addresses the *jus*, which was analyzed in the fourth chapter of this book. Subsequently, the Dutch seeks to unite the two terms and the first question that arises is whether there can be a just war. Since the law of war is based on Natural Law, on the *jus gentium* and on the Divine voluntary Law, the

[46]"(...) *sit bellum status per vim certantium, qua tales sunt*" (**DJBP**. I, 1, 2, 1).

[47]Haggenmacher (1983), p. 458.

[48]**DJBP**. III, 21, 1, 1.

[49]Haggenmacher (1983), p. 461.

most appropriate way to demonstrate the possibility of a just war is to confront war itself with these three sources.

Natural Law is confirmed *a priori* by the conformity of the thing with the rational nature, and *a posteriori* by the common testimony of men. The assessment of the justice of a war is made accordingly. *A priori*, it is necessary to perceive the creative impulses of Natural Law. Grotius borrows from Cicero the two Stoic inclinations of the *oikeiosis*: self-preservation and right reason. Now, he associates sociability with right reason itself, whilst in the book of youth, the former was a mere species of the latter. As seen in chapter IV, Grotius does so under the influence of Scholasticism, since it considers sociability to be the true driving force of Natural Law and thus responsible for minimizing the effects of the love for oneself. Again, Grotius reaffirms this preference:

> But from the knowledge of these principles, a notion arises of their being agreeable to reason, that part of a man, which is superior to the body. Now that agreement with reason, which is the basis of propriety, should have more weight than the impulse of appetite; because the principles of nature recommend right reason as a rule that ought to be of higher value than bare instinct. As the truth of this is easily assented to by all men of sound judgment without any other demonstration, it follows that in inquiring into the laws of nature the first object of consideration is, what is agreeable to those principles of nature, and then we come to the rules, which, though arising only out of the former, are of higher dignity, and not only to be embraced, when offered, but pursued by all the means in our power.[50]

In any case, nothing in war (in itself) is contrary to self-preservation. Rather, self-preservation seems to compel man to war, since it aims at ensuring the preservation of his life and body. Neither is the right reason opposed to war, for it seeks to preserve society and the rights of each man. When one wages war in search of peace and in pursuit of a right, one favors right reason.[51]

The testimony of history, the *a posteriori* evidence, also proves the justice of wars. First, Grotius turns to the Bible, the absolute document of (holy) history, and recounts many examples of conflicts approved by God. He then relies on the testimony of classical authors—historians like Josephus and Pliny, jurists as Gaius and Florentino, and the orator Cicero.[52]

Grotius dispenses only a few lines to examine the compliance of war with the Law of Nations. Since it is a voluntary law, the sole evidence of compliance thereto is the testimony of men. And as always, the author prefers ancient writers.

---

[50]"*At post cognita sequi notionem convenientiae rerum cum ipsa ratione quae corpore est potior; atque eam convenientiam, in qua honestum sit propositum, pluris faciendam, quam ad quae sola primum animi appetitio ferebatur; quia prima naturae commendent nos quidm rectae rationi, sed ipsa recta ratio carior nobis esse debeat quam, illa sint a quibus ad hanc venerimus. Haec cum veras int et ab omnibus, qui judicio sano sunt praediti; facile sine alia demonstratione assensum impetrent; sequitur in examinando jure naturae primum videndum quid illis naturae initiis congruat, deinde veniendum ad illud, quod quanquam post oritur, dignius tamen est; neque sumendum tantum, si detur, sed omni modo expetendum.*" (**DJBP**. I, 2, 1, 2).

[51]**DJBP**. I, 2, 1, 4-5.

[52]**DJBP**. I, 2, 2-3.

According to Hermogenian (who is quoted by Grotius), the *jus gentium* not only permits war, but would have actually introduced it. Grotius does not accept this interpretation: the Law of Nations only establishes certain formalities, such as the distinction between solemn and non-solemn war. While the latter is merely allowed, the former is actually supported by the *jus gentium.*[53]

Grotius focuses his efforts on demonstrating the legality of war pursuant to the voluntary Divine Law. He secures items 5 through 10 of the book (the rest of the chapter) to this analysis. Judging by its size, this *jus* would correspond to the main source of the law of war, followed by Natural Law and lastly by the *jus gentium*. While nothing besides the extension in which the subject is addressed supports such an understanding, the size itself is testimony to the relevance of religion in the composition of the law of war in the author's mind. Thus, Grotius must investigate the compatibility of the war with two divine laws: the Old and the New Testament. Regarding the Old Testament, Grotius' reasoning boils down to the idea of retribution: man may suffer and be punished, even with death, for the evils he commits. Justifying the law of war in the Gospels is in itself more intricate a task. Christ's teachings seem to demand absolute pacifism (an attitude that Grotius had repudiated in Erasmus); so, he employs extreme caution. The author seeks to distinguish the natural precepts from those of the New Testament. The first precepts would constitute a kind of minimum morality, while the last precepts would correspond to a maximum morality and would thus consist of advices rather than real obligations. For this reason, neither Christ nor the Church has ever condemned institutes such as military service and capital punishment.[54] Moreover, Grotius softens a large number of pacifist excerpts that seem to mitigate the seemingly anti-war position of the Gospels.[55] In any case, the Gospels do not explicitly condemn war and their admonitions against violence belong to a system of morality that lies above the Law: they belong to Charity.

In order to evaluate the justice of a war, Grotius abandons the system of the four Aristotelian causes in **De Jure Belli ac Pacis**. Instead, the author seems to adopt Aquinas' famous criteria of three causes. In the *prolegomena*, Grotius divides his work as follows. In the first book, he introduces the basic concepts, such as law, war, and just war. Then he presents the distinction between public and private wars (and, here, Grotius must explain the nature of sovereignty and the political duty to obey). This part corresponds to the study of the concept of competent authority. In the second book, Grotius affirms that he sought to expose every cause that may lead to war. Finally, in the third book, Grotius addresses everything that is permitted to do in a war and describes the many species of peace and all the conventions applicable to wars.[56]As seen, this last institute corresponds to what was called the law of peace, and the first to Aquinas' right intention. However, his exposition resembles that of the Spanish Scholastics, who mitigated the subjectivism in war.

[53]**DJBP**. I, 2, 4, 2.

[54]**DJBP**. I, 2, 5, 5.

[55]**DJBP**. I, 2, 8 (full).

[56]**DJBP**. *prolegomenon* 35.

Concerning the first condition, Grotius divides wars into public, private, and mixed (the latter between private individuals on the one side and those who hold *jurisdictio* in the other). The author modifies his previous classification, which did not contain this third element. Nothing indicates that Grotius had contact with Suárez's **De Bello**, but the similarities between their works are striking: according to Suárez, the external dispute is the genus of which war, strife, and sedition are species.[57] Suárez's Treaty of War was only published in 1621, which makes an influence on Grotius unlikely, albeit not impossible. Nevertheless, one thing is certain: the Grotian division falls within the Thomist cultural universe. As described in the previous chapter, the concept and terminology employed by Grotius observe, *grosso modo*, Aquinas' system, for whom the external struggle opposes external peace and hence Charity itself.[58] Even if Grotius had not read the **De Bello**, there is no doubt that from 1605 onward his thinking evolved toward Thomism.

Grotius then examines the legality of private wars. In the **De Jure Praedae**, he accepted the unrestricted validity of this type of conflict: all the causes that justify public war can legitimize a private war as well, since the "subjective rights" belong to both individuals and sovereign powers. Grotius now seems a little more reticent. Before the advent of courts, the freedom to engage in private wars was unrestricted. Afterwards, such freedom subsisted only when it was not possible to resort to the judicial body. The judicial process may be set aside shortly when its delay puts the rights at risk (this idea echoes the institutes of self-protection, state of necessity, and self-defense that exist in Positive Law). And it may cease permanently in two ways: either in law or in fact. The first form corresponds to the cases where there exists no neutral third party in the conflict: in the desert, in uninhabited islands, and outside the *cive*. This hypothesis legitimizes war itself in the "extra-national" relations. The second way corresponds to the cases in which people refuse to submit their claims to a judge or the judge himself refuses to recognize their claims.[59]

Grotius' entire reasoning above corresponds to the *a priori* proof of the lawfulness of private wars *vis a vis* Natural Law. Grotius employs the authority of the Bible, of the Twelve Tables, and of the Greek Solon[60] in his efforts to illustrate the consensus and thus to prove his point with *a posteriori* evidence.

Subsequently, Grotius shows the legitimacy of private war *vis a vis* the voluntary Divine Law. The author uses the same reasoning employed to confront this *jus* with war itself; he diminishes certain Biblical precepts and affirms that they refer to a higher morality, which, translated into legal language, would only constitute permission and not an obligation.[61]

---

[57]**De Bello**, *Proemium*. Haggenmacher himself had already called attention to this similarity (Haggenmacher, 1983, p. 529).

[58]**ST**. 2-2 q. 40-42.

[59]**DJBP**. I, 3, 2, 1.

[60]**DJBP**. I, 3, 2, 2.

[61]**DJBP**. I, 3, 3, 9.

The Grotian Law of Nations does not prohibit private wars, but establishes some formal requirements thereto. Grotius divides public war into solemn and non-solemn war. Solemn war is the one that typically qualifies as just (just like regular wills and equitable marriages oppose codicils and the union of slaves). However, such opposition does not imply that codicils are illegal or that slaves may not to take a spouse. The adjective "just" merely designates certain specific effects provided for in law, but their lack does not turn war unjust. Thus, solemn wars have two requirements: a competent authority and certain formalities that must be complied in the course of the conflict. And non-solemn public wars are carried out without these conditions; either there is a lack of formalities, or war is waged against private individuals or undertaken by non-sovereign magistrate authorities. Non-solemn wars may be mixed, that is, undertaken by a public authority that does not hold sovereignty (and this justifies Netherlands' struggle for independence).[62]

Later, I will discuss Grotius' thoughts on sovereignty and civil disobedience in the course of public and mixed wars. For now, it is worth mentioning the subtle decline in the relevance of private wars. The author still upholds their legality, but they may only take place, pursuant to Natural Law, in the event that it is not possible to resort to the judicial body: either because there is an emergency that cannot wait for the judicial proceeding, or because there is a state of anarchy in which people no longer trust the settlement of their disputes to the courts (failed State) or the magistrate himself refuses to hear their claims (and this would also constitute a failed State). Therefore, the validity of private war becomes an exception in Natural Law. In turn, while not expressly condemning private wars, Divine Law does not endorse them either. And the *jus gentium* simply ignores them and prefers to regulate public war. Thus, private wars end up fulfilling a residual and somewhat defensive position. It would be more appropriate if Grotius had simply prohibited this type of dispute altogether, maintaining only very few exceptions, as Suárez did. However, this would lead to a drastic change of his previous position. By affirming the legality of private wars at first and then restricting their application, Grotius makes a smoother transition from an engaged young jurist to an impartial unbiased mature philosopher prone to Scholasticism.

Grotius develops throughout book II the second condition established by Aquinas for a just war, which is the just cause. I have already disputed a highly spread view that this book would constitute an early form of "International Law of peace." If that is not the purpose of the book, then under what criteria did the author assemble institutes as diverse as the right to private property, the right of burial, embassies, and the right to punish?

In order to answer this question, it is essential to walk through the following reasoning. As if he were himself a Scholastic Priest, Grotius distinguishes between the *causa justifica* and the *causa suasoria*, the motive and the pretext for war.[63] This contrast distances Grotius from Gentili, who had a tendency to obscure this

[62]**DJBP**. I, 3, 4, 1-2 and I, 3, 5.

[63]**DJBP**. II, 1, 1, 1.

difference. The cause of a war should be a suffered *iniuria*, since the injured party may be able to defend its *jus* just like in a lawsuit. "There can be no other legitimate cause of war other than an incoming injury."[64] This formula is nothing new and Grotius himself quotes Augustine as its source. Nevertheless, the formula was spread by the Spanish Scholasticism. According to Vitória, the "sole and exclusive cause for waging war is the injustice received."[65] This is an essential part of the Christian and Scholastic Doctrine of Just War: the legitimacy of war lies in the search for justice, in the correction of an error.

Grotius attempts to assemble a comprehensive set of criteria that would allow anyone to unveil the just cause of a war. In the **De Jure Belli ac Pacis**, there is a direct correspondence between the causes of war and the injuries to subjective rights: self-defense, the vindication of an *in rem* right, the punishment of an offense, and the pursuit of an *in personam* right.[66] The causes that justify war boil down to the recovery of a *jus*, in the second sense of the term (as a subjective right). Even in the **De Jure Praedae**, Benjamin Straumann perceives the relation of these causes (and so of those rights) with the Roman actions from the **Digest**: *interdicta de non offendendo, vindicationes,* and *interdicta possessionis gratia, conditiones ex maleficio,* and *conditiones ex contractu,* respectively.[67] In his work of maturity, this connection stands out even more, as Grotius states that "as many are sources of a lawsuit, many are the causes of war."[68] The sources from 1625 slightly differ from those of 1605, but retain the idea of representing reasons for a lawsuit: returning what belongs or has belonged to someone (*in rem* and certain *in personam* lawsuits), paying what is owed due to a contract or quasi-contract, or in result of a tort, quasi-tort and of law (other *in personam* lawsuits) and the corresponding punishment for breaching such duties.

The author does not associate wars in general with judicial proceedings, but only those wars that are just, whether public or private. For that reason, book II features a list of unrelated institutions, some of which are of International Law, yet others from Domestic Law, and others even of Private Law. Grotius sought to establish an exhaustive list of rights which injury could justify public (solemn or non-solemn), private or mixed wars. The causes of war do not depend essentially on the quality of the belligerent or on formalities. That is the reason why the Grotian law of war may thus be inserted not in International Law itself, but in the field of extra-national relations.

---

[64]"*Causa iusta belli suscipiendi nulla esse alia potest, nisi injuria.*" (**DJBP**. II, 1, 1, 4).

[65]"*Unica est et sola causa iusta inferendi bellum, iniuria accepta.*" (**De indis II**. *De Jure Belli*, 13, p. 825).

[66]**DJBP**. II, 1, 2, 2. Many commentators (for example, Yasuaki, 1993, p. 79) tend to atribute to Grotius only three just causes for war. However, such attribution stems from a superficial reading of this passage: the author first states a general opinion, which he himself feels is not precise, and then differs *in personam* rights from *in rem* rights. This division is reflected in the very structure of book II of **DJBP**, in which Grotius adresses *in rem* rights from chapter 1 through 10 and *in personam* rights from chapter 11 through 19.

[67]Straumann, 2006, p. 13.

[68]"*Ac plane quot actionum forensium sunt fontes, totidem sunt belli*" (**DJBP**. II, 1, 2, 1).

Book III addresses the behavior of the belligerents during the state of war, which corresponds to an objective update of Aquinas' right intention. The text contrasts Natural Law (which is broad and applicable to all kinds of war) to the Law of Nations (more narrow and applicable only to some kinds of war, the reprisals and the formal public war). In general, Natural Law allows everything that is strictly necessary for the recovery of a *jus*, which is the cause of the conflict.

Yet, the Law of Nations changes this principle, although not always to restrict it. In public wars, the goods (but not the lives) of the subjects may be seized for the debt of the prince.[69] Moreover, formal war takes place between sovereigns of different peoples and is preceded by a public statement. This statement is not only dismissed by Natural Law (it is only required by the *jus gentium*), but removes the secrecy of the conflict—it is possible to know in advance the day and the place of the combat. The *jus gentium* also admits certain effects of bilateral justice: even a contender lacking a just cause may seize the property of another, kill and punish his enemy. Nations agreed on these effects in order to reduce the subjectivity of the requirement of right intention. Even in a just war, acknowledging the precise limit up to which one is allowed to defend himself, the recovery of a good, and the infliction of a punishment is not so simple a task. In addition, according to the *jus gentium*, the allies are not required to judge on which side lies justice and this is prudent.[70] Solemn war does not suppress considerations about justice, but it puts both sides on an equal footing because it authorizes the unfair belligerent to promote actions that would be forbidden in any other type of war.

These traces of bilateralism of justice in war actually distance Grotius from the Thomistic doctrine. Despite being cautious not to overstep the unilateral conception of justice, Grotius ends up straying from Aquinas' third condition by adopting a more objective interpretation thereof. However, it is a relative distance, since the Spaniards themselves had already adopted this posture, even if they were somewhat reluctant to reach the same conclusions as Grotius.

In any case, this deviation must have bothered the author himself, because he offers a way to control the righteousness of the acts of the belligerents after describing everything that the Law of Nations allows during war: the conformity of the act with the ideas of external and internal justices. Grotius attributes to external justice the abstract effects of the voluntary *jus gentium*; for this reason, he calls solemn war a *bellum iustum ex iure gentium*.[71] Thus, pursuant to external justice, all behaviors described heretofore are legitimate.

But internal justice is stricter:

> I must now retrace my steps and take away from those who wage war almost all the rights that I may seem to have granted them; which yet in reality I have not. For when I first undertook to explain this part of the Law of Nations, I then declared, that many things are said to be of right and lawful, because they escape punishment, and partly because the

[69]**DJBP**. III, 2, 2,1.

[70]**DJBP**. III, 4, 3 and 4.

[71]**DJBP**. III, 3, 11 and III, 6, 1, 1.

courts of justice have granted them authority. But these things are contrary to the rules, either of justice properly so called, or of other virtues; at least those who abstain from such things act in a manner more honest and more commendable in the opinion of good men.[72]

Grotius devotes one chapter on admonition (*monita*) and six on temperance (*temperamenta*) to examine how internal justice controls the actions of the contenders. Both parties seek to restrict the conduct of belligerents; admonition focuses on those who combat an unjust war, while temperance focuses on those who fight in a just war. The author considers the Law of Nations to be a rather lenient *jus* and so he appeals to a law in the strictest sense, the *facultas*, as well as to other virtues besides justice.

In the extra-national domain, faculties may only express precepts of Natural Law, since Domestic Law does not apply and Divine Voluntary Law does not address solemn wars. According to Basdevant, the *jus gentium* could revoke these rules of an allegedly superior law because, like the *facultas*, they belong to the individual (private or public), who can dispose of them. However, this Natural Law revoked by a practice that becomes law in the relations amongst the peoples still retains its value and is enforceable in the inner forum. It is a corrective measure of what Basdevant described as "initial inelegance" (having "less noble" rules derogating higher provisions).[73]

The temptation to attribute to Grotius a system of legal and another of moral control is almost irresistible. He seems to have conceived two types of the Law of Nations: one in accordance to Natural Law and the other more related to customs and dissociated from any abstract ideal of justice (as a more positivistic interpretation of International Law would entail). Nevertheless, this reasoning presupposes an anachronistic data: that Grotius' notions of Law and Moral would coincide with our current conceptions thereof, especially after the refinement carried out by the German Philosophy of the eighteenth century.

Haggenmacher affirms that the difference between internal and external justice corresponds to the Scholastic distinction between the judicial forum, which regulates the external actions, and the inner forum, which governs human consciousness.[74] As seen in chapter III, Suárez also displays this division and asserts that, since all authority comes from God, both Natural and human Laws produce bonds

72"*Legenda mihi retro vestigia, et eripienda bellum gerentibus pene omnia quae largitus videri possum, nec tamen largitus sum nam cum primum hanc juris gentium partem explicare sum aggressus, testatus sum juris esse aut licere multa dici eo quod impune fiant, partim etiam quod judicia coactiva sua illis auctoritatem accommodent, quae tamen aut exorbitent a recti regula, sive illa in jure stricte dicto, sive in aliarum virtutum praecepto posita est, aut certe omittantur sanctius et cum majori apud bonos laude*." (**DJBP**. III, 10, 1, 1).

73Basdevant (1904), p. 238.

74Haggenmacher (1983), p. 581.

of consciousness (although in Suárez, Positive Law does not apply to internal acts). There is no doubt that the idea of sin, a phenomenon alien to Law, lies at the bottom of this distinction. However, for the Scholastic theologians, who considered the study of the laws a part of Theology, the inner forum is not an extralegal reality. Apparently, neither for Grotius. Internal justice represents a true *jus*.

Still, at first glance, Natural Law does not seem to encompass all the precepts of internal justice. Throughout chapters X to XVI of Book III, Grotius appeals to many virtues in addition to justice itself: among others, *pietas, honestum,* and *modestia*. The *jus gentium* allows behaviors that Natural Law and other normative orders that govern human conduct as well deem excessive. Yet, one should not infer therefrom that internal justice is beyond the realm of Law. All these virtues are part of Law in a strict sense, in a stronger sense of the term. Whereas external justice requires a mere compliance with the rules of *jus gentium*, internal justice requires something more.

In order to explain the difference between internal and external justice, it is necessary to understand the relation that Grotius establishes between Natural and Positive Law. This division is not alien to the Grotian system. It does not appear solely in Book III, as a mere *ex machina*[75] expedient employed to solve a particular problem. In *prolegomenon* 41, Grotius alludes to a law that produces only external effects and to a stricter sense of law itself. A preliminary version of the chapters on *monita* and *temperamenta* also appear in the discussion on the *Honestum* of the **De Jure Praedae**, a virtue apparently distinct from Law. After demonstrating that the seizure of the **Santa Catarina** conforms to the *jus*, Grotius must rebut the opinions of those who considered the action legal, but dishonest. He is firm: these positions are inconsistent, because everything that is just is also honest. Grotius relies on the Ancient Socratic notion that justice embraces all other virtues. But there is an reservation thereto:

> For a better understanding of what we have said, it must be emphasized that we are not using the term "just" to describe what domestic law allows or is conivent. Because lawyers themselves believe that what is exempt from punishment is, to a certain extent, permissible, when, in fact, does not seem to be just or honest. However, it should be understood that what we are dealing with is decreed by the immutable Natural Law.[76]

That which Natural Law permits is honest too; however, this cannot be said of Civil Law. Grotius resumes the idea of separating honest from dishonest permissions in other passages of book III of the **De Jure Belli ac Pacis**. "For sometimes it is said to be lawful that which is altogether just and honest, yet perhaps some other more commendable thing may be done." And further: "sometimes one thing is considered permitted not because it may take place without prejudice to the rules of

---

[75]This expression belongs to Haggenmacher (1983), p. 584.

[76]"*Quod ut probe intelligatur, sciendum est justum nos non illud dicere, quod aliquo civili jure permittitur, aut potius, cui leges connivent: quod enim sic impune fertur atque adeo licere dicitur, cum revera justum non sit, ne honestum quidem est, ut jurisconsulti praedicant: sed de eo nos loqui, quod immutabili lege naturae decretum atque constitutum est.*" (**DJPC**, p. 301).

honesty and duties, but because, among men, such thing is not subject to a penalty."[77] It is in this second sense that the Law of Nations allows certain effects of the solemn war. These behaviors are prohibited by Natural Law, but Positive Law does not sanction them.

These two forms of permission are found even in Book I. In a passage that deals with the relation between Natural and the Divine Voluntary Law of the Old Testament, Grotius distinguishes between full permission, when the law (divine) grants complete freedom of action, and less than full permission, when the law grants mere impunity before men, and the right to act without being disrupted by others.[78] This last form of permission is contrary to Natural Law. Basdevant, for whom the difference between internal and external justice is merely a corrective measure within the Grotian system, is thus wrong. It is an idea that permeates the entirety of the Grotian system.

This subdivision of the permission category is already present throughout the Spanish Scholasticism. Amongst those theologians, Suárez addresses this issue in depth. He distinguishes the permission prescribed by law from that which results from the absence of a prohibitive law. The former is no mere negative prohibition, for it actually provides a faculty or sets forth a positive license. Such is the case of a law prescribing a reward for an action: the individual is free to decide whether to act, but if he does, he is entitled to the prize. The latter takes place when the law allows an evil and thus grants impunity before men.[79] The similarity with the Grotian conception is not a coincidence. Like Grotius would do later, Suárez applies this division to the relation between Natural Law and the *jus gentium*:

> The "lawful" expression should not be understood in a strict sense, as when referring to something lawful and honest. (…) We must understand the word "lawful" in a broad sense and in view of a human estimate, as when we say that it is lawful that which can be done with impunity and is tolerated by custom, which is the same as saying that it is allowed. That is equivalent to saying that an act is naturally lawful, that is, that the law of nations permit it, or does not prohibit it. Not because natural law in the strict sense does not prohibit it, but because the law of nations, by being human, contains no specific prohibition.[80]

As seen in chapter III, according to Suárez, Positive Law may indeed permit a behavior that Natural Law prohibits. The contradiction would only occur if the Law of Nations should command a behavior that the other prohibits. There is no direct

---

[77]"*Interdum enim licere dicitur id quod rectum ex omni parte piumque est, etiamsi forte aliud quid fieri possit laudabilius*" and "*Alias vero licere aliquid dicitur, non quod salva pietate et officiorum regulis fieri potest, sed quod apud homines poenae non subjacet*" (**DJBP**. III, 4, 2, 1 and 2).

[78]**DJBP**. I, 1, 17, 2.

[79]**DJBP**. I, 15, 11.

[80]"*(…) verbum licere non debere intelligi cum proprietate, ut dicitur de re licita et honesta. (…) Debet ergo verbum licere late sumi et in ordine ad humanum iudicium, prout licere dicitur quod impune fit et quod usu toleratur; quod perinde est ac permitti. Vel dici etiam potest et fere in idem redit naturaliter, id est, iure gentium id licere, id est, non prohiberi; non quia ius naturale rigorosum id non prohibeat, sed quia jus gentium, prout humanum est, non addit specialem prohibitionem*" (**DL.** II, 20, 4).

opposition between the deontic categories of what is allowed and what is forbidden, but between what is prohibited and what is ordered. However, even if Positive Law prescribes permission, this does not mean that the behavior is bad in itself.

In Grotius, as in Suárez, the foundation of the validity of Natural Law lies in necessity; however, voluntary law does not extend beyond the sphere of usefulness. Thus, nations may agree to allocate certain effects of bilateral justice to a particular conflict that meets some requirements. But they are still a sin.

Nevertheless, the Grotian *jus gentium* serves not only to permit what Natural Law forbids. It also prescribes valid behaviors before inner justice. For example, this is the case of the law of embassy, which is provided for by the Law of Nations and on which Natural Law is indifferent *ab initio*.[81] In Grotius, the only element shared by all precepts of the Law of Nations is the source: the common will of the peoples. There is no other feature that makes it a true system. From a substantive perspective, the rules of the Law of Nations may cover any topic: "international" issues such as war and embassies, matters of public law and even of private law, such as promises and oaths. From a formal point of view, the *jus gentium* may permit what is evil, prohibit or prescribe behaviors that are indifferent to Natural Law, or even concur with the prescriptions of this law. Except for its positive and human origin, the Grotian *jus gentium* does not resemble in anything today's International Law.

Grotius thus resorts to inner justice in order to establish the invalidity of certain acts deemed lawful by the *jus gentium*, yet not legal in a stronger sense of the term *jus*. Like any Positive Law, the Law of Nations does not aim at the righteousness of the soul, but Law as a whole does. This kind of thinking could only exist in an author who was greatly influenced by the theological (and hypertrophied) conception of Law of the Second Scholasticism.

Natural Law, which represents the most purest form of justice, encompasses all other virtues (in a more superficial analysis, that would ensure the interdisciplinary character of internal justice), but not Charity. Grotius presents that on several occasions: "the rules of Charity extend beyond the rules of Law (sic)." In another passage, the author makes it clear that Charity transcends law even in its strong sense: "often the love for one's neighbor would not allow us to make use of the strict sense of law."[82] Charity seems to be more merciful than Law. When examining the possibility of killing the opponent according to internal justice, Grotius states that

[81]**DJBP**. II, 18, 1.

[82]"*Saepe enim proximi caritas non permittet at summo jure utamur*" and "(...) *latius patere caritatis quam juris regulas*" (**DJBP**. III, 13, 4 and III, 1, 4, 2).

> No man can be deliberately killed with justice, unless for a capital crime, or because we cannot really secure our lives and estates without doing it. But that very thing, to kill a man on account of our estates, which are frail and perishable goods, **may not be repugnant to justice strictly taken, yet it is far from the law of Charity**.[83]

In the chapters on admonition and temperance, Grotius often uses Charity as another resource to moderate the bellicose impulses. However, the author only reminds the reader of the existence of an order of values higher than Law itself, but does not seek to incorporate it to internal justice.

Despite sharing so many similarities with Suárez, there is a difference regarding the very meaning of the law of war. Suárez's **De Bello** is part of his Treaty of Charity for various strategic reasons. The most important is the exclusion of any effects of the bilateralism of justice that a strictly legal analysis and an objective interpretation of Aquinas' third condition would entail. Another purpose thereof is to moderate the conduct of the belligerents during the state of war. These two features are also present in Grotius' internal justice. In Suárez; however, Charity fulfills an additional function: it enables the universalization of the law of war. Due to Charity, the suarezian *jus belli* ceases to be a specific law of a given people, or of European peoples, to become a worldwide phenomenon. In Suárez, both the Law of Nations and Natural Law encompass a number of provisions that are insufficient to ensure a minimum degree of civility. The Christian religion had already lost its unity within Europe, so it could not ensure peaceful living conditions. But Charity, even if striped of its religious elements, constitutes an objective order of values for a theologian; therefore it could be combined to the law of war in order to universalize it.

In Grotius, the law of war does not fulfill the role of preserving civility. Since Charity is beyond internal justice, the Grotian ethical minimum must settle for the lower standards of justice from Natural Law. The *jus belli* does not seek the legal and ethical unity of the entire human race, but only to offer a method for dispute settlement where courts are not available—it refers to an extra-national rather than international realm.

In fact, Grotius and Suárez faced the same problem and made different decisions: by realizing that religion could not be universalized, one generalizes Charity while the other reduces religion to a few rational precepts, as seen in chapter III. Suárez, a Catholic Theologian of the Counter-Reformation, could not abandon centuries of moral progress (European progress nonetheless, but Europeans are human) to ethical relativism that loomed over ever since Machiavelli and the discovery of the American people. Grotius, a Reformed Theologian, attacks ethical relativism by accepting to reduce mankind's values to the minimum envisaged by Natural Law (which is already above the Positive Law of Nations).

This distinction between the two authors exists because for Suárez the unity of mankind was a project. It had existed for centuries in Europe thanks to Christianity.

---

[83]"*Ex proposito juste interfici nemo potest, nisi aut in poenam justam aut quatenus absque eo vitam et res nostras tueri non possumus: quanquam illud ipsum ob res caducas hominem occidere, etiam si a justitia stricte dicta non abeat, a caritatis tamen lege discedit.*" (**DJBP**. III, 11, 2).

Ever since the world expanded, such unity needed repair, but Reformation and ethical relativism posed severe threats. For Grotius, in virtue of his readings of Cicero and of his ideas concerning a *humani generis societas*, the unity of all men was already a reality. He only needed to demonstrate how human beings should solve their own problems in the impossibility of applying Domestic Laws.

Indeed, the Grotian world society, although already existent, was less pretentious than Suárez's. But the difference between these two philosophers is smaller than their similarities. Both seek to establish the coexistence of values that transcend utility. This quality is present in Grotius' law of war, as he here reveals himself to be a legitimate follower of the Scholastic Doctrine of Just War. Yet, could this be said to one of the sources of the law of war, the *jus gentium*? Despite stemming from utility, does the Grotian Law of Nations have a moral foundation?

6.2 The Foundations of the Law of Nations

Grotius never addressed the *jus gentium* in itself. His considerations are part of larger studies on the law of war—of which the Law of Nations is but a source. Yet, paradoxically, Grotius became known for painting a more "Modern" and conclusive picture of this *jus*. As seen, he never intended to write a book on International Law, in the contemporary sense of the term. With this in mind, knowing that the Grotian Law of Nations does not play the same role of contemporary International Law, it seems possible to recreate the author's conception of the *jus gentium* from few scattered observations he made in the course of his research on the *jus belli*. Only after this reconstruction effort will it be possible to determine exactly how Modern and conclusive is Hugo Grotius' Law of Nations.

Like with Suárez, to investigate the basis of the Grotian *jus gentium* implies examining at least three related but autonomous aspects thereof: the subject of this law, its nature and the society to which it applies. These aspects correspond to the following questions "what does Grotius understand as 'people'?;" "how does the Grotian *jus gentium* manifest itself?;" and "what characterizes this Grotian *societas humani generis*?" This means studying, respectively, the theory of State, the formal source of a Positive (voluntary) Law that must not be mistaken for the formal source of Civil Law and the Grotian adaptation of the Stoic notion of moral unity of all men.

Finding the answer to each of these questions was more difficult than one may imagine. Unlike Suárez, strange as it may seem, the Dutch did not develop these topics at length. The Law of Nations was not a problem for Grotius; like every Positive Law, it seemed easy to prove its existence. Yet that rational law, the law that comes from nature and all its fruits, was more important.

Even so, Grotius offers us brief answers to each of these questions. The fact that he is so concise in his answers is proof of his loyalty to tradition. Still, in an author so eclectic as Grotius, "loyalty" and "tradition" are not univocal expressions.

6.2.1 The Theory of the State

For a long time Hugo Grotius was considered without any doubt a Modern author (perhaps even the first of them) not only because of his impious hypothesis, but also because of his Political Theory. He would have had developed several institutes that are characteristic of a Modern research on the subject: the social contract theory, the idea of sovereignty, the popular origin of power, State sovereignty (opposed to the sovereignty concentrated in the person of the Prince), and the right of resistance. These issues do appear in Grotius, but commentators often overlook some features that inevitably link him to the Scholastic or even to the Medieval universe as a whole. Grotius' study of politics is incidental to the study of the law of war. I shall address only those aspects of Grotius' theory that are of interest to the *jus gentium*; in other words, I will analyze whether the meaning of "people" in the term "Law of Nations" bears any resemblance to State.

Norberto Bobbio says that Hobbes not Grotius was the first Modern political writer because his naturalism differed from that of the Middle Ages. According to the Italian Jurist, Modern naturalism differs from the Medieval in the following aspects: men possess inherent rights which are prior to the organization of society and to the State; a state of nature, where equality reigns among men albeit in a precarious way precedes the civil status; and the passage from one state to another occurs through a social contract.[84] If these aspects define modern naturalism, then both Grotius and Suárez are Modern.

At the bottom of this reasoning lies a rather caricatured view of the Modern revolution, as if Modernity broke with tradition altogether and did not absorb anything of the preceding times. The authors prior to Hobbes would not have known the notion of a law emanating from the person and belonging to such person, and the *jus* would be reduced to a list of obligations. The duality of state of nature and civil state would be an unprecedented effort of reason to justify life in society, since society lacked legitimacy. Finally, the idea of social contract would forever bury the archaic ideology of the Aristotelian natural sociability.

However, in the field of Politics, Modernity seems to be less set by a break than by a gradual evolution. For a time, the new coexisted with the old. In late Scholastic authors, such as Suárez (and in philosophers heavily influenced by Scholasticism such as Grotius) the idea of social contract does not conflict with natural sociability. Even before the Spanish *maestros*, some writers have advocated that there would be a time governed by a primitive Natural Law, marked by the indivisibility of all things, prior to the advent of the civil state; yet this state, however precarious, did not entail something bad. Moreover, both Suárez and Grotius (the latter probably influenced by the former) conceived the idea of subjective rights.

Grotius delved into Politics as a lawyer, not as a political scientist. For him, this difference in approach has profound implications. "Thus one way of regarding the State is the community of rights and sovereignty, and the other is the mutual

[84] Bobbio (1991), pp. 134–137.

relation those that govern and those that are governed. This is the politician's business, and that the lawyer's (...)."[85] In order to keep himself within the sphere of Jurisprudence, Grotius spurns all the problems arising from the tension between rulers and subjects. Therefore, the author advocates no true theory of the right of resistance, as Suárez did. The Dutch is simply concerned with the origin of civil power, its structure, its functions, and the State's normative organization.

The first political theme that Grotius addresses in the **De Jure Belli ac Pacis** is civil power and consists of a sort of "moral right to govern a State."[86] Therefore, the power to command is a perfect *jus*, a mix between the *facultas* of the gender *potestas* and the *facultas* of the type *dominium*, since it is a right over persons and things. As seen in chapter IV, the *potestas* is divided into power over an individual or freedom (*libertas*), over one's home (*patria potestas*), or over slaves (*domenica potestas*). Those who hold the power to command require their orders to be obeyed; thus, if this right does not correspond to a freedom, then no other options are left and Grotius must identify the sovereign authority with the figure of the father over his children and/or the master over his slaves. The author prefers not to choose. The *facultas eminens* of the sovereign "has under his tutelage the powers of his father and his master."[87] In this regard, Grotius does not exceed the Medieval political ideas according to which the State was a broader parental authority and tyranny was accepted.

Grotius counterbalances the obsolescence of this definition with the substance of civil power. The king may govern a State by its own person or by representation—when magistrates and other public agents such as ambassadors exercise power. By acting in his own name, the sovereign dedicates his time to resolve general or specific businesses. In the first case, he is concerned with enacting or revoking laws (regarding temporal and spiritual matters). Specific businesses may be public or private. The former consists of actions directed to the common good: the decision to wage a war or to sign peace, tax collection, etc., whereas the latter involves settling disputes between his subjects.[88]

The contemporary reader may be surprised with the presence of the Legislative, Executive, and Judiciary branches of government in Grotius. Notwithstanding, it seems somewhat anachronistic to assume that the author, centuries before Montesquieu, would have conceived a theory of separation of powers. In fact, he does not envisage any mechanism of power control nor any work division: all these functions indistinctively belong to the person of the sovereign. Here, Grotius is not pioneering.

---

[85] "*Ita civitatis species una est, consociatio juris atque imperii; altera, relatio partium inter se earum quae regunt, et quae reguntur. Hanc spectat Politicus, illam Iurisconsultus* (...)" (**DJBP**. II, 9, 8, 2).

[86] "*Facultas ergo moralis civitatem gubernandi*" (**DJBP**. I, 3, 6, 1).

[87] "*Sic regia postestas sub se habet et patriam et dominicam potestatem*" (**DJBP**. I, 1, 6).

[88] **DJBP**. I, 3, 6, 2.

Grotius did not realize the difference in nature between the power of the father or the lord and that of the prince. Nonetheless, how Grotius conceives this old idea is new. Power is not legitimized by an immemorial tradition but by the free will of men. Soon after the creation of the world, God gave to all mankind a general right over all things which belonged to all indistinctively. "From hence it was, that every man converted what he would to his own use, and consumed whatever was to be consumed; and such a use of the right common to all men did at that time supply the place of property, for no man could justly take from another what he had thus first taken to himself."[89] Besides the common property, there was another birth right of men, the *libertas*. But Grotius advises that this initial state was precarious; it could have subsisted only if society did not become too complex or if all men lived in the most perfect practice of Charity.

In some passages of his work, Grotius refers to this idyllic stage of mankind as "state of nature." Despite the similarities, one must refrain from associating this primordial Grotian scenario with the Hobbesian state of nature. Both share only the fact that they were conceived as having existed prior to the institution of Civil Laws. Indeed, when writing about who had the right to decide on the succession to the throne (whether it was the king, the magistrates or the people), Grotius explains that the king cannot appoint his successor because such right precedes his jurisdiction and remains in the *status naturalis*.[90]

Still, there is much more to this Grotian state of nature than a mere opposition to the civil state. Here, Grotius reveals his great vocation: this state of nature is a category that belongs to both Theology and Law. In analyzing the validity of the marriage between two slaves or between a free man and a slave woman, Grotius opposes the *statu naturae* to the *statu legis Christianae*.[91] The Grotian state of nature designates a moment during which mankind is governed only by the primary Natural Law, before any voluntary law, whether Civil Law, the Law of Nations, or even the voluntary Divine Law.

The Grotian state of nature has more similarities with Suárez's than with Hobbes'. It does not designate a state of war of everyone against all, for sociability is innate to men. Before Civil Laws, men contracted nuptials and entered into contracts for the purchase and sale of goods.[92] This type of interaction reveals a union among humans stricter than the Hobbesian state of nature. The families already existed and practiced legal businesses.

However, if this state of nature is prior to any human institution, then there is not yet what Suárez calls (and Grotius accepts, as seen in chapter IV) "Dominative Natural Law": a natural obligation due after the introduction of a positive precept.

---

[89]"*Hinc factum ut statim quisque hominum ad suos usus arripere posset quod vellet, et quae consumi poterant consumere. Ac talis usus universalis juris erat tum vice proprietatis. Nam quod quisque sic arripuerat, id ei eripere alter nisi per injuriam non poterat.*" (**DJBP**. II, 2, 2, 1).

[90]**DJBP**. II, 7, 27, 1.

[91]**DJBP**. II, 5, 15, 2.

[92]**DJBP**. II, 2, 20 and 21, 1.

This means that there was no private property. However, at a given moment, sin, ambition, and the simple search for a more comfortable life destroyed this natural order. Therefore, when the community of goods became bothersome, men began to take things only for themselves, to the exclusion of all others. In order to prevent others from appropriating that which one had already taken for himself, it was necessary to have an express (the division of common assets) or implied (occupation) agreement thereon.[93]

This view does not imply a covenant for life in society. Private ownership was not introduced by a collective single act, but gradually and naturally. As mentioned above, common property was intended for everyone's use. However, use is always individual. And for some goods, such as food, use causes the destruction of the goods or prevents others from further using them. Therefore, in some goods, there is no way to separate use from domain. For the common enjoyment of these goods, men needed to institute private property.[94]

Although there was no political organization (and therefore no Civil Law), men enjoyed more complex relationships than those in the state of nature. The external "mine" and "yours" came before the advent of the State without needing to resort to Civil Law or to breach Natural Law. Moreover, since Natural Law establishes common property but does not prohibit private ownership (and even safeguards it, ever since it came into existence), man in the primitive state enjoys freedom, but may dispose of it.

> For when men are said to be by nature in a state of freedom, by nature is to be understood the right of nature, since it is antecedent to all human acts to the contrary; and the freedom there meant is an exemption from slavery and not an absolute incompatibility with slavery, that is, no man naturally is a slave, but no man has a right never to become such, for in this sense no body living is free (…)[95]

Only in the primitive state are men naturally born free. Yet, freedom is a disposable right, alienable by men. Men acquire rights over others by birth, by consent, or even due to a crime.[96] Therefore, slaves are men who were born as such, or that have consented to it or received a punishment of a court ruling or became prisoners in a just war.

However, even men who were born slaves descended from free men who, by their own will, lost their freedom. The element of "will" is essential. Grotius thus defines the State as a "perfect union of free men to enjoy the protection of the laws

---

[93]**DJBP**. II, 2, 2, 5.

[94]**ML**. *Caput* V, p. 18.

[95]"*Nam libertas cum natura competere hominibus aut populis dicitur, id intelligendum est de jure naturae praecedente factum omne humanum, et de libertate, non de ea quae est, hoc est ut natura quis servus non sit, non ut jus habeat ne unquam serviat*" (**DJBP**. II, 22, 11).

[96]**DJBP**. II, 5, 1.

and their common use."[97] Directly or indirectly, men agreed to create a State in order to enjoy life together. A State may also be formed by conquering another people; yet, ultimately, its power comes from a consent.

Except for the mention of the word "association," Grotius does not explain how a State emerges. At one point, the author employs the term "covenant,"[98] but in reference to a manner of instituting civil power. The other forms correspond to a conquest in a just war and to the spontaneous submission of a foreigner to the empire of another sovereign.[99] Although existent in Grotius, the idea of a social contract does not play a key role in the foundation of political power. Social contract merely represents one form of binding the subject to the State. The concept of the association of wills instead plays a central role. Human will has propelled the changes to the primordial state of nature. Since sociability is inherent to man, there was no rupture in the transition; there is a real *continuum* between isolated individuals and social groups, such as families and States. In a passage of the book, the author accepts the famous and ancient Aristotelian conception of the State as a gathering of families.[100]

Unlike Modern contractualists who use the figure of the contract less to describe a historical situation and more to justify the authority of the State, Grotius seeks to explain the historical origin of political organization. The author is not concerned with investigating the legitimacy of power; he simply seeks to understand it. In this sense, Grotius is much more "realistic" than the Moderns, but his Political Theory does not escape the Medieval domain.

In fact, Grotius' most important political concern was the *monarcomachi*, a group of pamphleteers, mainly of French origin, who supported tyrannicide and sought to restrict the power of the sovereign. Peter Borschberg says that Grotius owned a copy of the **Vindiciae contra tyrannus** by a writer named Stephanus Junius Brutus, a very popular pamphlet, well publicized at the time. Grotius was concerned with those who advocated Netherlands' war of independence against Spain based on this author, for they would be slandering a just cause.[101] It should not seem strange the fact that Grotius takes a long time in Chapter III of Book I (eighth paragraph) disputing those who believed in the popular source of power.

---

[97]"*Est autem civitas coetus perfectus liberorum hominum, juris fruendi et communis utilitatis causa sociatus.*" (**DJBP**. I, 1, 14, 1). It is importante to emphazise that the notion of "perfect community" brings the Grotian theory of the State closer to the Scholastic cultural universe. However, for an eclectic thinker such as Grotius, one influence is not enough. Del Vecchio discovered how Grotius' definition resembled that of his favorite ancient source, Cicero. In **República**. L, 1, 25, 39: "*Est igitur (...) res publica res populi, populus autem non omnis hominum coetus quoquo modo congregatus, sed coetus multitudinis juris consensu et utilitatis communione sociatus.*" (Del Vecchio, 1962, p. 261). This is another example of eclectic coincidence in Grotius.

[98]**DJBP**. II, 5, 24, 1.

[99]**DJBP**. I, 3, 8, 3-6.

[100]**DJBP**. II, 5, 23.

[101]Borschberg (2006), p. 10.

The initial sovereignty of the people existed only in the state of primitive nature. After that, the notion of popular sovereignty could instigate revolutionary theories such as tyrannicide.

For that reason, Grotius does not believe in the existence of a right of resistance against the orders of the State. Granted, everyone possessed a subjective right to protect their own lives and belongings; however, as seen in chapter III, the eminent domain of the sovereign power exceeds in force the ordinary domain that individuals have over their own lives and property. Grotius advocates a conservative approach, even if the prince were to enact unfair commands, contrary to Natural Law. Between peace and freedom, the author prefers the former: it is better to live as a slave than to die as a free man.[102] In fact, Grotius' position is based on the common good. The individual good cannot override the common good. In this case, the natural sociability of man justifies the individual liberticide.

Notwithstanding, the sovereign does not exercise an unlimited power: he must comply with the requirements of Natural, Civil Law, the Law of Nations, and the Divine Law. The king cannot violate an individual right, nor command a manifestly wrong or absurd behavior.[103] Yet the subjects cannot defend themselves against the sovereign.

Grounding civil power in the social contract theory does not imply necessarily a pact of submission. The substance of the social contract may vary. There is no natural form of government for Grotius. As a good jurist, he knows that the government depends on the terms and conditions of the social contract. There is a broad spectrum of possibilities, once one accepts that a people may agree to its own enslavement.

Many commentators see Grotius as a supporter of absolutism, since he disputed the right of resistance and popular sovereignty and supported the absolute loss of the *status libertatis*. However, the **De Jure Belli ac Pacis** has the "face of Janus, and his two mouths speak the language both of absolutism and freedom."[104] Grotius sought to establish the principles of a civilian power applicable to all kinds of States. There are absolutist, aristocratic, and democratic nations, so a universal system should encompass them all. The author does not favor any regime; the form of government depends on the constitutional arrangements set forth in the social contract for the exercise of sovereignty. There are States in which an assembly dictates the laws that bind the king; in others, the sovereign is restricted only by his own promises. There may also be a temporary dictator, like in Rome. A people may safeguard certain rights for itself when the kingdom is established so that its king exercises power in a rather limited shape. Beyond all these examples, there are several forms of mixed constitutions.[105]

---

[102]**DJBP**. II, 24, 6, 1-2.

[103]**DJBP**. II, 14, 8.

[104]Tuck (1979), p. 79.

[105]**DJBP**. I, 3, 8.

In accordance with nature, every man may protect his own rights; for that he has hands.[106] But this natural right of resistance may be restricted by Civil Law. On behalf of the common good, the individual good should be sacrificed. Yet, this right of resistance resurfaces only under extreme circumstances. In the state of necessity, even divine laws hold unspoken exceptions—exceptions which, in fact, are nothing if not the very precept which, for the sake of brevity, was not enunciated in full. This idea reflects the application of the good faith principle in interpreting agreements or, as some would say,[107] an "interpretive charity." In principle, all rights may be waived (up to total submission), but one should always presume that did not occur. Waiving them would not correspond to the will of the original parties

> I do not deny that some acts of courage may be commanded by a human law, in spite of the evident hazard of death. Such is the case of a soldier not to abandon his post; but it is not easily to imagine that such was the intention of the legislator and it is very probable that men have not received so extensive a power over themselves or others, except in cases where extreme necessity requires it. For all human laws are, and ought to be so enacted, as that there should be some allowance for human frailty. But this law (of which we now treat) seems to depend upon the intention of those who first entered into civil society, from whom the power of sovereigns is originally derived. Suppose then they had been asked whether they pretended to impose on all citizens the hard necessity of dying, rather than to take up arms in any case, to defend themselves against higher powers; I do not know whether they would have answered in the affirmative: on the contrary, it may be presumed they would have declared that one ought not to bear with every thing, unless resistance would infallibly occasion great disturbance within the state or prove the destruction of many innocents. For what charity recommends in such a case to be done, may, I doubt not, be prescribed by a human law.[108]

As stated above, there is no theory of civil disobedience in Grotius. These statements are scattered throughout the **De Jure Belli ac Pacis**. Still, they are enough to stress the difference between Grotius and Suárez. Suárez, much closer to the *monarcomachi* than Grotius (because of the influence of Juan de Mariana) supports popular sovereignty and regicide. But Grotius alternates between advocating a revolutionary and a passive stance. Unlike the Moderns who worried about the stability of power (Hobbes) or the freedom of the individuals (Locke)—issues that impregnated all classical liberal revolutions—Grotius is not concerned with such themes. As a result of the overall misperception regarding the Grotian legacy, is seems tempting to attribute to Grotius a role in a controversial discussion that

---

[106]**DJBP**. I, 5, 1.

[107]Tuck (1979), p. 80.

[108]"*Non nego a lege etiam humana quosdam virtutis actus posse praecepi, sub certo morris periculo, ut de statione non deferenda; sed nec temere ea voluntas legem condentis fuisse intelligitur, neque videntur homines in se, et alios tantum jus acepisse, nisi quatenus summa necessitas id exigat. Ferri enim legis ab hominibus solent et debent cum sensu humanae imbecillitatis.* (…) *Hi vero si interrogarentur an velint omnibus hoc onus imponere, ut mori praeoptent, quam ullo casu vim superiorum armis arcere, nescio an velle se sint responsuri, nisi forte cum hoc additamento, si resisit nequeat, nisi cum maxima reipublicae perturbatione, aut exitio plurimorum innocentium. Quod enim tali circusntantia caritas commendaret, id in legem quoque humanam deduci posse non dubito.*" (**DJBP**. I, 4, 7, 2).

lasted two centuries. That is why some commentators[109] even come as close as finding in Grotius, not without caution, the onset of a right to intervene. Nevertheless, here, Grotius belongs to an earlier time, a simpler time, when the king, albeit feared, was also loved and would never offend the divine plan or mistreat his subjects. The author's waivering position in relation to freedom and tyranny is a result of his Medieval belief in the naturalness of power and its benign nature.

Yet, Grotius is not so old as to accept the imperial monism. He would have even qualified this thesis as ridiculous, had not Bartolo, "the prince of the jurists," supported it.[110] In addition to not being advantageous (one government for so many men and so many lands), the right of the Roman Emperor no longer endured in the face of so many just wars and treaties on the subject (which generated just titles) after the dissolution of the Roman Empire. The author also disputes the Pontifical version of this thesis with the same arguments. For Grotius, the kingdom of God is not of this world. Moreover, the bishops, or the Pope, could not impose their authority by coercion but only by persuasion.[111]

Hence, Grotius treads a narrow path. He is Modern enough to dispute the more traditional of all political conceptions of the Middle Age, but still cannot (or refuses to) perceive the tension between freedom and authority that already marked some political writers of his time and also those of the following years. In this regard, Suárez appears more Modern than Grotius.

However, both authors do not develop the Modern notion of sovereignty. As seen, Suárez comes very close with his idea of "perfect community," which consists of a mystical body that exceeds its parts in rights. The authority of the perfect community does not stem from individuals, but from the association itself. The source of power in Suárez is popular, but does not lie in the individual rights: only the assembly of people has jurisdiction.

In turn, Grotius does not seem to find the concept of sovereignty useful, since both men and States enjoy the same rights, as reflected in this passage from the **De Jure Praedae**:

> (…) It seems clear that the causes of punishment are natural and derive from that precept which we call the first law. Even so, the power to punish would not be a power that belongs essentially to the State? Not at all! Rather, as every power of the magistrate comes from the State, the power of the State comes from individuals (…). Therefore, since it is not possible to transfer something that it has never owned, it is clear that the right to punish was exercised by private individuals before the State. (…)[112]

---

[109]Vincent (2002), p. 241 et seq.

[110]**DJBP**. II, 22, 13, 1.

[111]**DJBP**. II, 22, 14, 1-3.

[112]"*Ex his apparet puniendi causas esse naturales et ex ea lege procedere, quam nos primam descripsimus. Quid ergo, nonne puniendi potestas reipublicae propria est? Imo vero ut a republica ad magistratum, ita ad rempublicam jus omne a singulis devenit (...). Quare cum transferre nemo possit, quod non habuit, jus illud antiquius penes privatos fuisse quam penes rempublicam necesse videtur.*" (**DJPC**, p. 91).

However, in the **De Jure Belli ac Pacis**, Grotius allots a prerogative solely to sovereign entities: the solemn war. Only the sovereign States may take part in an agreement of *jus gentium* enabling some effects of bilateral justice. Therefore, "peoples" devoid of sovereignty cannot create the authentic Law of Nations. During the gap between his works of youth and maturity, Grotius seems to have elaborated on his concept of sovereignty.

Indeed, Grotius addressed the issue of sovereignty between 1605 and 1625. He devoted an important study thereto, the **De Imperio Summarum Potestatum circa Sacra**. At the beginning of this book, the author defines sovereignty as the supreme organ, the *summus magistratus*, which may be an individual or a collegiate body that governs a people. It is a unique and exclusive power, inferior only to God, but not abstract. The holder of the *summa potestas* is not an abstract collectivity called State, but a single person, a king, or an assembly of men.[113]

In the **De Jure Belli ac Pacis**, sovereignty becomes a *facultas*, the "moral right to govern a State," as described above. Indeed, although it does not encompass a greater amount of rights, the eminent *facultas* surpasses the ordinary *facultas* in strength. Thus, the State possesses rights that are stronger than those of the individuals.

At first glance, Grotius seems to have developed the idea of State sovereignty. "Let us then see what is the object of this supreme power. It is either common or proper: such as the body is the common object of sight and the eye the proper; so the common object of supreme power is the State; which I have before called a perfect society of men." And then: "the State then is, in the sense I have just mentioned, the common object of sovereignty. The proper object is one or more persons, according to the laws and customs of each nation."[114] This difference between common and proper object seems to demonstrate that the author already attempted to dissociate sovereignty from the person of the ruler to that of the State.

However, much like in his previous works, despite these statements, the title of the sovereignty does not yet belong to the State, but to certain people. To Haggenmacher, despite his apparent Modernity, Grotius did not conceive the concept of State sovereignty. Grotius places his analysis of the *summa potestas* immediately after the *civilis potestas*; between them, there is no contradiction, only a relation of genus and specie, from a perspective that today would be perceived as "constitutional." The civil power designates the public authority as a whole and the supreme power encompasses only the most "decisive" part of that public authority, the supreme organ, whose command is not subject to appeal. Grotius' whole problem boils down to using this distinction to justify the possibility of several

---

[113]Grotius, Hugo. **Traité du Pouvoir du Magistrat Politique sur les choses sacrées**. Trad. Lescalopier de Nourar. Londres: s/n, 1751, p. 2.

[114]"*Haec ergo summa potestas, quod subjectum habeat videamus. Subjectum aliud est commune, aliud proprium: ut visus subjectum commune est corpus, proprium oculos. ita summae potestatis subjectum commune est civitas, quam perfectum coetum esse supra diximus.*" and "*Subjectum ergo commune summae potestatis esto civitas, ita ut jam diximus intellecta. Subjectum proprium est persona uma pluresve, pro cujusque gentis legibus ac moribus*" (**DJBP**. I, 3, 7, 1 and 3).

people being subject to only one sovereign. Since there may be several inferior magistrates, it is necessary to find out in which one rests the supreme power. In fact, the sovereignty of the State begins to take shape in the notion of common object, but Grotius does not elaborate more. In all other passages in which Grotius addresses the *summa potestas*, he refers to the proper object. The common object is nothing more than a reflex.[115]

Grotius' view does not surpass national law, the Constitutional Law. The author does not develop the idea of independence among several States. He sought only to find, within the State, that organ which holds the ultimate power. Grotius built a paradoxical situation: the Law of Nations is created solely by the confluence of wills of sovereign entities, but does not apply in a scenario of independent States. The subjects of the Grotian *jus gentium* are sovereign peoples, but non-sovereign peoples should also comply with it. In Grotius, "Peoples" do not mean an abstract collectivity called "State," but "persons," "men" in the plural. Although valid for almost all men, almost all peoples, the Grotian Law of Nations stems from a very special kind of people: the sovereign ones.

6.2.2 The Positivity and the Formal Source of the Law of Nations

The **De Jure Praedae** presents two categories of the *jus gentium*: the *primarium jus gentium* (also known as *jus naturae secundarium*) and the *secundarium jus gentium*. In this work, Grotius created an axiomatic–deductive structure according to which every rule derives from a specific will. The first *jus* emanates from the common will of all men, but only to the extent that such will represents a common effect of a universal and singular cause: the rational and social nature of men. The fact that different men from different places have the same judgment concerning what is right and wrong is not a coincidence. All of them reach the same conclusion because they share the same nature. As seen in chapter IV, for this reason some commentators soften the voluntarist aspect of Grotius' work of youth. Ultimately, the Secondary Natural Law, or the Primary Law of Nations, stems from human nature.

Therefore, albeit voluntary, the *jus gentium primarium* cannot be characterized as Positive Law. The common will of all men is more an effect than a cause of this law. But Grotius only clarifies this in the **De Jure Belli ac Pacis**; still, in 1605, the author seemed uncomfortable with the idea that this first *jus gentium* would originate from a human lawmaker: "Cicero said that the informative principle of this

[115]Haggenmacher (1983), pp. 540–541. It is worth pointing out that the common and proper objects correspond to the Scholastic distiction between the universal and the singular. See chapter III.

right is the right reason proceeded from gods' will."[116] The voluntarist tone of the work hinders some distinctions (such as, for instance, the difference between the Primary Natural Law and the Voluntary Divine Law), even those pertaining to the two categories of the Law of Nations.

Nevertheless, there is a significant difference between the Primary and the Secondary Law of Nations. The *jus gentium secundarium* derives from the common will of the States: "the law is what the States have indicated as their will."[117] There seems be no doubt regarding the positivity of this law. However, Grotius believes that the *jus gentium secundarium* is a "mixed" law, part Primary Law of Nations and part Civil Law. The author gives some examples of this *jus*: the inviolability of the ambassadors, matters related to the burial of the dead and other "similar institutes."

In fact, Grotius' examples confuse more than enlighten the reader. What do the inviolability of the ambassadors and the burial of the dead have in common to be placed within the same category? Besides, the hybrid nature of the *jus gentium secundarium* could raise several doubts regarding the positivity of this law. Would it be a law which rules are natural in origin but become valid after the consent of the States? This would mean that the *jus gentium* does not stem from utility like the rest of Positive Law, but from necessity; hence, the *jus gentium* would address good and evil behaviors in themselves. However, these critics on the author's lack of clarity are not accurate, for they presuppose an *ex post* reading that looks for elements of contemporary International Law in his Law of Nations. Grotius would have needed to infuse more "internationality" in his *jus gentium* in order to reduce its aloofness, but that was not his intention.

In order to find out Grotius' purpose regarding the "international" character of the Law of Nations, it is crucial to first unveil the mystery of the positivity of the Secondary Law of Nations. In the **De Jure Belli ac Pacis**, this issue is no longer a problem, since he associates Positive Law with voluntary law. However, in the **De Jure Praedae**, all species of the *jus* are voluntary.

The uncertainty seems to disappear with the **Nova Declaratio** that Grotius inserts in the form of a separate sheet to the manuscript of this work. In it, he divides the *jus gentium secundarium* into two classes. One has the strength of a pact between the peoples ("*pacti vim habent inter respublicas*"). The other does not have as much authority and Grotius prefers to label it as a custom, not as Law ("*receptae potius consuetudinis nomine, quam juris appellaverim*"). That is the case of slavery, of some types of contracts and of the law of succession. These provisions appear in all or almost all of nations, in an isolated way, as a fruit of mutual imitation or mere coincidence, in accordance with the individual interests of each State. Therefore, each State can revoke these rules given that they do not derive of a mutual agreement, because they derive from the particular will of the States, from their

---

[116] "(...) *cujus legem Cicero nihil aliud esse ait, nisi rectam et a numine Deorum tractam rationem*" (**DJPC**, p. 12).

[117] "(...) *quicquid pmnes republicae significarunt se velle id in omnes ius est*" (**DJPC**, p. 26).

Civil Law, pursuant to Grotius' eighth rule. After establishing this difference, the author can argue that the main precept of the true *jus gentium* consisted of the *lex duodecima*: "no State, nor its citizen, may exercise its own right against another State, or its citizen, except through a legal procedure."[118] Both divisions refer to institutes from Positive Law.

The difference between the improper Law of Nations (not enunciated in the rule) and the authentic Law of Nations resembles the difference enunciated by Suárez between the *jus gentium per similitudinem* and the *jus gentium propiissime dictum*. In light of so many similarities, Jan Kosters defended the idea that Suárez exerted influence over Grotius on this issue. However, as one would expect, there is no reference to Suárez. Besides, the **De Jure Praedae** was published in 1605, while the **De Legibus** was published in 1612 (which could invalidate this thesis), but the **Nova Declaratio** was written after the original version. The graphological studies were not conclusive and the insertion could have taken place at any time.[119]

Haggenmacher disputes this Suarezian influence. He believes that Grotius added the two amendments (sheets 12'a and a sentence at the end of 12') at the same time he wrote his work, although they do not appear in the first edition. They evidence a progressive comprehension of the Law of Nations acquired in the course of writing the subsequent chapters of the book.[120] The two modifications reflect an internal and dynamic evolution of Grotius' system, rather than an external influence thereon.

It is possible thus to identify three distinct stages of Grotius' concept of *jus gentium* in the **De Jure Praedae**. In the original version, Grotius offers us only the notion of a mixed law, halfway between Natural and Civil Law, the enunciation of the eighth rule and examples such as the inviolability of ambassadors and the right of burial. After that, Grotius proclaims in sheet 13 his twelfth law—which is the most important precept of this *jus gentium secundarium*. The author has not called this mixed law the Secondary Law of Nations yet. He only contends that there exists a mixed law.

The amendments attempt to establish the validity not of a whole set of legal rules, but of one especial rule—the individual's and State's obligation to not exercise their rights by their own hands, but through a judiciary power. At the margin of the excerpts, the author quotes the **Semestria** by Petrus Faber. Grotius extracted from him even the two already referred examples of *jus gentium secundarium*. In this quote, Faber analyzes the legal bases of the declarations of war, a *sine qua non* condition for this judicial procedure named war, announced by the twelfth law. Furthermore, in Faber as in Gentili, the Law of Nations may be mistaken for Natural Law, but its provisions undertake a conventional and positive form. Therefore, the expression "mixed law" need to be comprehended in its literal

[118]"*Ne respublica neu civis in alteram rempublicam alteriusve civem jus suum nisi judicio exsequatur*" (**DJPC**, p. 27; sheets 12'a and 12').

[119]Kosters (1925), p. 43.

[120]Haggenmacher (1983), p. 361.

meaning: it means a mixture of the two previous orders, the Secondary Natural Law and Civil Law, rather than an autonomous legal system.[121] Grotius' main focus is not on the Secondary Law of Nations, but on a command prescribing a necessary obligation for war to be regarded as a judicial procedure.

In the second stage of his writing, Grotius adds the following sentence, right after mentioning the mixed law: "that is correctly and properly called Secondary Law of Nations."[122] At the margin of the page, he writes in capital letter "JUS GENTIUM SECUNDARIUM" and inserts a reference to the **Controversiae** of Vázquez. By naming the mixture, he thinks it forms something autonomous from its constituents. Hence, he starts to believe in the existence of a new source of the law of war, different from the previous ones.

This designation is unexpected: there is no other mark or anything else preparing the reader to this new law. Haggenmacher believes that this change came as a result of Grotius reading Vázquez's work, which identifies the *jus naturae secundarium* with the *jus gentium primarium*. This seems to not have any relation to the excerpt, but the ink that was used to write the Secondary Law of Nations matches the one that, a few pages before, Grotius used to write JUS NATURAE and the JUS GENTIUM PRIMARIUM, also at the margins of the page. The notes at the margins referring to the main sources of the law of were made under Vásquez's influence. And there is more. Up to the eighth chapter of the **De Jure Praedae**, Grotius does not distinguish among the institutes of the *jus gentium* those that proceed from the primary *jus gentium* from those that proceed from the secondary *jus gentium*. Only in the 53th sheet (which corresponds to the page 119 of the Hamaker's edition) does the author explore this difference. In this excerpt, there is also a reference to the **Controversiae** and another to the **Nova Declaratio**.[123]

In chapter eight, Grotius addresses the just ways of conducting a war. In this passage, the author introduces a second corollary according to which the right of booty and prize in regard to nonvoluntary agents (soldiers) may be just for both combatants, if the order received was not manifestly against reason.[124] In other words, Grotius affirms that there exists bilateral effects of justice. Like in his work of maturity, this kind of precept could only appear as a result of the *jus gentium secundarium*. Although without the clarity of twenty years later, Grotius realizes the bilateral effects of justice cannot fit into a narrower notion of law and justice. Therefore, the bilaterality could not derive from the Primary Law of Nations, also called Secondary Natural Law, because this one is based on the rational nature (albeit being expressed by the common will of all men). It could only be part of Positive Law, which does not address good and evil actions in themselves. But there are not many options. If such permission does not stem from Natural Law and, due to its cross-border aspect, it cannot come from Civil Law either, then it must

[121] Haggenmacher (1983), p. 363.

[122] "(...) *sive jus gentium quod recte ac proprie secundarium dicitur*" (**DJPC**, p. 26; sheet 12').

[123] Haggenmacher (1983), p. 366.

[124] **DJPC**, p. 119.

derive from a Positive Law that is able to extend across the same spatial validity of Natural Law. It is at this moment that Grotius, with no remarkable influence of Suárez, surpasses the Roman conception of *jus gentium.*

In page 53 (and even prior to that), Grotius establishes the bilateral right of prize and booty based on a tacit agreement among States. Indeed, it resembles the solemn war of the **De Jure Belli ac Pacis**, although there is no difference in the justice of private and public wars in Grotius' work of youth. This positive *jus gentium* results from a *tacitus consensus civitatum.*

Yet this agreement can justify possession during the conflict, but once the war comes to an end, Grotius says that the goods should return to their true owners pursuant to the Primary Law of Nations. It is only possible to acquire irrevocable ownership of a good by force of a statutory period of limitation, an institute of Positive and Civil Law by excellence. Curiously, this provision appears in all internal legal systems; for the common good of the State, the lapse of time always turn permanent those acquisitions that were once precarious. Therefore, one may already envisage at this second stage two classes of the Secondary Law of Nations: a *jus inter gentes* and a *jus intra gentes.*[125]

Grotius will separate these two classes at the third stage of his writing, in which he alternates between one and the other. Except for this passage, the author only displays the same clarity in chapter X, which focuses on the distribution of the seized prize. In page 59 of the manuscript (page 157 of the Hamaker's edition), Grotius asserts that the booty is the most appropriate way to pay a subject in consideration for his military services. This way, the enemy becomes poorer while the soldier has one more reason to fight. Subordinates may adjudicate movable goods, but immovable goods belong to the State, by force of a generally accepted custom.

> This principle does not result from what we call Primary Law of Nations, but from the kind Positive Law that is composed in its major part by customs. Furthermore, this principle is not based on a general agreement that binds many States, but it is based on a coincidence, which can be denied by each country when it is considered convenient to do so.[126]

Indeed, as Grotius sets the Primary Law of Nations aside, the right of seizing immovable assets could only be part of the Secondary Law of Nations. And it is based on a custom, not on an agreement among States and so each nation may revoke it at will.

In this passage, Grotius mentions the two elements that characterize the two classes of the Secondary Law of Nations: the custom and the general agreement. At first glance, he seems to base this entire law on customs. However, this is just an impression. In fact, Grotius presented the origins of each type of *jus gentium* before excluding one of them, indicating that the distinction between these two classes was

---

[125]Haggenmacher (1983), p. 370.

[126]"*Id enim non ex primario ut diximus gentium jure procedit, sed ex jure positivo, cujus pars magna sunt consuetudines. Deinde non ex condicto venit, ut respublicas obliget, sed quasi fortuito consensu, a quo singulis populis, ubi ita videtur, recedere liberum est*" (**DJPC**, p. 157).

already sufficiently evidenced, at least in his mind. According to Haggenmacher, it was at this stage that those two pages were included (53'a and 53'a,' which, in the Hamaker edition, correspond, respectively, to pages 121 and 122), following up on the subject of the bilateral acquisition of goods by subordinates. At the end of the initial text, without the included pages and just before introducing the third corollary, Grotius asserts that this right of acquisition results from the "Law of Nations, not in its natural stage, but in its positive one."[127] The added text attempts to prepare the reader for this assertive. Grotius abandons the frugality of the **De Jure Praedae** (according to which both private and public wars are legitimate) and explains that only the soldiers of an external public war (civil wars are excluded then) may acquire permanently the properties that were seized during the conflict. The exclusion of civil wars is due to the fact that these wars involve an authority that is not public and thus could not have taken part in the tacit agreement among States allowing such practice. Therefore, in this passage, the consensus among States is the source of the Secondary Law of Nations; in another passage dated of this same period, the origin is found in customs, as Grotius sets aside the tacit agreement.[128]

There is no doubt that Grotius already perceived two categories of the same law, based on two different grounds. When he expressly excludes the right of bilateral acquisition of the seized goods on a permanent basis by soldiers of civil wars, he stresses that the agreement is made *inter gentes* and not *intra gentes*. On the other hand, the common custom is a result of a coincidence and may thus be revoked by each nation. The joint analysis of these two passages allows the reader to understand that this Positive Law of Nations is applied between the States (through a tacit agreement), but also permeates all nations (as a generalized custom).

In these passages, as well as in the *prolegomena*, Grotius does not hide his disdain for custom. Customs seem to lack the strength of a true *lex*. Indeed, in his youth, he attempted to diminish the role of custom, a nonlegal source of *jus* associated with the Middle Ages. At the beginning of the **Mare Liberum**, Grotius stresses this problem:

> It is about an ancient and detestable illusion with which a lot of men, especially the ones that have more influence because of their wealth and power, convince themselves (or try to do so, as I prefer to believe) that justice and injustice are different not because of their own nature, but, in some way, only because of opinion and customs.[129]

As the central power was eroded, the Middle Ages knew the enactment of very few laws. The Law was mostly composed of customary precepts, which were associated with a Germanic comprehension of the juridical phenomenon (that was

---

[127]"(...) *ex jure gentium, non illo naturali, sed positivo*" (**DJPC**, p. 122).

[128]Haggenmacher (1983), p. 376.

[129]"*Error est non minus vetus quam pestilens, quo multi mortales, ii autem maxime, qui plurimum vi ataque opibus valent, persuadent sibi, aut, quod verius puto, persuadere conantur, justum atque injustum non suapte natura, sed hominum inani quadam opinione, atque consuetudine distingui.*" (**ML**. *Ad Principes Populosque Líberos Orbis Christiani*, p. 10).

deemed less evolved than the Roman). Grotius addresses the custom in chapter VII of **Mare Liberum** along with the acquisite prescription and does not distinguish them with clarity. By establishing a sort of equivalence between the two, the author treats custom less as a source of law and more as an institute that belongs to Civil Law.[130]

At this point, one may begin to see the differences between the first Grotian conception of *jus gentium* and the Suárez's concept. As seen in the last chapter, Suárez is one of the few Scholastics to value extralegal modalities of law and to carefully distinguish custom from acquisite prescription. In addition, the custom is the formal source of his entire concept of *jus gentium*, there comprised the *jus gentium inter gentes* and the *jus gentium intra gentes* both. Because of the relative effect of treaties, Suárez did not believe that they could create a real "international legislation" and thus the *mores omnium nationum* fulfilled this role. However, Grotius does not trust the normative power of the custom and considers it the source of a non-authentic Law of Nations only.

Furthermore, each author employs different examples to corroborate their understanding. To Suárez, the *ius gentium propiissime dictum* includes commercial agreements, the law of war, peace treaties, truces, and the ambassadors' inviolability; and the *ius gentium per similitudinem* encompasses religious cults and a good part of Isidore's list: the occupation of territories, the building of houses, the fortification, the use of money, and the *postliminium.* In Grotius, the *authentic jus gentium* encompasses the subordinates' right of bilateral war, the declaration of war, the ambassadors' inviolability, and the right of burial, whereas the false *jus gentium* would encompass the rights of succession, some types of contracts and slavery. There are too many differences between the two theologians to consider that one influenced the other. It is more probable that Grotius and Suárez reached similar conclusions due to the internal dynamics of their respective reasoning.

Nevertheless, Grotius' conception of the Law of Nations did not stay static. Not long after 1605, the author would promote a change so delicate that would go unnoticed by most of commentators,[131] but is of utmost importance once he revised his previous opinion. He introduces this change around 1613–14 in a work entitled the **Defensio Capitis quinti Maris liberi oppugnati a Guilielmo Welwodo**.

The story behind this text may help understanding this change. Although Grotius had the **De Jure Praedae Commentarius** ready and expressed in his letters the desire to publish the work, to which he referred to as **De Rebus indicis** (the title, as it became known, was given by the publisher), the fact is that this work remained a manuscript until it was found in the papers of the De Groot family in 1864. Notwithstanding, the thirteenth chapter thereof, entitled **Mare Liberum**, was published in 1609 anonymously. This was possibly one of the most controversial works of the seventeenth century. Grotius' ideas on freedom of navigation, trade,

---

[130]**ML**. *Caput* VII, p. 28.

[131]Peter Haggenmacher is one of the few commentators of Grotius to examine the text referred to above and to suggest its connection with Suárez (Haggenmacher, 1983, pp. 388–397).

and fishing were already ill received in the politically sensitive European countries and still Grotius did not refrain from disputing the Papal Bull *Inter Coetera*. In the following year, the Church enlisted the book in the Index. But that was not enough; its message was too radical. Several lawyers wrote elaborate answers: the Scot William of Welwod wrote **An Abridgement of all Sea-Lawes** in 1613 and **Dominio De Mares** in 1615; the Englishman John Selden wrote **Mare Clausum** in 1618, the Portuguese Francisco Seraphim de Freitas wrote **De Justo Imperium Lusitanorum Asiatico** in 1625, and the Spaniard Juan de Solórzano Pereira wrote **De Indiarum Jure** in 1629.[132]

Grotius seems to have read every criticism that his **Mare Liberum** received. In a letter of April 1640 to his brother, he claims to know the works of Selden and Seraphim de Freitas and expresses his desire to rebut the arguments of the latter. However, hurt by a forced exile, he restrains himself from aiding "that ungrateful Dutch people."[133]

Yet, before the political and religious tribulations that led him to prison, Grotius wrote between 1613 and 1614 twenty pages in response to **Abridgement of all Sea-Lawes** of Welwod. The **Defensio Capitis quinti Maris liberi oppugnati the Guilielmo Welwodo** remained a manuscript, and, unlike the **De Jure Praedae**, it was never ready for publication: Grotius stopped writing in the fifth part of the text possibly due to the political persecution that the work would entail. Therefore, throughout the text, Grotius' references seem incomplete. Moreover, in the unfinished final part of the work, the author indicated that he would analyze the contemporary literature on the subject. If Grotius had already read Suárez's **De Legibus**, he would have offered his comments in this very part.

The main thesis of the **Mare Liberum** refers to the impossibility of owning the seas. In accordance with the Primitive Law of Nations, which coincides with Natural Law itself, during an idyllic period called the "Golden Age" or "Kingdom of Saturn," men shared all goods and there was no private property. Private property arose out of the use of certain goods such as food, whose use led to the destruction of the good or to the impossibility of using them again. Therefore, there was no way to separate the use from the domain. By an intellectual process of *aggiornamento*, this appropriation of goods was extended to a second category of things, such as clothing, furniture and even some living things. The immovable properties also fell victim of this *aggiornamento*: although they were not for consumption, in a way they ended being in fact consumed. For instance, the fields should be cultivated for food. However, there were not enough immovable properties to satisfy the needs of every person. Therefore, scarcity required that the immovable properties should be acquired by occupation. Yet, the sea, like the air, is unfit for appropriation because it cannot be grasped physically. Therefore, it remains in its original regime of *res communis*.[134]

---

132 Armitage, 2004, p. xviii.

133 Burigny, 1754. pp. 26–27.

134 **ML**. *Caput* V. pp. 17–21.

Welwod contends that the States may take possession of the shores and thus have the exclusive right of fishing thereon. In order to demonstrate this, he must refute the notion that the seas are unsusceptible of appropriation. Grotius had identified two Roman expressions that referred to those goods that are kept for the use of all, even after the appropriation process began: the *publica juris gentium* and the *communia omnium jure naturali.* However, Welwod employs these terms in a much more narrower sense. In chapter XXVII of the **Abridgement of all Sea-Lawes**, *Of the Community and Property of the Seas*, the Scot turns to Roman sources and reinterprets the concept of common property. "For *commune* there is nothing else but *publicum, quasi populicum*, signifying a thing common for the usage of any of one sort of people and not for all of all nations, according to that of Modestinus: '*Roma communis patria est'*." So, Welwod had another meaning for the Law of Nations:

> Neither yet doth that word *jure gentium* mean any law set down by common consent of all nations, but only notes the example of the law or custom of other nations, as if they would say the liberty of fishing on our seas and of other doing there and at shore should be common to everyone of the Roman Empire, like as the same is common to all of all other nations on their seas and their shores.[135]

Therefore, according to Welwod, "common" is opposed to "specific" and "public" to "private." The coastal waters are public property of the States. In turn, the Law of Nations does not correspond to a common law among nations, but only to that part of the Civil Law of each nation that is also found in others.

Grotius' rejoinder is simple: once again, now by the use of the terms "common" and "public," he needs to explain the distinction outlined in the **De Jure Praedae** between the *jus inter gentes* and the *jus intra gentes*. Welwod was mistaken. Yet, Grotius does resume the distinction on the same basis of the division of 1605, but rather introduces some minor changes that bring it closer to Suárez. First, the Dutch considers this *jus intra gentes* true Civil Law:

> I do not want to deny that sometimes, especially for historians, the Law of Nations is improperly taken for that law that nations have established between themselves, but for what certain nations, one following the example of another, has determined as law to them, ie, as a Civil Law of different peoples.[136]

Although naming the false Law of Nations as "Civil Law" does not collide with Grotius' explanation in the **De Jure Praedae**, Grotius was careful not to use this term in this work. He prefers to designate this class of *jus gentium* as a custom,

---

[135]Welwod (2004), p. 69.

[136]"*Negare nolo interdum, apud historicos maxime, jus gentium abusive sumi non pro eo jure quod inter se habent gentes, sed pro eo quod quaedam nations altera alterius exemplum secuta sibi juris statuerunt, hoc est pro jure civili diversorum populorum.*" (Grotius, Hugo. **Defensio Capitis quinti Maris Liberi oppugnati a Guilielmo Welwodo Iuris Civilis professore capite XXVII eius libri scripti Anglico sermone cui titulum fecit Compedium legum Maritimarum. A Collotype Reproduction of the Manuscript**. New York: Carnegie Endowment for International Peace, s.a. Sheet 10'a. Henceforth, **DCQ**).

something that does not have the same legal strength as law. For the Grotius of 1605, Civil Law may tolerate the existence of a custom, but it would not be composed entirely out of customary norms. At best, the custom was an institute, never a formal source of any kind of law.

However, in 1613, Grotius seems to value custom more. This is his second subtle change. After stating that the ancients called some natural precepts *jus gentium* (which would correspond to the Primary Law of Nations), the author argues that there are other provisions of the Law of Nations that originate from a tacit consensus. And he examines how this occurs.

> Between a single people, even if it is not prepared for the law, uses and customs, which are the elements of tacit consensus, make law. Likewise, the primitive custom of mankind has the force of law. And thus it is said that the Law of Nations was introduced by custom.[137]

In the **De Jure Praedae**, Grotius had considered the tacit agreement among nations and the customs true and false sources of the *jus gentium*, respectively. He does not elaborate how this tacit agreement came to be, but seems to exclude permanently the customary way. However, in defense of the **Mare Liberum**, Grotius revisits his old offensive opinion and adds the custom as the mediate origin of the Law of Nations itself. As seen, in Suárez, the international custom is the formal source of the *jus gentium*. In an author who does not despise the will in the formation of law, such as the Jesuit, the custom is a necessary element for the internal coherence of the system. As there is not a world authority, the only way for a Positive Law of Nations to exist is through custom. It is worth remembering that Grotius shares Suárez's syncretic voluntarism. Thus, this change of opinion should not seem strange.

There is one last argument for the Suarezian influence on the Grotian *jus gentium* of the **Defensio**: the fact that Grotius employs the notion of subjective right in the same page (10'a) in which he explains the difference between the two types of Law of Nations.

> Moreover, the lawyers say that the sea is common not only because of the law between nations, but also because it is a **right** between nations. Law here does not mean a standard of justice, but a moral faculty about one thing, as when we say that one thing is my right, that is, I have ownership over it, or use or something similar.[138]

Before Grotius, only Suárez had developed the concept of subjective right (and employed the same term, "moral faculty"). The presence of this notion in the excerpt above shows that Grotius and Suárez thought alike.

---

[137]"*Nam sicut in uno populo, etiamsi populos non convenerit ipse tamen usus et consuetudo taciti consensus index jus facit, ita et humani generis prisca consuetudo vim habet legis. Et hinc est quod multa Juris gentium dicuntur introducta moribus.*" (**DCQ**. sheet 10').

[138]"*Adde iam quod Mare non tantum dicitur a Jurisconsultis esse commune gentium jure, sed sine ulla adjectione dicitur esse Juris gentium, quibus in locis jus non potest significare normam aliquam justi, sed facultatem moralem in re: ut cum dicimus haec res est juris mei, id est habeo in ea dominium aut usum aut simile aliquid.*" (**DCQ**. sheet 10'a).

Nevertheless, all these similarities evidence a probable, but not peremptory, influence of Suárez on Grotius' *jus gentium*. They are hints, not definitive proofs. In authors so different but at the same time so similar such as Suárez and Grotius, coincidences appear more frequently than one would imagine. Still, this case deserves more attention. In chapter IV, when James St. Leger and Richard Tuck's hypotheses were dismissed, I looked for answers not in exogenous determinations, but within Grotius' own thoughts. I also supported the hypothesis that favored the internal dynamics of Grotius' system over Jan Kosters' thesis. But now, there has been an actual change in Grotius' position. In 1613, Grotius gave greater importance to custom than before and considered it the formal source of all Secondary Law of Nations.

Moreover, in the **De Jure Belli ac Pacis**, Grotius confirms this change. Similar to Natural Law, Grotius unites the two classes of the Law of Nations, the primary and the secondary, but the prior division still appears in some passages as reminiscence.[139] One would imagine that, by elimination, since in this work Natural Law corresponds to the *jus gentium primarium* of his work of youth, that Grotius would grant the title of Law of Nations only to the Secondary Law of Nations. Indeed, that is precisely what happens. However, Grotius does not reason by elimination: he is fully aware that he has stepped out of the cultural orbit of the Roman Jurists who mistook this law for Natural Law.

> We have thought fit to observe that when someone finds the term Law of Nations in Roman law authors, he should not understand that as the law that cannot be altered, but that he should distinguish with caution **natural precepts** from those that exist only because of certain circumstances and **the laws that are common to several peoples but stem from each of them separately** from those that oblige and are **the bond of all human society**.[140] (emphasis added).

In this excerpt, Grotius distinguishes the authentic Law of Nations from Natural Law and from the improper Law of Nations. Natural Law cannot be changed; it may be easily mistaken for the introduction of a given provision (through Civil Law or the *jus gentium*) which then ends up binding by Natural Law itself. Such is case of the *traditio* as a means of acquiring property. In principle, Natural Law does not require the effective transfer, but, once this requirement is established, it becomes mandatory by its very nature. But this does not imply denying the positivity of the precept.

Furthermore, The Romans did not separate the law common to several peoples (considered separately), the *jus intra gentes*, from that law which binds human societies, the *jus inter gentes*. Therefore, Grotius openly leaves the Roman tradition: the Grotian Law of Nations is unambiguously positive and does not designate any

---

[139]**DJBP**. I, 2, 4, 1 and 2.

[140]"*Haec ideo annotavimus, neque reperta juris gentium voce apud Romani juris auctores statim id jus intelligat quod mutari non possit: sed diligenter distinguat naturalia praecepta ab his quae pro certo statu sunt naturalia, et jura multis populis feorfim communia, ab his quae societatis humanae vinculum continent.*" (**DJBP**. II, 8, 26).

law common to several peoples. The previous reference to proper and improper Law of Nations (which resembles Suárez's *jus gentium propiissime dictum*) persists and Grotius resumes it in the following passage with the expression *jure gentium improprie dicto.*

Elsewhere, Grotius discusses the same issue:

> When they treat of the acquisition of property, the Roman lawyers reckon up many methods, which they say are according to the Law of Nations. But a diligent examiner will find that all of them, except that gained by the law of war, do not belong to that Law of Nations, which we are now treating. They should either be referred to the law of nature, but not to that which flows purely and simply from nature, but to that which takes place in consequence of establishing property and before all civil law, **or alongside with the Civil Law**, not only that of the people of Rome, but of many other nations surrounding them.[141]

In this excerpt, Grotius clearly establishes a distinction between the true and the false Law of Nations. The markup is intended to show that, as in the **Defensio**, the false Law of Nations relates to the Civil Laws of many different peoples.

For the first time, Grotius addresses the *jus gentium* right at the very first chapter, when he introduces the classification of *jus*. The Law of Nations corresponds to a subdivision of the human voluntary law—as seen, a clarity that Alberico Gentili lacked. It is broader than Civil Law, but its scope does not coincide precisely with that of Natural Law.

> But the more extensive law [than Civil Law] is the Law of Nations, which derives its authority from the will of all, or at least of many, nations. I say of many, because there is scarcely any law common to all nations, except that of nature, which is also called [by the Romans] as the Law of Nations.[142]

Concluding that it is a law of a "great number of nations," Grotius elaborates the same position of Suárez and Isidore, for whom the *jus gentium* applied to "almost" all nations. Suárez did not influence this feature, since Grotius himself had already endorsed it in the **Nova Declaratio** of the **De Jure Praedae**. Yet, since the author heavily relied on Gentili, the presence of this idea is noteworthy.

As seen, Natural Law is evidenced by the conformity of its precepts to the right reason and by the unanimous testimony of history, because similar effects must have a single cause. In turn, Positive Law is proven in a simpler way: by the act that enacts the law. However, especially after changing his mind on the relevance of customs, Grotius understood that there could be a non-written Positive Law, the proof of which was problematic. Grotius inserts the Law of Nations into this

---

[141]"*Romani Iurisconsulti ubi de acquirendo rerum dominio agunt, complutes ejus acquirendi recensent modos, quo juris gentium vocant: sed si quis recte advertat, inveniet eo omnes, excepto belli jure, non pertinere ad jus gentium illud de quo agimus: seda ut referendos ad jus naturae, non quidem merum, sed quod sequatur introductum jam dominium, et legem omnem civilem antecedat, aut ad ipsam legem civilem, non solius populi Romani, sed multarum circa nationum*" (**DJBP**. II, 8, 1, 1).

[142]*Latius autem patens est jus Gentium, id est quod Gentium omnium aut multarum voluntate vim obligandi accepit. Multarum addidi, quia vix ullum jus reperitur extra jus naturale, quod ipsum quoque gentium dici solet, omnibus gentibus commune.*" (**DJBP**. I, 1, 14, 1).

category, together with the unwritten Civil Law: "Now the proofs on which the Law of Nations is founded are the same with those of the unwritten Civil Law, through a **continual use** and the testimony of men skilled in the Laws."[143] (emphasis added).

Besides the word of the experts (the authority of lawyers), the existence of an unwritten Positive Law, such as the *jus gentium*, is proved by the customs. Grotius does not differentiate the use from the custom; this *jus* is based on "time and use" (*usus et repertum temporis*). As in the **Defensio**, the custom becomes the formal source of the Law of Nations in the **De Jure Belli ac Pacis**. The author does not abandon the idea of a tacit pact set forth in his work of 1605, he only unveils the process according to which this silent and unwritten agreement takes shape. Therefore, in the passage that serves as a general overview of the work, *prolegomena* 17 and 26, Grotius decides to simplify things and teaches that the *jus gentium* is based on the consensus between the peoples.

Therefore, the Law of Nations is demonstrated by custom. So is the false Law of Nations (which, in fact, is part of Civil Law) as well: "and therefore might be altered by any one people, without consulting the others; and it may also happen that in some other places and at some other times a very different common custom, and so another Law of Nations improperly so called, might be introduced."[144] Grotius' prior reluctance in considering this *jus gentium* a Civil Law comes from his belief that custom did not have the status of law. The value of the custom is the element that separates Grotius' work of youth from the works he wrote after 1613.

Much like the **De Legibus**, the **De Jure Belli ac Pacis** provides no detailed account of the custom. However, there is one single and brief reference thereto when Grotius examines the legal prescription and the acquisitive prescription. The very place of such reference does little to support the hypothesis that Suárez influenced Grotius, since Grotius maintained the frugality of **De Jure Praedae** and thus his belief in the custom's lack of legal force. Still, the content of the passage surprises.

> There is something very similar [to the acquisitive prescription] in the establishment of a custom. For this too (setting aside Civil Law, which regulates the time and manner of it) may be introduced by the subjects, if the sovereign tolerates and connives at it. It is true, the time required to give this custom **any effect of law** has in general no fixed limits; but it ought to be sufficiently long, in order to give room to suppose the consent of the prince.[145] (emphasis added).

---

[143]"*Probatur autem hoc jus gentium pari modo quo jus non scriptum civile, uso continuo et testimonio peritorum.*" (**DJBP**. I, 1, 14, 2).

[144]"(…) *unde et ab uno populo aliis inconsultis mutari potuit, imo et hoc evenire ut aliis locis atque tem.*

[145]"*Cui simillimum quid in consuetudine apparet. Nam haec quoque, semotis legibus civilibus quae certo tempore ac modo eam introduci volunt, a populo súbdito introduci potest ex eo quod ab imperium habente toleratur: tempus vero quo illa consuetudo effectum juris accipit, non est definitum, sed arbitrarium, quantum fatis est ut concurrat ad significandum consensum.*" (**DJBP**. II, 4, 5, 2).

Therefore, Grotius does grant the custom "some effect of law." Yet, in this excerpt there lies an even more important feature. As seen in Suárez, there is a division of the authority responsible for creating the custom: the will of the people who regularly practice the behavior and the approval of the prince who accepts this repeated behavior. The similarity is not fortuitous: this excerpt is one of the four explicit references to Suárez's **De Legibus**. Grotius quotes Book VII, chapter XV, in which Suárez addresses the duration of the custom.

Therefore, Francisco Suárez in fact influences Grotius' concept of *jus gentium*. Nevertheless, the influence of the former in the thoughts of the latter is less prominent than Jan Kosters (or even James St. Leger) advocate. Even before reading Suárez, the Grotian Law of Nations belonged to Positive Law and displayed the famous Suarezian distinction between *jus intra gentes* and *jus inter gentes*. Although less comprehensive, the influence of Suárez is no less striking: it focuses on the basis of this law. The custom is the element that binds (almost) all human societies.

6.2.3 The International Society

The foundation of Grotius's *jus gentium* is close to being completed. So far, I have displayed that the meaning of peoples to Grotius is not limited to the State, but to all peoples exercising civil power, even the non-sovereign peoples. Paradoxically, despite the fact that the Law of Nations applies to almost all peoples, it stems from an agreement of will among the sovereign peoples only. I have also contended that in his maturity work, Grotius clarifies the nature of this consensus and accepts the Suarezian thesis on the customs being the formal source of the *jus gentium*. Therefore, despite being a voluntary law, the Law of Nations does not conform to a voluntary system of law, since its legislator is lost in memorial times and it is not possible to establish a relation between its will and the law resulting from it. The question remains whether Grotius, like Suárez, conceived the notion of an international society.

In the **De Jure Praedae**, the Law of Nations is divided into two: the Primary and the Secondary Law of Nations. This division is a reminiscent from the glossators, who divided Natural Law and/or the Law of Nations into stages according to chronological or genetic criteria. Grotius reproduces this idea. However, between the two categories of the Law of Nations, there exists a considerable time lapse. They are two forms of *jus* that only share the name.

In order to understand this, it is important to look into the axiomatic–deductive structure of the *prolegomena*, at the beginning of Grotius' 1605 work. According to such structure, the origin of all sources of the law of the war is always the same: the will of a legislator. While this will seems to vary, in truth it is only one, ramified into many others. All other legislators are a reflection of the first and are only the immediate causes of the *lex*.

Therefore, the Primary Natural Law, the law that is common to all creation, comes from the divine will. God created men as rational and social beings, so the collective will of mankind generates the Secondary Natural Law, also called Primary Law of Nations. This one corresponds to Natural Law of the **De Jure Belli ac Pacis**. The consensus of all man is an effect of a universal cause: had God not infused this nature into men, this Secondary Natural Law would never have existed. Indirectly, God is responsible for the creation of this *jus*. However, his participation is subtle, for the domain of validity of this law is still secular and human.

The contracts and especially the social contract that establishes the political society are a result of the individual will of men. In turn, the magistrate appointed by the State creates Civil Law. Grotius then adds a mixed law, the Secondary Law of Nations, composed of the Primary Law of Nations and of Civil Law. The will that enacts such law is the will of all States.

There is no continuity between the *jus gentium primarium* (Natural Law) and the *jus gentium secundarium* (Positive Law, the Law of Nations of 1625); Civil Law lies between them. This is quite significant. When Medieval authors promoted this distinction, they did not understand very well the difference between Natural Law and the Law of Nations, but sought to reduce the gap between Natural and Civil Law. In Suárez, although there is no doubt that the *jus gentium* belongs to Positive Law, it seems to fulfill the same purpose of achieving a common good that is slightly higher than that of Civil Law and a little lower than that of Natural Law.

Had Grotius employed the same logic, the Secondary Law of Nations should appear after Civil Law, but it does not. Indeed, Grotius is very precise in explaining its nature: the Secondary Law of Nations is a hybrid, a mixture between Natural and Civil Law. He was not mistaken in placing the *jus gentium secondarium* where he did. The existence of this law presupposes the existence of Civil Law. The difference between the *jus gentium primarium* and the *jus gentium secundarium* may seem obscure due to the similarity of their names. They share a similar designation because they share the same scope, as they both apply to mankind. However, mankind may be approached from two different perspectives: as a community of men or as a society of States (according to the author's conception of State). In Grotius, what separates both kinds of *jus gentium* is their addressee.

The Secondary Law of Nations only appears after Civil Law, because it stems from the will of the States, a fruit of Civil Law. In the **De Jure Praedae**, Grotius does not hesitate to classify the Secondary Law of Nations as a voluntary or Positive Law. The *jus gentium secundarium* does not link Natural and Civil Law; in fact, Civil Law is closer to Natural Law (and hence to its divine source) than the Secondary Law of Nations itself. The creation of this *jus* presupposes the organization of men into political groups. As will be seen, this assumption is both ontological and chronological. The *jus gentium secundarium* presupposes the existence of States.

There is another feature of this *jus gentium secundarium* that flows from this axiomatic–deductive structure. In Suárez, as in Grotius, Positive Law derives from utility and not from necessity. Yet, in comparison to the common good of Civil Law, the common good of Suárez's Law of Nations is found at the end of the utility scale, closer to the first degrees of necessity, signaling that the global common good for Suárez is "ethically superior" to the common good of one singular State.

The same does not occur to the common good of Grotius' *jus gentium secundarium*, which presents itself as "less pure" than Civil Law itself. That is why the law of war that originates from the Law of Nations allows some effects of bilateral justice in the **De Jure Belli ac Pacis**. However, Grotius' global common good does not flow entirely from the *jus gentium secumndarium*, but also from Natural Law. That is why in his maturity work the author applies the internal justice to correct the consequences of the solemn war—which are less "just" than the wars permitted by Natural Law.

Therefore, in the **De Jure Praedae**, should the society composed by all States depended solely on the (Secondary) Law of Nations, it would be morally inferior to the State itself. However, a Natural Law of Nations (the Primary Law of Nations) ensures an ethical minimum to this domain.

Actually, it is on the *jus gentium primarium* (the Secondary Natural Law) that Grotius mentions for the first time the expression *mundi civitas*. He explains this world society by quoting Seneca:

> Just like the members of a body work in mutual harmony because it is an advantage to the entire body that the individual pieces are preserved, also humanity must take care of men because we are born to the common life. Society should be safeguarded only by the love and care of its component parts.[146]

There is not one single element of "internationality" in this world society. Grotius mentions Seneca to describe the second tendency of the Stoic *oikeiosis*: the love for others and the solidarity among individuals, not among States. The author here is referring to the natural sociability of men. Sometimes he calls this group of men *mundi civitas*, others mankind. Grotius does not conceive an essential difference between peoples and men in plural. For that reason, the (Secondary) Natural Law can also be called (Primary) Law of Nations.

Grotius has no doubt that the *jus gentium secundarium* also regulates this global association. He introduces this law by using comparisons. As the common good of the individuals shaped the previous precepts (of Civil Law), the common good of the States (*commune rerumpublicarum inter se bonum*) creates the Secondary Law of Nations.[147] However, the Secondary Natural Law, or the Primary Law of Nations, which share the same spatial scope, also intervenes in this *inter gentes* society—a society that may be understood as between States or between men. Grotius shows that his world society does not correspond to an **international** dominion, but to an **extra-national** one, coinciding with mankind.

As seen in the previous chapter, Suárez also associates his version of world society with mankind, although for him mankind was already divided into States.

---

[146]"(…) *ut omnia inter se membra consentiunt, quia singula servari totius interest, ita homines singulis parcent, quia ad coetum geniti sumus. Salva autem esse societas, nisi amore et custodia partium non potest.*" (**DJPC**, p. 13).

[147]**DJPC**, p. 26.

That primitive moment of unity (if it actually existed) has long passed. Men have a duty to reconstruct this unity through the Law of Nations. However, Suárez perceives this international society as a project, as something yet to be fulfilled.

As I have presented in the second chapter, Vitória's idea of *totus orbis* no longer existed either; it was a memory of a time when all Christians were united under the *orbis Christianus*. The *orbis Christianus* had historically existed, but the world had changed: the Great Navigations expanded its frontiers and now encompassed "barbarian peoples." Like the *jus gentium* of the Roman Empire, this new Law of Nations applied to foreigners within a new World Christian Empire. But this political organization was not established yet. The Pope's donation was not a valid title and thus it was necessary to find another title of acquisition.

In Scholastic authors, the natural sociability is insufficient to preserve the unity of men after they form independent political communities. That is why the international society is a project, something that should exist. In Suárez, the natural society is reached through the Law of Nations (propelled by a minimum content of Charity), whereas in Vitória the natural society is driven by this *jus* and by Natural Law (which may be part of a single phenomenon).

To Grotius, in the **De Jure Praedae**, this world society is a fact, the Stoic *magna communitas humani generis*. Unlike Suárez, Grotius seems to accept the historical existence of a primordial state of nature whenever he refers to it, as follows from this excerpt: "during the first periods of human history, property [*dominium*] bore a distinct concept from its current meaning nowadays."[148] In this sentence, the author contrasts the common property of the ancient human history with the current concept of property. In the next page, he refers to this period in history as "other times" (*eo tempore*).

In the **De Jure Belli ac Pacis**, Grotius also refers to the historical existence of this primitive state. "The Almighty God at the Creation, and again after the Deluge, gave to mankind in general a dominion over things of this inferior world."[149] Therefore, the community of peoples and things existed in two moments: immediately after the creation of the world and after the Deluge. As seen in chapter IV, the Bible is an important historical source for Grotius. The *mundi civitas* existed as a sociological fact at the beginning of human race.

In his work of maturity, this primordial state of nature corresponds to the international society. Grotius names the assembly of States *magnae universitatis*,[150] in contrast with the *coetuum singulorum*: men may gather in private groups, in States or even in larger associations. But both the *civitas* and the *magnae universitatis* are comprised of individuals. Therefore, there is no difference between the society of the *respublicas* and the natural community of men. Civil Law creates an

---

[148]"*Sciendum est igitur in primordiis vitae humanae aliud quam nunc est dominium, aliud communionem fuisse.*" (**DJPC**, p. 214).

[149]"*Deus humano generi generaliter contulit jus in res hujus inferiores naturae statim a mundo condito, atque interum mundo post diluvio reparato.*" (**DJBP**. II, 2, 2, 1).

[150]**DJBP**. *prolegomenon* 17.

association that differs from the natural association, but not the Law of Nations. The Law of Nations only enhances, through utility, a reality already created by nature.

For Grotius, the natural solidarity between men is based on biological connections:

> Besides, regardless of what is in its precepts, the Holy History does not stimulate in a mediocre manner this tendency to social life, teaching us that all men were born from the same first parents. Consequently, it is possible to affirm that nature, according to Florentino, established a bond between us all.[151]

The *magna communitas humani generis* does not correspond to the contemporary concept of nation. The reference to kinship bonds implies that all men share one essence of mankind, which comes from the common nature and from the fact that all men are from the same species.

Once more, there is a crucial difference in relation to Suárez. The human unity created by the *jus gentium* to which Suárez referes transcends pure biology. The connection that binds (or should bind, since it is only a project) men is Charity, the material source of his Law of Nations. Yet, in Grotius, the natural community (of Stoic origin) is based on a biological fact: the two drives of *oikeiosis*. Furthermore, Charity does not fulfill the same purpose. As previously described, Grotius always distinguishes this legal order from the Law of Nations. For him, Charity sets forth a stricter moral pattern and at times is used to correct the permissiveness of the Law of Nations.

The Suarezian perfect community is an autocracy. States do not actually need each other but, because of Charity, they want to. However, the Grotian State is not so auto-sufficient. According to Grotius, some people make the mistake of thinking that justice applies only to individuals and not to States themselves—since they seem to have everything necessary to the social life. Nevertheless, "there is no such thing as a nation so strong that will never need help from others, whether in relation to trading activities or to repel foreign nations united against it."[152] Grotius' *summa potestas* means only that a single entity holds the ultimate power to make decisions within a political body. It does not imply that States are independent from the each other.

Therefore, Grotius' world society lacks the element of "internationality." It corresponds solely to the natural union of the human species, a Stoic concept that actually existed in history. The Law of Nations may be combined with Natural Law within this preexistent domain in order to improve the legal community through utility.

---

[151]"*Sed et historia sacra, praeter id quod in praeceptis consistit, affectum illum socialem non parum etiam eo excitat quod nos docet ab iisdem primis parentibus ortos homines omnes, ita ut eo quoque sensu dici recte possit quod alio dixit Florentinus, cognationem inter nos a natura constituam*" (**DJBP**. *prolegomenon* 14).

[152]"*(...) nulla est tam valida civitas quae non aliquando aliorum extra se ope indigere possit, vel ad comercia, vel etiam ad arcendas multarum externarum gentium junctas in se vires" (***DJBP.** *prolegomenon 22).*

Suárez says that the union of all men is more an idea of reason than an actual historical event. Therefore, men must build it; it is a project. Since men divided themselves into different States, they no longer require assistance from others. But men do not have only biology in common; they are all sons of God and because of love, they wish the company and the well-being of even those who do not share their citizenship. For Grotius, men do not want, they actually need mutual assistance because the State itself is not sufficient to attend to the requirements of social life. The Dutch does not use Charity to lay the foundation of his *jus gentium* because the human society already exists, and where society exists so does law. Grotius' basis of the Law of Nations seems to be beneath Suárez's simply because there is no need to justify an empirical data.

Neither Grotius nor Suárez developed the concept of International Law, in the current sense of the term, in their notions of *jus gentium*. Neither knew the idea of sovereign States. However, they both conceived a notion of the Law of Nations that escaped the Roman cultural universe: a **Positive** Law applicable **between** peoples. Subsequent writers also endeavored to conceive a positive *inter gentes* law, but this *jus* gained two features: it began to govern only the conduct of States and became a law detached from the idea of justice. According to Grotius and Suárez both, despite applying to the peoples, the *jus gentium* also applied to men: although voluntary, their *jus gentium* left no room for ethical relativism. It is a narrow, but viable path.

6.3 Summary

Grotius did not exactly develop a true theory of the Law of Nations. This *jus* appears in the course of his studies on the law of war. Grotius embarked on a millenary Christian tradition in order to limit the role of violence in the resolution of conflicts among peoples, in a world that was far from ideal and morally imperfect. The Doctrine of Just War emerges to govern a reality in which it was not possible to abandon war or to accept it unconditionally. In fact, Humanist jurists (of which Grotius is himself an heir) softened the ethical content of this tradition, even if only marginally. But Grotius kept true to what Alfred Vanderpol has called "the Scholastic Soctrine of Just War." The Dutch Theologian disputes the "realistic" arguments of his main contemporary role model, Alberico Gentili, and adopts some opinions that bring him closer to the Spanish Scholastics.

Grotius makes some peripheral considerations on the *jus gentium*, given that this kind of law is one of the sources of the law of war. The author uses extra-national sources to build his *jus belli*: the Law of Nations, Divine and Natural Law. His analysis is limited to the *materia belli*, which could not be governed by Civil Law because of its very nature. Therefore, in order to understand the law of war, Grotius must study the sources that were broader than Civil Law.

At first glance, after studying the same institute from Suárez's perspective, it feels strange to note that Grotius' Law of Nations fulfills a role of softening the prescriptions of Natural Law in the law of war. Indeed, as a Positive Law, the *jus gentium* owes its origin to utility, not necessity. Therefore, the provisions thereof may well temper the morality of Natural Law on war, such as permitting some effects of bilateral justice. Nevertheless, just like a Scholastic Theologian, Grotius has a broader notion of Law, in the sense that not all licit behaviors are legitimate from the perspective of consciousness. Therefore, he reviews the permissiveness of the Law of Nations in accordance with the inner justice of each act. Beyond Natural Law, other orders, amongst them Charity, function as a corrective tool of the internal justice—even if, not rarely, they coincide with the provisions of Natural Law.

Although the *jus gentium* was not Grotius' main subject of study, it seems possible to build a concept thereof based on his meager observations. The first question concerns the recipient of this *jus*. By answering it, Grotious displays his notion of "people." The author's Political Theory is pre-Modern: he does not elaborate on issues that would mark the debates of the following centuries, such as civil disobedience and tyranny. The reason behind this is that Grotius does not accept the popular origin of power, as Modern authors do. In a primitive period of the human race, power was vested in each person. But the same power could be alienated or lost in a just war. Therefore, after this period, some peoples kept their sovereignty while others did not. Grotius did not accept Suárez's thesis that power would return to the people in the event the king would breach the precepts of Natural Law. Then, Grotius' "peoples" were organized in sovereign or non-sovereign States. The author does not elaborate on the idea of State sovereignty; sovereign is a body within the *civitas*. Therefore, even the peoples that form a sovereign State are not independent—as assumed in the contemporary notion of sovereignty in International Law.

Since Grotius' *jus gentium* is voluntary and there is no world authority to create laws, the second problem addressed by Grotius refers to the formal source of this law. Here, Suárez' influence is decisive, but not in the way Jan Kosters has presented it to be. During his youth, Grotius developed on his own the distinction that would make Suárez known and that would forever dismantle the Roman heritage: it is necessary to distinguish the authentic Law of Nations (the *jus inter gentes*) from the false one (the *jus intra gentes*), the precepts of which belong to Civil Law and are copied by all peoples. The true *jus gentium* arises out of an agreement between nations, but Grotius did not know how this agreement took place and disputed that the custom could ever become a source of law. However, he changes his opinion when he reads the **De Legibus**. Grotius perceives the normative power of custom and begins to consider it a source of the Law of Nations. One may sense this change in an unfinished manuscript from 1613 to 14 and it takes its final shape in **De Jure Belli ac Pacis**: one of Grotius' four references to Suárez pertains to his analysis of the custom as a source for law.

Since the Grotiam *jus gentium* has no ethical content, his international society faced the risk of serving only the selfish purposes of the *respublicas*, in the context of politics of power. However, this society is perfectioned by the Law of Nations, but is created by Natural Law. The Law of Nations becomes part of a preexistent reality in order only to improve it. By doing this, the author ensures the morality of this domain. Grotius' *civitas mundi* matches the Stoic *magna communitas humani generis*, an initial period of human history. Hence, Grotius' world society coincides with mankind itself: it does not consist of an association of independent States, but of an association of peoples, i.e., of human beings.

References

Armitage, David. Introduction. In: Grotius, Hugo. **The Free Seas**. With William Welwod's critique and Grotius's Reply. Trad. Richard Hakluyt. Edited by David Armitage. Indianapolis: Liberty Fund, 2004. (Natural Law and Enlightenment Classics).

Basdevant, Jules. Hugo Grotius. In: Pillet, Antoine (ed.). **Les Fondateurs du Droit International**. Paris: V. Giard & E. Brière, 1904.

Bobbio, Norberto. **Thomas Hobbes**. Trad. Carlos Nelson Coutinho. Rio de Janeiro: Campus, 1991.

Borschberg, Peter. **Grotius, the Social Contract and Political Resistance**: a study of the unpublished Theses LVI. IILJ Working Paper 2006/7 (History and Theory of International Law Series). New York: New York University School of Law, 2006. Available at <http://www.iilj.org>.

Burigny, Jean-Levesque de. **Vie de Grotius, avec l'histoire de ses ouvrages, et de négociations auxquelles il fut employé**. Amsterdam: M.M. Rey, 1754.

Del Vecchio, Giorgio. Grotius and the Foundation of International Law. **New York University Law Review**, v. 37, n. 260, pp. 260-266, April 1962.

Erasmo de Roterdão. **A Guerra e a Queixa da Paz**. Translated by A. Guimarães Pinto. Lisboa: Edições 70, 1999.

Grotius, Hugo. **Defensio Capitis quinti Maris Liberi oppugnati a Guilielmo Welwodo Iuris Civilis professore capite XXVII eius libri scripti Anglico sermone cui titulum fecit Compedium legum Maritimarum. A Collotype Reproduction of the Manuscript**. New York: Carnegie Endowment for International Peace, s.a.

Grotius, Hugo. **The Freedom of the Seas, or the right which belongs to the Dutch to take part in the East Indian Trade**. Translated by Ralph van Deman Magoffin. Introduction by James Brown Scott. New York: Oxford University Press, 1916.

Grotius, Hugo. **De Iure Belli ac Pacis libri tres**. *In quibus ius naturae et Gentium: item iuris publici praecipua explicantur.* Parisiis: Nicolaum Buon, 1625.

Grotius, Hugo. **De Iure Belli ac Pacis libri tres**. *In quibus ius naturae et Gentium: item iuris publici praecipua explicantur.* Amsterdã: I. Blaeu, 1646. Edited by James Brown Scott. Oxford, London: Clarendon Press, Geoffrey Cumberlege, 1925. (The Classics of International Law).

Grotius, Hugo. **De Iure Belli ac Pacis libri tres**. *In quibus ius naturae et Gentium: item iuris publici praecipua explicantur.* Cum Annotationibus Auctoris, ejusdemque Dissertatione de Mari Libero; Ac Libello singulari *De Aequitate, Indulgentia et Facilitate*: Nec non Joann. Frid. Gronovii Notis in totum opus de Jure Belli ac Pacis, Ex altera recensione Joannis Barbeyracii. Amsterdã: apud Janssonio-Waesbergios, 1735.

Grotius, Hugo. **De Jure Praedae Commentarius**. La Haye: Hamaker, Nijhoff, 1868.

Grotius, Hugo. **De Jure Praedae Commentarius**. I: Trad. Gwladys Williams e Walter Zeidel. II: **The Collotype Reproduction of the Original Manuscript of 1604 in the Handwriting of Grotius**. Edited by James Brown Scott. Oxford, London: Clarendon Press, Geoffrey Cumberlege, 1950. 2 v. (The Classics of International Law).

Grotius, Hugo. **Traité du Pouvoir du Magistrat Politique sur les choses sacrées**. Trad. Lescalopier de Nourar. Londres: s/n, 1751.

Guimarães Pinto, António. Introdução. ERASMO DE ROTERDÃO. **A Guerra e a Queixa da Paz**. Trad. A. Guimarães Pinto. Lisboa: Edições 70, 1999.

Haggenmacher, Peter. **Grotius et la doctrine de la guerre juste**. Genève, Paris: Heige, Presses Universitaires de France, 1983.

Kissinger, Henry. **Diplomacy**. New York: Simon & Schuster, 1994.

Kosters, Jan. **Les Fondements du Droit des Gens**. Contribution à la théorie générale du droit des gens. La Hague: Lugduno-Batavae, 1925. (Biblioteca Visseriana, v. IX, t. IV).

Straumann, **Benjamin. Is Modern Liberty Ancient?** Roman Remedies and Natural Rights in Hugo Grotius' Early Works on Natural Law. IILJ Working Paper 2006/11 (History and Theory of International Law Series). New York: New York University School of Law, 2006. Available at <http://www.iilj.org>.

Tucídides. **História da Guerra do Peloponeso**. Trad. Mário da Gama Kury. 4.ed. Brasília: UNB; São Paulo: Imprensa Oficial do Estado de São Paulo, 2001.

Tuck, Richard. **Natural Rights Theories**: their origin and development. New York: Cambridge University Press, 1979.

Vincent, R.J. Grotius, Human Rights and Intervention. In: Bull, Hedley; Kingsbury, Benedict; Roberts, Adam (ed.). **Hugo Grotius and International Relations**. Oxford, New York: Oxford University, Clarendon Press, 2002.

Vitoria, Francisco de. De Indis II. De Jure Belli. In: ______. **Obras de Francisco de Vitória**. Relecciones Teologicas. Elaboradas bajo la dirección de Teofilo Urdanoz. Madrid: Biblioteca de Autores Cristianos, 1960.

Welwod, William. Of the Community and Property of the Seas. In: Grotius, Hugo. **The Free Seas**. With William Welwod's critique and Grotius's Reply. Translated by Richard Hakluyt and edited by David Armitage. Indianapolis: Liberty Fund, 2004. (Natural Law and Enlightenment Classics).

Yasuaki, Onuma. War. In: Yasuaki, Onuma (ed.). **A Normative Approach to War**: peace, war and justice in Hugo Grotius. Oxford: Clarendom Press, 1993.

Chapter 7
Conclusion

This book has fulfilled its purpose to demonstrate Francisco Suárez's influence on Hugo Grotius' conception of *jus gentium*. Notwithstanding, this influence is much more circumscribed and less comprehensive than many commentators, such as Jan Kosters, James St. Leger, Paul Merea and Scott Brown have pictured it to be. Suárez is responsible for the change that takes place in Grotius' two main works in the author's assessment of custom as a formal source of the Law of Nations as well as an element of Law creation. Custom enables the positive character of the Law of Nations and ensures a spatial domain of validity similar to that of Natural Law. In addition, for these two authors, the fact that the *jus gentium* is expressed through custom prevents the emergence of a more rigid voluntarism as basis of this law. Since the legislative authority is lost in ancient times in the formation of custom, the Law of Nations is positive, but does not exactly reflect the circumstancial and individual interests of the States. This denotes a subtle but very significant influence: despite being a human construction, the *jus gentium* is not divorced from Ethics.

There is no doubt that this is a Christian morality (thus subject to all the criticism that it has already been subject to). Both lawyers were theologians and did not keep Theology out of their legal texts. However, what matters in this topic is not the emphasis on a particular religious ethos, but the very choice of abiding by one. Suárez and Grotius no longer lived in the time of Francisco de Vitória, a time when Christianity still seemed an indisputable truth. The world had expanded its horizons. In the mid-sixteenth century, it was a question of universalizing the Christian religion, even in its most basic precepts, and the Law of Nations was an instrument for this purpose. However, when these two writers emerged, Reformation was already well under way and Catholicism was no longer unanimous even in Europe. The separation of the two cities was a reality of fact and a universal Christian morality was simply implausible. It is not a coincidence that skepticism resurfaced in those years and soon after arose a branch of Modernity based on the most primary and selfish instinct of man: the instinct of self-preservation.

P.E. Vauthier Borges de Macedo, *Catholic and Reformed Traditions in International Law*, Studies in the History of Law and Justice 9,
DOI 10.1007/978-3-319-59403-3_7

If universalizing Christian morality was no longer possible, the alternative seemed giving up on any ideal of absolute values. Machiavelli and Hobbes embodied the most pure and novel form of this inclination, since they escaped nihilism (the temptation of every skeptical), but still conceived society in an amoral basis. The Legal Humanism of an Alberico Gentili dissociated the Law of Nations from Ethics even in the Medieval Law of war, a Christian and moral tradition. Christianity alone was simply not capable of supporting a universal (or almost universal) Positive Law.

Suárez and Grotius wrote in this context: Ethics was no longer absolute, but they did not accept the ethical relativism. Hence, the *jus gentium* should belong to Positive Law, but could not be a mere product of the will of the States. For both the authors, having the custom as a formal source of the Law of Nations ensured its positivity without turning it into a (arbitrary) product of the will of the States.

Like every worthy enterprise, the journey seems more interesting than the outcome itself. The reason behind the choice of these two jurists ended up being more appropriate than previously assumed. This requires an explanation. This oeuvre does not seek to unveil the paternity of International Law, despite reviewing the origins of this branch. For 300 years, Grotius held the title of the single founder of this discipline and of the Modern Legal Philosophy as well. However, each and every commentator of his work drew the Dutch out of his own time and out of his own concerns; so, in order to meet the expectations of readers from centuries later, he became a myth.

When the **De Jure Praedae** came to light (and its references to the Spanish Scholastics, especially to Francisco de Vitória), Grotius gradually loses importance. From mere precursors, the Scholastics became the true founders of International Law. The obsession with looking for a single founder ended only in 1904 with **Les fondateurs du droit international**, by Antoine Pillet. Since then, the perception that the International Law is the collective work of several founders instead of just one has gradually settled. Grotius' status now is not as admirable. Many commentators such as James Brown Scott even deem him a mere disciple of the Iberians. Scott and other authors made generic comparisons between Grotius and the Scholastics; each intended to accentuate the similarity of their concepts or even Grotius' intellectual debt to the Spanish authors. Once again they exaggerate, but this time to the opposite direction: from myth, Grotius becomes a mere follower, devoid of any originality. As Vollenhoven evidences, in every language there has been published a text proclaiming what Grotius should have done to write a more satisfactory book in International Law.[1] The content of the debates on the paternity of International Law may have shifted, but the interpretations thereof still remained largely anachronistic.

[1]Vollenhoven, 1925, p. 1.

Wihout any doubt, Vitória was the precursor of International Law, but Suárez is a much denser writer, and this compels commentators such as Paulo Merêa to consider Grotius inferior to him.[2] Comparisons like his and Brown Scott's are so generic that cannot possibly be conclusive. Even in more specific assessments, such as the ones carried out by St. Leger and Jan Kosters, Grotius loses all of his originality to Suárez. In addition, classic Grotian ideas, such as the distinction between *jus inter gentes* and *jus intra gentes*, also end up being attributed solely to Suárez. However, these theories face serious obstacles: the timing (**De Legibus** was published only in 1612, while the **De Jure Praedae** was written in 1604–1605) and the fact that there are so few references to Suárez in Grotius' *magna opus*.

In order to understand the work of an author accurately, two essential requirements must be complied with. First, the reading must take into account the issues of his time and the concrete readers that the author seeks to address. Second, one must accept that the author says what he wants to, not what contemporary readers would like to read. Fulfilling these requirements is not a simple task; to a greater or lesser extent, commentators often fail to leave their preconceived notions behind. Grotius and Suárez are part of a same tradition: the Doctrine of Just War. That is why the Dutch resembles the Spaniard so much; he did not exactly embraced Thomism, but he did adhere to the most basic assumptions of a political-legal theoretical body strongly influenced by Aquinas, which predates him and remained alive centuries after him.

This common origin is quite controversial and may thwart those who seek to find all the elements of Modernity in Grotius. However, one must not imagine that there was only one single trend of Modernity that broke all links with the past. In accordance with a fortunate analogy from Haggenmacher, the development of International Law can be compared to a plant: if International Law is the flower, then the Medieval Law of war is its stalk.[3]

Grotius and Suárez stand out amongst the thinkers of this tradition. Both are not only theologians, but know, in depth, the classical canons of Law, the Roman sources. They know them so well that they are able to distance themselves from them. Hence the choice of these authors: among all those involved in the Doctrine of Just War, Suárez and Grotius developed a notion of *jus gentium* that actually escapes the Roman cultural orbit (an internal law of the Empire that often is mistaken with Natural Law). Even though their systems exercised a considerable influence over these two authors, neither Vitória nor Gentili displayed this awareness. Grotius and Suárez deserve a special chapter in the history of International Law not because they employ the term *jus gentium*, but because they used it with a meaning that none of the Roman jurists and the subsequent writers of the Just War tradition ever did.

---

[2]Merêa (2004), pp. 178–179.

[3]Haggenmacher (1988), p. 77.

Since Grotius and Suárez belong to the same tradition, comparing them in a general basis is of little use to assess whether one influenced the other's concept of Law of Nations. Such a scale of analysis is unsatisfactory. It is necessary to expose every nuance of their concepts of *jus gentium*. This is no easy task, since some features of their Law of Nations (the custom as a formal source and positivity) depend on other concepts, the understanding of which requires incursions in Legal Philosophy and even Theology: among others, the *analogia entis*, the balance between voluntarism and intellectualism, the state of nature and the social contract, the source of power and the idea of sovereignty. Even more specific comparisons, such as those of Kosters and St. Leger, do not expose these subtleties.

An analysis of this magnitude produces surprising results. On the one hand, readers who are unfamiliar with Grotius' successive trends of interpretation may discover how close he was to Suárez. On the other hand, scholars who are familiar with the debate should conclude that the two are so distinct. In truth, these authors developed very similar concepts of the Law of Nations, but many of these similarities are merely fortuitous. The two theologians read the same authors and had similar intellectual concerns. It should not come as a surprise that their concepts of *jus gentium* come mainly from the internal dynamics of their own systems.

Therefore, Grotius did not "plagiarized" Suárez. When the Dutch inserts the *jus gentium* into the domain of Positive Law and differentiates the *jus inter gentes* (the real Law of Nations) from the *jus intra gentes* (the fake Law of Nations), in his work of youth, he had not yet come into contact with Suárez' **De Legibus**. The differentiation is in line with the logic of the axiomatic-deductive structure of the **De Jure Praedae**. What Grotius lacked was clarity over the basis of the Law of Nations itself: like all Positive Law, the Law of Nations should derive from the human will (the agreement between States), but in his youth, the Dutch did not believe that customs could be the manifestation of that consensus. Customs could not constitute a legal source.

In the course of his writings, Grotius retains a consistency that is surprising for an eclectic thinker. The changes are thus mere developments of his previous ideas. Still, the custom in the **De Jure Belli ac Pacis** acquires the status of a formal source of law, a change which requires overcoming prejudices. One of the only four references to the **De Legibus** concerns the custom as a true source for Law.

Albeit quite specific, this change is of utmost relevance. Because it stems from custom, the *jus gentium* is able to exceed the boundaries of Civil Law and address a scope almost as broad as that of Natural Law. Moreover, the custom dilutes the will of the legislative authority and with it the voluntarist character of the Law of Nations. Grotius left the Roman conception by himself, but he needed Suárez to infuse an ethical essence into his *jus gentium*.

References

Haggenmacher, Peter. La place de Francisco de Vitoria parmi les fondateurs du droit international. In: Truyol y Serra, Antonio et al. **Actualité de la Pensée Juridique de Francisco de Vitoria**. Bruxelles: Bruylant, Centre Charles de Visscher pour le droit international, 1988.

Merêa, Paulo. **Estudos de Filosofia Jurídica e de História das Doutrinas Políticas**. Lisboa: Imprensa Nacional-Casa da Moeda, 2004.

Vollenhoven, Cornelius van. Grotius and the Study of Law. **The American Journal of International Law**, v. 19, n. 1, pp. 1–11, January 1925.

Printed by Printforce, the Netherlands